The Civil Rights Movement

MAGILL'S CHOICE

The Civil Rights Movement

Volume 1
Abolition – Lincoln-Douglas debates
1 - 384

edited by

The Editors of Salem Press

SALEM PRESS, INC.

PASADENA, CALIFORNIA   HACKENSACK, NEW JERSEY

Most of these essays originally appeared in *Racial and Ethnic
Relations in America*, 1999. The rest first appeared in *Survey of Social
Science: Government and Politics*, 1995; *American Justice*, 1996; and
Great Lives from History: American Series, 1987. New material has
been added.

∞ The paper used in these volumes conforms to the American
National Standard for Permanence of Paper for Printed Library
Materials, Z39.48-1992 (R1997).

Library of Congress Cataloging-in-Publication Data
The Civil Rights movement / edited by the editors of Salem Press.
    p. cm. — (Magill's choice)
  Includes bibliographical references and index.
  ISBN 0-89356-170-3 (v. 1 : alk. paper) — ISBN 0-89356-171-1
  (v. 2 : alk. paper) — ISBN 0-89356-169-X (set : alk. paper)
    1. Afro-Americans—Civil rights—History—20th century—Dictio-
naries. 2. Civil rights movements—United States—History—20th cen-
tury—Dictionaries. 3. United States—Race relations—Dictionaries.
I. Salem Press. II. Series.
E185.61 .C6124 2000
305.896′073—dc21
                                                                99-046715
                                                                CIP

First Printing

Contents

Contents

Contents

Publisher's Note

This contribution to Salem Press's Magill's Choice series is a broadly conceived survey of the Civil Rights movement in the United States. In 319 alphabetically arranged essays, *The Civil Rights Movement* examines racial issues in all their manifestations, providing a strong emphasis on the role of African Americans—who, by all measures, were at the heart of the Civil Rights movement and provided its primary leaders.

Among books published on the Civil Rights movement, the breadth of this set may be unique. Its articles, ranging in length from 200 to 2,500 words, examine the Civil Rights movement in all its dimensions. The forces underlying the modern Civil Rights movement began taking shape well before the 1950's, when it developed into a powerful and dramatic national force that could not be ignored. In addition to the many articles in these volumes specifically addressing major aspects of African American history, nearly one hundred articles examine what lay behind the prejudice and discrimination that African Americans—and members of other racial and ethnic minorities—faced. To explain the concepts behind this reference work, it will it helpful to review what is meant by the phrase "Civil Rights movement."

The term "civil rights" has been applied in many different ways and is often treated as synonymous with "civil liberties." In narrower usage, however, these concepts have distinct meanings. Civil rights are generally understood to be positive government actions undertaken to protect members of minority groups against forms of discrimination leveled at them because of their membership in those groups. By contrast, civil liberties are generally understood to be negative government guarantees against restricting rights belonging to *all* citizens. Most of the rights outlined in the U.S. Constitution's Bill of Rights are thus civil liberties. For example, the First Amendment prohibits Congress from abridging the rights of free speech, free press, freedom of assembly and petition, and religion. (These protections were later extended to apply to all levels of government, not just the federal Congress.) In principle, at least, *all* American citizens are entitled to enjoy these and many other civil liberties without fear of government hindrance.

The concept of civil rights is an outgrowth of historical situations in which rights have been denied, not to all citizens, but only to members of certain groups. For this reason, civil rights are often called "minority rights." In U.S. history, groups whose members have been denied rights have been defined mainly by race, sex, age, and sexual orientation. Especially pervasive examples have included denial of the vote to African Americans living in the South in the century following the Civil War and the almost total denial of the vote to women until passage of the Nineteenth Amendment in 1920.

The need for government to take positive steps to correct civil rights abuses was first recognized around the time of the Civil War, when the impending abolition of slavery was raising questions of what rights former slaves were to have. After the war ended, the Thirteenth, Fourteenth, and Fifteenth Amendments to the Constitution were passed to abolish slavery, guarantee citizenship to all persons born in the United States—regardless of past servitude—and to prohibit denying the vote to citizens on the basis of race. These amendments alone, however, were not sufficient to protect African American rights, so Congress went further by passing a series of civil rights acts that spelled out other, more specific, rights and empowered the federal government to enforce them. Within a decade, however, the courts overturned these laws, effectively removing civil rights protections of African Americans until well into the twentieth century. Moreover, not only did the federal government retreat from protecting African American rights, it stood by while state governments—particularly those of the former Confederacy—passed discriminatory legislation making the condition of their African American citizens even worse. Eventually, the federal government again intervened to protect minority rights.

The epoch commonly known as the Civil Rights movement is generally regarded as having begun in the mid-1950's. In 1954 the U.S. Supreme Court outlawed racial discrimination in public schools in its *Brown v. Board of Education* decision. A few years later, an African American boycott of segregated buses in Montgomery, Alabama, launched a decade-long era of antidiscrimination protest campaigns and voter-registration drives that culminated in the first significant civil rights legislation in nearly a century. By the end of the 1960's, virtually all major forms of legally enforced or protected racial discrimination were outlawed, and for the first time in American history it could be said that something approximating racial equality existed—at least on paper. Afterward, the struggle for real equality continued, but without most of the legal barriers it had previously encountered.

The political and social gains made by the Civil Rights movement were not merely products of government generosity or goodwill, they were won through relentless campaigning by Americans who refused to be denied rights on the basis of their membership in racial and ethnic groups. Because of their numbers and the distance they had to travel to attain legal equality, African Americans were the driving force behind the Civil Rights movement. They are also the focus of this two-volume set on the movement.

Many civil rights issues were debated in the courts, with most finally being settled in the U.S. Supreme Court. Individual court cases are the subject of forty-six articles. Since "civil rights" are, in effect, defined around positive government actions, it follows that legislation is a central part of civil rights history. Thirty of this set's articles, therefore, discuss individual pieces of legislation, including key constitutional amendments. Organizations advocating civil rights were also important components of the Civil Rights movement, and the set contains forty-two articles on black churches, the National Association for the Advancement of Colored People (NAACP), the Congress of Racial Equality (CORE), the Student Nonviolent Coordinating

Committee (SNCC), and the Southern Christian Leadership Conference (SCLC), as well as government agencies and other bodies.

Articles in this set are arranged alphabetically under simple, straightforward titles. Additional help in finding information is provided by extensive cross-references listed at the end of each essay and by a comprehensive index. The 138 longest articles contain up-to-date bibliographical notes on core sources. Additional bibliographical material can be found in a comprehensive bibliographical appendix at the end of volume 2. Other appendices include a directory of profiles of eighty leading figures in civil rights history, the complete text of the U.S. Constitution, and a time line.

The overwhelming majority of essays in this set are taken from Salem's new reference work, *Racial and Ethnic Relations in America*. The rest have been adapted from other Salem works, such as *American Justice* and *Great Lives from History: American Series*. All of the essays were written with the needs of students and general readers in mind. This project draws on the work of 187 scholars, to whom we once again express our thanks.

Contributors

McCrea Adams
Independent Scholar

Candace E. Andrews
San Joaquin Delta College

Mary Welek Atwell
Radford University

Barbara Bair
Duke University

Thomas E. Baker
*Texas Tech University
Law School*

Carl L. Bankston III
*University of Southwestern
Louisiana*

Gregg Barak
Eastern Michigan University

Bernice McNair Barnett
University of Illinois at Urbana

Paul Barton-Kriese
Indiana University—East

Patricia A. Behlar
Pittsburgh State University

Alvin K. Benson
Brigham Young University

Joseph M. Bessette
Claremont McKenna College

Tej K. Bhatia
Syracuse University

Cynthia A. Bily
Adrian College

Steve D. Boilard
Independent Scholar

James J. Bolner
*Louisiana State University,
Baton Rouge*

Aubrey W. Bonnett
*State University of New York,
Old Westbury*

Dallas L. Browne
*Southern Illinois University
at Edwardsville*

Fred Buchstein
John Carroll University
Dix & Eaton

Michael H. Burchett
Limestone College

Malcolm B. Campbell
Bowling Green State University

Terri L. Canaday
Mississippi State University

Byron D. Cannon
University of Utah

Glenn Canyon
Independent Scholar

Richard K. Caputo
Barry University

Sharon Carson
University of North Dakota

Paul J. Chara, Jr.
Loras College

Cheryl D. Childers
Washburn University

Erica Childs
Fordham University

John G. Clark
University of Kansas

Michael J. Clark
*California State University,
Hayward*

Thomas Clarkin
University of Texas

Philip N. Cohen
*University of Maryland,
College Park*

William H. Coogan
University of Southern Maine

Tom Cook
Wayne State College

William J. Cooper, Jr.
*Louisiana State University,
Baton Rouge*

Randall Coyne
*University of Oklahoma
Law School*

Stephen Cresswell
West Virginia Wesleyan College

Laura A. Croghan
College of William and Mary

Edward R. Crowther
Adams State College

Richard V. Damms
Mississippi State University

G. Reginald Daniel
*University of California,
Santa Barbara*

Sudipta Das
*Southern University
at New Orleans*

Jane Davis
Fordham University

Héctor L. Delgado
University of Arizona

Ione Y. DeOllos
Ball State University

Thomas E. DeWolfe
Hampden-Sydney College

Davison M. Douglas
William and Mary Law School

Jennifer Eastman
Clark University

Craig M. Eckert
Eastern Illinois University

Sharon Elise
*California State University,
San Marcos*

Robert P. Ellis
Worcester State College

James B. Epps
University of South Florida

John W. Fiero
*University of Southwestern
Louisiana*

Brian L. Fife
Ball State University

Alan M. Fisher
*California State University,
Dominguez Hills*

R. M. Frumkin
Center for Democratic Values

John C. Gardner
*Louisiana State University,
Baton Rouge*

Karen Garner
University of Texas at Austin

Phyllis B. Gerstenfeld
*California State University,
Stanislaus*

Contributors

Robert F. Gorman
Southwest Texas State University

Jennifer Lynn Gossett
University of Cincinnati

Lewis L. Gould
University of Texas, Austin

William H. Green
University of Missouri, Columbia

Michael Haas
University of Hawaii at Manoa

Frank E. Hagan
Mercyhurst College

Irwin Halfond
McKendree College

Timothy L. Hall
University of Mississippi Law School

Roger D. Hardaway
Northwestern Oklahoma State University

Keith Harper
Mississippi College

William M. Harris, Sr.
Jackson State University

Stanley Harrold
South Carolina State University

Donald M. Hayes
Sam Houston State University

James Hayes-Bohanan
University of Arizona

Chalis Holton
Independent Scholar

Ronald W. Howard
Mississippi College

William L. Howard
Chicago State University

Charles C. Jackson
Augusta State University

John Jacob
Northwestern University

Robert Jacobs
Central Washington University

Joyce P. Jacobsen
Rhodes College

Duncan R. Jamieson
Ashland University

Robert L. Jenkins
Mississippi State University

K. Sue Jewell
Ohio State University

Charles L. Kammer
College of Wooster

Mathew J. Kanjirathinkal
Independent Scholar

Valli Kanuha
University of Hawaii

Kathleen Odell Korgen
William Paterson University

Jeri Kurtzleben
University of Northern Iowa

M. Bahati Kuumba
Buffalo State College

Linda Rochell Lane
Tuskegee University

Lisa Langenbach
Middle Tennessee State University

Eleanor A. LaPointe
Ocean County College

Sharon L. Larson
University of Nebraska—Lincoln

Abraham D. Lavender
Florida International University

Thomas T. Lewis
Mt. Senario College

Anne C. Loveland
Louisiana State University, Baton Rouge

William C. Lowe
Mount St. Clare College

Donna Echols Mabus
PLATO Associates

Grace McEntee
Appalachian State University

Robert E. McFarland
Truett-McConnell College

Susan Mackey-Kallis
Villanova University

Paul D. Mageli
Independent Scholar

Scott Magnuson-Martinson
Normandale Community College

Robert D. Manning
Georgetown University

Jonathan Markovitz
University of California, San Diego

Thomas D. Matijasic
Prestonsburg Community College

Steve J. Mazurana
University of Northern Colorado

Edward V. Mednick
New Jersey City University

Diane P. Michelfelder
Utah State University

Liesel A. Miller
Mississippi State University

Kesha S. Moore
University of Pennsylvania

William V. Moore
College of Charleston

Christina Moose
Independent Scholar

Gil Richard Musolf
Central Michigan University

Eileen O'Brien
University of Florida

Oladele A. Ogunseitan
University of California, Irvine

Gwenelle S. O'Neal
Rutgers University

Max Orezzoli
Florida International University

William Osborne
Florida International University

Maria A. Pacino
Azusa Pacific University

Lisa Paddock
Independent Scholar

Jason Pasch
Independent Scholar

Craig S. Pascoe
University of Tennessee, Knoxville

Darryl Paulson
University of South Florida

Thomas R. Peake
King College

William E. Pemberton
*University of Wisconsin—
La Crosse*

Marilyn Elizabeth Perry
Independent Scholar

Marjorie Podolsky
Penn State University—Erie

David L. Porter
William Penn College

John Powell
Penn State University—Erie

Steven Pressman
Monmouth University

Lillian M. Range
*University of Southern
Mississippi*

Samory Rashid
Indiana State University

R. Kent Rasmussen
Independent Scholar

E. A. Reed
Baylor University

Thomas D. Reins
*California State University,
Fullerton*

Douglas W. Richmond
University of Texas, Arlington

Jaclyn Rodriguez
Occidental College

Courtney B. Ross
*Louisiana State University,
Baton Rouge*

Joseph R. Rudolph, Jr.
Towson State University

Dorothy C. Salem
*Cleveland State
University/Cuyahoga
Community College*

J. Christopher Schnell
*Southeast Missouri State
University*

Larry Schweikart
University of Dayton

Rebecca Lovell Scott
College of Health Sciences

Aristide Sechandice
University of Georgia

Terry L. Seip
*Louisiana State University,
Baton Rouge*

R. Baird Shuman
*University of Illinois,
Urbana-Champaign*

Malik Simba
*California State University,
Fresno*

Donald C. Simmons, Jr.
Mississippi Humanities Council

Donna Addkison Simmons
Independent Scholar

Kevin F. Sims
Cedarville College

Andrew C. Skinner
Brigham Young University

James Smallwood
Oklahoma State University

Charles V. Smedley
Charleston Southern University

Christopher E. Smith
Michigan State University

Robert Sobel
Hofstra University

John A. Sondey
South Dakota State University

David L. Sterling
University of Cincinnati

Leslie Stricker
Park College

James Tackach
Roger Williams University

Harold D. Tallant
Georgetown College

Emily Teipe
Fullerton College

Vincent Michael Thur
Wenatchee Valley College

Leslie V. Tischauser
Prairie State College

Brian G. Tobin
Lassen College

Paul B. Trescott
Southern Illinois University

Mfanya D. Tryman
Mississippi State University

Harry van der Linden
Butler University

Fred R. van Hartesveldt
Fort Valley State College

Milton D. Vickerman
Bloomfield College

Mary E. Virginia
Independent Scholar

Randolph Meade Walker
Le Moyne-Owen College

Thomas J. Edward Walker
*Pennsylvania College of
Technology*

Claudia A. Pavone Watson
University of Hawaii, Hilo

Elwood David Watson
East Tennessee State University

Robert P. Watson
University of Hawaii, Hilo

William L. Waugh, Jr.
Georgia State University

Ashton Wesley Welch
Creighton University

Richard Whitworth
Ball State University

Richard L. Wilson
*University of Tennessee
at Chattanooga*

Thomas Winter
University of Cincinnati

Michael Witkoski
Independent Scholar

Trudi D. Witonsky
*University of Wisconsin,
Madison*

Gene Redding Wynne, Jr.
Tri-County Technical College

Cynthia Gwynne Yaudes
Indiana University

Clifton K. Yearley
*State University of New York
at Buffalo*

Abolition

The abolition movement attempted to apply the concepts of Christian brotherhood and democratic egalitarianism to race relations; it helped to end slavery in the United States.

By the mid-eighteenth century, American Quakers such as John Woolman and Benjamin Lay were denouncing slavery as un-Christian. The rationalism of the Enlightenment, with its stress upon natural law, added ammunition to the arsenal of critics of slavery.

The egalitarian rhetoric of the Revolutionary era illustrated the irony of slaveholders fighting for liberty. As a result, most Northern states abolished slavery by 1784. New York and New Jersey did so afterward. Southern whites felt that they could not afford to abolish slavery, yet they too felt the need to justify the institution on ethical grounds. They concentrated on humanizing the institution and argued that it was a "necessary evil."

Antislavery feeling receded after 1793 because of fear of slave revolts, the increasing profitability of slavery following the invention of the cotton gin, and new scientific theories that reinforced racism. The leading antislavery organization in the early nineteenth century was the American Colonization Society (ACS). The ACS attempted to resettle free blacks in Africa and encouraged voluntary emancipation without challenging the right to own human property. The colonization plan allowed liberal slaveholders and moderate members of the clergy to rationalize their guilt over slavery.

In 1825, a great Protestant religious revival swept the northeastern region of the country. Ministers such as Charles Grandison Finney preached a new perfectionist theology that sought to counter the growing worldliness of Americans. This revival sparked a host of humanitarian crusades designed to protect the rights of the disadvantaged and to cleanse American institutions of contamination.

By the early 1830's, many evangelical reformers began to view slavery and racism as sinful because racism violated the Christian ethic of equality. Known as immediate abolitionists, these reformers demanded the immediate and unqualified liberation of slaves and an end to racial discrimination. With the formation of the American Anti-Slavery Society in 1833, abolitionist speakers toured the Northern states attempting to rally support for their cause. Abolitionists were frequently attacked by angry mobs, and their literature was destroyed in Southern post offices.

The abolition movement failed to end racism in the North. It did, however, spark anti-Southern feelings, which led to increased controversy within the national government. This conflict led directly to the Civil War. During the war, abolitionists pressured the federal government to transform the conflict from a war to preserve the Union into a war to end slavery. Abolition advocates were disappointed by the Emancipation Proclamation because it was based upon military necessity rather than moral principle, but they accomplished their central purpose with the passage of the Thirteenth Amendment, which ended slavery in the United States.

Garrisonian Ethics One major faction within the abolition movement was led by editor William Lloyd Garrison. In a real sense, the publication of the first issue of *The Liberator* on January 1, 1831, established Garrison as the foremost abolitionist in the country. Garrison's harsh attacks upon slaveholders and colonizationists caused a national sensation even though the circulation of his newspaper never exceeded three thousand.

Like all abolitionists, Garrison demanded that everyone recognize a personal responsibility to improve society. The three major tenets of his ethical philosophy were human liberation, moral suasion, and no compromise with evil. Garrison actively campaigned on behalf of legal equality for African Americans, temperance, and equality for women. Garrison rejected force and violence in human affairs. He sought the moral reformation of slave owners, not their destruction. He never advocated slave revolts, and he wanted the Northern states to allow the South to secede during the crisis of 1860-1861.

Garrison sincerely believed in all that he advocated, and he would not compromise his principles. He rejected any solution to the issue of slavery that involved a program that would delay emancipation. He also demanded that his followers reject participation in the American political system because the Constitution was a proslavery document. Other abolitionists, such as Gerrit Smith and James Birney, attempted to use the political system as a way to gain publicity for the cause of abolition.

African American Abolitionism In a sense, there were two abolition movements. The white movement was based on a moral abstraction, but African Americans were forced to confront the everyday realities of racism in nineteenth century America.

Frederick Douglass emerged as the major spokesperson for African Americans during the antebellum period. Douglass self-consciously attempted to use his life as an example to repudiate racist stereotypes. Because of his eloquence, Douglass gained an international reputation as a public speaker, and in doing so, he proved the humanity of African Americans.

Like Garrison, Douglass strongly supported temperance and women's rights. He was, however, willing to use any means to achieve the liberation of slaves, including violence and political action. He approved of John Brown's idea of using the southern Appalachians as an armed sanctuary for runaways. He also supported the Free-Soil and Republican Parties even though neither advocated the emancipation of Southern slaves. He justified his positions as part of a larger struggle to advance the cause of racial equality in America. For Douglass, as for other African Americans involved in the cause of abolition, equality was the only acceptable ethical standard for a free society.

Thomas D. Matijasic

Core Resources

Books that provide additional information on the abolition movement include Gilbert Hobbs Barnes's *The Antislavery Impulse: 1830-1844* (New York: Harcourt, Brace & World, 1964), *The Antislavery Vanguard: New Essays on the Abolitionists* (Princeton, N.J.: Princeton University Press, 1965), edited by Martin Duberman, Gerald Sorin's *Abolitionism: A New Perspective* (New York: Praeger, 1972), James Brewer Stewart's *Holy Warriors: The Abolitionists and American Slavery* (New York: Hill & Wang, 1976), and Alice Felt Tyler's *Freedom's Ferment: Phases of American Social History to 1860* (Minneapolis: University of Minnesota Press, 1944). Nathan Irvin Huggins's *Slave and Citizen: The Life of Frederick Douglass* (Boston: Little, Brown, 1980) looks at the African American abolitionist, and Russel B. Nye's *William Lloyd Garrison and the Humanitarian Reformers* (Boston: Little, Brown, 1955) examines the prominent white abolitionist.

See also: American Anti-Slavery Society; Emancipation Proclamation; *Liberator, The*; Slave rebellions; Slavery and race relations; Slavery: history; Slavery: North American beginnings; Thirteenth Amendment.

Accommodationism

Accommodationism refers to the outward acceptance of racial inequality by African Americans to obtain concessions from a white-dominated society. This ideology is most commonly associated with black educator and activist Booker T. Washington. During Reconstruction, many blacks called for bringing about change through militant means, but Washington instead advocated downplaying white racism and focusing on black economic solidarity, racial pride, vocational education, and political passivity. In a speech delivered at the Atlanta Exposition in 1895, now commonly known as the Atlanta Compromise address, Washington declared that blacks and whites could remain socially separate while cooperating economically, and implored whites to be patient while blacks established a foothold at the bottom of the socioeconomic order. The address established Washington as the dominant African American political figure until his death in 1915.

By focusing on economic empowerment and separate community development, accommodationists managed to achieve modest successes in a violently oppressive sociopolitical climate. Nevertheless, institutionalized racism continued to encumber southern blacks, who migrated in increasing numbers to northern cities. Within a decade of Washington's Atlanta Compromise address, new ways of thought arose to challenge accommodationism. In 1905, W. E. B. Du Bois, a former ally who had become a critic of Washington, organized the Niagara Movement as a radical alternative to accommodationism. The Niagara Movement precipitated the establishment of the National Association for the Advancement of Colored People (NAACP) in 1909, ushering in a new era of protest through legalism and direct action.

"Accommodationism" remains in general use as an academic term among students of racial relations. "Accommmodation" suggests a necessity to assimilate or "melt" into the dominant society without a forthright willingness to do so, unlike "conformity," which suggests some level of willingness to blend into mainstream society.

Michael H. Burchett

See also: Atlanta Compromise; National Association for the Advancement of Colored People; Niagara Movement.

Adarand Constructors v. Peña

In *Adarand Constructors v. Peña*, the U.S. Supreme Court held that broad affirmative action programs involving employment and contracts were unconstitutional but preserved the applicability of affirmative action to specific and limited circumstances of discrimination.

Randy Pech, a white contractor in Colorado Springs, Colorado, submitted the lowest bid for a federal road-repair project. The contract, however, was awarded to a company owned by a Latino man because of a 1987 law requiring that the Department of Transportation award at least 10 percent of its funds to companies owned by minorities or women. Pech took his complaint to the courts. The case was decided by the Supreme Court at a time when criticism of affirmative action had become widespread both among the public and in Congress. In addition, the makeup of the Court itself had changed since the last federal affirmative action case in 1990; notably, Thurgood Marshall, a staunch liberal, had retired and been replaced by another African American jurist, Clarence Thomas, a conservative.

Overturning previous decisions offering support of federal affirmative action, on June 12, 1995, the Court voted 5 to 4 that the type of affirmative action program involved in the case was unconstitutional. In an opinion written by Justice Sandra Day O'Connor, the Supreme Court stated that the Constitution protects individuals but was not intended to offer special protections to groups. Treating "any person unequally because of his or her race" causes the person to suffer an injury that is not acceptable under the Constitution's guarantee of equal protection under the law. The law can treat people differently because of race "only for the most compelling reasons," and racial classifications by government agencies are "inherently suspect and presumptively invalid." The Court did say, however, that affirmative action programs could be acceptable to remedy specific, provable cases of discrimination.

The decision severely undercut all federal affirmative action programs, most notably those involving jobs or contracts required to go to minorities ("minority set-asides"). In addition, federal law at the time of *Adarand* required firms that did more than fifty thousand dollars of business a year with the federal government and had more than fifty employees to have a written affirmative action policy, which meant that the *Adarand* decision could affect the policies of nearly all major employers in the United States. Reaction to the decision was strong and immediate. A leader of the Anti-Defamation League called it a "sea change" in the law. Many civil rights leaders protested the decision and urged the government not to abolish all affirmative action efforts. Conservative Republican leaders in Congress, in contrast, vowed to pass legislation to eliminate all "racial preferences" in federal hiring and contracting.

McCrea Adams

See also: Affirmative action; *Bakke* case; *Fullilove v. Klutznick*; *Griggs v. Duke Power Company*; Set-asides; *United Steelworkers of America v. Weber*.

Affirmative action

Since the 1960's, affirmative action has been considered a major strategy in the attempt to eliminate institutional discrimination in the areas of employment and education by providing minorities and women with greater access to opportunity; it has also been controversial and widely debated.

Affirmative action policies and programs, which are specifically designed to increase the numbers of minorities and women in employment and education where their representation has been sparse or nonexistent, have created tremendous controversy since their introduction in the 1960's under the John F. Kennedy and Lyndon B. Johnson administrations. Affirmative action programs involve strategies designed to increase the participation of women and minorities, particularly in the areas of employment and education. Typically, affirmative action programs are gender-conscious and/or race-conscious measures designed to assist minorities in overcoming past and present discrimination.

Purpose of Affirmative Action   Affirmative action policies have been applied to a host of situations involving discrimination in employment and education. The underlying purpose is to increase the prospect for equality of opportunity while eliminating systemic discrimination against specific populations. Equality of opportunity has historically been the social agenda pushed by civil rights organizations. They believe that affirmative action is an important strategy in the struggle for equal opportunity.

The enforcement of affirmative action is predicated on Titles VI and VII of the Civil Rights Act of 1964 (and to a lesser degree on Executive Order 11246, a 1965 order requiring equal employment opportunity clauses in all federal contracts). The U.S. Department of Justice, the Equal Employment Opportunity Commission, the Office of Federal Contract Compliance Programs (of the Department of Labor), and the federal courts have used Title VII to dismantle long-standing patterns of discrimination in employment and education. Affirmative action programs are actually considered remedial strategies.

Ideally, affirmative action is a twofold approach. First, it is an analysis of the existing workforce to determine if the percentages of "protected groups" in a given job classification are similar to the percentages of those groups in the surrounding community. Second, if it can be substantiated that certain practices have an exclusionary effect in the selection process, affirmative (race- and gender-conscious) measures may be required to remedy the situation. A number of steps may be taken to alter the existing selection process, including the establishment of goals and timetables for hiring, the development of recruitment programs, a redesigning of jobs and job descriptions, substantiation of the use of testing as a selection instrument, and attempting to improve the opportunity for advancement training for those in positions with limited career paths.

An affirmative action program may involve some or all of these steps. Additionally, affirmative action may be either voluntary or mandated by the courts. A court order or consent decree may force an offending enterprise to make restitution and to submit a detailed plan specifying its intentions to provide back pay and strategies for equitable promotion opportunities to those it has victimized. It may also include a provision on how it proposes to restructure its recruitment and hiring practices to come into compliance with federal guidelines. A primary concern of affirmative action is to encourage that additional measures be taken that go beyond the mere cessation of discriminatory practices.

Without the invoking of goals and timetables, the responsibility for providing equal opportunity would rest solely with the employer. Goals and timetables provide a type of indicator for employers; they are different from quotas, which are rigid and inflexible. Quotas do not allow for flexibility above or below the stated numbers.

Distributive and Compensatory Justice   Since the Supreme Court's decision in the "reverse discrimination" case of *Regents of the University of California v. Bakke* in 1978, the debate on affirmative action has been framed within interpretations of Title VI of the Civil Rights Act of 1964, the 1965 Executive Order 11246, and subsequent decisions by the Supreme Court.

James Meredith's enrollment in the University of Mississippi in 1962 was a harbinger of future affirmative action legislation; he decided to crack the university's color barrier after John F. Kennedy was elected president, as he knew that the new Democratic administration would be more supportive of civil rights than a Republican administration. *(Library of Congress)*

The Court's decisions have appeared to oscillate between limiting and expanding affirmative action. Two major questions are considered in such decisions: whether affirmative action is permissible and appropriate under the law and whether it should be limited to victims of discrimination or should include distributive remedies.

According to Kathanne W. Greene, in *Affirmative Action and Principles of Justice* (1989), affirmative action rests on two basic principles: distributive justice and compensatory justice. Distributive justice is concerned with the distribution of the benefits, rights, and burdens shared by members of society. These benefits and rights can be distributed in several ways; they may be based on equality of opportunity, for example, or based on need, effort, and utility. Therefore, there is no one best way to effectuate distributive justice.

Compensatory justice is essentially concerned with compensation (or reparation) for past injustices against individuals or groups by the government: A victim is entitled to fair compensation or entitled to be returned to a situation comparable to that which existed before the injustice. There is little debate that the U.S. government was a participant in the injustices perpetuated against certain groups (as in *Plessy v. Ferguson*, 1896).

Levels of Preferential Consideration   There are arguably three levels at which preferential considerations or affirmative measures may be accorded women and minorities in employment and education under affirmative action. First, an affirmative measure can be accorded minorities or women who are less qualified than their white male counterparts. Second, an affirmative measure can be granted to minorities and women when they and their white male counterparts are equally qualified. Third, minorities and women can be accorded an affirmative measure when they are more qualified than their white male counterparts.

The Controversy   Critics of affirmative action argue that it accords special privilege to entire categories of people whose individual members may or may not have experienced discrimination. Moreover, they maintain that affirmative action policies establish rigid quotas and may therefore extend opportunities to individuals who are otherwise unqualified. The resulting argument is that affirmative action programs create "reverse discrimination" against white males. Proponents, on the other hand, argue that race-conscious and gender-conscious measures are needed because race and gender have long been bases for discrimination. Race and gender, they say, still limit opportunities for minorities and women in certain areas of society. Consequently, minorities and women will only be able to achieve equal opportunity through the use of race- and gender-conscious strategies.

Affirmative action and equality of opportunity have been inextricably linked in the minds of some Americans. Yet over the years affirmative action has become associated with concepts that have served to bias many others against it. For example, terms such as "preferential treatment," "minority set-asides," "quotas," "managing diversity," and "reverse discrimination" have caused many whites to become hostile to the concept of affirmative action. Few Americans would dispute the fact that minority populations and women have experienced widespread discrimination in the past. Many, however, disagree that they continue to experience discrimination. One reason has to do with the perception that there is already widespread application of affirmative action programs in both the public and private sectors.

"Reverse" Discrimination   Some opponents of affirmative action insist that such policies and programs amount to social engineering and violate the Constitution: They virtually sanction discrimination against white males, thereby simply reversing the object of discrimination. The reverse discrimination argument maintains that women and members of minority groups receive preferential treatment in employment (for example, in obtaining promotions) and in admission to institutions of higher education, particularly where a past history of discrimination can be documented. In such situations, white males who may demonstrate greater academic skill, may have accrued more seniority on the job, or may have scored higher on an entrance examination may be passed over so that the institution can increase the numbers of an underrepresented population. Consequently, and controversially, such decisions are not based on merit. It might be noted that very little objection has been heard concerning episodes of nepotism and widespread preferential treatment offered to veterans (which are clearly not based on merit).

In the well-known 1978 *Regents of the University of California v. Bakke* litigation, a white applicant with a higher score on a medical school entrance examination than some minority applicants was rejected because of the practice of reserving fifteen spaces for minority applicants. Tremendous controversy ensued. (Little was said about the sons and daughters of upper-level university officials who also happened to receive special consideration over more qualified applicants.) Although affirmative action policies are attempts to rectify past and present discriminatory practices, they do undeniably have a negative impact on the opportunities of some white males (as argued in *Weber v. Kaiser Aluminum and Chemical Corporation*). Opponents of affirmative action argue that all that can be hoped to be achieved legally is the eradication of discrimination. Nothing else, constitutionally, can be done. Any attempt to compensate victims of discrimination—especially if they are given preferential consideration in hiring, promotion, or admission to an institution of higher education—simply results in another form of discrimination. Compensation, if it were to be considered, should be offered only to the actual victims of discrimination, not to individuals simply because they belong to a particular group. Departing from its previous rulings on affirmative action, the Supreme Court gave support to this view in 1995 in its decision in *Adarand Constructors v. Peña*.

Limited Success of Affirmative Action It has been argued that affirmative action programs have experienced only limited success, despite the fact that they have been an accepted strategy for many years. Augustus J. Jones, Jr., in *Affirmative Talk, Affirmative Action: A Comparative Study of the Politics of Affirmative Action*, suggests a number of reasons for this. First is poor communication between policymakers and those responsible for implementing the policies. If policies are not clearly delineated, they cannot be effectively administered. Second, a lack of adequate resources may prohibit successful implementation. Money, information, authority, and the necessary staff must all be in place. Third, those responsible for implementation may be antagonistic to affirmative action and may operate opposite to their directives. Fourth, dysfunctional organization structure may preclude the effective implementation of policies. Fifth, political leadership (especially at the national level) may sour the social climate for the acceptance of affirmative action. In particular, inflammatory rhetoric using such terms as "preferential treatment," "racial quotas," and "reverse discrimination" has helped to create reservation and even anger among some whites regarding the legitimacy of affirmative action. Presidents Ronald Reagan and George Bush, for example, consistently referred to affirmative action policies as reverse discrimination and quota legislation.

Reagan, in particular, was an outspoken critic of affirmative action policies and programs. He believed that they were unfair and that they led to rigid quotas, and during his administration he appointed men and women that shared his views. It has been noted that Reagan put together a conservative team of legal experts in the Department of Justice that shared his opposition to affirmative action. His administration also challenged the use of statistical data as a means of substantiating discriminatory patterns by employers.

Both Reagan and Bush appointed minority individuals who opposed affirmative action to posts in their administrations and in federal agencies. Reagan completely restructured the U.S. Commission on Civil Rights and selected Clarence Pendleton, an African American, to be chairman of the commission. Pendleton proved to be so extreme in his opposition to affirmative action that he was rejected by much of the African American community and rebuffed by black Republicans. Linda Chávez, a Hispanic, was selected staff director of the U.S. Civil Rights Commission. Criticizing affirmative action programs in a number of speeches, she argued that affirmative action actually endangered the progress made by African Americans since *Brown v. Board of Education* (1954) and that it was a new type of paternalism.

Clarence Thomas, as chairman of the Equal Employment Opportunity Commission (EEOC), applied a more restrictive interpretation of Title VII than his predecessors had. He decided that the EEOC would pursue only individual claims of discrimination that could be explicitly proved. Therefore, neither statistical data nor the underrepresentation of certain populations in the workforce would be sufficient to demonstrate systemic discrimination. The individual complainant had to provide undeniable proof of discrimination. This policy virtually eliminated the conception of "pattern and practice" discrimination for filing suit.

Congress and the federal courts also manifested some degree of retrenchment regarding affirmative action during the 1980's. Amendments were introduced in Congress to eliminate affirmative action, while the federal courts, in particular the Supreme Court, vacillated on the applicability of affirmative action policies. A number of decisions by the Court in the 1980's and 1990's, particularly *Adarand Constructors v. Peña*, called into question the use of broad affirmative action programs.

In the 1990's, affirmative action suffered some serious setbacks. In 1995, the Regents of the University of California decided to end affirmative action in admissions and hiring. Other states, including Texas, began dismantling affirmative action programs. The results were mixed, with some prestigious universities reporting a significant drop in minority admissions. The following year, California voters approved Proposition 209, the California Civil Rights Initiative, a proposal to amend the California state constitution. The proposition declared that the state should "not discriminate against, or grant preferential treatment to, any individual or group on the basis of race, sex, color, ethnicity, or national origin in the operation of public employment, public education, or public contracting." The proposition drew support from Ward Connerly, a black businessman from Sacramento, because it provided for equal treatment under the law, in accordance with a "color-blind" society, and opposition from organizations such as the American Civil Liberties Union and the National Association for the Advancement of Colored People, which believed the measure was designed to end state-supported affirmative action. Legal challenges against the proposition were for the most part unsuccessful, and California governor Pete Wilson implemented the proposition in March, 1998.

Charles C. Jackson

Core Resources

An excellent explanation of affirmative action goals and discussion of timetables versus quotas can be found in Robert K. Fullinwider's *The Reverse Discrimination Controversy: A Moral and Legal Analysis* (Totowa, N.J.: Rowman & Littlefield, 1980). A discussion of the justification for reverse discrimination can be found in chapter 3 of Tom Regan and Donald VanDeVeer's *And Justice for All: New Introductory Essays in Ethics and Public Policy* (Totowa, N.J.: Rowman & Allanheld, 1982). An analysis of the effort to dismantle affirmative action is provided by Charles C. Jackson in "Affirmative Action: Controversy and Retrenchment," *The Western Journal of Black Studies* 16 (no. 4, Winter, 1992). William G. Bowen and Derek Bok's *The Shape of the River: Long-term Consequences of Considering Race in College and University Admissions* (Princeton, N.J.: Princeton University Press, 1998) provides a defense of affirmative action. Black conservative Shelby Steele's *A Dream Deferred: The Second Betrayal of Black Freedom in America* (New York: HarperCollins, 1998) is sharply critical of affirmative action, calling it redemptive liberalism meant to make whites feel better. A good look at the application of affirmative action programs at the local level can be found in Augustus J. Jones, *Affirmative Talk, Affirmative Action: A Comparative Study of the Politics of Affirmative Action* (New York: Praeger, 1991).

See also: *Adarand Constructors v. Peña; Bakke* case; Civil Rights Act of 1964; College admissions; Equality of opportunity; *Griggs v. Duke Power Company; Proposition 209; "Reverse" racism; *Richmond v. J. A. Croson Company; Weber v. Kaiser Aluminum and Chemical Corporation.*

African American-American Indian relations

Traditional American racial history, by focusing on American Indian-white or black-white relations, has ignored the important cultural contributions of American Indian-black interactions.

Since the 1960's, revisionist historians have shown great interest in the histories of American Indians and African Americans. The study of the history of the contact between these two groups has been a logical development, and much new evidence has emerged. For example, significant contact between American Indians and Africans occurred in Europe at the time of Portuguese encounters with Africans. In the sixteenth century, American Indians were traded for West African slaves, who were needed to work on Brazilian plantations.

The Spanish were the first major users of African slaves in the New World. An initial function of Africans, because of their knowledge of Indian culture, was to aid in exploration as guides and interpreters. The first African in the New World known by name was Estevanico, a Muslim native of Acamor. He accompanied the expedition of Pánfilo de Narváez, which was shipwrecked off the coast of Florida in 1529. Francisco Vásquez de Coronado was also accompanied by Africans as he explored central Kansas in 1541.

Indigenous forms of servitude were modified by the Spanish to serve the labor needs of their mines and plantations. Beginning with Hernando de Soto in 1538, the Spanish transported thousands of Indians from the Southeast to the West Indies. By 1540, however, Indian slavery was deemed unsuitable because of the Indians' susceptibility to disease; thereafter African labor began to be used. The mixing of Native American and African slave populations in sixteenth century Spanish America created a solidarity between the two groups, as seen in numerous revolts and insurrections.

American Colonization   Contacts among the races in the age of exploration were minor compared with those that occurred in the period of colonization. The main areas of interaction can be divided geographically into, first, New England, the Middle Colonies, and the Chesapeake, and second, the Southeast and Indian Territory. Except for the case of the Seminole Wars in Spanish Florida, the relations between blacks and Indians were not as amicable in English North America as they were in Spanish America. This was attributable in large part to demographics. The numbers of Indian and African slaves from New England to the Chesapeake were small in the early seventeenth century. Over time the Indian population diminished, and the black population increased. Although the two groups were initially few in number and spread over a large geographical area, there was extensive intermingling, which served to modify the physical appearance of both in Massachusetts, Connecticut, New York, New Jersey, Delaware, Maryland, and Virginia. The main form of relationship during this time was intermarriage between free blacks and reservation Indians. Reservations, in fact, were centers of racial fusion all the way from Cape Cod to the Chesapeake. Crispus Attucks, Paul Cuffe, and Frederick Douglass were famous men of mixed blood.

A mulatto named York, the first black to cross the continent, was critical to the success of the Lewis and Clark expedition of 1804-1806. The explorers would have turned back at the Rocky Mountains had not York befriended the Shoshone, who provided needed supplies and horses. York, the son of two slaves, was known as Big Medicine by the Indians. He spoke several Indian languages as well as French. The Indian woman Sacagawea was his constant companion during the expedition.

Indian Slavery The most massive contact between Indians and African Americans arose within the system of slavery developed by the so-called Five Civilized Tribes of the Southeast—the Cherokee, Chickasaw, Choctaw, Creek, and Seminole. Predominant among the Five Tribes were the Cherokee, whose 12,395-member nation held 583 slaves in 1809. By 1824, the numbers had grown to 15,560 and 1,277 respectively. Although it seems that the Cherokee were not unduly harsh masters, they refused to allow intermixture with blacks. The Chickasaw and Choctaw tribes together counted 25,000 members, with 5,000 slaves. Believing, like the Cherokee, in racial separation,

Home of an African American family living among the Creek in Oklahoma at the end of the nineteenth century. *(National Archives)*

these two tribes were crueler masters. The Chickasaw, who on occasion murdered the slaves of other owners, were especially cruel.

The Creek and Seminole were considered the least civilized of the Five Tribes, partly because they had the least prejudice toward blacks. This was especially true of the Seminole, who allowed their "slaves" to live in separate farming communities while paying a small annual tribute. The Creek, a patriarchal society, had children by slave women. The Creek reared these children as equals to their full-blooded progeny. A famous Creek chief, Tustennuggee Emartha, or Jim Boy, was of such mixed breed. The Seminole, who numbered about 3,900 in 1822, owned 800 slaves. These slaves were "maroons"—they had escaped the plantations of Georgia and the Carolinas. It was the presence of the maroons that initiated the Florida Wars.

War and Politics   Native American and African American military cooperation occurred in two campaigns closely related in time, geography, and cause. The second decade of the nineteenth century saw, in the Southeast, the outbreak of the Creek War and the First Seminole War. Both were precipitated by the anger of white slave owners who sought the return of their runaways from neighboring reservations. Andrew Jackson led the assault that crushed the Creek Red Stick Revolt in 1814, and he ended the First Seminole War in 1818 by capturing a Seminole stronghold in Florida.

African Americans figured prominently in both of these wars, since they had the most to lose in the event of a defeat. In numerous battles, Indians and blacks fought and died together. Jim Bowlegs, who was a slave of Chief Billy Bowlegs and served as his interpreter and adviser, later became a Seminole maroon leader, organizing a resettlement for his group in Mexico in 1850. The Indians and blacks continued to fight for their independence in two successive wars until the Civil War broke out.

The participation of slave-holding Indians in the Civil War (1861-1865) was determined by their respective views on slavery. The Chickasaw and Choctaw tribes, who were the most prejudiced against blacks, supported the Confederacy; the Creek and Seminole opposed it. The Cherokee held a divided position; mixed-bloods (part Indian, part white) generally supported the South, while full-bloods tended to sympathize with the North. In the confusion of war, the slaves were left largely on their own, attacking both Unionists and Confederates. After the war some blacks sought incorporation into the various tribes. This action was resisted by the Choctaw and Chickasaw. After the tribes' removal to Indian Territory, the legacy of Indian slave-holding was clearly evident. By 1907, no Seminole family was free of black intermixing, and almost no Creek families were pure-blooded. The other three tribes, however, had practically no mixture.

Since the 1960's a new alliance has occurred between Native Americans and African Americans in the arena of political activity. The Black Power and Civil Rights movements inspired Red Power organizations such as the American Indian Movement (AIM). Black theology has been the model for the

Troops of the 25th Infantry Colored garrisoning Fort Randall in Dakota Territory, where Sioux prisoners were held in the late nineteenth century. *(Library of Congress)*

development of what has been called "red theology." Such political actions have spread to international bodies such as the United Nations and the Organization of Indigenous Peoples, in which African and indigenous New World peoples sustain positive contact.

William H. Green

Core Resources

Jack D. Forbes's *Black Africans and Native Americans: Color, Race, and Caste in the Evolution of Red-Black Peoples* (New York: Basil Blackwell, 1988) uses ethnohistorical and philological methods to break new ground in the study of American culture by stressing Native American contributions to the ethnic complexity of the nation. Gary B. Nash's *Red, White, and Black: The Peoples of Early America* (Englewood Cliffs, N.J.: Prentice-Hall, 1974) argues that American culture arose as the product of three centuries of intense mixing and contact between three cultures: red, black, and white. Dwight W. Hoover's *The Red and the Black* (Chicago: Rand McNally, 1976) presents a detailed history of Indian-black interaction from the fifteenth century, with special attention to the distinct development of each culture. William Loren Katz's *Black Indians: A Hidden Heritage* (New York: Atheneum, 1986) examines how European Americans sought to discourage contacts between Indians and blacks from the age of exploration to Reconstruction. R. Halliburton, Jr.'s *Red over Black: Black Slavery Among the Cherokee Indians* (Westport, Conn.: Greenwood Press, 1977) and Theda Perdue's *Slavery and the Evolution of Cherokee Society, 1540-1886* (Knoxville: University of Tennessee Press, 1979) look at slavery within the Cherokee Nation. Daniel F. Littlefield, Jr., examines the rise and development of Creek slavery from its beginnings to the aftermath of the Red Stick Rebellion in *Africans and Creeks: From the Colonial Period to the Civil War* (Westport, Conn.: Greenwood Press, 1979) and shows the influence of African slaves on the Seminoles' activities as they fought and signed treaties with the federal government from the time of the removal policy to the Civil War in *Africans and Seminoles: From Removal to Emancipation* (Westport, Conn.: Greenwood Press, 1978). Kevin Mulroy's *Freedom on the Border: The Seminole Maroons in Florida, the Indian Territory, Coahuila, and Texas* (Lubbock: Texas Tech University Press, 1993) describes the long interaction between black Seminoles and their native masters as both sought to cooperate and survive destructive federal policies.

See also: African American cowboys; Slavery: history.

African American Baptist Church

An amalgamation of African and European forms of religious worship found expression beginning in the late 1700's.

The religious revivals of the 1730's collectively known as the first Great Awakening transformed the spiritual climate of British North America by the mid-eighteenth century. Church membership grew and evangelical religious ideas, which emphasized a person's own relationship with God, began to acquire hegemony over the religious values propagated by the established churches. Among those people who embraced evangelical ideals were African American slaves, who found attractive the notion of a personal God, the hope for salvation, and the less formal style of evangelical worship. This was especially true in the South, where African Americans benefited from a practice among some white evangelicals of allowing blacks to preach to other blacks and where African Americans were the targets of white missionary activity.

The Baptist Church   African Americans were particularly drawn to the Baptist faith, especially in the latter part of the eighteenth century. White Baptists, themselves often among the poorest in southern society, actively recruited African Americans. Furthermore, Baptists did not require formal education as part of ministerial training, and what learning they did encourage centered on mastering the contents of the Bible. Even African Americans held in bondage and denied opportunities for formal education could fulfill these expectations, and more than a few became ministers. African American slaves not only joined biracial Baptist churches but also fashioned their own fellowships, where they blended the traditional folk religions they brought from Africa with the evangelical nostrums of the Europeans, thus creating a hybrid African American religion.

In the Savannah River Valley, which connected the hinterlands around Augusta, Georgia, with the port city of Savannah, evangelical revivals among whites and blacks bore organizational fruit among African Americans, who formed their own Baptist church at Silver Bluff, near Augusta, in 1773.

About that time, a slave named George Liele heard a sermon preached by the Reverend Matthew Moore, a white minister, and became convinced that he needed to respond to the gospel. Baptized by Moore, Liele became a preacher and began to exhort other slaves in the vicinity of Augusta to become Christians. Liele's master temporarily had to flee Georgia for his life and freed Liele. For the next several years, Liele and a colleague, David George, preached regularly at the Baptist church in Silver Bluff. George, who was born a slave in Virginia and had run away from a cruel master before coming to the Deep South as the slave of George Galphin, was converted after hearing sermons in the mid-1770's by several African American preachers, including Liele. George and Liele organized other churches, including the congregation at Yama Craw, outside Savannah, in 1777.

Among those who heard Liele preach at Yama Craw was Andrew Bryan, a South Carolina slave baptized by Liele in 1782. Bryan eventually purchased his freedom and devoted himself to his ministry. Although whites who feared an unshackled black man whipped Bryan twice and imprisoned him once, he continued to preach to ever-larger congregations, which often contained both blacks and whites. In 1788, his congregation constituted itself into the Savannah Georgia First Colored Church, commonly called the Savannah Church. At the time, it boasted 575 members, and it would grow to more than 800 by the time of Bryan's death.

A Fusion of Beliefs   The religious teachings of Liele, George, and Bryan fused the African concepts of a unitary universe where the sacred and profane are not segregated, the European mythologies of Heaven, Hell, and redemption, and their present reality of slavery. God would help Africans through their travail of slavery and would one day lead them out of bondage. In this melding process, certain African religious practices were proscribed. The church covenant of Liele's Yama Craw Church specifically banned the consumption of blood and strangled meat of animals offered to idols, which had been a part of some West African religious rituals. Other African practices were given an important place, such as moaning as part of religious singing. This practice originated in ecstatic African religious rituals, and moaning and wailing have been preserved in southern gospel singing. This hybrid religious ritual did not confine itself to African American communities. The emotional shouts and ritual cadences of African worship affected the rhythms of white discourse as well, especially the sermon form, in which the preacher and congregation engage in something of a dialogue.

Both Liele and George eventually fled the South for the British Empire, seeking to continue their ministerial work without the specter of slavery hanging over them. Liele went to Jamaica, establishing the first Baptist churches there. George went to Canada, where he worked with both blacks and whites before organizing a Back-to-Africa movement, in which a thousand Canadian blacks went with George to Sierra Leone in 1792. Bryan, however, remained in the South, calling upon African Americans to lead better lives and, sometimes stealthily, urging whites to live out the Golden Rule in dealing with blacks. By establishing churches that counseled patience while teaching a theology of ultimate deliverance, African American leaders like Liele, George, and Bryan helped African Americans survive slavery by encouraging them to expect freedom soon.

Edward R. Crowther

Core Resources

LeRoy Fitts's *A History of Black Baptists* (Nashville, Tenn.: Broadman Press, 1985) presents a sympathetic and readable account of black Baptist leaders and churches. C. Eric Lincoln and Lawrence H. Mamiya's *The Black Church in the African American Experience* (Durham, N.C.: Duke University Press, 1990) is a well-written survey of African American churches since their earliest times and their meaning in the African American struggle in the United States. Editor Gayraud S. Wilmore's *African American Religious Studies: An Interdisciplinary Anthology* (Durham, N.C.: Duke University Press, 1989) contains a series of essays that may help readers interpret the fragmentary documentary record of early African American religious life. Milton C. Sernett's *Afro-American Religious History: A Documentary Witness* (Durham, N.C.: Duke University Press, 1985) contains letters from Bryan and Liele and many other representative documents of the African American religious experience.

See also: AME Church; AME Zion Churches; Black church; Slavery: history.

African American cowboys

Despite the predominantly white images in television and film Westerns, many cowboys were African American. Attracted by the high wages and the pull of the open range, the cowboys were a diverse lot that included former Civil War soldiers, former African American slaves, Mexicans, and American Indians. Evidence suggests that perhaps as many as 25 percent of cowboys were African American. Most of the African Americans were unable to read or write, so few records of their daily life exist, but like their peers, they spent as many as four months in the saddle, working the long drives. The cowboy's job was dangerous, hard, and lonely. Because the cowboys had to work together to herd the cattle up the trail, segregation was impractical, but African American cowboys were constantly reminded of the inequalities of the

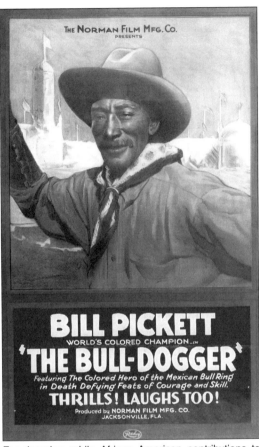

For decades, while African American contributions to opening the West were ignored by the white-dominated film industry, a parallel black film industry celebrated its own western heroes. (Library of Congress)

time. Pay for African American cowboys was frequently less than for their white counterparts, and segregation was common in cattle towns along the trail. Despite the discrimination they faced, however, the contribution of the African American cowboy to the westward movement and the settlement of the western United States is indisputable.

Donald C. Simmons, Jr.

See also: African American-American Indian relations; Segregation on the frontier.

African American women

African American women, who constitute the largest segment of the nonwhite population in the United States, as a group have done much to effect greater social equality based on race, gender, and social class.

In spite of the many social and economic hardships that African American women have endured in the more than four hundred years since they were brought to America, as a group they have made significant contributions to the United States, both to the survival and progress of the African American community and to the social and economic development of the larger society. The challenges that African American women have faced include slavery, segregation, and institutional race, gender, and class discrimination. Nevertheless, they have made notable accomplishments in education, politics, government, the social sciences, entertainment, human services, journalism, law, medicine, business, sports, and the military. African American women have also played a key role in sustaining vital institutions within the African American community, such as the African American family, the black church, black colleges and universities, and black-owned businesses. A major factor that has enabled African American women to continue to survive and progress despite enormous structural barriers is their strong sense of community. Their belief in strong kinship bonds and reliance on mutual aid networks, consisting of family, friends, and neighbors, have helped African American women to function as agents of social change.

Sociodemographic Characteristics

According to the 1990 U.S. Census, there were 16,138,000 African American females in the United States, constituting 6.6 percent of the population. When African American males are included, the entire African American population makes up 12 percent of the U.S. population. As a group, African American women have made strides in education over the years. In 1990, they had a median of 12.8 years of education and made up approximately 60 percent of the nearly 800,000 African Americans enrolled in colleges and universities in the United States. In 1990, 14.5 percent of all African American women graduated from college.

Although the number of African American women represented in white-collar occupations increased from the 1960's to the 1990's, the majority work at the lower end of the pay scale in these positions. Generally, African American women are employed in clerical, technical, retail sales, and administrative support positions. They continue to be underrepresented in professional and managerial positions and to be overrepresented in low-paying service occupations. In 1990, only 18.8 percent of African American women worked in professional and managerial positions, while 27 percent were employed in service occupations. Their income remained relatively low. In

1990, the median annual income for African American women was $8,327, compared with $10,316 for white women, $12,867 for African American men, and $21,169 for white men.

In spite of the social and economic gains that African Americans experienced in the 1960's and 1970's, African American women, along with African American men and children, continue to be overrepresented in the impoverished class. In fact, in 1990 the percentage of African Americans with incomes below the poverty level was 33 percent, compared to 11 percent for whites. Among the primary factors contributing to an inordinate number of African Americans having incomes below the poverty level are social policies that have resulted in occupational displacement and an inequality in economic and educational systems that has destabilized families and contributed to an increase in the rates of marital disruption. In 1990, 43.8 percent of African American families were headed by women. An inordinate number of these families maintained by women were poor.

Social and Economic Issues   African American women continue to be confronted with social and economic factors that impede their upward mobility in the United States. In many respects, various laws, policies, and practices have contributed to the marginal status of African American women. In spite of the fact that they have increased their participation in the private sector and government, they remain largely outside decision-making positions. Therefore, as workers, African American women are not well positioned to influence policies and practices that limit their full participation in the workplace. Other factors that continue to prevent African American women from experiencing social equality in the United States include negative cultural images, factory closings, the relocation of factories to foreign markets, business development outside central cities, lack of adequate funding for inner-city schools, federal cuts to financial aid to higher education, employment discrimination, and housing discrimination.

Cultural images that portray African American women negatively and suggest that they are better suited for domestic service and other low-paying, service-related occupations contribute significantly to the societal perception that African American women are intellectually incapable of assuming meaningful and responsible positions.

The decline in old-line industries such as the automobile and steel industries beginning in the 1970's, in conjunction with the relocation of many factories to foreign markets where labor is cheaper, has meant the occupational dislocation of many African American women and men who once depended on these industries. Living primarily in central cities, African American women have also been adversely affected by the trend of businesses moving from the central cities to suburban communities and other areas peripheral to cities. Given the fact that many cities do not have adequate mass-transit systems, many African American women, and their husbands, have lost their jobs because of their inability to travel to these locations.

A longtime activist, Ella Baker (1903-1986), helped found the Student Nonviolent Coordinating Committee, and was one of many women who played prominent roles in the Civil Rights movement. *(Schomburg Center for Research in Black Culture, New York Public Library)*

The traditional funding of public schools is also a factor that affects how well African American girls are academically prepared and skilled in marketable technologies. When inner-city schools are compared with suburban schools, the former have inadequate resources, including facilities, textbooks, equipment, and other educational materials. The fact that property taxes serve as the primary source of funding for public schools means schools within the inner-city are economically disadvantaged in comparison with suburban schools. Federal cutbacks in aid to institutions of higher education have also lowered the participation and graduation rates of African American students.

Employment discrimination adversely affects the participation rates and mobility of African American workers. Employment discrimination manifests itself most frequently in the refusal of employers to hire African American women. These women also experience glass ceilings, in which employers limit how far they can rise within the company or agency. In addition, they face tokenism, whereby employers set a limit on the number of African American women whom they are willing to hire in order to meet affirmative action requirements.

Housing discrimination continues to affect African American women. In many communities, financial institutions use various, often insidious methods to refuse property loans to African American women. In addition, discrimination is directed against African Americans who rent. In the past, the most common practice found among savings and loan institutions to prevent African Americans from purchasing property was to retain their applications in the pending file until their contract on the property expired.

The Response of African American Women African American women have challenged unjust policies and practices in courts, in legislatures, and before school boards and other policy-making bodies. They have done so through voting and other forms of political participation and by establishing schools, businesses, and civic organizations within their own communities. African American women have also challenged the television, film, and music industries to eliminate their negative and nonrepresentative images and messages and to replace them with positive imagery and accurate information.

African American women have recognized that while they have concerns that are unique because of race, gender, and social class, they also share common interests with women who are members of other racial and ethnic groups. Some of these issues are the need for affordable child care and health care, pay equity, and the need for policies and legislation that can eliminate race, gender, and class inequities within societal institutions.

K. Sue Jewell

Core Resources

Books on African American women and the issues that surround them include Angela Davis's *Women, Race, and Class* (New York: Random House, 1981) and K. Sue Jewell's *From Mammy to Miss America and Beyond: Cultural Images and the Shaping of U.S. Social Policy* (New York: Routledge, 1993). Three articles dealing with African American women and economics are Elizabeth Higginbotham's "We Were Never on a Pedestal: Women of Color Continue to Struggle with Poverty, Racism, and Sexism," in *For Crying out Loud: Women and Poverty in the United States* (New York: Pilgrim Press, 1986), edited by Rochelle Lefkowitz and Ann Withorn, Julianne Malveaux's "The Economic Interests of Black and White Women: Are They Similar?" in *The Review of Black Political Economy* (13, Summer, 1985), and Margaret C. Simms's "Black Women Who Head Families: An Economic Struggle," in *Slipping Through the Cracks: The Status of Black Women* (New Brunswick, N.J.: Transaction Books, 1986), edited by Simms and Malveaux.

See also: Affirmative action; Colored Women's League; Discrimination: racial and ethnic; Education and African Americans; Employment among African Americans.

African Liberation Day

In 1963, thirty-one African heads of state convened in Ethiopia for the Summit Conference of the Independent African States, with the overall goal of freeing African people from the yoke of European domination and white supremacy. On May 25, 1963, the Charter of the Organization of African Unity was signed, and it was decided to celebrate African Liberation Day (ALD) every year on May 25. Sponsored by the All African People's Revolutionary Party, ALD has led to the concerted action of the member states of the Organization of African Unity to pool financial aid to revive, strengthen, and intensify liberation movements throughout Africa. As much as possible, the goal is to end exploitation and oppression of Africans at home and abroad by finding peaceful solutions through deliberations and frank exchange of views among the nations that are involved.

ALD has become an institution throughout the African world, being a day when all African people rally for unity and denounce racism, capitalism, and Zionism. On ALD, African people focus on what they share—their common past, set of problems, and future—as they pause to think about the plight of their African brothers who are under foreign rule and who are seeking to win their freedom and fundamental human rights.

Alvin K. Benson

See also: All African People's Revolutionary Party; Black nationalism; Pan-Africanism.

Afrocentrism

A philosophy of historical analysis and education put forth by Molefi Kete Asante, professor of African American studies at Temple University, in his works *The Afrocentricity Idea* (1987), *Afrocentricity* (1988), and *Kemet, Afrocentricity, and Knowledge* (1990). In these works, Asante defines Afrocentrism as the perspective on history that allows students to observe the world from the point of view of the African and African American. Asante created Afrocentrism as a reaction to "Eurocentric" interpretations of history, which, in Asante's view, marginalize ethnic and racial minorities by portraying them as victims and passive participants in European-dominated history.

Asante's philosophy advocates a "multi-centered multiculturalism" in which all racial groups are encouraged to write history from their perspective to replace the "monocentric," or European-dominated, historical perspective. Asante's philosophy does not advocate the elimination of the European perspective but rather invites the European perspective to be presented alongside the interpretations of other racial groups. Opponents of the Afrocentric model, however, accuse Asante and his supporters of historical inaccuracy and of using history to promote a racist political agenda. The philosophy of Afrocentrism borrows heavily from the writings of Carter G. Woodson, Asa Hilliard, and Cheikh Anta Diop.

Jason Pasch

See also: Critical race theory; Ideological racism; Racial formation theory; Racism: history of the concept; Underclass theories.

Aid to Families with Dependent Children

By 1930, mothers' pension programs, which provided meager financial support to poor children in their homes, were in effect in most states for widows and divorced women with children. These programs were funded through counties or cities and served only a limited number of women, few of which were African Americans. Those women who received aid had to undergo a grueling and humiliating investigation to prove their character and "fitness" to have custody of their children.

In 1935, President Franklin D. Roosevelt signed into law the Social Security Act, part of which established Aid to Dependent Children (ADC). ADC shifted care for dependent children to the federal government and the states from the cities and localities. The original law provided aid for children up to the age of sixteen in families where the breadwinner was disabled or unemployed or even underemployed. ADC was limited, until 1961, to single-parent families. However, ADC entitlements often remained linked to the character and moral fitness of the primary caretaker, most often a single mother. As the program evolved, states created rules that denied aid to unwed mothers, African American women, or those women whose lifestyles did not adhere to the community's mores.

Congress, from the beginning, appropriated fewer funds and established lower matching and reimbursement rates for ADC than other public assistance programs. A 1962 amendment to the Social Security Act, Section 1115, gave the states free rein to experiment with the renamed program, Aid to Families with Dependent Children (AFDC). That same year, federal law allowed states to require adult recipients to work in order to qualify for aid for themselves and their children. Work and training programs became a focus of "helping the poor to help themselves" in the late 1960's and in the 1970's; these programs were limited in scope, however, and were often punitive rather than helpful. In the 1960's and early 1970's, the National Welfare Rights Organization, under the leadership of Johnnie Tillmon, a welfare mother, helped publicize the idea that AFDC was a basic, fundamental human right.

Although AFDC provided some money and services to mothers and children in desperate need, the bureaucracy and stigma attached to welfare cut deep into a woman's pride and self-esteem. Since every state provided only enough funds to AFDC recipients to help them exist below the poverty level, the program contributed to the "feminization of poverty."

Public attitudes toward the poor and destitute continue to be negative and punitive; many people believe that being poor in the United States has more to do with character than with economic and social issues. This often causes single mothers to be accused of being morally deficient and lazy.

In August, 1996, Congress passed the Personal Responsibility and Work Opportunity Reconciliation Act. The law, effective October 1, 1996, gave states authority over AFDC, food stamps, and Supplemental Security Income (SSI). Federal guidelines limited able-bodied welfare recipients to two years of benefits and five years over a lifetime.

Candace E. Andrews

See also: Poverty and race; Welfare reform: impact on racial/ethnic relations.

AIDS conspiracy theory

Various media polls taken during the 1980's and 1990's showed that approximately one-third of African Americans believed in the AIDS conspiracy theory—that the acquired immunodeficiency syndrome (AIDS) is caused by a virus engineered to eliminate nonwhite populations. Another third of those polled were not sure, and the remainder did not believe in a conspiracy. Stories of accidental or deliberate development of the human immunodeficiency virus (HIV) and its dissemination among nonwhite populations have been dismissed by health officials and scientific researchers.

African Americans' suspicions were fueled, in part, by public scrutiny of the Tuskegee experiment (1932-1972), in which treatment for syphilis was withheld from poor black men in order to study the natural consequences of the disease. A leading doctor for the Nation of Islam has also promoted the idea that the U.S. government invented HIV/AIDS to eliminate blacks. In 1997, a black American biochemist attempted to stop a polio vaccination campaign in Ghana by claiming that the polio vaccine and other drugs being shipped to Africa from the United States might contain the virus. He claimed the West wanted to wipe out black Africans in order to obtain the many rich resources found on the African continent.

AIDS conspiracy theorists cite as evidence the similarities between HIV and other viruses and testimony by a Pentagon official to Congress in 1969 requesting funding for development of a biological warfare agent to attack the human immune system. One version of the conspiracy theory is that a new virus was developed and tested on prisoners who participated in the experiment in exchange for early release. The researchers did not recognize the long incubation period for HIV infection and released the apparently healthy prisoners. Many went to New York City, where they later became ill. The former prisoners passed the virus to others through homosexual activity. Another version of this story is that the virus was deliberately released among the poor and disenfranchised as a form of genocide.

HIV is, in fact, quite similar to a number of viruses, including HTLV-1 (a leukemia virus) and SIV (a virus that infects monkeys). Genetic and

HIV/AIDS researchers refute the conspiracy theory on a number of grounds. First, they say it was not technologically possible nor was it practical to engineer as complex a virus as HIV in the late 1960's and early 1970's. Second, given what is known about the sequence of genes in HIV, it is not possible to splice known viruses together to produce this sequence. Finally, the thrust of research into biological weapons in the 1970's was not on splicing viruses but on other techniques.

Public health officials are concerned that people who believe in the conspiracy theory are less likely to get tested for HIV or to take appropriate precautions to avoid exposure to others' body fluids. Early identification of HIV carriers allows them to be started on medications that prolong the period before they develop symptoms of AIDS.

Rebecca Lovell Scott

See also: Culture of poverty; Homelessness.

Alexander v. Holmes County Board of Education

In the late 1960's, a group of African American parents in Mississippi filed lawsuits challenging segregation in thirty of the state's school districts. In 1969, the U.S. Court of Appeals for the Fifth Circuit ordered the districts to file desegregation plans by August 11, 1969, to take effect by the beginning of the 1969-1970 school year. With the support of President Richard M. Nixon's Department of Justice, however, the school districts requested the court to allow them to postpone the submission of school desegregation plans until December 1, 1969. The court granted the request, and the parents who had filed the original suits appealed to the U.S. Supreme Court.

On October 29, 1969—only twenty days after deciding to hear the case and only six days after oral argument—the Supreme Court held that the court of appeals had erred in permitting the delay. The Court's decision stated that "the obligation of every school district is to terminate dual school systems at once." The Court ordered every affected school district to "begin immediately to operate as unitary school systems."

Courts throughout the South began to insist on immediate desegregation, in some instances in the middle of the school year. The *Alexander* decision, by rejecting the previous policy of "all deliberate speed," dramatically altered the time frame within which school boards were required to meet their desegregation obligations.

Davison M. Douglas

See also: Busing and integration; Desegregation: public schools.

All African People's Revolutionary Party

The All African People's Revolutionary Party (AAPRP) is a Pan-African socialist political organization for people of African descent. The party has chapters in the United States, Africa, Canada, the Caribbean, and Europe. The AAPRP was founded in 1968 in response to a call by Kwame Nkrumah, the first president of independent Ghana, for a political party that would unify independent African nation-states into a "United States of Africa" and link African people globally. The AAPRP is often associated with one of its founders, Kwame Toure (previously Stokely Carmichael), a key organizer during the Civil Rights and Black Power movements.

The AAPRP adheres to an ideology predicated on the philosophies of Nkrumah and Sekou Toure of Guinea. The party calls for unity among all people of African descent; a focus of efforts toward the liberation and empowerment of Africa; and opposition to colonial, capitalist, and imperialist relations. The party's approach thus runs directly counter to the racial integrationist philosophy of the era previous to its emergence.

The AAPRP is organized in work-study political education structures; it sponsors political events on college campuses and in the African descendant community. The AAPRP also has a women's wing, the All African Women's Revolutionary Union, and a youth component, the Young Pioneers League. The professed objective of the AAPRP is "the total liberation of Africa under scientific socialism."

M. Bahati Kuumba

See also: African Liberation Day; Black nationalism; Black Power movement; Pan-Africanism.

AME Church

A radically distinct denomination becomes an advocate for the cause of abolition and a bulwark of the African American community.

Sixteen African Methodist delegates met in Philadelphia on April 9, 1816, to unite as the African Methodist Episcopal Church. Delegates from Philadelphia and Attleborough, Pennsylvania, joined representatives from Baltimore, Wilmington, and Salem to elect a bishop. They elected Richard Allen, who was consecrated as the first bishop of the African-Methodist Episcopal Church (AME Church) on April 11, 1816. From the original sixteen delegates in 1816, membership grew to 7,257 by 1822.

Allen, known as the father of African American religion, was born a slave in 1760 in Philadelphia. Sold to the Stokeley plantation near Dover, Delaware, Allen attended evangelical tent meetings and experienced a religious conversion when he was seventeen years of age. He joined the Methodist Society, which held classes in the forest under the leadership of a white man, Benjamin Wells. Allen became a convincing proselytizer, converting first his family and then his owner, who agreed to Allen's proposal to purchase his own freedom in 1777. Allen worked at many jobs and preached at his regular stops, developing broad contacts through his travels. As an aide to other itinerant preachers, he met Bishop Francis Asbury, who established the first General Conference of the Methodist Church in America in 1784. Allen declined to accompany Asbury on a trip through the South and returned to Philadelphia in February, 1786.

Allen joined such Philadelphia leaders as former slave clerk and handyman Absalom Jones and other members of the St. Thomas vestry: James Forten, William White, Jacob Tapisco, and James Champion. Allen and Jones became lay preachers throughout the city, including early-morning and evening services at St. George's Methodist Episcopal Church. As African American attendance increased, racial conflict became apparent. In November, 1787, African Americans worshiping at St. George's were ordered to the gallery. After mistaking the section of the gallery assigned for their worship, Allen, Jones, and White were physically removed while praying at the Sunday morning worship service.

The Free African Society   The humiliation of this incident led to a mass exodus of African Americans from this church and a movement to create a separate church. In the spring, these African American leaders established the Free African Society, the first mutual aid society established to serve their community. By 1791, they held regular Sunday services, assumed lay leadership positions, and made plans for construction of a church building.

The leaders differed over the issue of church affiliation, with the majority voting to unite with the Episcopal church. On July 17, 1794, the St. Thomas African Church was dedicated as the first African church in Philadelphia, a Protestant Episcopal church with Jones as pastor. Jones became the first African American priest in 1804.

Allen withdrew from the Free African Society to form a separate church, the Bethel African Methodist Episcopal Church, on July 29, 1794. Allen declared the church independent in management but did not sever all relations with the Methodist Episcopal Church. The articles of incorporation ensured independence by allowing membership only to African Americans. Allen became the first African American to receive ordination from the Methodist Episcopal Church in the United States.

A Force for Change   Such church independence helped African Americans resist the insults and subordination resulting from slavery and racial prejudice and reflected a growing role of the church in the community. Sermons underscored the need for the African American community to become self-reliant through the church, schools, and economic organizations in order to gain group solidarity and recognition. Christian character, in turn, depended upon Christian education.

In 1804, Allen established the Society of Free People of Color for Promoting the Instruction and School Education of Children of African Descent. In 1809, he helped Forten and Jones organize the Society for the Suppression of Vice and Immorality in Philadelphia, to provide community supervision of the morality of African Americans and to establish means for their moral uplift. These leaders recruited three thousand members for the Black Legion during the War of 1812. The successful functions associated with African American churches led to greater membership. By 1813, St. Thomas had a membership of 560, while Bethel Church had 1,272 communicants.

The movement spread to other cities and along the seaboard states. Church leaders continued their pioneering efforts for group solidarity. In January, 1817, the First Negro Convention met at the Bethel Church to protest the plans of the American Colonization Society for emigration of free blacks to Africa. Also in 1817, Allen and Tapisco published the First Church Discipline as well as a book of hymns compiled by Allen, Daniel Coker, and Champion.

The church continued to improve the conditions for African Americans. It supported the use of boycotts to protest the economic basis of slavery through the Free Produce Society of Philadelphia, which was organized at an assembly at Bethel Church on December 20, 1830, to advocate purchase of produce grown only by free labor. The First Annual Convention of the People of Color, convened in Philadelphia in 1831, elected Allen as its leader shortly before his death on March 26, 1831. The African Methodist Episcopal Church has survived as an integral part of the African American community and continued its strong leadership role.

Dorothy C. Salem

Core Resources

Katharine L. Dvorak's *An African American Exodus* (Brooklyn, N.Y.: Carlson, 1991) provides the history and theology of the nineteenth century African Methodist Episcopal Church. A number of books and articles describe Richard Allen and his life and work, including Allen's own *The Life, Experience, and Gospel Labors of the Right Reverent Richard Allen*, originally published in 1833 (Nashville, Tenn.: Abingdon Press, 1983), Carol V. R. George's *Segregated Sabbaths: Richard Allen and the Rise of Independent Black Churches, 1760-1840* (New York: Oxford University Press, 1973), *Richard Allen: The First Exemplar of African American Education* (New York: ECA Associates, 1985) by Mwalimu I. Mwadilitu (E. Curtis Alexander), Charles Wesley's *Richard Allen: Apostle of Freedom* (Washington, D.C.: Associated Publishers, 1935), and Gary Nash's "New Light on Richard Allen: The Early Years of Freedom" in *William and Mary Quarterly* 46 (April, 1989).

See also: African American Baptist Church; AME Zion Churches; Black church; Free African Society.

AME Zion Churches

The African Methodist Episcopal (AME) Zion Church is one of several black Methodist churches that originated in the northern United States in the late eighteenth and early nineteenth centuries. Organized in 1821, the AME Zion Church was conceived in the 1790's, when a handful of black congregations broke away from the predominantly white Methodist Episcopal denomination in search of greater autonomy and freedom of worship. These independent black Methodist churches eventually organized into three separate denominations: the Union Church of Africans; the African Methodist Episcopal (AME) Church; and the New York City-based AME Zion Church. Although largely similar in doctrine, these and other black Methodist churches operated separately, occasionally clashing over competition for membership and the question of which denomination was established first.

The AME Zion Church grew steadily before the Civil War, establishing congregations as far south as Louisville, Kentucky, and rousing white suspicion for its emphasis on abolitionism and religious self-determination. Emancipation and Reconstruction opened the postbellum South to black Methodist churches, sparking a dramatic expansion of AME Zion missionary activity in North America, the Caribbean, and Africa that increased AME Zion Church membership from 4,600 in 1860 to around 350,000 in 1896. In addition to missionary activity, the AME Zion Church has historically emphasized advancement of black citizenship rights, expanded roles for women in church government, and ecumenicism among black and white Methodist churches.

Michael H. Burchett

See also: AME Church; Black church.

American Anti-Slavery Society

The American Anti-Slavery Society, which unified two centers of radical abolitionism, called for immediate eradication of slavery.

In December, 1833, sixty delegates gathered in Philadelphia to form the American Anti-Slavery Society, electing Arthur Tappan, a wealthy New York businessman, as president. They also approved a Declaration of Sentiments, drawn up by William Lloyd Garrison, Samuel May, and John Greenleaf

Whittier, that called for immediate, uncompensated, total abolition of slavery through moral and political action. In signing the declaration, the delegates pledged to "do all that in us lies, consisting with this declaration of our principles, to overthrow the most execrable system of slavery that has ever been witnessed upon earth . . . and to secure to the colored population of the United States, all the rights and privileges which belong to them as men and Americans." The American Anti-Slavery Society organized a system of state and local auxiliaries, sent out agents to convert people to its views, and published pamphlets and journals supporting its position. The society grew rapidly; by 1838, it reported approximately 250,000 members and 1,350 auxiliaries.

Immediatism   Before the 1830's, most opponents of slavery advocated moderate methods such as gradual and "compensated" emancipation, which would reimburse former slave owners who released slaves, or removal of free African Americans to Liberia by the American Colonization Society, founded in 1817. The formation of a national organization based on the principle of immediatism, or immediate and total emancipation, symbolized the new phase that antislavery agitation had entered in the early 1830's—radical, uncompromising, and intensely moralistic. The shift to immediatism was a result of several factors, including the failure of moderate methods; the example of the British, who abolished slavery in the empire in 1833; and, probably most important, evangelical religion. Abolitionists of the 1830's inherited from earlier antislavery reformers the notion that slavery was a sin. This notion, coupled with the contemporaneous evangelical doctrine of immediate repentance, shaped the abolitionist doctrine of immediate emancipation. Abolitionists emphasized moral suasion over political methods. They hoped to persuade people to emancipate the slaves voluntarily and to form a conviction of guilt as participants in the national sin of slavery.

The American Anti-Slavery Society represented the union of two centers of radical abolitionism, one in Boston, the other around Cincinnati. Garrison, the key figure among New England abolitionists, began publishing *The Liberator* in 1831 and soon organized the New England Anti-Slavery Society, based on the principle of immediate abolition. In the Midwest, Western Reserve College and Lane Seminary were seedbeds for the doctrine of immediate emancipation. Theodore Dwight Weld, a young man who had been converted to evangelical Christianity by Charles Finney, organized a group of antislavery agents known as The Seventy, who preached the gospel of immediatism throughout the Midwest.

Although the leadership of the antislavery movement remained predominantly white, free African Americans played a significant role in its ranks. Before 1800, the Free African Society of Philadelphia and black spokespersons such as astronomer Benjamin Banneker and church leader Richard Allen had denounced slavery in the harshest terms. By 1830, there were fifty antislavery societies organized by blacks, and African Americans contributed to the formation of the American Anti-Slavery Society in 1833. African American orators, especially escaped slaves such as Frederick Douglass and Sojourner Truth, moved large audiences with their impassioned and electrifying oratory. African Americans also helped run the Underground Railroad; Harriet Tubman led more than three hundred blacks to freedom. Generally, African American abolitionists shared the nonviolent philosophy of the Garrisonians, but black anger often flared because of the racism they found within the antislavery ranks. Influenced by tactical and race consid-

Fanciful painting of President Abraham Lincoln, the "Great Emancipator," meeting with Sojourner Truth, a tireless opponent of slavery. *(Library of Congress)*

erations, white abolitionist leaders such as Garrison and Weld limited their African American counterparts to peripheral roles or excluded them from local organizations.

Internal Divisions   The late 1830's marked the high point of the movement for immediate abolition through moral suasion. Abolitionism was hard hit by the Panic of 1837, which reduced funds and distracted attention away from reform. At the same time, abolitionists faced an internal challenge as the American Anti-Slavery Society divided into radicals and moderates. One issue causing the split was women's rights. Moderate abolitionists tolerated and even welcomed women in the society, as long as their activities were confined to forming auxiliary societies, raising money, and circulating petitions. They refused, however, the request that women be allowed to speak in public on behalf of abolitionism or to help shape the organization's policies.

The other issue that divided abolitionist ranks was that of political action. Some abolitionists, convinced that political action, not merely moral suasion, was necessary to effect emancipation, formed the Liberty Party in 1840. In the 1840's and 1850's, the majority of abolitionists moved gradually into the political arena, where they became involved in the Free-Soil movement and other aspects of the sectional conflict leading to the Civil War.

Anne C. Loveland, updated by Sudipta Das

Core Resources

Louis Filler's *The Crusade Against Slavery, 1830-1860* (New York: Harper & Row, 1960) is a comprehensive treatment of the people and groups who made up the antislavery movement and the relation of the movement to other reform activities of the period. Lawrence J. Friedman's *Gregarious Saints: Self and Community in American Abolitionism, 1830-1870* (New York: Cambridge University Press, 1982) presents a fresh, challenging analysis of the antislavery movement, written from a psychological perspective and focusing on the first-generation immediatists. *Antislavery Reconsidered: New Perspectives on the Abolitionists* (Baton Rouge: Louisiana State University Press, 1979) edited by Lewis Perry and Michael Fellman contains fourteen original, thought-provoking essays based on a variety of interpretive and methodological approaches. Richard H. Abbott's *Cotton and Capital: Boston Businessmen and Antislavery Reform, 1854-1868* (Amherst: University of Massachusetts Press, 1991) examines the activities and ideology of a group of Bostonian businessmen who fostered abolition. In *The Liberator: William Lloyd Garrison* (Boston: Little, Brown, 1963), John L. Thomas surveys not only the antislavery movement but also the many other reforms in which the well-known editor was engaged.

See also: Abolition; American Colonization Society; Free African Society; Free-Soil Party; *Liberator, The*; Underground Railroad.

American Colonization Society

Organized in 1816, the American Society for Colonizing the Free People of Color of the United States, commonly known as the American Colonization Society, attempted to resolve conflicts over slavery and racism by removing African Americans from the United States. Popular in many northern cities and in the upper South, it counted among its members national figures such as Henry Clay, Daniel Webster, and Francis Scott Key. The society planned to establish a colony in Africa to which free African Americans could voluntarily migrate. Although the society did not address the issue of emancipating enslaved African Americans, it hoped that the colonization scheme would prompt slaveowners to free their slaves, secure in the knowledge that the free blacks would not remain in the South. In 1822, the society helped to found Liberia, on the western coast of Africa, and supported a small settlement there. However, lack of financial support and the commitment to slavery in the lower South doomed the unrealistic plan to failure. Most important, almost all African Americans rejected the notion of colonization, declaring the United States to be their rightful home. Only fifteen thousand made the journey to Liberia in the years before the Civil War (1861-1865).

Thomas Clarkin

See also: Abolition; American Anti-Slavery Society; Pan-Africanism.

American Council on Race Relations

The American Council on Race Relations was founded by liberal whites in 1944, with the goal of obtaining justice for African Americans. Its first president was Charles Pickett of the American Friends Service Committee, supported by other white men of scholarly and religious background. The organization was committed to five strategies for working toward equality: calling for scientific study to dispel misinformation and misunderstanding about African Americans; working with public and private agencies to spread study results; assisting grassroots organizations in developing organizational skills; developing instructional materials for schools; and urging the popular media to use their influence to educate the general public about race.

The council soon became known for levelheadedness and organizational skill. In 1947, the council was asked by a group of city human relations commissioners to host a national conference in Chicago for leaders of groups working for racial justice, including the National Association for the Advancement of Colored People (NAACP), the Anti-Defamation League of B'nai

B'rith, and the Japanese American Citizens League. At this conference a new group, the National Association of Intergroup Relations Officials, was founded. In the 1950's, the American Council on Race Relations worked actively in the Midwest to challenge segregation laws, especially in the public schools.

Cynthia A. Bily

See also: Desegregation: public schools; National Association for the Advancement of Colored People.

Amistad slave revolt

Abolitionists win a victory in the judicial battle that follows an illegal importation of Africans as slaves.

Although the British-Spanish Treaty of 1817 banned African slave trading as of 1820, a highly lucrative covert slave trade existed, especially between Africa and Cuba. In April, 1839, a Portuguese slave ship left West Africa bound for Havana filled with more than five hundred illegally purchased Africans, mostly Mendis. After a two-month passage in which one-third of the Africans died, the ship reached Havana. Government officials receiving kickbacks provided paperwork declaring these Africans to be *ladinos*, slaves residing in Cuba prior to 1820, which would make their sale legal. Within a few days, José Ruiz purchased forty-nine adult African men, and Pedro Montes bought four children, three girls and a boy.

The Uprising   The slaves were loaded onto the schooner *Amistad*, which set sail for Puerto Príncipe, a few days' journey away. The Africans, unable to communicate with the Spanish-speaking owners or crew, became convinced that they were to be eaten. On the third night out, Joseph Cinqué picked the lock on his iron collar and broke into the cargo hold, where he and others found cane knives. The Africans took over the ship, killing the captain and the cook. The two crew members disappeared, perhaps having jumped overboard. Ruiz, Montes, and Antonio, the captain's slave cabin boy, were spared.

The Africans demanded to be taken to Sierra Leone. For almost two months, Ruiz and Montes pretended to comply. During the day they sailed southeast, occasionally landing to scavenge for food and water, but at night they headed north and northeast, in hopes of finding help. The schooner's decrepit condition and the many blacks on board aroused suspicion. The *Amistad* came to the attention of the USS *Washington*, whose captain, Thomas Gedney, ordered the schooner boarded. The thirty-nine surviving slaves, by now almost starved and unable to resist, were taken into custody.

Contemporary illustration of the revolt aboard the *Amistad* in 1839. *(Library of Congress)*

The Legal Battle   Ruiz and Montes filed suits to have their slave property returned to them; Gedney claimed salvage rights to the *Amistad* and its cargo, including the slaves; the Spanish government demanded the fugitives be handed over to it; U.S. abolitionists clamored for the Africans to be set free. Although African slave trade was banned, slavery in Cuba was legal, and Ruiz and Montes had paperwork documenting their ownership. Moreover, there were U.S.-Spanish relations to be considered in determining whether or not the United States should recognize Spanish property rights to the Africans. Precedents from an earlier slaver incident, the *Antelope* case, had to be analyzed also. Perhaps most important, the *Amistad* affair carried grave implications for the slavery issue in the United States—and President Martin Van Buren hoped to avoid that issue in his upcoming reelection campaign, knowing that his success depended on maintaining his coalition of Northern and Southern supporters.

Newspapers across the land kept an interested public informed of the status of the case. For the most part, Northerners were sympathetic toward the Africans, while Southerners felt they should be returned to the Spanish government to be tried for piracy and murder. The affair probably would have been handled quietly and quickly if the abolitionists had not recognized its potential to raise the public's awareness of the moral and legal issues at stake in the slavery question.

Abolitionists and other opponents of slavery quickly formed the *Amistad* Committee, made up of Simeon Jocelyn, Joshua Leavitt, and Lewis Tappan, to raise money for legal counsel and to appeal to President Van Buren to allow the case to be decided by the United States court system rather than turning the prisoners over to the Spanish government. The committee employed James Covey, a native African who could speak the Mendi language, to communicate with the *Amistad* blacks, for so far depositions had been given only by the Spaniards and the cabin boy.

The legal proceedings began in mid-September, 1839, in the United States Circuit Court convened in Hartford, Connecticut. The case worked its way over the next eighteen months from Circuit Court to District Court, back to the Circuit Court and finally to the Supreme Court. The abolitionists made sure that the case stayed before the public. The public, although ambivalent in its responses to the legal and moral questions, stayed interested.

The case also excited international interest, and the cause of the abolitionists was substantially aided when Richard Robert Madden, a British official living in Havana, gave a moving and informed deposition concerning the state of the slave trade in Cuba. He spelled out the means and extent of illegal activities and clarified the status of *ladinos*. He also stated that the children on board the *Amistad* were without doubt too young to be pre-1820 Cuban residents, and that he strongly believed that all the *Amistad* captives were *bozales*, newly imported Africans, not *ladinos*.

The Conclusion   In January, 1840, Judge Andrew T. Judson of the U.S. District Court of Connecticut ruled that the Africans could not be counted as property in the calculation of salvage value, nor could they legally be held as slaves, because their initial purchase had been illegal. The government appealed the case, and a few months later, Judge Smith Thompson of the U.S. Circuit Court concurred in Judson's decision. The government again appealed, and the case came before the United States Supreme Court in early 1841. John Quincy Adams argued passionately on behalf of the defendants. On March 9, 1841, the Supreme Court also ruled that Africans brought to Cuba illegally were not property, that as illegally held free men they had a right to mutiny, and that they should therefore be released. In November, 1841, the Africans sailed to Sierra Leone, accompanied by a small group of New England missionaries.

The *Amistad* decision was a great victory for abolitionists and raised the public's awareness of the slavery issue. The case fed secessionist sentiments in the Southern states but helped opponents of slavery focus on legal attacks against the institution.

Grace McEntee

Core Resources

Christopher Martin's *The "Amistad" Affair* (New York: Abelard-Schuman, 1970) and Howard Jones's *Mutiny on the "Amistad": The Saga of a Slave Revolt and Its Impact on American Abolition, Law, and Diplomacy* (New York: Oxford University Press, 1987) describe the case and its effects. William A. Owens's *Black Mutiny: The Revolt on the Schooner "Amistad"* (Philadelphia: Pilgrim Press, 1968) is a dramatized but well-researched rendering of the incident that includes information on the fate of the Africans after the trial. *The "Amistad" Case: The Most Celebrated Slave Mutiny of the Nineteenth Century* (New York: Johnson Reprint, 1968) contains correspondence between the U.S. and Spanish governments concerning the *Amistad* case.

See also: Abolition; Slave rebellions; Slavery: history.

Antislavery laws
of 1777 and 1807

On July 2, 1777, Vermont became the first of eight northeastern states to end slavery. On March 2, 1807, a federal bill outlawed the slave trade but failed to condemn slavery outright, reflecting the young nation's moral ambiguity.

On July 2, 1777, Vermont became the first state to abolish slavery fully. Its 1777 Constitution outlawed "holding anyone by law to serve any person" as a servant, slave, or apprentice after he or she reached twenty-one years of age. In 1780, Pennsylvania passed a law gradually abolishing slavery. An attempt five years earlier had failed, partly because opponents argued that abolishing slavery would antagonize the South, where slavery was a deeply embedded institution, and break up the Union during the war for independence from England. Under the Pennsylvania law, any African American not registered as a slave by the end of the year would be considered free; however, children born slaves in 1780 would remain in service to their owners until they were twenty-eight years of age to compensate the owners for the cost of raising them. The law also enabled blacks to testify against whites in courts and legalized interracial marriage.

In Massachusetts, opponents defeated a gradual emancipation bill in 1777, and three years later, voters rejected a constitution that declared all men free and equal and provided voting rights for free blacks. In 1781, however, a slave named Quork Walker sued for his freedom in a state court because his owner had severely abused him. The trial judge, Caleb Cushing, instructed the jury that the idea of slavery conflicted with state law, so Walker was ordered freed. Although the legislature refused to act, by 1790, slavery no longer existed in Massachusetts because of similar court actions in dozens of other cases.

During the American Revolution, the New Hampshire legislature gave freedom to any of the state's six hundred slaves who volunteered for the militia. Other slaves gained their liberty by running away and joining the British military. Thus, when the state's 1783 constitution declared all men equal and independent from birth, only fifty slaves remained in the state. Although slavery was never abolished legally, slave property was removed from tax roles in 1789 and eleven years later, only eight slaves remained in the state.

In 1783, Rhode Island passed a gradual emancipation bill after six Quakers petitioned the state assembly for immediate liberation for all human beings kept as property. The bill stipulated that all slave children born after March 1 would be apprentices; girls became free at age eighteen, boys at age twenty-one. After slaves were freed, their masters were required to post bonds with the state guaranteeing that the former slaves would never require public assistance.

Connecticut, the New England state with the largest population of African Americans, granted freedom to slaves who fought against England but three times—in 1777, 1779, and 1780—rejected gradual emancipation. In 1784, however, the legislature declared that all adult slaves would be free by the end of the year and that black and mulatto (mixed-race) children would become free at twenty-five years of age. The state also passed discriminatory laws forbidding free blacks to vote, serve on juries, or marry whites.

Both New York and New Jersey freed African Americans who served in the army, but these states were slow to enact antislavery laws. New York's legislature rejected gradual emancipation in 1777. Eight years later, a freedom bill supported by the New York Manumission Society, whose membership included Alexander Hamilton, John Jay, and Aaron Burr, was defeated. In 1785, New York prohibited the sale and importation of slaves and allowed masters to manumit (free) their slaves, but only if they guaranteed that they would not require public assistance. The next year, New Jersey passed similar laws. In 1788, New York declared that slaves would no longer be judged or punished under standards different from those used to judge whites. Although slave auctions ended in both states by 1790, New York did not pass an emancipation bill until 1799. The bill allowed owners to free their slaves regardless of age or condition but permitted them to keep boys until twenty-eight years of age and girls until the age of twenty-five. In 1804, New Jersey became the last of the original Northern states to end slavery legally. Neither state allowed free African Americans the right to vote.

The 1807 Bill   Although these northeastern states had ended slavery, the invention in 1793 of the cotton gin by Eli Whitney had made cotton a more profitable crop by greatly increasing the speed at which seeds could be separated from the picked cotton, thus increasing plantation owners' desire for more cotton pickers. It has been estimated that no fewer than twenty thousand new slaves were imported in Georgia and South Carolina in 1803.

In December, 1805, Senator Stephen R. Bradley of Vermont introduced legislation that would prohibit the slave trade beginning in 1808, but the bill was stalled for some months. A similar bill was offered in the House of Representatives by Barnabas Bidwell of Massachusetts, again to no effect. Later that year, President Thomas Jefferson urged passage of the bill in his message to Congress. On March 2, 1807, Congress enacted a law specifying a twenty-thousand-dollar fine and forfeiture of ship and cargo for importing slaves, as well as other penalties for acts ranging from equipping a slave ship to knowingly buying an imported slave. The disposition of illegally imported slaves was left to the states, however. Enforcement of the law was delegated first to the secretary of the treasury and later to the secretary of the navy.

Antislavery forces rejoiced in this new and symbolically important law, but enforcement proved weak. An exhaustive census of the slave trade published in 1969 estimated that 1.9 million slaves were imported illegally between 1811 and 1870; more recent research has called that estimate low. Although more than one hundred slave vessels were seized and their officers arrested in the years between 1837 and 1862, and nearly as many cases were prosecuted, convictions were difficult to obtain, and judges often gave light sentences. Another weakness of the 1807 law was that it permitted the continuation of slave traffic between states. An owner could take his slaves into another slave state or, according to the Missouri Compromise of 1820, into a western territory south of 36°30′.

Adapted from essays by Robert P. Ellis
and Leslie V. Tischauser

Core Resources

Books that discuss the end of slavery in the northeastern states include Gary B. Nash and Jean R. Soderlund's *Freedom by Degrees: Emancipation in Pennsylvania and Its Aftermath* (New York: Oxford University Press, 1991), Arthur Zilversmit's *The First Emancipation: The Abolition of Slavery in the North* (Chicago: University of Chicago Press, 1967), and Robin Blackburn's *The Overthrow of Colonial Slavery, 1776-1848* (New York: Verso, 1988). John Hope Franklin's *From Slavery to Freedom: A History of Negro Americans* (5th ed., New York: Alfred A. Knopf, 1980), first published in 1947, is a pioneering study by an African American historian that contains a succinct summary of the enactment of the 1807 law and its aftermath. Warren S. Howard's *American Slavers and the Federal Law: 1837-1862* (Berkeley: University of California Press, 1963) is a copiously documented study of violations of the 1807 law during the quarter century before the outbreak of the Civil War. James A. Rawley's *The Transatlantic Slave Trade: A History* (New York: W. W. Norton, 1981) surveys the slave trade from its fifteenth century beginnings and places U.S. involvement in its international context.

See also: Abolition; Missouri Compromise; Proslavery argument; Slave codes; Slavery: history; Slavery: North American beginnings.

Atlanta Compromise

Booker T. Washington's controversial advocacy of accommodationism had a major influence on African American political and economic strategies.

Booker T. Washington, born a slave on a small Virginia plantation, gained his freedom at the end of the Civil War in 1865. He learned to read by studying spelling books and occasionally attending a school for African American children. In 1872, Washington enrolled at Hampton Institute in Virginia, a technical and agricultural school established for emancipated slaves. After graduation, he taught in Malden, West Virginia, then later returned to Hampton Institute.

As the head of the Tuskegee Institute, Booker T. Washington was considered the leading African American educator of his time and was regarded by whites as the leading spokesperson for all African Americans. *(Library of Congress)*

In May, 1881, Washington received an invitation to join a group of educators from Tuskegee, Alabama, to help establish a technical and agricultural college for African American students. Tuskegee Institute opened on July 4, 1881, with Washington as its principal. Washington raised funds, acquired land, supervised the construction of buildings, and recruited talented faculty members. Within a decade, the school had gained a national reputation for providing outstanding technical and occupational training for African American students.

In the spring of 1895, Washington was invited to join a planning committee for the forthcoming Atlanta Cotton States and International Exposition, which would highlight the South's most recent developments in agricultural technology. Washington was asked to deliver one of the key addresses during the exposition's opening ceremonies, a speech that would focus on the role of African Americans in the South's agricultural economy.

The Address Washington delivered his Atlanta Exposition address on September 18, 1895, to an audience of several thousand listeners. He opened by thanking the directors of the Atlanta Exposition for including African Americans in the event and expressing his hope that the exposition would do more to "cement the friendship of the two races than any occurrence since the dawn of our freedom."

Washington went on to predict that the exposition would awaken among both white and black southerners "a new era of industrial progress." He illustrated his point by telling a parable of a ship lost at sea whose crew members were desperate for fresh water. The captain of another ship, hearing the pleas for water by the captain of the distressed vessel, urged the lost sailors, "Cast down your bucket where you are." When the captain of the lost ship followed that advice, his crew members brought aboard sparkling fresh water from the Amazon River.

Washington then urged his African American listeners to cast down their buckets "in agriculture, mechanics, in commerce, in domestic service, and in the professions." He said that African Americans would prosper "in proportion as we learn to dignify and glorify common labour and put brains and skill into the common occupations of life." He added that "no race can prosper till it learns that there is as much dignity in tilling a field as in writing a poem."

Washington also told his white listeners to cast down their buckets among the South's African Americans, "who have, without strikes and labour wars, tilled your fields, cleared your forests, builded your railroads and cities, and brought forth treasures from the bowels of the earth, and helped make possible this magnificent representation of the progress of the South." He encouraged white Southerners to educate African Americans in "head, heart, and hand" so that they would remain "the most patient, faithful, law-abiding, and unresentful people that the world has seen." He asserted that in "all things purely social we can be as separate as the fingers, yet one as the hand in all things essential to mutual progress."

Washington concluded his speech by expressing his belief that the "wisest among my race understand that the agitation of questions of social equality is the extremest folly, and that progress in the enjoyment of all the privileges that will come to us must be the result of severe and constant struggle rather than of artificial forcing." He emphasized that African Americans must achieve economic self-reliance before they received "all the privileges of the law."

Washington's address was enthusiastically received by those present and the press. President Grover Cleveland wrote a congratulatory note. Washington received dozens of invitations to speak around the country and deliver his pragmatic message of economic self-reliance and political accommodationism.

Critics   Nevertheless, critics of Washington's philosophy soon surfaced, accusing Washington of making an unsatisfactory compromise by accepting an inferior social and political position for African Americans in exchange for economic opportunities. These critics argued that the tools for economic independence alone would not lead African Americans toward full citizenship and that the widespread segregation of and discrimination against African Americans in the United States, especially in the South, was proof of the flaws of Washington's reasoning.

Perhaps the most eloquent critic of Washington's message was W. E. B. Du Bois. In *The Souls of Black Folk* (1903), Du Bois, who would later found the National Association for the Advancement of Colored People (NAACP), asserted that Washington "represents in Negro thought the old attitude of adjustment and submission," that the ideas expressed in what he called Washington's "Atlanta Compromise" were merely "a gospel of Work and Money" that prompted African Americans to surrender political power, civil rights, and opportunities for higher education. In contrast to Washington, Du Bois advocated that African Americans receive the right to vote, civic equality, and opportunities for higher academic education, as opposed to the kind of occupational training offered at Tuskegee Institute.

James Tackach

Core Resources

Two biographies of Booker T. Washington that discuss the Atlanta address are Louis R. Harlan's *Booker T. Washington: The Making of a Black Leader, 1856-1901* (New York: Oxford University Press, 1972) and Arna Bontemps's *Young Booker: Booker T. Washington's Early Days* (New York: Dodd, Mead, 1972). Booker T. Washington's *Up from Slavery* (1901; reprint, New York: Bantam Books, 1970) contains the entire address and a discussion of the events surrounding it. In his *The Souls of Black Folk* (1903; reprint, New York: Penguin Books, 1989), W. E. B. Du Bois critiques the ideas expressed in Washington's Atlanta Exposition address.

See also: Accommodationism; Education and African Americans; National Association for the Advancement of Colored People.

Bakke case

Allan Bakke had applied to the medical school of the University of California at Davis, but he was not among the one hundred applicants finally accepted by the school. Pursuant to university policy, sixteen of the hundred slots had been reserved for racial minority students. Bakke, who was white, claimed that since he was better qualified than some of the applicants accepted for the sixteen minority positions, the university had discriminated against him on the basis of race.

The California Supreme Court ruled in favor of Bakke, and the case was appealed to the U.S. Supreme Court. The case drew national attention, attracting a record-breaking number of *amicus curiae* briefs. On June 28, 1978, the Court, sharply divided, issued its decision in favor of Bakke. In a 5 to 4 vote, the Court held that the University of California at Davis' practice of reserving positions strictly on the basis of race violated Title VI of the Civil Rights Act of 1964. Title VI provides that "[n]o person in the United States shall, on the ground of race, color, or national origin, be excluded from participation in . . . any program or activity receiving Federal financial assistance." Davis did not contest the fact that it was receiving federal financial assistance. Although the decision was not based on constitutional grounds, Justice Lewis Powell, writing for the majority, noted that the guarantees of Title VI are grounded in principles found in the equal protection clause of the Fourteenth Amendment.

A different 5 to 4 majority, however, also declared that race could be considered as one of several criteria for admission to a university. One's status as a racial minority presumably could help one secure admission, but only if the position being contested were formally available to all, irrespective of race. The Court thus did not rule out affirmative action programs in general, only those provisions that amount to strict racial quotas. The decision can therefore be seen as a compromise between those who would abolish all forms of affirmative action as reverse discrimination and those who would guarantee outcomes based on race.

The narrowness of *Regents of the University of California v. Bakke* ensured the continuation of affirmative action programs in various forms. Less than a week after the *Bakke* decision, the Court let stand a lower court's ruling that permitted quantitative "goals" for the hiring and promotion of women and minorities. For almost fifteen years after *Bakke* the Court seemed to agree that the lingering effects of slavery, segregation, and blatant discrimination—and perhaps the continuation of more subtle biases—justified some institutionalized efforts to provide special assistance to racial minorities in employment and education. In the mid-1990's, however, those assumpions were challenged anew. The Supreme Court decision in *Adarand Constructors v. Peña* (1995), for example, ruled that a federal policy mandating that a certain percentage of construction projects receiving funding from the Department of Transportation be set aside for minority-owned companies was unconstitutional.

Steve D. Boilard

See also: *Adarand Constructors v. Peña*; Affirmative action; Civil Rights Act of 1964; "Reverse" racism.

Banking practices

The extension of legally protected civil rights to minorities in the United States has intensified intergroup conflict over socioeconomic mobility. Bank practices regarding the extension of consumer credit—critical in purchasing a home, starting a small business, or obtaining a college education—have shifted from overt to covert forms of discrimination. This trend has helped create the two-tiered financial services system.

The Civil Rights movement of the 1960's provided the moral and legal impetus for redressing the disadvantaged conditions of racial and ethnic minorities in the United States. In the 1970's and 1980's, minorities made substantial progress in overcoming obstacles to socioeconomic mobility as mirrored in their rising educational and occupational levels. As middle-class minorities grew, however, overt discrimination began to be replaced by subtler but no less pernicious forms of racism. One of the most devastating—because of its long-term consequences—is the unequal access to consumer financial services from first-tier, or traditional, banks. This has contributed to the persistence of racial inequality through lower rates of minority home ownership, small business development, and college graduation. Furthermore, the concentration of minorities in urban communities and the consolidation of corporate banking operations in the late 1990's have led to the rapid expansion of second-tier, or fringe, banks that offer high-cost financial services. The second tier of the banking system features check-cashing outlets, rent-to-own stores, and pawnshops, all of which market expensive financial services to primarily poor and minority groups.

Overt Discrimination and First-tier Banks   The institutionalization of race and class discrimination in bank lending practices dates to the inception of the Home Owner Loan Corporation (HOLC) in 1933. As Kenneth T. Jackson explains in his book *Crabgrass Frontier* (1985), the HOLC's goal of stabilizing the home mortgage market was based on appraising property values according to the general characteristics of the surrounding neighborhood rather than the specific properties to be mortgaged. This four-category, color-coded rating system devalued neighborhoods that were densely populated, racially mixed, or aging. Ratings ranged from first grade (green) homogeneous neighborhoods populated by white American (not Jewish) businesspeople and professionals to fourth grade (red) "declining" areas with deteriorating housing stock, low rents, and a racially or ethnically mixed population. This appraisal method is the historical basis of contemporary financial "redlining" or racially discriminatory lending practices, often employed against African Americans.

Overt discrimination by first-tier banks, prohibited by the Civil Rights Act of 1964 and other legislation, has disappeared. However, in subsequent decades, researchers have found that minorities continue to be more likely to be rejected for personal loans (mortgages, car loans, credit cards) than whites with the same socioeconomic characteristics. Although the negative consequences appear to be borne by individuals, the impact is much more profound in that these practices tend to concentrate minorities in declining urban neighborhoods where crime is high, jobs are scarce, and public schools are inadequate. Furthermore, as illustrated in Robert D. Manning's "Multicultural Washington, D.C.," in *Ethnic and Racial Studies* (1998), the postindustrial shift of economic activities away from the central city, which resulted in the exodus of the most successful urban minorities to the suburbs, creates a decline in investment in the inner city. In 1977, the Community Reinvestment Act was enacted to fight redlining policies by requiring banks to invest a small proportion of their loans in underserved areas. This legal commitment has been assailed by the banking industry, and because of the large numbers of corporate mergers in the late 1990's, regulatory enforcement is uncertain although members of minority communities continue to find it difficult to obtain loans.

Covert Discrimination and Second-tier Banks   The deregulation of the U.S. banking industry beginning in 1980 has dramatically affected the cost and availability of consumer financial services. As bank mergers produce fewer branch offices in urban—especially minority—communities and higher fees for bank accounts, including substantially greater minimum cash balances, the numbers of alternative financial service facilities are increasing. John P. Caskey's *Fringe Banking: Check Cashing Outlets, Pawnshops, and the Poor* (1994) documents the rapid increase in the numbers of second-tier, or "fringe," banks that offer high-cost services to poor and minority clients. Second-tier financial service providers include regional and national chains of check-cashing outlets (which charge 1.5 percent to 3 percent for essentially a two- to three-day loan), pawnshops (which charge 10 percent to 15 percent per month plus storage fees), rent-to-own stores (annual cost of credit from 150 percent to 450 percent), and finance companies (which charge 24 percent to 38 percent per year and require costly insurance). The most usurious loans are postdated, personal "payday" checks that typically cost 25 percent for a one-week loan or 1,250 percent per year.

The shift from overt to covert bank discrimination, which is manifest in the dramatic growth of second-tier financial services, generates billions of dollars in annual corporate profits. Michael Hudson, in *Merchants of Misery: How Corporate America Profits from Poverty* (1996), documents the direct and indirect linkages between second-tier banks and major financial corporations such as BankAmerica, Fleet Financial, Ford, NationsBank, and Western Union. These include providing profitable lines of credit, purchasing publicly traded stock, and "flipping" or buying high-interest loans from small companies for a small percentage or "finder's fee." In addition, the U.S. government's shift to paperless financial transactions at the end of the 1990's is likely to force those excluded from top-tier banks to cultivate new and more costly relations with second-tier financial services providers. The profit motive and linkage between the first- and second-tier banks have been suggested as the reason that "fringe" banks are more accommodating and hospitable to racial and ethnic minorities at the same time that first-tier banks are abandoning racial and ethnic neighborhoods. More disturbing, this subtle form of financial discrimination is creating a modern form of debt peonage that perpetuates economic inequality and therefore will exacerbate intergroup tensions.

Robert D. Manning

Core Resources

Kenneth T. Jackson's *Crabgrass Frontier: The Suburbanization of the United States* (New York: Oxford University Press, 1985) documents the historic role of the U.S. government in institutionalizing discriminatory bank lending practices as well as promoting the postwar boom in racially exclusionary suburban communities. *From Redlining to Reinvestment: Community Responses to Urban Disinvestment*, edited by Gregory D. Squires (Philadelphia: Temple University Press, 1992) illuminates the financial origins of the United States' urban decline and examines efforts to revitalize predominantly minority communities through a series of case studies. The historic transformation of the U.S. metropolis, guided by the postindustrial economy, and the changing patterns of racial inequality are the focus of Robert D. Manning's "Multicultural Washington, D.C.: The Changing Social and Economic Landscape of a Post-industrial Metropolis," in *Ethnic and Racial Studies* (volume 21, no. 2, March, 1998). David Caplovitz's sociological classic *The Poor Pay More: Consumer Practices of Low-Income Families* (New York: Free Press, 1963) explores the high cost of consumer credit to America's neediest citizens. Economist John P. Caskey's *Fringe Banking: Check Cashing Outlets, Pawnshops, and the Poor* (New York: Russell Sage Foundation, 1994) examines the exodus of corporate banks from minority neighborhoods and the accompanying growth of bottom-tier financial services. *Merchants of Misery: How Corporate America Profits from Poverty*, edited by investigative journalist Michael Hudson (Monroe, Maine: Common Courage Press, 1996), shows how the high cost of consumer credit for the poor generates huge profits for the United States' largest corporations.

See also: Culture of poverty; Housing; Poverty and race; Redlining; Segregation: de facto and de jure.

Baseball

Brothers named Welday and Moses Walker were the first African American baseball players in the major leagues. They played for a Toledo, Ohio, team in 1884. Racially integrated baseball, however, was poorly accepted, and by the 1920's, major league baseball's first commissioner, Judge Landis, prohibited black players. African American players, with the door to the major leagues closed to them, formed all-black teams in order to pursue their playing activities.

Initially black baseball teams were formed to play exhibition games against white teams or other black teams. The Cuban Giants, formed on Long Island, New York, in 1885, was the first all-black team. Although some short-lived black leagues were formed in the early twentieth century, the first successful one was the Negro National League, founded by "Rube" Foster in 1920. In 1923, a second black league, the Eastern Colored League, was formed. Because of the financial instability of the first black leagues, many teams survived by barnstorming—making exhibition tours—across the

United States. A notable barnstorming was undertaken by the Kansas City Monarchs, who, beginning in 1931, traveled the country with a portable lighting system and played night games several years before the first white major league night game.

In 1936, the Negro American League was formed to replace its failed predecessors. The two most successful teams were the Kansas City Monarchs, who won seven championships, and the Homestead Grays (originally based in Pittsburgh, Pennsylvania), who won nine pennants. Several members of these teams, including catcher Josh Gibson, pitcher Satchel Paige, and infielder Jackie Robinson, were eventually elected to the Baseball Hall of Fame.

The beginning of the end for the all-black leagues came in 1945 when Branch Rickey of the Brooklyn Dodgers signed African American stars Jackie Robinson and John Wright to play on a Brooklyn farm team. Robinson broke the color barrier in 1947 with Brooklyn and was named rookie of the year. The door opened by Robinson was soon entered by Larry Doby, the first African American in the American League (Cleveland), and other black players. By the 1940's, the Negro American League, while retaining older stars such as Gibson, was losing most of its younger talent—Roy Campanella, Willie Mays, and Hank Aaron—to the major leagues. The drain of talent and subsequent declining attendance resulted in the folding of the Negro American League in 1960.

The impact of African Americans on major league baseball was dramatic: The sudden influx of talented players significantly raised the level of play. The composition of the Baseball Hall of Fame illustrates this impact. Even though black players were omitted from the hall from 1936 until 1962 (Robinson's induction), by the close of the twentieth century, more than 10 percent of inductees were African Americans. Progress in other areas of the game was slower. It was 1974 before an African American, Frank Robinson, became a manager. By the late 1990's there were no more than a sprinkling of African American managers during any one season, and few African Americans held higher administrative positions.

Paul J. Chara, Jr.

See also: Sports.

Batson v. Kentucky

On the surface, *Batson v. Kentucky* (decided 1986) was one of a long string of efforts to eliminate discrimination from the judicial system. It departed from the Supreme Court's 1965 holding in *Swain v. Alabama*, in which the Court first considered the use of the peremptory challenge for discriminatory purposes.

In *Swain*, asked whether the equal protection clause of the Fourteenth Amendment prevented the total exclusion of blacks from a jury, the Supreme Court declared that the "presumption in any particular case must be that the prosecutor is using the State's challenges to obtain a fair and impartial jury . . .[even if] all Negroes were removed because they were Negroes." To overcome the presumption, the Court ruled, a defendant would have to demonstrate that the state followed a consistent pattern of discrimination in "case after case."

Swain prevailed until 1986. Challengers were unable to meet the standards of systematic exclusion established in the decision. State and federal courts alike refused to countenance presentation of evidence from only cases that involved black defendants. Over the repeated objections of Justice Thurgood Marshall, the Supreme Court waited to allow "states to serve as laboratories in which the issue receives further study before it is addressed by this Court" again. Marshall called the experimentation cruel, noting that "there is no point in taking elaborate steps to ensure Negroes are included in venires [pools of prospective jurors] simply so they can be struck because of their race by a prosecutor's use of peremptory challenges."

The reconsideration came in *Batson v. Kentucky*. Batson's counsel asked the Court:

In a criminal case, does a state trial court err when, over the objection of a black defendant, it swears an all-white jury constituted only after the prosecutor had exercised four of his six peremptory challenges to strike all of the black veniremen from the panel in violation of constitutional provisions guaranteeing the defendant an impartial jury and a jury composed of persons representing a fair cross section of the community?

James Kirkland Batson had been charged with burglary and the receipt of stolen goods. The prosecutor used four of his six peremptory challenges to create, in his words, an "all-white jury." The defense counsel's motion to discharge the panel before it was sworn in on grounds that the panel did not represent a cross-section of the community and that to use it would be a denial of equal protection was denied by the trial judge. Tried and convicted, Batson appealed to the Kentucky Supreme Court, which upheld the conviction in 1984, based on the *Swain* doctrine. The U.S. Supreme Court disagreed. Reversing the conviction in April of 1986, it held that the impaneling of the jury resulted in a denial of equal protection. It ruled that when objection is lodged against an alleged racially discriminatory use of the peremptory challenge, the trial court must examine the validity of the claim. Thus, for the first time, a federal court agreed that an attorney can be forced to explain his or her reason for invoking a peremptory challenge.

Ashton Wesley Welch

See also: Criminal justice system; Jury selection.

Bigotry

Bigotry is the obstinate and unreasonable attachment to one's own opinions or beliefs. Bigots are intolerant of beliefs that oppose their own. Often, such people are very emotional and may become stubbornly intolerant or even hostile toward others who differ with them regarding religion, race, sexual orientation, or other issues. This state of mind encourages stereotyping, overgeneralization, and other errors that suggest the absence of critical thinking.

Bigoted attitudes can be culturally transmitted as part of the education of children or adults. Bigotry is a learned prejudice that is founded on inaccurate and inflexible overgeneralizations. Bigots may believe, for example, that "all blacks are thieves," despite the fact that they have no experience on which to base this belief. Even if they know a very honest African American individual, they will state that this person is the exception to the rule or has yet to reveal his or her true character. When confronted with new information that contradicts their beliefs, bigots are unwilling to change but instead perceive the contradictory evidence as exceptional and may become excited and emotional.

Bigotry is not confined to race. Some bigots dislike fat people, redheads, or the elderly and discriminate against these populations without cause. However, bigotry, being a learned behavior, is not immutable but can be ameliorated through social policy.

Dallas L. Browne

See also: Discrimination: behaviors; Individual racism; Internalized racism; Psychology of racism; Racism as an ideology; Racism: changing nature of; Racism: history of the concept; "Reverse" racism.

Biracialism

Mixed-race Americans occupy a hidden or virtually invisible place in society, partly because they are not identified under traditional, one-race categorization systems. They are increasing in number and influence and struggling for acceptance.

Mixed-race people have been called biracial, brown, interracial, mestizo, multiracial, mixed, and rainbow. Strictly speaking, the term's use of the prefix *bi-* indicates two races; however, the concept of race itself is open to debate. Between 1870 and 1920, people of black and white parentage were called "mulatto." Historically, people of racially mixed parentage have been considered to be of the same race as the nonwhite parent—if one parent is black, then the child is considered to be black. If both parents are nonwhite and one is a Native American, then the child is considered to be a Native American. Mixed-race people who appear to be white sometimes "pass" for white and hide their true racial makeup. However, some mixed-race Americans dislike one-race classifications and want to be considered as belonging to more than one race. They argue that generally accepted racial categories do not fit them.

The number of mixed-race births in the United States increased noticeably during the last quarter of the twentieth century. U.S. Census Bureau figures showed that the number of interracial marriages increased from 310,000 in 1970 to 994,000 in 1991. Between 1968 and 1989, children born to parents of different races increased from 1 percent to 3.4 percent of all births. About three-quarters of African Americans are multiracial, and perhaps as many as one-third have some Indian ancestry. Virtually all Latinos and Filipino Americans are multiracial, as are most American Indians. Millions of people who consider themselves white have multiracial roots.

History   The first recorded interracial marriage in U.S. history was between adventurer John Rolfe and Pocahontas, the North American Indian princess reputed to have saved Captain John Smith from execution. Fur traders, trappers, mountain men, and Indians often married and produced racially mixed children throughout the eighteenth and nineteenth centuries.

As more white settlers entered the Americas, laws defining an individual's race and against intermarriage began to be passed. In 1785, a Virginia law defined a black person as anyone with a black parent or grandparent. People were considered white if they were one-eighth black. In 1830, Virginia adopted the notorious "one-drop" law—defining as black anyone with one drop of African blood. Whether a person was black was determined by genealogy, physical appearance, claims to identity and heritage, and blood. In essence, the one-drop law excluded everyone with a black ancestry from white society.

Laws prohibiting sexual relations or marriage between a man and a woman of different races—called miscegenation laws—were in force from the 1660's through the 1960's. The laws, created shortly after African slaves were first brought to colonial America, were attempts to restrict mixing of the races and were among the longest lasting of U.S. racial restrictions and the most prominent examples of white supremacy in action. These laws criminalized mixed-race marriages and illegitimized the children. Legislators passed miscegenation laws, and judges and juries enforced them, because they believed setting racial boundaries and categories was crucial to the maintenance of an orderly society. They were determined to protect "white purity." These laws were issues in civil cases about marriage and divorce, inheritance, and child legitimacy and in criminal cases about sexual misconduct.

A state miscegenation law was first held to be unconstitutional in *Perez v.*

Lippold in 1948. The laws prohibiting miscegenation began to fall in the western states in the 1950's and 1960's but persisted in the South until after the landmark *Loving v. Virginia* decision, ruled on by the U.S. Supreme Court in 1967. The Court declared the Virginia miscegenation law unconstitutional because it violated the equal protection and due process clauses of the Fourteenth Amendment. The justices said the Virginia statute was designed to maintain white supremacy through racial categories and argued that culture—not race—determined meaningful human differences. The Court's ruling made racial categories synonymous with racism. In its 1954 ruling on *Brown v. Board of Education*, the Court took another step toward eradicating racism by its deliberate nonrecognition of race. Because of *Brown*, during the 1960's and 1970's, most U.S. states repealed statutes that defined race through blood proportion. The states then attempted to erase racial terminology from their laws.

As the U.S. Supreme Court was trying to limit or eliminate racial categories, the U.S. Office of Management and Budget began to emphasize racial categories. In 1977, it issued a directive that divided Americans into five major groups—American Indian or Alaska native, Asian or Pacific islander, black, white, and Hispanic. The categories were created because the government was mandated by new laws to monitor voting rights and equal access for minorities in housing, education, and employment. These categories and the statistics they generated helped determine everything from census data to eligibility for inclusion in affirmative action programs to the drawing of voting districts. During the biracial baby boom that began in the late 1960's, people who did not fit neatly into these categories were instructed to choose the category that most closely reflected how they were perceived in their communities.

During the late 1970's and 1980's, interracial groups were formed around the country to challenge the official one-category-only classification of multiracial, multiethnic people, particularly in public schools. Some multiracial parents complained that their children were being forced to favor one parent and his or her racial heritage over the other. They argued that forcing children to select one race was a denial of their right to choose who and what they were. In 1990, the U.S. Census Bureau came under mounting pressure to recognize multiracial as a distinct racial category. People who did not want to identify themselves or their children as monoracial led the lobbying campaign to add a multiracial category to the census form. Organizations such as the Association of MultiEthnic Americans argued that monoracial categories were a form of bigotry against racially mixed Americans. They wanted the federal government to establish a public policy that explicitly acknowledged the existence of multiracial/multiethnic people. The government decided against including a multiracial category on the 2000 census; however, it allowed multiracial or multiethnic people to check as many categories as applied.

Fred Buchstein

Core Resources

To understand the feelings and experiences of Americans who live in multiracial families, read *Of Many Colors: Portraits of Multiracial Families* (Amherst: University of Massachusetts Press, 1997) by Gigi Kaeser and *Black, White, Other: Biracial Americans Talk About Race and Identity* (New York: Morrow, 1994) by Lise Funderburg. The cultural, psychological, and social development, identity, and heritage of mixed-race people are explored in *Racially Mixed People in America* (Newbury Park, Calif.: Sage Publications, 1992), edited by Maria P. P. Root, *The New Colored People: The Mixed-Race Movement in America* (New York: New York University Press, 1997), by Jon Michael Spencer, and *Race and Mixed Race* (Philadelphia: Temple University Press, 1993), by Naomi Zack. The culture and diversity of interracial people are treated in *Culture and Difference: Critical Perspectives on the Bicultural Experience in the United States* (Westport, Conn.: Bergin & Garvey, 1995), edited by Antonia Darder, *English Is Broken Here: Notes on Cultural Fusion in the Americas* (New York: The New Press, 1995), by Coco Fusco, and Naomi Zack's *American Mixed Race: The Culture of Microdiversity* (Lanham, Md.: Rowman & Littlefield, 1995).

See also: *Brown v. Board of Education*; Censuses, U.S.; Interracial and interethnic marriage; Miscegenation laws; Multiracial movement; One-drop rule; Passing; Race as a concept.

Black cabinet

The black cabinet was formed by more than a dozen African American men and women who had been appointed to federal positions by President Franklin D. Roosevelt by the year 1935. Known as the Federal Council on Negro Affairs after 1935, it was an informal gathering of African American advisers from various New Deal agencies led unofficially by Mary McLeod Bethune, the director of the National Youth Administration's Division of Negro Affairs. Its members included Robert Weaver, the Negro Affairs adviser in the Public Works Administration, and William Hastie, assistant solicitor in the Department of the Interior. Several other cabinet members later became nationally prominent. They usually met at the home of Bethune or Weaver and informally had some impact on New Deal agencies. Eleanor Roosevelt often provided the impetus behind certain changes after meeting with Bethune.

The appointment of blacks to federal positions symbolized the attempt by some New Dealers to eradicate racial injustice in the United States and influenced some blacks to convert from the Republican to the Democratic Party. President Roosevelt, however, ultimately did not challenge the more intransigent elements of a still segregated society. Still, although the black cabinet did not dramatically alter federal government policies toward African Americans because the appointments were not at the highest levels and its membership was fluctuating, it made white New Dealers more responsive to African American problems.

David L. Porter

See also: Roosevelt coalition; Summit Meeting of National Negro Leaders.

Black church

The term "black church" refers collectively to the many autonomous denominations of African American Christian churches. The black church evolved as a highly visible social institution in response to white racism in American society and racism in white-defined Christianity.

Although African American religious experience is diverse and social forms of religious life vary greatly, the black church has historically been the most visible religious institution in African American culture. As a visible institution controlled from within the black community, the black church has played a central role in African American social and political history. This history has evolved within the broader historical context of American racism and racial politics. The church, also evolving within that broader context, has been an important center for the development of African American Christian theology and for community identity. In fact, the black church originated as a formal institution when African American religious leaders in Philadelphia were forcibly removed from worshiping on the main "whites only" floor of St. George's Methodist Episcopal Church. When Richard Allen and Absalom Jones were evicted from the church in 1787, they and their fellow black Christians concluded that the racism of white-defined Christianity precluded full Christian expression for blacks in white-controlled congregations. Their formation of the Free African Society that year paved the way for the later creation of the fully autonomous African Methodist Episcopal (AME) Church, one of the earliest black churches in the United States. An institutionalized form of distinct African American Christian theology began to emerge.

Lincoln/Mamiya Model   In their expansive sociological study entitled *The Black Church in the African-American Experience* (1990), C. Eric Lincoln and Lawrence H. Mamiya propose a dynamic model for interpreting the sociology of black churches in their diversity and complexity. Lincoln and Mamiya identify the major black denominations as the AME Church, the AME Zion

Church, the Christian Methodist Episcopal (CME) church, the National Baptist Convention, U.S.A., Incorporated (NBCA), the Progressive National Baptist Convention (PNBC), and the Church of God in Christ (COGIC). These denominations, as well as many other smaller ones and local churches, provide institutional structure for the religious (and often political) life of millions of African American Christians.

Although sociologists and political historians debate the nature of the black church and its political role, Lincoln and Mamiya offer a "dialectical model of the black church" that encourages an open and ongoing analysis. The Lincoln/Mamiya model offers a way of analyzing the ongoing tensions, both theological and political, within African American Christianity as those tensions are embodied in the structure of the black church. The model proposes the following six "dialectically related" pairs, or opposites. With these pairs the focus is on the ways that human experience shifts back and forth between the two opposites, sometimes tending more toward one idea, sometimes tending more toward the other.

For example, the first dialectic is that between "priestly" and "prophetic" functions of the church. In other words, it concerns how the church balances its role as the center for worship (priestly) in relation to its role as an agent for social change in the community (prophetic). Second, there is a dialectic tension in the black church between the "other-worldly" and the "this-worldly." Does the church focus on individual spiritual salvation for the "life to come" or does it focus on social justice in the here-and-now? The third

Christian churches have long been one of the most rigidly segregated sectors of American society. *(Library of Congress)*

dialectic proposed by Lincoln and Mamiya is between "universalism" and "particularism": how the black church negotiates its role in Christianity, broadly speaking, and its very particular role in African American history. The black church is part of a universal religious institution but is also a very particular response to white racism in American Christianity. A fourth dialectic is between the "communal" and the "privatistic": How does the church address individual spiritual life in the context of the social realities of African American experience? The fifth dialectic is especially important politically; it is between the "charismatic" and the "bureaucratic." This involves how the church uses the power of personalized and local leadership in relation to developing larger-scale institutional structure and national leadership as well as how it handles the tensions inherent in doing both. Finally, Lincoln and Mamiya join many African American historians and cultural critics when they identify the dialectical tension between "accommodation" and "resistance." Given the realities of white racism and African American history's origins in the experience of slavery, how has a primary social institution such as the black church moved between accommodating and resisting white mainstream culture in the United States?

Politics and the Church It is in this final dialectic that much of the debate over the role of the black church in the twentieth century Civil Rights movement evolved. It is debated, for example, whether the church served as an accommodationist spiritual escape that diluted the intensity of its members, whether the church served as a fundamental source of activism and militancy, or whether the black church did both.

During the 1950's and the 1960's, the Civil Rights movement accelerated and moved to the center of the national political stage. Beginning with efforts to integrate schools following the Supreme Court's *Brown v. Board of Education* decision in 1954 and continuing through the Montgomery bus boycott (1955-1956), the formation of the Southern Christian Leadership Conference (1957), the Freedom Rides summer (1961), and the March on Washington (1963), hundreds of thousands of African Americans confronted American racism and fought for fulfillment of the United States' stated commitment to freedom for all its people. The black church played a central role during these years, providing people and resources for grassroots organizing while cultivating leadership for the national movement.

During this period, tensions arose in the black community that illustrate the sociological complexity of the church as a social institution. From the perspective of the emerging Black Power movement, the church was suspect in its adherence to Christian principles of nonviolence in the face of white racial violence and was deluded in its emphasis on integration into mainstream American society. For black nationalists, this mainstream society remained white-dominated and white-controlled. Some nationalists argued that African American Christianity itself was flawed because of its origins as a religion of enslavement.

From another perspective, political and religious leaders such as Martin Luther King, Jr., proposed that African American Christianity provided both the spiritual and material bases for a militant liberation theology, one that posed a radical challenge to the white-supremacist status quo of the mid-twentieth century United States. King was a nationally recognized Christian leader, but with him were thousands of African American Christian women and men who argued that the black church provided the path of most, rather than least, resistance to white racism. As Lincoln and Mamiya point out, the fact that white racists bombed several hundred black churches during the civil rights period indicates that the threat posed to white supremacy by the black church was substantial.

A second debate that highlights some of the issues from the Lincoln/Mamiya model concerns the role of women in the black church. During the Civil Rights movement, women provided the "rank and file" of many organizing efforts, working together with men to form the core of the movement. In the church, however, men still maintained a monopoly in terms of formal congregational leadership. On the national level, this trend was even more pronounced; the nationally recognized black leadership of the Civil Rights movement was almost exclusively male. Women such as Rosa Parks, Fannie Lou Hamer, and Mamie Bradley (Emmett Till's mother) were recognized on a national level, but the political leadership of black women in many key political battles, especially on the local level, went unacknowledged both in the national media and in the formal leadership structure of the church.

Gender politics are significant because they highlight tensions within the church when issues that are often expressed in secular political terms (such as women's oppression) are also engaged in theological and spiritual terms. This can result in significant structural change within a social institution such as the black church. In the case of women and the church, the political becomes religious and the religious becomes political, bringing into play the dynamic tensions between the "this-worldly" and the "other-worldly," between the "priestly" and the "prophetic."

Sharon Carson

Core Resources

E. Franklin Frazier and C. Eric Lincoln's *The Negro Church in America: The Black Church Since Frazier* (New York: Schocken Books, 1974) is an important sociological study that offers the comparative perspectives of two important scholars of the black church. C. Eric Lincoln and Lawrence H. Mamiya's *The Black Church in the African-American Experience* (Durham, N.C.: Duke University Press, 1990) covers theoretical and historical issues as well as providing in-depth denominational histories and useful statistical data. Peter J. Paris's *The Social Teaching of the Black Churches* (Philadelphia: Fortress Press, 1985) is a very good source for more detailed discussion of the ways that the black church, as a social institution, has participated in African American culture. *African American Religious Studies: An Interdisciplinary Anthology* (edited by

Gayraud S. Wilmore, Durham, N.C.: Duke University Press, 1989) offers both a wide range of readings in the subject of African American religion and an introduction to many important scholars in the field.

See also: African American Baptist Church; AME Church; AME Zion Churches; Church burnings; Civil Rights movement; Free African Society.

Black codes

In their broadest sense, black codes were laws aimed at controlling African American life in the nineteenth century. Some of these laws, the slave codes, applied only to slaves. As America's indigenous black population grew, free blacks became increasingly subject to discriminatory laws designed to ensure their acquiescence to white rule. For example, some states refused to allow black people to carry canes, a widely recognized symbol of authority, and free blacks in nearly all states could be sold into slavery for failure to pay their taxes. Moreover, fearing that free blacks might incite or assist slave insurrections, especially in the wake of Nat Turner's revolt (1831), antebellum black codes became increasingly severe. In most southern states, free black status was barely distinguishable from slave status on the eve of the Civil War.

The term "black codes" most commonly refers to laws passed by former Confederate state legislatures in response to the Thirteenth Amendment to the Constitution (1865). These laws bestowed certain civil rights on the newly freed black population. While these codes varied from state to state, all black codes legitimized African American marriages, recognized their right to own property, and permitted blacks to sue and be sued, enter into contracts, and testify in court cases involving other blacks. On the other hand, most black codes forbade interracial marriage, denied blacks the right to bear arms, and prohibited blacks from testifying against whites in courts of law. On an even more negative note, the black codes merely granted African Americans an apprentice-like status that in no way conferred genuine freedom. They also attempted to tie black employment to a socioeconomic system that closely resembled slavery. Most states required newly freed blacks to secure employment with a local landowner or face involuntary service in plantation labor. Free blacks were also subject to involuntary service for civil offenses ranging from vagrancy and derogatory gestures to "mischief" and preaching the Gospel without a license. Moreover, in some states white landowners were subject to a fine or imprisonment for attempting to hire black laborers who were already under contract to someone else.

Appalled by southern actions, northern congressmen began calling for legislation that would ensure civil rights for all African Americans. The result was the Fourteenth Amendment to the Constitution, which forbade denial of "life, liberty, and property without due process of law" and guaranteed citizenship to all persons born or naturalized in the United States. This amendment, ratified on July 28, 1868, constitutionally guaranteed civil rights that had been stipulated earlier in the Civil Rights Act of 1866. It would take nearly a century, as well as the 1964 Civil Rights Act, however, for African Americans to gain their full civil rights under this constitutional amendment.

Keith Harper

See also: Civil rights; Civil Rights Act of 1964; Civil Rights Acts of 1866-1875; Fourteenth Amendment; Grandfather clauses; Jim Crow laws; Literacy tests; Miscegenation laws; Turner's slave insurrection.

Black colleges and universities

Black colleges and universities are historic institutions of higher education that have targeted African American students. They have been a major education vehicle for African Americans, allowing them to become credentialed to interact with others at work and socially and have enhanced intergroup understanding and relations.

Lincoln University in Lincoln, Pennsylvania, established by Presbyterians in 1854, is the oldest black institution of its kind still in existence, and Wilberforce University in Ohio, established by Methodists two years later, is the second oldest. Both facilities have remained in their original locations. However, the first separate educational facilities for blacks were private African schools established by free blacks after the Revolutionary War. Like later black colleges and universities, the early schools provided a strong sense of black identity as well as a way in which students could prepare for employment. Work opportunities, however, were often limited to manual labor or two professions that the larger society felt were less threatening: the ministry and teaching.

Many private and public historically black colleges and universities were established during the post-Civil War era and became the primary means by which African Americans could obtain a higher education in a society that restricted them from attending white institutions, either by law or by social norms. When they were created, many of these colleges were called "universities" or "colleges" but were actually secondary-school-level institutions. When studies that led to the professions of minister and teacher were incorporated into their curricula, these institutions rose to a post-high-school level. In most cases, the post-Civil War historically black colleges and universities included a theological purpose for all students: the instilling of what were considered Christian values.

Founded by the federal government in 1867, Howard University in Washington, D.C., quickly became one of the most prestigious black colleges in the nation. *(Library of Congress)*

By the early part of the twentieth century, American philanthropic organizations had started to help support black colleges and universities through financial gifts. In the North and West, these gifts were not considered problematic, but in the South, many whites insisted that fiscal support go to institutions that emphasized vocational and industrial training. Two major black academics of that era, Booker T. Washington of Tuskegee Institute in Alabama and W. E. B. Du Bois of Atlanta University in Georgia, debated the type of education that African Americans, especially in the South, should receive. Washington emphasized the need for vocational and industrial training, while Du Bois focused on education that would lead to the professions. By the 1930's, however, the debate was moot: Most historically black colleges and universities had developed into full-fledged colleges that required a high school diploma for entrance, and many were increasing graduate studies. These developments began to be supported in the 1940's with the establishment of the United Negro College Fund, which pooled the fiscal resources of financially fragile private institutions. By the end of the twentieth century, enrollment at black colleges and universities had increased to its highest levels, which demonstrates that they retained their appeal to African Americans.

Demographics   Historically black colleges and universities are predominantly black academic institutions established before 1964 whose main purpose has historically been the educating of African Americans. Each must be state authorized to provide either a junior college education or a four-year bachelor's degree, and each must be accredited by an association recognized by the U.S. Department of Education or show progress toward achieving that accreditation.

There were 109 historically black colleges and universities in 1995. Fifty of these, or 46 percent of the total, were public institutions, and the remainder were private institutions. They were located in fourteen southern states, three northern states, and three midwestern states plus the District of Columbia and the U.S. Virgin Islands. The institutions offered more than 450 academic programs in the liberal arts, sciences, education, business administration, social work, law, medicine, dentistry, engineering, military science, theology, and other fields. Most of the institutions offered associate or bachelor's degrees. Thirty-eight of the schools offered master's degrees, and twelve offered doctorate degrees. Some offered professional degrees.

Enrollments in black colleges and universities represented about 3 percent of total higher educational institution enrollments in the United States in the mid-1990's. Black enrollments increased from the 1960's to 1980, decreased from 1981 to 1986, and then increased in the late 1980's and the 1990's. Generally, black male enrollment has slightly decreased over these periods, while black female enrollment has increased significantly. Historically black colleges and universities welcome nonblack students. In 1976, white enrollment in these institutions was more than 18,000; by 1989, this had increased to more than 26,000. Some institutions in gateway cities, such as Florida Memorial College in Miami, have had as much as one-third of their total student enrollments come from Hispanic communities. The majority of faculty and staff at these institutions are black, and the remainder are white, Latino, and nonblack foreign nationals. Although the institutions enroll just 20 percent of all African American undergraduates, they produce 30 percent of those who graduate.

Impact   American higher education has always been pluralistic; certain institutions were created primarily to serve students of a particular gender, race, ethnicity, or religion. Black colleges and universities fit this national pattern, even though their histories and original needs may have differed. The impact of these institutions on the African American communities of the United States has been significant: Many of the local and regional African American leaders—ministers, educators, politicians, businesspeople, writers, artists—throughout the latter part of the nineteenth and the entire twentieth century have been graduates of black colleges. One of the more famous graduates is civil rights leader Martin Luther King, Jr. Black colleges and universities, first established from necessity, have continued to be prominent in American educational life because they have a purpose that appeals to their majority clientele, the encouragement and credentialing of an ethnically aware population. At historically black colleges and universities, many black students thrive academically in an environment they consider supportive and socially acceptable.

William Osborne and Max Orezzoli

Core Resources

Historically Black Colleges and Universities: Their Place in American Higher Education, by Julian Roebuck and Komanduri Murty (Westport, Conn.: Praeger, 1993), includes very specific data from studies of race relations among students on both black and white campuses. A fine, older anthology that considers many issues faced by black educational institutions is *Black Colleges in America: Challenge, Development, Survival*, edited by Charles Willie and Ronald Edmonds (New York: Teachers College Press, 1978). Many scholars have contributed to this volume, which includes discussions of the self-concept of the colleges, the role of the graduate, the interaction of black college faculty and students, and teaching in key areas of the sciences and humanities. The United Negro College Fund has edited studies of black colleges and universities that provide continuing statistics and changing data, such as B. Quarles's "History of Black Education," in *United Negro College Fund Archives: A Guide and Index to the Microfiche* (New York: University Microfilms, 1985). The American Council on Education's Office of Minority Concerns publishes *Minorities in Higher Education: Annual Reports* (Washington, D.C., various years), an annual document full of data and statistics.

See also: Atlanta Compromise; Desegregation: public schools; Education and African Americans; United Negro College Fund.

Black conservatism

Black conservatives tend to oppose treating people as members of racial groups; therefore, they tend not to support programs that aim at improving the situations of disadvantaged groups by means of what they term "racial preferences," including affirmative action. They usually place little emphasis on discrimination as a cause of minority disadvantages and maintain that individual self-help is the best way to overcome these disadvantages.

Contemporary black conservatism is the product of two related historical developments, the elimination of legal discrimination and the rise of the black middle class. The Civil Rights movement of the 1950's and 1960's was successful in overcoming segregation and overt discrimination by law in the United States. By the end of the 1960's, laws enforcing segregation had been struck down almost everywhere in the United States, and blacks had registered to vote in large numbers. African Americans and whites who believed that racial justice could be achieved simply by the government's ceasing to maintain unequal laws concluded that the Civil Rights movement had achieved its goal of equality between the races. Some argued that any remaining inequality would disappear as individual African Americans achieved higher levels of education and acquired attitudes consistent with upward mobility.

With the disappearance of discriminatory laws, a substantial group of well-educated, financially successful black Americans began to appear. Between 1960 and 1981, the percentage of blacks in the middle class almost tripled, from 13 percent to 38 percent of the black population. In general, the higher the social and economic position of an individual, the more likely that individual is to hold conservative views on matters such as economics and the role of government in society. Black success, then, has tended to encourage black conservatism.

Conservative Black Intellectuals   Thomas Sowell, an economist with degrees from Harvard, Columbia, and the University of Chicago, was one of the earliest and most influential of contemporary black conservatives. From the early 1970's onward, Sowell produced a long string of books in which he argued that liberal attempts to help blacks had simply made them dependent and led them to see themselves as victims. He argued that success is a product of a culture of achievement and that blacks could create such a culture by striving for individual self-sufficiency.

Many of Sowell's themes were adopted by other black academics. Glenn Loury, an economist at Harvard who later moved to Boston University, became well known in the 1980's for his opposition to affirmative action and his advocacy of black self-help. Loury, who expressed discomfort with being labeled as a conservative, argued that many of the problems of inner-city blacks were the result of irresponsible behavior. English professor Shelby Steele sounded many of the same notes in his books, *The Content of Our Character: A New Vision of Race in America* (1991) and *A Dream Deferred* (1998). Steele argued that many African Americans had adopted a view of themselves as victims and that they should concentrate on getting ahead by their own efforts.

The ideas set forth by black conservatives influenced African Americans usually not considered conservative, such as sociologist William Julius Wilson. Wilson maintained that discrimination was no longer as responsible for black disadvantage. The lack of jobs, combined with attitudes and forms of behavior created by dependency, produced the black underclass in the inner city, according to Wilson.

Conservative Blacks in Politics   Conservative black public figures attracted a great deal of attention in the 1980's and 1990's. In 1991, President

George Bush nominated Clarence Thomas, an outspoken opponent of affirmative action, to the U.S. Supreme Court. As head of the Equal Employment Opportunity Commission during the administration of President Ronald Reagan, Thomas had rejected lawsuits on behalf of minority members as a group and pursued only lawsuits regarding individual acts of discrimination. Thomas's nomination, despite charges of sexual harassment, was confirmed.

In 1991, Gary Franks of Connecticut became the first black Republican elected to the House of Representatives since 1932. Franks always maintained a conservative position and opposed the Civil Rights Act of 1991. Although Franks was defeated in his majority-white district in 1996, most observers agreed that race was not the reason for his loss.

In the 1996 presidential primaries, black Republican Alan Keyes sought the Republican presidential nomination. Keyes, a former U.S. State Department official with a doctorate in government from Harvard, had headed the conservative organization Citizens Against Government Waste. He had run unsuccessfully for U.S. senator from Maryland in 1988 and 1992. His presidential campaign, in which he opposed affirmative action and abortion, also failed to win him the nomination.

Ward Connerly, a former real estate investor who had been appointed by California governor Pete Wilson to the University of California Board of Regents, focused national attention on the campaign against affirmative action. Connerly led the attack on affirmative action programs in the state's university system. He became the foremost proponent of the state's Proposition 209, an initiative banning affirmative action in California that passed in 1997 and was later challenged in the courts.

Criticisms and Defenses Critics of black conservatives have accused them of saying things that please whites in order to further their own careers and of turning against programs such as affirmative action after benefiting from them. They have pointed out that the majority of black conservatives in political office, including Thomas and Connerly, have been appointed and not elected. Civil rights activist Julian Bond has argued that black conservatives receive attention because they get corporate sponsorship. Critics have pointed out that Thomas was nominated as Supreme Court justice after serving as a federal appellate court judge for only sixteen months. Connerly has been accused of having used minority set-aside programs to make money during his career in real estate.

In response, black conservatives and their defenders have pointed to the continuing existence of a large, poverty-stricken black population in the United States. They have maintained that liberal programs have failed to improve the lives of those in this population. Further, they have accused their critics of stereotyping African Americans as monolithically liberal and of demanding intellectual conformity.

Carl L. Bankston III

Core Resources

The views of black conservatives are presented in *Black and Right: The New Bold Voice of Black Conservatives in America* (Westport, Conn.: Greenwood, 1997), edited by Stan Faryna, Brad Stetson, and Joseph G. Conti. This collection of twenty-five essays contains writings by Justice Clarence Thomas, Shelby Steele, and former Connecticut congressman Gary Franks. Many of the goals and arguments of black conservatives are presented in *A Conservative Agenda for Black Americans* (Washington, D.C.: Heritage Foundation, 1990), edited by Joseph Perkins. Stephen L. Carter presents the view that affirmative action is unnecessary and harmful to blacks in *Reflections of an Affirmative Action Baby* (New York: Basic Books, 1992), a book about his own experiences as a student at Yale law school. Another highly personal book that presents a perspective usually associated with black conservatism is Shelby Steele's *The Content of Our Character: A New Vision of Race in America* (New York: Harper Perennial, 1991) and *A Dream Deferred* (1998). The essays in Glenn C. Loury's *One by One from the Inside Out: Essays and Reviews on Race and Responsibility in America* (New York: Free Press, 1995) consider the problem of racial inequality in the United States. Although often classified as a conservative, Loury rejects this label and argues that Americans must move beyond the liberal-conservative categories in thinking about race. Economist Thomas Sowell's views on race are in *Race and Culture: A World View* (New York: Basic Books, 1994).

See also: Affirmative action; Black middle class/black underclass relations; Civil Rights movement; Poverty and race; Proposition 209; Set-asides; Thomas/Hill hearings; Wilson-Willie debate.

Black flight

Movement from urban to suburban areas is often thought of as occurring primarily among whites. However, middle-class African Americans have also been leaving cities for suburbs, often settling in primarily black suburbs.

In the decades following World War II, the United States became an increasingly suburban nation as Americans left cities for suburbs. During the 1940's, the federal government began guaranteeing mortgage loans in order to encourage Americans to become homeowners. These mortgage guarantees went primarily to those buying homes in the suburbs, and they frequently underwrote home ownership in neighborhoods that intentionally excluded blacks. At the same time, the growing use of private automobiles and the construction of the freeway network encouraged movement to the suburbs.

As whites became more suburban, blacks became more urban. Early in the twentieth century, the African American population had been primarily rural. As agriculture became more mechanized, blacks moved to urban areas. Black concentration in cities, like white concentration in suburbs, was encouraged by the federal government. The federal Public Housing Authority established public housing largely in central city areas and restricted residence in public housing to the most economically disadvantaged. Because blacks were proportionately much more likely to be poor than whites were, the availability of public housing in cities combined with housing discrimination in the suburbs to bring black Americans into urban areas.

By the 1970's, white movement from the cities to the suburbs had become known as "white flight." Many observers of current events believed that whites were fleeing the cities to get away from blacks. The racial integration of schools, and especially the busing of children to achieve racial integration, may have contributed to the movement of whites out of the cities, although social scientists continue to debate this point.

Whites, however, were not the only ones to move to the suburbs. After the 1960's, the middle-class African American population grew rapidly, and suburban housing became more widely available for them. During the 1970's, the African American suburban population of the United States grew at an annual rate of 4 percent, while the white suburban population grew at a rate of only 1.5 percent. African American movement to the suburbs, labeled "black flight" by some social scientists, continued throughout the 1980's and 1990's. It was driven by many of the same factors that had been driving "white flight": the concentration of the poor in central city areas, the deteriorating condition of urban neighborhoods and schools, and the availability of suburban housing.

Black movement to the suburbs did not, however, lead to fully integrated neighborhoods across the United States. Instead, as authors Douglas S. Massey and Nancy A. Denton maintained in their influential book, *American Apartheid* (1993), African Americans tended to move into majority black suburban neighborhoods. Thus, "black flight" further concentrated minority poverty in the inner city by removing the middle class from inner city neighborhoods, while largely failing to integrate the American suburbs.

Carl L. Bankston III

See also: Black middle class/black underclass relations; Discrimination: racial and ethnic; Housing.

Black Is Beautiful movement

The Black Is Beautiful movement, part of a broader drive to change political, economic, and social conditions for African Americans, emphasized the importance of countering stereotyped representations. Originating in the

Black Power movement of 1965-1975, the phrase "black is beautiful" appealed to large segments of the black community not directly involved with movement organizations. Music and visual arts were central to this appeal: James Brown's "Say It Loud, I'm Black and I'm Proud" and Aretha Franklin's "Respect" signified the change in spirit from earlier integrationist phrases of the movement.

Movement theorists, including Kwanza founder Ron (Maulana) Karenga, declared the necessity of an art connected with the African American community and committed to its well-being and proposed that black art should "praise the people" as well as "expose the enemy" and "support the revolution." The Black Is Beautiful movement initiated sustained investigations of African traditions and history and celebrated the distinctiveness of African American culture. The success of evocations of "soul" in black music, food, speech, physical beauty, body language, and clothing inspired the creation of independent presses and bookstores and student demands for African American studies departments. Though the Black Power movement lost most of its impetus by 1975, the Black Is Beautiful ethos exerts a continuing influence on the struggles for multicultural, feminist, and homosexual self-definition.

Trudi D. Witonsky

See also: Black Panther Party; Black Power movement; Universal Negro Improvement Association.

Black middle class/black underclass relations

Much scholarly debate has taken place on the extent and consequences of the interactions between the black middle class and black underclass, in particular the effect of middle-class presence on the lives of poor urban blacks. A number of theories of urban poverty identify the lack of a connection between the black underclass and black middle class as a factor in the perpetuation of poverty.

The first step in understanding the relationship between the black middle class and the black underclass is to examine the concept of the underclass. The meaning and usefulness of the term have been debated frequently among scholars; however, the concept is potentially beneficial because it describes the new form of poverty that exists in urban areas. This inner-city poverty, unlike that of earlier decades, is characterized by chronic and persistent joblessness, concentration in a particular geographic area, and racial segregation.

The Underclass The term "underclass" implies a lack of social and economic mobility. Although considerable progress was made toward racial equality in the 1950's and 1960's, some researchers believe that this progress has stopped and perhaps even reversed itself since the early 1970's. As signs of persistent inequality, they cite a growing gap in the incomes of blacks and whites, lower economic rewards for higher educational attainments on the part of blacks, and greater segregation and isolation of the races rather than increased mobility. The concept of an underclass, therefore, they argue, is an appropriate portrayal of the urban poor.

However, regardless of its potential, the term "underclass" has been stigmatized to the point that it has lost much of its usefulness as an analytical tool. Much of the discussion about the underclass does not focus on the structural factors that have segmented this population and constrained its members' mobility. Instead, the discussion tends to focus on crime and other negative products of poverty. This negative image has diverted attention from scholarly analysis and instead produced racism-tinged discussions of the immorality of the poor. The idea that people are impoverished because of their immorality and unwillingness to work is deeply rooted in American ideology. Many people believe that the United States is a meritocracy, in which all people are rewarded for their hard work on the basis of merit, and that no inequities factor into this equation. Therefore, many Americans equate the underclass with the "undeserving poor." This emphasis on the supposed immorality and deviance of the poor stigmatizes the underclass and turns the urban poor into scapegoats for many of the nation's problems. For example, some people believe that economic strain is caused primarily not by changes in the economy or the effects of inflation but by the use of tax money to support the underclass.

The concept of the underclass also evokes images of poor, young, urban African Americans that often produce feelings of fear, anger, and disdain among members of the white middle and upper classes. Although it is no longer socially acceptable to speak of members of racial minorities in disparaging terms, some of the harsh criticisms of the supposed immorality and criminal tendencies of the poor inner-city African Americans mask lingering racist attitudes toward blacks. The moral and racist connotations of the term "underclass" have made it ineffective as a conceptual framework for understanding the truly disadvantaged and the structural forces that have produced their poverty.

Community The degree of community believed to exist between the black middle class and the black underclass varies. Some scholars suggest that the African American community has diverged so much that the two groups share very little in common. In *The Declining Significance of Race* (1978), sociologist William Julius Wilson suggests that class, not race, is becoming the fundamental category of stratification in U.S. society. Therefore, he argues that members of the black middle class have much more in common with their white peers than with the poor and working-class members of their racial group.

The Declining Significance of Race produced heated debate among academics and numerous scholars who argued that race was still a primary determinant of life opportunities in the United States. They said that although no one could deny the increasing class differentiation within the African American community, the stratification could not be said to measure racial equality. Racial inequality could still be observed in differences between whites and blacks in income, education, mortality, housing, psychological well-being, and other measures of the quality of life. The black middle class still suffers from lingering racism and discrimination in spite of civil rights legislation and affirmative action policies. Its increasing prosperity, occurring as it does alongside the severe hardship of the black underclass, is not a sign of the amelioration of racial discrimination.

Wilson suggests that when segregation was legal, the black community experienced a much stronger form of class integration. The black middle class lived and worked among poor and working-class blacks. The black middle class provided valuable social and material resources to their less advantaged neighbors. However, with the post-World War II economic boom and the passing of legislation against racial discrimination and segregation, the black middle class expanded and separated itself from the rest of the community. The class structure within the black community became more differentiated and hierarchical.

However, researchers warn against forming too communal a view of the segregated ghetto. Closer inspection of historical studies of the black ghetto during segregation shows that the African American community evidenced a highly stratified society within a compact geographical space. Although they were not totally able to separate themselves from the rest of the black community, the black middle class continuously attempted to form discrete enclaves within the geographic area. Without the forced segregation resulting from white racism, the black middle class would probably have been more successful at separating themselves spatially from poor and working-class blacks. Although researchers agree that the black middle class lived in close proximity to poor blacks, almost no data exist about the frequency and quality of their interactions.

Implications   Many scholars as well as community activists are hoping that the black middle class will become more involved in improving the opportunities of poor African Americans. Through mentoring and youth development programs, members of the black middle class are encouraged to share their knowledge, social networks, and values with black urban youth. A strong political movement within the African American community is seeking resources to address its social needs. Specifically, the disillusionment with liberal politics has led many African American activists to emphasize themes of empowerment and self-determination. This new political agenda, known as black empowerment, places much more emphasis on the dimensions of class and community. It focuses on the control of land in urban communities, emphasizing the economic and cultural strengthening of African American communities. Such a political agenda requires a strong interclass coalition and a commitment of the black middle class to share material and social resources.

Kesha S. Moore

Core Resources

Numerous books address the issues of race, class, and community. These include Elijah Anderson's *Streetwise: Race, Class, and Change in an Urban Community* (Chicago: University of Chicago Press, 1990), Oliver C. Cox's *Caste, Class, and Race: A Study in Social Dynamics* (New York: Doubleday, 1948), Edward Franklin Frazier's *Black Bourgeoisie* (New York: Free Press, 1965), Douglas Massey and Nancy A. Denton's *American Apartheid: Segregation and the Making of the Underclass* (Cambridge: Harvard University Press, 1993), W. J. Wilson's *The Declining Significance of Race: Blacks and Changing American Institutions* (Chicago: University of Chicago Press, 1978), St. Clair Drake and Horace Cayton's *Black Metropolis: A Study of Negro Life in a Northern City* (1945; reprint, Chicago: University of Chicago Press, 1993), and W. E. B. Du Bois's *The Philadelphia Negro: A Social Study* (1899; reprint, Philadelphia: University of Pennsylvania Press, 1996).

See also: Class theories of racial/ethnic relations; Economics and race; Poverty and race; Wilson-Willie debate.

Black nationalism

Black nationalism is an identity movement that emphasizes the distinctiveness of black heritage and culture and a revitalization movement that seeks to empower black communities so that they direct their own futures and have more control over their relations with other racial and ethnic groups.

Black nationalism, a historical movement that dates back to the sixteenth century, first appeared as protests by enslaved blacks who were being transported to the Americas and continued in the form of organized slave revolts that lasted until the Emancipation Proclamation. These protests could be termed nationalistic because the participants attempted to reclaim historic identities and rejected the power that whites had over them. One of the earliest, best-organized black nationalist movements was started by Paul Cuffe between 1811 and 1815. Cuffe was a black sea captain who transported several dozen black Americans to Africa in an attempt to establish a colony in Sierra Leone. Although black nationalism took various forms in the history of the United States, blacks who emphasized their identity and power have always existed.

The International Aspect Black nationalism has been most explicitly expressed and most broadly studied in the United States, but the movement is not limited to one nation. Black nationalists have asserted their distinctiveness and attempted to achieve self-empowerment in many postcolonial countries in the world, including Caribbean basin nations such as Jamaica, the Bahamas, Trinidad and Tobago, and earlier in history, Haiti. Nationalistic feelings not only helped black people in these nations rid themselves of the European powers that had colonized them but also continue to affirm their distinctiveness. Black nationalist organizations have been active in Brazil, South Africa, and western Europe, particularly Great Britain. Many of the movements outside the United States have influenced blacks in America, and American black nationalists have had an effect on blacks in other countries, especially during the latter half of the twentieth century.

Black Nationalist Leaders Throughout U.S. history, the black nationalist movement has been led by members of the clergy. In slave eras, some religious leaders would sing black spirituals that often had a political and social meaning in addition to their theological intent. Some of these songs, such as "Steal Away to Jesus," were used to gather plantation slaves who would escape to freedom. In post-slave eras, African American ministers often became the major organizers of nationalistic movements because they were the primary leaders of black communities. In their sermons, ministers often drew analogies between the enslaved people of Israel in the Old Testament and disfranchised African Americans. Some black theologians such as Joseph Washington have suggested that black churches functioned as political organizations whose main goal was freedom from white oppression. In the early twentieth century, African American sociologist W. E. B. Du Bois advocated a dual-consciousness for blacks that emphasized their distinctiveness while recognizing them as Americans. Eventually Du Bois became disenchanted with the limitations on black status in the United States and explicitly promoted a Pan-African movement that would coordinate freedom movements between blacks in America and Africa. Toward the end of his life, he considered Africa the national homeland for all blacks and encouraged them to migrate there.

Marcus Garvey, a West Indian who had immigrated to the United States, was the creator of the largest mass movement of nationalistic blacks in the history of the nation. Under the auspices of his Universal Negro Improvement Association (UNIA), millions of American blacks were recruited to one of the institutions and businesses he set up as alternatives to white-dominated facilities. These included black capitalist enterprises such as restaurants, grocery stores, hotels, and entertainment centers and a steamship line that served to transport black Americans wishing to migrate to Africa. Most important, he also established the African Orthodox Church, a religious denomination that symbolized the highest values of a people seeking freedom and empowerment. White hostility and organizational mismanagement diminished the UNIA's influence, but Garvey had demonstrated how separate institutions could help African Americans maintain their group identity and be empowered to express it.

Contemporary Black Nationalism   Many black movements followed in Garvey's footsteps, but one, in particular, has been successful in continuing parts of his legacy while rejecting any notion of moving back to Africa. The Nation of Islam, whose members are sometimes called Black Muslims, flourished under the leadership of Elijah Muhammad between the 1930's and the 1960's, reaching a peak membership of more than 100,000. The group's membership, however, does not reflect the many African Americans who did not join the organization but admired its tenets. The Nation of Islam shared Garvey's insistence that African Americans have their own separate organizations in a white-dominated nation and claimed that the black nation in the United States had a right to be an independent nation with its own land. The Nation of Islam claimed that blacks were the original people of creation and, therefore, the pure race. Blacks were to remain separate from nonblacks because interacting with nonblacks could only make them less pure. The Nation of Islam emphasizes the central role of the man in the family, the importance of economic self-sufficiency, the necessity to abstain from degrading habits such as alcohol, drugs, and casual sex, and the worship of Allah, the creator. Their institutions are primarily mosques and religious houses of teaching and worship, but they also have agricultural areas in the South, small businesses in the North, and some educational facilities such as elementary schools in their headquarters, Chicago, Illinois.

The death of Elijah Muhammad and the division of his organization into several groups has not diminished the influence of some of his followers. Louis Farrakhan, the leader of the most important of these groups, has expanded membership, accepted some Latinos and other minorities into the Nation, and correlated the Nation of Islam's agenda with non-Muslim organizations including black Christian churches and black community-based political groups.

The Impact of Black Nationalism   The two major debates among black nationalists in the United States center on whether African Americans need to return to Africa or at least live separately and on what kind of alliances they should form with other organizations and people. Many people question whether a group can be seriously nationalistic without going back to Africa or establishing a separate territory within a previously white-dominated country. Malcolm X, who was Elijah Muhammad's primary spokesperson while he was a member of the Nation of Islam, first believed in setting up a separate nation within United States boundaries but later perceived nationalism as a commitment and act that did not require geographical separation. Huey P. Newton and Bobby Seale, cofounders of the nationalistic Black Panther Party for Self-Defense, interpreted existing African American communities as unofficial black "places" that should be allowed self-determination and the expression of racial pride. Farrakhan has played down the notion of a separate land and instead emphasized the idea of separate thought. The second debate involves how closely black nationalists should ally themselves with either blacks who are not nationalistic or nonblacks. Malcolm X's organization, founded after he left the Nation of Islam, Newton's Black Panther Party, and even Farrakhan's organization have worked with nonblacks, and all three have interacted with African American Christian clergy, who remain important black community spokespersons and organizers.

In the 1960's, when the U.S. Congress passed a series of desegregation laws, some people believed it would result in the demise of black nationalism. However, because the legal changes did not substantially affect discriminatory customs and attitudes, and African Americans remained the object of subtler forms of racism in their economic, political, and social lives, nationalism survived and grew. African Americans, even if they do not belong to a black nationalistic organization, continue to feel nationalistic pride and to attempt to empower themselves. As long as the United States is not a racially blind nation, it is likely that black nationalistic thinking and acts will affect American life. Black communal pride and black self-determination, the marks of identity and revitalization movements, remain relevant as long as the social implications of black "inferiority" persist.

HERE AND NOW FOR BOBBY SEALE

We must save Bobby Seale because we must save the Black Panther Party because we must save the revolutionary spirit in America.

Poster issued by the Black Panther Party in support of its cofounder Bobby Seale when he was being tried for conspiracy to riot in 1968. *(Library of Congress)*

William Osborne and
Max Orezzoli

Core Resources

Modern Black Nationalism: From Marcus Garvey to Louis Farrakhan (New York: New York University Press, 1997), an exceptional anthology, relates the major black power era leaders' ideas and discusses contemporary movements through the 1990's. The major academic proponent of black nationalism, W. E. B. Du Bois, traces his own evolving thinking and contradicts some of his earlier social ideas in *Dusk of Dawn: An Essay Toward an Autobiography of a Race Concept* (New York: Harcourt Brace, 1940). For interviews of major figures of the movement, see *The Negro Protest: James Baldwin, Malcolm X, Martin Luther King Talk with Kenneth B. Clark*, edited by Kenneth B. Clark (Boston: Beacon Press, 1963). An incisive interpretation of the changes in Malcolm X's life and thought appear in George Breitman's *Last Year of Malcolm X: The Evolution of a Revolutionary* (New York: Merit Publishers, 1967). One of the most important historical works on the Nation of Islam is C. Eric Lincoln's *The Black Muslims in America* (Boston: Beacon Press, 1961). The Black Panther Party's minister of information, Eldridge Cleaver, wrote the twentieth century classic autobiography evidencing black identity problems called *Soul on Ice* (New York: McGraw-Hill, 1968).

See also: Afrocentrism; Black church; Black Is Beautiful movement; Black Panther Party; Black Power movement; Nation of Islam; Universal Negro Improvement Association.

Black-on-black violence

Black-on-black violence reached epidemic proportions in the United States in the 1990's. This particular manifestation of intraethnic violence is frequently miscast as a relatively recent (post-1960's) phenomenon. However, social historian James W. Clarke documents an increased prevalence of violence within African American urban and rural communities since the nineteenth century. What has changed is the rate of increase of such violent confrontations and the youth of the victims. In the late 1990's, homicide surpassed disease and accident as the number-one cause of death in male African Americans age fifteen to thirty-four, and the lifetime risk of death by homicide was six times greater for African Americans than for whites. Earlier notions of the causes of black-on-black violence were based on presumed racial (biologically/genetically based) differences in aggression. Later, more psychologically oriented views portrayed black-on-black violence as compensation for self-perceived inferiority, manifested as self-hate.

Such views, while persistent among the general population, have been largely discredited. Black-on-black violence may be more reasonably viewed as a cultural phenomenon rather than as a racially or psychologically based act. Contemporary theory on black-on-black violence is typified by that of sociologist William J. Wilson, who postulates that disadvantage in community structure predicts violence equally in both African American and white neighborhoods. The fact that more African Americans than whites live in the conditions that promote violent behavior results in the different rates of intraethnic violence between African Americans and whites. Isolation from the society at large, diminished access to traditional role models, and dimmer job prospects make systematic upward mobility a dream that is not likely to be visualized or attained. The result is an erosion in the ability of traditional social controls such as schools and community self-supervision to govern violent behavior.

The black-on-black violence witnessed at the end of the 1990's may be attributed to several factors. The number of poverty-stricken communities, along with the magnitude of poverty in the most disadvantaged neighborhoods, has risen steadily since the 1970's. The resultant increase in stressors, plus context-specific attitudes advocating extreme response to relatively minor infractions, has a synergistic effect, creating a vicious cycle in which young persons witness routinized violence as a problem-solving tool, come to view such violence as a norm, and adopt this behavior as teenagers and adults, effectively modeling this behavior for subsequent generations. If handguns are readily available, people may tend to settle perceived challenges using guns rather than their fists, with devastating consequences.

The single best predictor of aggressive behavior as an adult is aggressive behavior as a child or adolescent. It is likely, therefore, that the surge in black-on-black violence has not yet crested. Systemic problems require systemic solutions. Such solutions are aided by a rising reconceptualization of black-on-black violence as a major public health issue requiring society-wide prevention and intervention techniques to stem the epidemic. According to sociologist William Oliver, steps in the solution include providing greater access to education and jobs, greater dispersal of African Americans into the society at large, more stringent gun-control laws, strategically placed violence-prevention programs, and renewed community dedication toward the functional socialization of African American youth.

James B. Epps

See also: Crime and race/ethnicity; Criminal justice system.

Black Panther Party

The Black Panther Party for Self-Defense was considered a militant organization of African Americans that grew rapidly in major U.S. cities between 1966 and the mid-1970's. The party's confrontational approach to race and ethnic relations marked a change in focus of the Civil Rights movement from nonviolence to self-defense and black power.

The Black Panther Party was founded in 1966 by Huey P. Newton and Bobby Seale, two African American college students, in Oakland, California. The organization grew rapidly in urban areas of the United States and is estimated to have increased to between two thousand and five thousand members in its first three years. The overall objective of the Black Panthers was political, economic, and social equality for the African American community. Their philosophy and strategies differed from the nonviolent and civil disobedience tactics of the earlier Civil Rights movement. From the Black Panther viewpoint, the African American community was exploited and dominated by the United States' capitalist power structure, which used the police as a controlling force. Emphasis was therefore placed on self-defense, black unity, and achieving equal rights "by any means necessary."

Party Philosophy   The Black Panthers promoted a "revolutionary nationalist" philosophy that called for African American liberation and black community empowerment through self-reliance and the destruction of capitalism. Their teachings combined the black nationalist philosophies of Malcolm X with Maoist socialist philosophy. The Black Panthers' philosophy is summarized in its Ten Point Program, called "What We Want, What We Believe":

1. We want freedom. We want power to determine the destiny of our Black Community.
2. We want full employment for our people.
3. We want an end to the robbery by the capitalist of our Black Community.
4. We want decent housing, fit for shelter of human beings.
5. We want education for our people that exposes the true nature of this decadent American society. We want education that teaches us our true history and our role in the present-day society.
6. We want all Black men to be exempt from military service.
7. We want an immediate end to POLICE BRUTALITY and MURDER of Black people.
8. We want freedom for all Black men held in federal, state, county, and city prisons and jails.
9. We want all Black people when brought to trial to be tried in court by a jury of their peer group or people from their Black communities, as defined by the Constitution of the United States.
10. We want land, bread, housing, education, clothing, justice, and peace. And as our major political objective, a United Nations-supervised plebiscite to be held throughout the Black colony in which only Black colonial subjects will be allowed to participate, for the purposes of determining the will of Black people as to their national destiny.

Party Programs   The Black Panther Party, identified by the distinctive black leather jackets and berets worn by members, was best known for its

This official propaganda poster of the Black Panther Party uses two of the movement's primary icons: a gun and a book. *(Library of Congress)*

confrontational activities. These included openly carrying guns (then legal in California if unloaded), directly challenging the local police, and espousing antigovernment rhetoric. One of the Black Panthers' earliest strategies was monitoring the activities of the police in the African American community. In their role of "policing the police," Black Panthers would observe police interactions with community residents and inform the community members of their rights.

The Black Panthers were also known for the "survival programs" that they initiated. The first and most popular of these programs was the Free Breakfast for School Children Program, which began in 1970. It provided breakfasts for children in the community with food donated by local merchants. The survival programs in various Black Panther chapters included free clothing programs, legal assistance, and preventive health care services. The Black Panthers also sought to distribute alternative newspapers within the community. The Black Panther newspaper, *Black Panther: Black Community News Service*, was established in 1967 to facilitate this goal. The Black Panthers joined with other radical organizations of that period, including the Students for a Democratic Society (SDS) and the Student Nonviolent Coordinating Committee (SNCC).

The Destruction of the Party   The Black Panthers were viewed with great apprehension and disdain by the larger American population. The media emphasized their criminality and portrayed them as a violent, antiwhite organization. From the federal government's perspective, the Black Panther Party was an internal threat to the country. As head of the Federal Bureau of Investigation (FBI), J. Edgar Hoover spearheaded systematic efforts to infiltrate, attack, and destroy the Black Panthers through the Counterintelligence Program (COINTELPRO) administered by the FBI. This strategy, which began in the late 1960's, fueled internal conflicts between Black Panther Party members and external tensions between the party and other African American organizations. Other tactics employed included police raids on Black Panther headquarters, killing and jailing of members, and the use of infiltrators and informers. These actions hastened the Black Panther Party's destabilization and demise in the mid-1970's.

M. Bahati Kuumba

Core Resources

Huey P. Newton, founder of the Black Panther Party, wrote two books, *To Die for the People* (New York: Random House, 1972) and *Revolutionary Suicide* (New York: Harcourt Brace Jovanovich, 1973). Bobby Seale's *Seize the Time: The Story of the Black Panther Party and Huey P. Newton* (New York: Random House, 1968) chronicles the emergence and philosophy of the Black Panther Party from an insider's perspective. Panther minister of information Eldridge Cleaver's version of the Black Panther philosophy and ideology appears in *Soul on Ice* (New York: Dell, 1968). Elaine Brown's autobiography, *A Taste of Power* (New York: Pantheon, 1993), provides an insider woman's perspective of the Black Panthers. The historical documents of the Black Panther Party have been compiled by Philip Foner in *The Black Panthers Speak—The Manifesto of the Party: The First Complete Documentary Record of the Panthers Program.* For an illustrated introduction to the Black Panther Party, see Herb Boyd's *Black Panthers for Beginners* (New York: Writers and Readers, 1995).

See also: Black Is Beautiful movement; Black Power movement; Civil Rights movement.

Black Power movement

In 1967, Stokely Carmichael (later Kwame Toure) and Charles V. Hamilton, in their book *Black Power* (1967), argued that "black power" as a concept rests on the premise that before a group can enter the open society it must first close ranks. Carmichael, head of the Student Nonviolent Coordinating Committee (SNCC), and Hamilton, a professor at Columbia University, captured the mood of many young blacks in 1966 who rejected the nonviolent, assimilationist, Civil Rights movement led by Martin Luther King, Jr. Carmichael, who had marched with King in the South, split with King to adopt a more militant approach to combating American racism. By the summer of 1966, black power became the rallying cry for angry young blacks. As a movement it demanded an end to social injustice and a redefinition of the black liberation struggle that would be shaped by blacks themselves.

Although the movement was first associated with Carmichael, other prominent leaders of the movement included H. Rap Brown (later Jamil al-Amin), who led a protest delegation to the United Nations, Huey P.

Newton and Eldridge Cleaver, major figures in the Black Panther Party in Oakland, California, Bobby Seale of the Black Panthers, author-poet LeRoi Jones (later Imamu Amiri Baraka), author-professor Angela Davis, and Ron (Maulana) Karenga, founder of the black cultural holiday known as Kwanza.

Although united by their militant opposition to what they saw as injustice toward blacks, black power groups differed in their vision of the future and in the political strategies they embraced. For example, groups associated with Karenga redefined black culture in terms of Kwanza, while Jones and Brown redefined black culture in terms of Islam. Cleaver and Newton's Black Panthers gained notoriety for violent encounters, including shootouts with police. Regardless of their ideological differences, black power groups frightened many whites. Another aspect of the Black Power movement was the joining of some black militants with white radicals to forge a potent antiwar movement (members of the Black Panther Party, for example, worked with white radical groups such as Students for a Democratic Society).

Like many white radicals, black power leaders modified their political views over time, creating a decline in the movement. For example, Carmichael became a pan-Africanist and emigrated to the West Africa state of Guinea. Newton earned a Ph.D. degree but died violently in 1989 at the hands of drug lords in California. Karenga and Davis became college professors in California. Cleaver, who became a born-again Christian and a Republican, died in 1998. Jamil al-Amin became the leader of a large Islamic community in Atlanta, Baraka became a Marxist college professor in New York, and Seale wrote a cookbook in the early 1990's. The presence of blacks in various fields in the 1990's can be seen as a reminder of the legacy of both the Civil Rights and Black Power movements and their impact on social justice in the United States.

Samory Rashid

See also: Black Panther Party; Civil Rights movement; Student Nonviolent Coordinating Committee.

Blackness and whiteness: legal definitions

The inconsistencies in racial categories over the course of U.S. history reveal the inherent social construction of race. The federal government has never legally defined "whiteness" and "blackness," but individual states have done so in myriad ways that have fluctuated with changes in racial attitudes.

The United States Census illustrates the fluidity of racial definitions on a national level. The Office of Management and Budget (OMB), which constructs the racial options on the census, continues to alter the number and description of these categories. These determinations are influenced by common usage in the population. For example, in 1790, the first U.S. Census divided the population into free white males, free white females, slaves, and other persons (these included free blacks and American Indians residing in or near white settlements).

Throughout most of the nineteenth century, the U.S. census broke African Americans down into black and mulatto (mixed-race) racial categories. The 1890 census created the categories of quadroon and octoroon (one-quarter and one-eighth black, respectively) to distinguish between various black-white biracial persons. Toward the beginning of the twentieth century, as the "one-drop rule" ("one drop" of black blood made the person black) became entrenched in U.S. society, the census no longer included any mixed-race categories. After 1920, the census classified persons with any African ancestry as black.

Through 1950, census enumerators determined the racial classification of the individuals they recorded. In 1960, the bureau collected data through a combination of observation, direct interviews, and self-classification. Since the 1970 census, the primary means of collecting data has been through self-administered surveys. Debate over methods of data collection escalated toward the end of the 1990's, with some advocating statistical sampling as a means of obtaining a more accurate count of U.S. residents.

Although the majority of Americans with African heritage also have American Indian and/or white ancestors, there was no significant change in the percentage of Americans racially classified as black when the census became self-administered. This indicates the internalization of the "one-drop rule" among Americans with African American ancestry and may also be attributed to the lack of a multiracial option and census instructions to choose only one racial category. In 1998, the OMB, in response to the requests of the growing multiracial movement, decided to include instructions to "check all that apply" among the racial category options on the 2000 census.

No national legal definitions of "white" and "black" exist in the United States. The race of Americans is determined by the legislation of individual states. The census describes white Americans as those "having origins in any of the original peoples of Europe, the Middle East, or North Africa" and black or African Americans as those persons "having origins in any of the black racial groups of Africa." It is unclear how much longer these categories will exist. The categorization of persons by race and the very concept of race are increasingly challenged throughout all levels of American society. Just as racial categories on the census face an uncertain future, states' legal definitions of "whiteness" and "blackness" may soon be under fire.

Kathleen Odell Korgen

See also: Biracialism; Censuses, U.S.; Race as a concept.

Bleeding Kansas

A territorial war between free-soil and proslavery elements presages a national civil war.

With the opening of Kansas Territory to settlement in 1854 through the Kansas-Nebraska Act, a contest began between groups supporting slavery (mainly persons from Missouri) and settlers from the Northwestern states who were Free-Soilers in practice, if not ideology. The Missourians seized control of the territorial government and immediately enacted proslavery legislation. President Franklin Pierce and his successor, James Buchanan of Pennsylvania, accepted the proslavery Kansas government and committed the Democratic Party to the admission of Kansas as a slave state.

By September, 1855, enough Free-Soilers had entered the state to enable them to repudiate the territorial legislature, organize a Free State Party, and call for a constitutional convention to meet in Topeka. A free-state constitution was written in October and November, 1855, and in January, 1856, the party elected a governor and legislature. Kansas found itself with two governments—one supporting slavery and considered legal by the Democratic administration in Washington but resting upon a small minority of the population; and the other representing majority opinion in Kansas but condemned as an act of rebellion by President Pierce and Senator Stephen A. Douglas of Illinois. Douglas, who had drafted the Kansas-Nebraska Act of 1854 as a way to extend a railroad westward across the territories, favored the theory of popular sovereignty, letting the people decide the issue of slavery. That doctrine, however, was exposed—eventually by Abraham Lincoln in the Lincoln-Douglas debates—as unconstitutional: The will of the people could not be held above constitutionally protected rights.

The Violence Begins   Although proslave and free-soil groups moved into Kansas, actual bloodshed remained at a minimum through 1855; nevertheless, the territory quickly came to symbolize the sectional dispute. Violence became commonplace in Kansas through the spring and summer of 1856. Armed free-soil and proslavery parties skirmished along the Wakarusa River south of Lawrence as early as December, 1855; but it was the sack of Lawrence in May, 1856, by a large band of proslavery Border Ruffians from Missouri, that ignited the conflict. Retaliation was demanded: John Brown, the abolitionist crusader, his four sons, and three others struck at Pottawatomie, where they executed five settlers who were reputed to be proslavers. That act of terrorism sparked further retaliation. Early in August, free-soil forces captured the slavery stronghold of Franklin; later that month, Free-Soilers, led by Brown, repelled an attack by a large party of proslavers at Osawatomie. Guerrilla warfare raged throughout the territory until September, when a temporary armistice was achieved by the arrival of federal troops and a new territorial governor, John W. Geary. However, a solution to the travail of Kansas could come only from Washington, D.C., and it would have to overcome the determination of the Democratic administration and its Southern supporters to bring Kansas into the Union as a slave state. Meeting at Lecompton in January and February, 1857, the proslave territorial legislature called for an election of delegates to a constitutional convention. The measure passed over Governor Geary's veto.

The Lecompton Constitution   The constitutional convention that met in Lecompton in September, 1857, hammered out a document to the electorate; the proslavery leadership would agree only to submit the document to the people with the choice of accepting it with or without the clause explicitly guaranteeing slavery. However, ample protection for slavery was woven into the fabric of the constitution. Opponents refused to go to the polls, and the proslavery Lecompton Constitution was approved in December, 1857.

The Free-Soil Party, meanwhile, had captured control of the territorial legislature and had successfully requested the new territorial governor, Frederick P. Stanton, to convene the legislature in order to call for another election. On January 4, 1858, the Lecompton Constitution met overwhelming defeat. Kansas was, by that time, free-soil in sentiment, but the Buchanan administration supported the Lecompton Constitution, which became a test of Democratic Party loyalty. Although Douglas came out against the administration's position, the Senate voted in March, 1858, to admit Kansas under the Lecompton Constitution. Public sentiment in the North opposed such a policy, and the House of Representatives voted to admit Kansas as a state only on the condition that the state constitution be submitted in its entirety to the voters at a carefully controlled election. That proviso was rejected by the Senate.

A House-Senate conference proposed the English Bill, a compromise measure that stipulated that the Lecompton Constitution should be submitted to the people of Kansas again: If the bill were approved, the new state would receive a federal land grant; if it were rejected, statehood would be postponed until the population of the territory reached ninety-three thousand. Although Congress passed the bill in May, the voters of Kansas rejected the Lecompton Constitution again, this time by a margin of six to one. In January, 1861, after several Southern states announced secession, Kansas entered the Union as a free state under the Wyandotte Constitution.

John G. Clark, updated by Larry Schweikart

Core Resources

Roy F. Nichols's *The Disruption of American Democracy* (New York: Macmillan, 1948) is a traditional, yet effective, analysis of the 1850's, emphasizing the destruction of the Democrats as the national party. William E. Gienapp's *The Origins of the Republican Party, 1852-1856* (New York: Oxford University

Press, 1987) emphasizes the rise of the Republican Party as the crucial element in ending the earlier U.S. party system. Argues that the formation of the Republican Party represented a realignment that started with the demise of the Whigs, continued with the rise of the Know-Nothings, and culminated with the events in Kansas that galvanized the disparate elements.

See also: Compromise of 1850; Free-Soil Party; John Brown's raid; Kansas-Nebraska Act; Lincoln-Douglas debates; Proslavery argument.

Body of Liberties

The Body of Liberties of 1641 granted slavery in Massachusetts Bay Colony a formal status, making it an institution in the British colonies.

From its outset, the Massachusetts Bay Colony endorsed the idea of unfree labor. One hundred eighty indentured servants arrived with the original colonists. Food shortages led to the surviving servants' being set free in 1830. Unfree labor, however, continued on a private basis, and some white criminals were made slaves of court-appointed masters. Captives from the Pequot War of 1636-1637 were given over into slavery. Some of these captives were subsequently transported to a Puritan enclave off the coast of Nicaragua, and black slaves were introduced from there to the Massachusetts colony. The colony, however, remained without a formal endorsement of slavery until the promulgation of the Body of Liberties in 1641.

The Creation of the Document The Body of Liberties evolved out of the gradually weakening authority of Governor John Winthrop and his first Board of Assistants, and the emergence of the General Court as a representative body of freemen. In 1635, the General Court had appointed a committee to draw up a body of laws for the rights and duties of the colonists. This committee stalled over the church-state conflict, and another committee was impaneled in 1636. John Cotton sat on this committee. Cotton was a devout churchman who drafted a document that derived much of its authority from scripture. Cotton did, however, believe in limitations on authority and resisted adopting biblical statutes wholesale. Winthrop, who was lukewarm to the entire idea, called Cotton's code, "Moses his Judicialls."

Cotton's counterpart in drawing up the code was Nathaniel Ward. Ward was a Puritan with a sense of humor and a literary bent. Like most Puritans, he was a friend to strict discipline, but he also was a foe to arbitrary authority. He agreed with Winthrop and Cotton that all law was the law of God, but he insisted that the code be based on English common law rather than on the Bible. He became the chief architect and intellectual godfather of the Body of Liberties. The Pequot War slowed deliberations, but by 1639, the committee had created a document that combined Cotton's and Ward's work. The final document was adopted in November, 1641.

The Slavery Issue In many ways, the Body of Liberties was an enlightened document and certainly remarkable by seventeenth century standards. A compilation of one hundred laws, the Body of Liberties allowed for wide judicial discretion and for each case to be judged on its merits. It also effectively barred the legal profession from defending anyone for pay, and it protected married women from assault. It addressed the liberties of servants in humanitarian terms for those times, limiting the number of lashes given to servants to forty. The capital laws were more lenient than those of England. The one problem, however, was slavery. This bold document addressed the slavery issue thus:

> There shall never be any bond slaverie, villainage or captivitie amongst us unles it be lawfull captive, taken in just warres, and such strangers as willingly selle themselves or are sold to us. And these shall have all the liberties and Christian usages which the law of God established in Israell concerning such persons doeth morally require. This exempts none from servitude who shall be judged thereto by authoritie.

Although not a ringing endorsement of slavery, the Body of Liberties nevertheless admits of it, opening the way for the official sanction of slavery. Later and stricter codes would formalize the institution in New England on a colony-by-colony basis, largely because trading in slaves was profitable. Yankee traders found that slaves were more valuable as cargo to be sold to the plantation colonies or in the West Indies than as laborers in the northern economy.

By 1680, Governor Simon Bradstreet estimated the number of "blacks or slaves" in the Massachusetts colony at one hundred to two hundred. The equation of race ("blacks") with slavery here is important. Some special laws were passed restricting the movement of African Americans in white society, but the Puritans encouraged Christian conversion and honored marriages between blacks. The conditions of slavery were not as harsh as in the plantation colonies. Slaves needed to read and write to do their jobs. Although there were occasional isolated rebellions, the slaves benefited from the New England love for learning and the strong Puritan emphasis on marriage and family.

Slavery gradually faded away in Massachusetts, perhaps because of its vague legal status. In the aftermath of the American Revolution, a national clamor for a Bill of Rights led individual colonies to adopt their own. While none expressly forbade slavery, the institution seemed at odds with the rhetoric. By 1776, the white population of Massachusetts was 343,845 and the black population was 5,249. The census of 1790 showed Massachusetts as the only state in which no slaves were listed.

Despite the legalization of slavery in the Body of Liberties, slavery was never popular in Massachusetts except as incidental to trade—and the slave trade was an accepted practice by seventeenth century European standards. The Puritans themselves were products of a rigorous, harsh, isolated experience. They were humanists and intellectuals with contradictions. They prized sincerity and truthfulness, yet practiced repression and inhibition to steel themselves against life's ills. They had a strong element of individualism in their creed, believing that each person must face his maker alone. Puritan humanism therefore never squared with the institution of slavery.

Brian G. Tobin

Core Resources

Ulrich B. Phillips's *American Negro Slavery* (Baton Rouge: Louisiana State University Press, 1966) is rich in original source material about the development of slavery. John Hope Franklin's *From Slavery to Freedom: A History of Negro Americans* (3d ed., New York: Alfred A. Knopf, 1967) is a classic text on the evolution of American slavery that contains a chapter on "Puritan Masters." *The American Puritans: Their Prose and Poetry* (edited by Perry Miller, New York: Columbia University Press, 1982) includes selected writings from John Cotton, Nathaniel Ward, and John Winthrop. Samuel Eliot Morison's *Builders of the Bay Colony* (Boston: Northeastern University Press, 1981) contains chapters on the Elizabethan architects of Massachusetts, including John Cotton, Nathaniel Ward, and John Winthrop.

See also: Slave codes; Slavery: history; Slavery: North American beginnings.

Bolling v. Sharpe

In *Bolling v. Sharpe* (decided December, 1954), a companion case to *Brown v. Board of Education* (decided May, 1954), the issue of segregated public schools in the nation's capital, a matter of congressional jurisdiction, was treated in an opinion separate from *Brown* because the Fourteenth Amendment did not apply to the federal government and because the applicable Fifth Amendment did not include an equal protection clause. From the perspective of practical politics, it would have been highly embarrassing for the Court to allow segregated schools in Washington, D.C., while ruling them unconstitutional in the rest of the country.

Speaking for a unanimous Supreme Court, Chief Justice Earl Warren first noted that the petitioners were African American minors who had been refused admission to a public school "solely because of their race." He then declared that the Court had long recognized that certain forms of governmental discrimination violated the constitutional mandate for due process of law. For precedents, he looked to an 1896 *dictum* by Joseph M. Harlan and to *Buchanan v. Warley*, a 1917 decision that had defended the equal right of citizens to own property based on a substantive due process reading of the Fourteenth Amendment. Also, Warren referred to *obiter dicta* in the Japanese American cases that acknowledged that racial classifications were inherently suspect, requiring that they be "scrutinized with particular care."

Warren gave an expansive interpretation of the "liberty" protected by the Fifth Amendment, explaining that it extended to the "full range of conduct which the individual is free to pursue." The government could restrict liberty only when justified by a "proper governmental objective," and racial segregation in education was not related to such an objective. Thus, the Washington schools were imposing an "arbitrary deprivation" on the liberty of black children. In addition, Warren noted that it was "unthinkable" that the federal government might practice the kind of discrimination prohibited in the states.

Bolling v. Sharpe had major theoretical implications, for the case indicated that the Supreme Court continued to interpret the due process clauses as protecting substantive rights as well as procedures, although the substantive focus had shifted from property interests to liberty interests. Also, the decision affirmed that the ideas of liberty and equality are often overlapping and that constitutional due process of law prohibits government from practicing invidious discrimination.

Thomas T. Lewis

See also: *Brown v. Board of Education*; *Buchanan v. Warley*; Civil rights; Desegregation: public schools; Segregation.

Brotherhood of Sleeping Car Porters

A small group of men gathered in 1925 and organized the Brotherhood of Sleeping Car Porters in an effort to improve the Pullman Company's treatment of African American employees. Since the 1860's, black porters had been providing personalized service to rail passengers traveling in the finely furnished sleeping cars first introduced by George Pullman. Pullman cars, as they were known, were comparable to the nation's most luxurious hotels. The porters carried luggage, provided room service, made beds, and cleaned the cars. Despite their many duties, the porters were paid exceptionally low wages. In the summer of 1925, with assistance from magazine publisher A. Philip Randolph, leaders of the New York branch of Pullman porters met to organize a union, the Brotherhood of Sleeping Car Porters. For twelve years, the union struggled to reach a compromise with the Pullman Company, nearly abandoning the effort on several occasions. Finally in 1937, the Brotherhood of Sleeping Car Porters won the wage and work-hour concessions it was demanding, thus becoming the first African American labor union to sign an agreement with a major U.S. corporation.

Donald C. Simmons, Jr.

See also: Employment among African Americans; Labor movement.

Brown v. Board of Education

This landmark case struck down the "separate but equal" doctrine upheld by the U.S. Supreme Court in Plessy v. Ferguson *(1896) and subsequent court decisions, ending legal racial segregation in public schools.*

Oliver Brown et al. v. Board of Education of Topeka, Kansas, et al., usually referred to as *Brown v. Board of Education*, was but one case dealing with segregation in public schools that came before the Supreme Court in 1954. Similar suits were filed in South Carolina (*Briggs v. Eliot*), Virginia (*Davis v. County School Board*), and Delaware (*Gebbart v. Belton*). The cases all addressed the same basic problem: the exclusion of black children from all-white schools by state laws maintaining racial segregation.

Litigants and the District Court Ruling The plaintiffs in the Kansas case were elementary schoolchildren in Topeka. The case was initiated in 1951, after the daughter of a black clergyman was denied admission to an all-white public school. As a class-action suit, it went before the U.S. District Court for the District of Kansas. Although the three-judge court found that public school segregation had a "detrimental effect upon the colored children," contributing to "a sense of inferiority," it denied them relief, upholding the separate but equal doctrine. The case then went to the U.S. Supreme Court, which reversed the lower court's decision unanimously.

The Supreme Court's Argument In writing the Court's decision, issued May 17, 1954, Chief Justice Earl Warren stated that "in the field of public education the doctrine of 'separate but equal' has no place" because segregated schools are "inherently unequal." The decision held that the plaintiffs were in fact "deprived of the equal protection of the laws guaranteed by the Fourteenth Amendment."

A second *Brown* opinion, generally known as *Brown II*, was issued a year later, on May 31, 1955. It remanded impending desegregation cases to lower federal courts, ordering them to issue equitable decrees in accordance with "varied local school problems." Although this decision directed the district courts and school boards to desegregate public schools "with all deliberate speed," it opened the door to judicial and political evasion at the local level. Thus, despite the fact that in *Cooper v. Aaron* (1958) the Court unequivocally reaffirmed the 1954 decision, strong resistance to the ending of both de jure (by law) and de facto (by custom) segregation delayed the implementation of the Supreme Court's ruling for many years.

Brown and the Civil Rights Movement   Although the *Brown* decision theoretically ended legal segregation in public education, it did not bring an immediate end to the segregation of schools or any other public facilities. In the South, change was particularly painful and slow, in both urban and rural areas. According to the U.S. Commission on Civil Rights, in 1963, nine years after the *Brown* ruling, less than half of 1 percent of southern black students were attending integrated schools. It would take marches, boycotts, sit-ins, and more aggressive racial agitation by blacks and sympathetic whites, plus growing media coverage and strong public pressure, to force change.

The Civil Rights movement took a dramatic turn in 1955, in Montgomery, Alabama, when Rosa Parks, a black woman, refused to surrender her bus seat and move to a section reserved for blacks. Her action began a boycott that led to other demonstrations throughout the South under the leadership of Martin Luther King, Jr. The movement culminated in the Civil Rights Act of 1964, the Voting Rights Act of 1965, and the Fair Housing Act of 1968.

However, the *Brown* decision was the most important legal precedent in the Civil Rights movement. It was also inevitable. In earlier cases, the Supreme Court, even while upholding the "separate but equal" doctrine, had begun to undermine it. As early as 1938, in *Missouri ex rel. Gaines v. Canada*, the Court rejected the practice of funding law schooling for blacks outside a state in lieu of providing equal facilities within the state. In 1950, in *Sweatt v. Painter*, the Court further determined that a separate public law school for blacks (in Texas) violated the equal protection clause of the Fourteenth Amendment because the school was not equal to the state's white law school in prestige or quality of faculty and facilities. Thereafter, by 1952, the Court had begun to review cases dealing with public schools, not only the professional schools.

Brown's Legal Legacy   *Brown v. Board of Education* set a legal precedent that would be used to overturn laws upholding segregation not only in public schools but also in other public facilities. The argument that separate facilities are "inherently unequal" is the cornerstone of much civil rights legislation that has effectively ended apartheid in the United States. New ground would be broken two decades later, in 1976, when the Supreme

Court, in *Runyon v. McCrary*, ruled that even private, nonsectarian schools violated federal civil rights laws if they denied admission to students because they were black. Although some problems implementing these important rulings remain, the landmark decision in *Brown* made it clear that segregation would no longer be tolerated in a democratic society.

John W. Fiero

Core Resources

The role of the U.S. Supreme Court in school desegregation and the general impact of school integration are extensively covered in several studies, including Leon Jones's *From Brown to Boston: Desegregation in Education, 1954-1974* (Metuchen, N.J.: Scarecrow Press, 1979), *The Consequences of School Desegregation* (edited by Christine H. Rossell and Willis D. Hawley, Philadelphia: Temple University Press, 1983), *Shades of Brown: New Perspectives on School Desegregation* (edited by Derrick Bell, New York: Teachers College Press, 1980), and Larry W. Hughes, William M. Gordon, and Larry W. Hillman's *Desegregating American Schools* (New York: Longman, 1980).

See also: *Bolling v. Sharpe*; Busing and integration; Civil Rights movement; *Cooper v. Aaron*; Discrimination: racial and ethnic; Little Rock school desegregation; National Association for the Advancement of Colored People Legal Defense and Educational Fund; *Plessy v. Ferguson*; *Runyon v. McCrary*; Segregation: de facto and de jure; *Sweatt v. Painter*.

Buchanan v. Warley

In May, 1914, Louisville, Kentucky, passed an ordinance that made it unlawful for "any colored person" to move into a house on a block where the majority of houses were occupied by whites. Whites were similarly disqualified from moving to a block where the majority of the occupants were black. William Warley, who was black, contracted to buy a house lot from Charles Buchanan, a white man. Part of the contract between them was a proviso by Warley that said "I shall not be required to accept a deed to the above property unless I have the right under the laws of the state of Kentucky and the city of Louisville, to occupy said property as a residence." Warley refused to pay on the contract, alleging that the Louisville ordinance forbade him from living on the property. Buchanan sued Warley to force him to perform on the contract, attacking the ordinance as unconstitutional under the due process clause of the Fourteenth Amendment.

The U.S. Supreme Court unanimously held that the ordinance was unconstitutional. Justice William R. Day wrote that the Louisville law deprived both black and white people of the right to own and dispose of property in violation of the command of the Fourteenth Amendment that no person shall be deprived of life, liberty, or property without due process of law.

Robert Jacobs

See also: Discrimination: racial and ethnic; Fair Housing Act; Fourteenth Amendment; Housing.

Busing and integration

Busing as a tool for desegregating public schools has been controversial, and both Congress and the Supreme Court have dealt with the issue.

School desegregation has been the most controversial American educational issue of the twentieth century. Busing, one of the more feasible strategies for achieving school desegregation, generated tremendous controversy as desegregation plans were implemented during the late 1960's, 1970's, and 1980's. Consequently, school desegregation and busing have become inextricably linked in the minds of many people. Busing actually predates school desegregation by many decades, and it was originally simply a means of transporting students in rural areas to schools that were better equipped and staffed than traditional one-room country schools. In rural areas of the South, however, busing simultaneously served as a means of facilitating school segregation.

Busing to Facilitate Segregation   Many school districts in the South encompass entire rural counties, so transportation to school must be provided to students. Busing proved to be the most feasible means to transport large numbers of students. Until the Supreme Court's *Brown v. Board of Education* decision in 1954, segregated schools were legal in the South. Typically, segregation meant busing black and white children to different schools regardless of what school was closest to a child's house. Black children could be bused many miles even if a white school was right next door. Similar circumstances would apply for the white child if the nearest school was a black one.

The 1954 *Brown* decision was supposed to bring an end to de jure (by law) segregation, the practice of state-imposed segregation. A subsequent decision (*Brown II*) in 1955 addressed the issue of remediation and ordered that the elimination of segregated dual school systems proceed "with all deliberate speed." Yet thirteen years passed before the Supreme Court became disillusioned with the delay tactics and obstructions employed by many southern school districts and began enforcement of its desegregation de-

African American children in Boston boarding a bus that will be taking them to predominantly white suburban schools. *(Library of Congress)*

cree. During that time, an entire generation of schoolchildren, both black and white, was subjected to the continuation of busing that facilitated segregation.

Busing to Facilitate Integration   Busing became an effective strategy for transporting students reassigned under desegregation plans. In *Swann v. Charlotte-Mecklenburg Board of Education* (1971), the Supreme Court established that busing was an acceptable strategy for desegregating school systems. In upholding the use of busing, the Supreme Court was aware that it might prove to be administratively awkward for school districts and that it might impose a degree of hardship on some districts. Although busing was sanctioned in the *Swann* decision, it was done so only in regard to de jure (by law) segregation. In *Keyes v. Denver School District No. 1* (1973), busing was ordered for the first time outside the South. In this case, the Supreme Court ruled on the issue of de facto segregation (segregation "in fact," generally resulting from discriminatory residential patterns) for the first time. In evaluating the Denver school system, the Court concluded that when segregative intent exists in a substantial portion of the school system, then a systemwide remedy to assure nondiscrimination is acceptable. A systemwide remedy necessitates the reassignment of significant numbers of students, which typically requires some degree of busing. In a number of desegregation cases, the federal courts used busing when forced to develop their own desegregation plans, especially when recalcitrant school districts refused to restructure long-standing dual systems of education.

A number of school districts in the South developed desegregation plans that were premised on voluntary integration strategies, such as freedom-of-choice plans, voluntary transfer plans, and magnet schools. The Fifth Circuit Court, in *United States v. Jefferson County Board of Education* (1966), argued that the only desegregation plans that would be acceptable to the federal courts would be those that work—those that are practical and that actually accomplish the goal of desegregation.

In *Green v. County School Board of New Kent County* (1968), the Supreme Court rejected the freedom-of-choice plan implemented by the New Kent County school board. The Court concluded that freedom-of-choice plans did not demonstrate significant levels of desegregation and did not remove the racial identification attached to specific schools. Although freedom of choice was rejected as the primary strategy in a desegregation plan, however, it was not precluded from being used as a supplemental component in a more comprehensive desegregation plan.

The federal courts came to a similar conclusion regarding voluntary transfer plans. White parents saw no benefit in having their children attend a segregated black school that was perceived to be educationally inferior. On the other hand, many African American parents did not see the value in having their children attend segregated white schools where they were unwelcome. They were hesitant to expose their children to the physical threat posed by some segregated white schools.

Magnet schools have unquestionably been the most successful of the voluntary desegregation plans. Magnet schools have grown tremendously since their inception in 1972. Generally, these are racially integrated public schools that have innovative programs and activities that attract students from throughout a school district.

Freedom-of-choice, voluntary transfer, and magnet programs all required some degree of busing if they were to be properly executed. In some instances, voluntary desegregation plans involved a greater degree of busing than did the mandatory pupil reassignment plans initiated by the federal courts. Yet parents had little difficulty in accepting the notion of a voluntary desegregation plan. Voluntary plans permit parents and children who do not wish to participate in the desegregation effort to remain outside the process while remaining within the public schools. Many of the voluntary desegregation plans, however, proved to be unacceptable to the courts.

Resistance to Busing   Busing to achieve integration met with considerable opposition at the local, state, and federal levels. Although busing was merely a strategy to facilitate meaningful integration, it eventually became symbolic of all that some people found distasteful about the desegregation process. Opponents of desegregation characterized it as "forced busing."

The issue of forced busing, for many, was associated with the reluctance of white parents to send their children to what had previously been inferior all-black schools. Actually, considerably more minority students (African American and Hispanic) than white students were bused for desegregation purposes. Over the decades of the 1960's, 1970's, and early 1980's, white parents took to the streets in their opposition to forced busing. The problem was exacerbated when some political leaders—instead of seeking to mollify and encourage the desegregation process—took advantage of the controversy for political gain.

During the time of the *Keyes* decision, when the use of busing was being established as a remedy in de facto segregation cases, there was substantial political force growing in opposition to busing. According to Derrick A. Bell, Jr., in *Race, Racism, and American Law* (1980), Richard M. Nixon used an antidesegregation plank in his presidential campaign in 1968 to help defeat the Democratic presidential candidate, Hubert H. Humphrey. Nixon's opposition to forced busing assumed an even greater role in his reelection campaign for 1972.

Although the legitimacy of busing was upheld in the *Keyes* decision, the parameters for its use were questioned the following year in *Milliken v. Bradley*

Opposition to busing often unleashed virulent emotions; here opponents of busing attack a civil rights attorney at the entrance to Boston's city hall in 1976. *(Library of Congress)*

(1974). The Supreme Court failed to support metropolitan busing in Michigan that would have involved the city of Detroit and fifty-three surrounding suburban school districts. Detroit, at the time, was more than 63 percent African American, while the neighboring suburban districts were almost exclusively white. The Supreme Court reasoned that the plaintiffs did not demonstrate constitutional violations on the part of the suburban communities. The plaintiffs' request to include the suburban school districts in the desegregation effort was denied.

During this same period, Congress was reevaluating busing and its proper place in school desegregation. Congress attempted to pass legislation that would have either eliminated or limited the use of busing. It failed to pass antibusing legislation designed to reduce federal jurisdiction. It succeeded, however, in passing legislation that placed restrictions on the use of busing for desegregation beyond the next-nearest school. This permitted many students to remain at their neighborhood school, and since many neighborhoods were racially segregated, the legislation actually contributed to school segregation. Congress also passed legislation that prioritized remedies in school desegregation cases and prohibited the issuance of administrative or judicial orders requiring student reassignment at any time other than the beginning of an academic year.

Despite the guidelines established in the *Milliken* decision regarding metropolitan busing, the restrictive busing legislation passed by Congress, and other precedent-setting decisions in the federal courts, school desegregation continued to move forward. The responsibility of proof had changed, however—from demonstrating the mere existence of segregation in a school system to the more difficult to prove standard of segregative intent on the part of school officials.

Much concern surfaced in Congress and in the federal courts about "white flight," the movement of white families to areas outside racially mixed school districts as well as the increasing tendency of white parents to place their children in private schools. Although part of the decline in the number of white students can be attributed to desegregation and busing, white enrollment had actually begun to decline almost a decade before integration began. This decrease was a function of the declining white birthrate, departures to private schools, and departures to the suburbs. It should be noted that some suburban school districts not subject to desegregation actually lost more students proportionally than did city districts undergoing desegregation.

Although the phenomenon of white flight is generally associated with the desire to avoid school desegregation, technically the term is a misnomer. It would be more accurately characterized as middle-class flight. The African American middle class, along with other minority middle class populations, has continually sought to remove itself from the inner cities when presented with the opportunity.

Diminished Opposition to Busing Opposition to busing appeared to diminish in the 1980's. The administration of Ronald Reagan tended to focus on other domestic and foreign issues. Nevertheless, the Reagan administration was firmly opposed to busing. It even threatened to reopen desegregation cases already settled through extensive busing if it believed that the remedy was too drastic. The Reagan administration argued that desegregation should occur on a voluntary basis. Consequently, it supported voluntary desegregation plans such as magnet schools, tuition tax credits, and school "choice" programs. Busing became a side issue as debates focused on the impact that tuition tax credits and choice programs would have on public schools.

Charles C. Jackson

Core Resources

A thorough examination of busing can be found in *School Desegregation: Hearings Before the Subcommittee on Civil and Constitutional Rights of the Committee on the Judiciary, House of Representatives, Ninety-seventh Congress* (Washington, D.C.: U.S. Government Printing Office, 1982). Other excellent discussions are the Citizens Commission on Civil Rights, *"There Is No Liberty . . ."* (Washington, D.C.: Citizens Commission on Civil Rights, 1982); Derrick A. Bell, Jr., *Race, Racism, and American Law* (2d ed. Boston: Little, Brown, 1980); Harvard Sitkoff, *The Struggle for Black Equality: 1954-1992* (New York: Hill and Wang, 1993); and S. Alexander Rippa, *Education in a Free Society: An American History* (7th ed. New York: Longman, 1992).

See also: *Brown v. Board of Education*; Civil rights; Civil Rights movement; Desegregation: public schools; *Green v. County School Board of New Kent County*; *Keyes v. Denver School District No. 1*; *Milliken v. Bradley*; *Swann v. Charlotte-Mecklenburg Board of Education*.

Censuses, U.S.

Every ten years, a federal census counts all the people residing in the United States. The information obtained includes each person's ethnic or racial background. This enables the size of each ethnic or racial group to be compared over time and allows governmental programs to take the size of an ethnic or racial group into account when determining policy.

The United States Constitution requires that population be the basis for determining the number of seats apportioned to each state in the U.S. House of Representatives. As the population of the country shifts, the decennial census permits a readjustment in the number of seats for each state. Census reports have also been used to calculate how many immigrants from particular countries are allowed admission into the United States as well as to determine what constitutes unlawful discrimination.

Censuses   A population census is a complete count of all persons residing in a particular area. A census differs from a population sample, which scientifically selects a percentage of persons in an area in order to estimate characteristics of the entire population of the territory.

To undertake a population census, census takers must identify the dwelling units in the area to be covered; then they must go to each abode and obtain information from all persons residing therein. Inevitably, census takers miss some people because not everyone is at home when the census taker arrives, some people choose to evade being counted, others are homeless or transient, and not all dwelling units are easy to identify. Censuses, thus, generally undercount population, especially in areas where less affluent minorities reside. That is why, some argue, a method known as "statistical sampling" may be more accurate than an actual headcount, provided that the census has identified all dwelling units.

Legal Requirements   The Constitution of the United States requires a population census every ten years. Because the Constitution requires that each state's representation in the federal House of Representatives be based on population, a major purpose of the decennial census is to increase or decrease the number of seats in the House of Representatives apportioned to each state in accordance with relative changes in the population of each state. The Constitution did not consider Native Americans to be citizens of the United States, so they were not originally counted in the census; those living on reservations did not affect the allocation of seats in the House of Representatives until after 1924, when they were granted American citizenship. Those of African descent were counted in each state, but before the Civil War (1861-1865), when they were not considered citizens, their number was multiplied by three-fifths for the purpose of reapportioning representation in the House of Representatives.

Beginning in the 1960's, affirmative action began to be applied to remedy employment discrimination in the United States. One aspect of the policy is that federal government employers and those with federal contracts are supposed to hire men and women of the various ethnic or racial groups in the same proportions as their relative availability in the workforce. To determine the composition of the workforce, employers usually rely on census data, which are disseminated by the U.S. Department of Labor.

Ethnic/Racial Categories   In the first federal census of 1790, each individual was assigned membership in one of two racial groups: white and colored. The colored population was divided into free colored and slaves, and both categories were divided into black or mulatto. These census categories were used until 1860, when the Asiatic category was added and a count was made of the people in various Indian tribes. The 1870 census used four categories: white, colored, Chinese, and Indian. In 1880, Japanese became the fifth category, and the term "Negro" replaced "colored." These five categories remained on census reports through 1900. The 1910 census added several new categories: Filipinos, Hindus, and Koreans. A footnote in the census report noted that Hindus were Caucasians but still were counted separately from whites. The 1920 census added Hawaiians and part Hawaiians, but these two categories were removed from the national enumeration in 1930 and 1940. Mexicans joined the category list in 1930 and 1940. In 1950, the only racial categories were white and nonwhite. In 1960, six categories were used: white, Negro, Japanese, Chinese, Filipino, and Indian. In 1970, Hawaiians and Koreans returned to the list, making eight categories. In 1980, the category black replaced Negro, and the list of Asian and Pacific races expanded to include Asian Indians, Samoans, and Vietnamese. In 1990, nearly every country in Asia was represented as a separate category.

Although Mexicans appeared as a category in 1930 and 1940, they did not reappear in national statistics for forty years. In 1970, the census counted "Persons of Spanish Heritage," but in 1980, the census counted Cubans, Mexicans, and Puerto Ricans separately. In 1990, the census reported the number of persons from almost all countries in the Caribbean, Central America, and South America.

Census reports on the territories of Alaska and Hawaii used unique category schemes. For Alaska, the census counted Aleuts, Eskimos, and Alaskan Indians; Aleuts and Eskimos became national categories in 1980 and 1990, but Alaskan Indians were pooled with all other American Indians in both years. For Hawaii, the indigenous Hawaiians were counted, although up to 1930, they were divided into pure Hawaiians, Asiatic Hawaiians, and Caucasian Hawaiians.

From the beginning, the census had separate subcategories for European ethnic groups (British, French, German, and so on), all of which were counted as white. The breakdown was made to record the number of foreign-born individuals in the population. Due to concerns among the earlier immigrants from western and northern Europe that too many eastern and southern Europeans were arriving, Congress passed the Immigration Act of 1924. This act replaced a temporary immigration law, passed in 1921, which had restricted immigrants to 3 percent of each admissible nationality residing in the United States as of 1910. According to the 1924 act, known as the National Origins Act, the maximum from each European country was calculated as 2 percent of the nationality group already inside the United States as determined by the federal census of 1890. Most Asians, effectively, were barred from immigration under the law with the exception of Filipinos, as the Philippines was an American possession as of 1898. The restrictive 1924 immigration law imposed no quota on immigrants from the Western

Hemisphere. With the Immigration and Nationality Act of 1965, Congress established equal quotas for all countries, regardless of hemisphere.

With the advent of affirmative action, a five-category scheme was developed by federal civil rights enforcement agencies. The so-called COINS categories stood for Caucasian, Oriental, Indian, Negro, and Spanish. Later, the term "Oriental" was replaced by the term "Asian and Pacific Islander," and the term "Hispanic" replaced the term "Spanish."

Census for the Year 2000   During the 1990's, considerable pressure was brought to bear to change the categories for the census for the year 2000. Some blacks wanted to be called "African Americans." Hispanics wanted to be counted as "Latinos" and as members of a race rather than an ethnic group. Native Hawaiians wanted to be moved from the category "Asians and Pacific Islanders" and included with "American Indians and Native Alaskans." Middle Easterners, particularly those from Islamic countries, wanted separate status. Finally, some mixed-race or multiethnic people who spanned two or more of the categories wanted to be counted as "multiracial." Advocates of a society in which ethnic and racial distinctions would not be recognized officially wanted to drop all references to race and ethnicity in the census.

After many hearings and studies on the subject, the U.S. Office of Management and Budget decided to keep the previous categorizations with one modification: "Asians" would be counted separately from "Native Hawaiians and Other Pacific Islanders." The proposal for a separate "multiracial" category was rejected, but persons with multiracial backgrounds would be allowed to check more than one category. Thus, data on ethnic backgrounds of people in the United States have been collapsed into five racial categories: African American or black, American Indian or Native Alaskan, Asian, Native Hawaiian or Other Pacific Islander, and White. The census of the year 2000 permits a member of any of these five categories to also check "Hispanic or Latino."

Impact on Public Policy   The ethnic and racial diversity of the United States is best documented by the decennial federal census. The count of each ethnic or racial group is crucial in determining whether discrimination occurs, but questions about ethnic group membership or race on a census deeply affect the identity of many persons, who in turn may support efforts either to abolish ethnic and racial counts or to change categories.

Michael Haas

Core Resources

The best source on ethnic data in the census is the census report itself, which is found in most documents sections of university libraries, as well as on the Internet at www.census.gov. Bryant Robey's *Two Hundred Years and Counting: The 1990 Census* (Washington, D.C.: Population Reference Bureau,

1989) provides an overview of the census with a focus on the 1990 census. Margo J. Anderson's *The American Census: A Social History* (New Haven, Conn.: Yale University Press, 1988) is a historical account of the taking of censuses that includes many of the associated controversies. On the tendency to undercount minorities, see Harvey M. Choldin's *Looking for the Last Percent: The Controversy over Census Undercounts* (New Brunswick, N.J.: Rutgers University Press, 1994); Barbara Everett Bryant and William Dunn's *Moving Power and Money: The Politics of Census Taking* (Ithaca, N.Y.: New Strategic Publications, 1995). For the thesis that racial divisions have been artificially promoted by the census, see Michael Omi and Howard Winant's *Racial Formation in the United States: From the 1960's to the 1980's* (New York: Routledge & Kegan Paul, 1986).

See also: Affirmative action; Biracialism; Multiracial movement; Quotas; Race as a concept; Racial and ethnic demographics: trends.

Charleston race riots

After the Civil War ended in 1865, South Carolina was controlled by Northern-born whites and Southern blacks with support from the U.S. federal government. Southern whites who were allied with some Southern blacks attempted to regain control of the local government. By 1876, a tense atmosphere had developed between the two forces as a gubernatorial election approached between Republican Daniel H. Chamberlain, the incumbent and a Massachusetts-born former Union army officer, and Democrat Wade Hampton, a former slaveowner and Confederate lieutenant general. Political corruption and intimidation characterized both sides. On September 6, black Democrats rallied in Charleston to support Hampton. A group of black Republicans attacked the black Democrats and their white escorts, and a riot ensued. The riot lasted for several days with black Republicans destroying property and attacking whites. One black man and one white man died, and about one hundred people were injured. Tensions remained high until the election on November 7, and the next day, as people were awaiting the election results, gunfire erupted in Charleston. Black police officers loyal to the Republicans began firing at the rioters. One black man and one white man were killed, and about a dozen other people were injured. Federal troops intervened and restored order. Both candidates claimed victory in the election, but by 1877, power had returned to white Democrats because of a political deal with the Republican presidential candidate.

Abraham D. Lavender

See also: Colfax massacre; Race riots of 1866; Reconstruction.

Children in the Civil Rights movement

Many African American children—from the very young to teenagers—were involved in the Civil Rights movement of the 1950's and 1960's in the United States. They participated in marches, demonstrations, boycotts, pickets, sit-ins, desegregation of schools, voter registration campaigns, and freedom rides. Some children accompanied their activist parents to organizing meetings, which were often held in black churches and conducted by members of the National Association for the Advancement of Colored People (NAACP), the Student Nonviolent Coordinating Committee (SNCC), the Southern Christian Leadership Conference (SCLC), the Council of Federated Organizations (COFO), and other civil rights organizations. The children were primarily involved in the movement in the South, especially Mississippi, Alabama, Georgia, Tennessee, Arkansas, Tennessee, and Florida, where both de jure (by law) and de facto (by custom) segregation existed. Although the movement was nonviolent, it elicited violent acts from angry white mobs who gathered around protests, local authorities trying to break up demonstrations and arrest protesters, and racist groups who bombed churches and attacked African Americans in an effort to intimidate them. In the course of the struggle to obtain civil rights, African American children

Thousands of people attended the funeral of fourteen-year-old Carol Robertson, one of the girls killed in the bombing of Birmingham's Sixteenth Street Baptist Church in 1963. *(Library of Congress)*

were beaten, clubbed, gassed, threatened by lynch mobs, attacked by police dogs, blasted by high-power water hoses, arrested, jailed, and even killed.

In May of 1963, in Birmingham, Alabama, thousands of children marched for civil rights as part of the Children's Crusade. Birmingham police commissioner Eugene "Bull" Connor, a staunch segregationist, gave the order for police to attack the children with nightsticks, police dogs, and high-power water hoses. The police arrested the children, filling the city jails and then imprisoning children in a makeshift jail at the fairgrounds. In September, 1963, a bomb exploded in the Sixteenth Street Baptist Church in Birmingham, killing four young girls who had been attending Sunday school. The church had been selected as a target because civil rights activists gathered there and organized protests.

Children also played an important, and difficult, role in school desegregation. Their parents filed lawsuits on their behalf, but it was the children who attended these schools who bore the brunt of racially motivated attacks, verbal and physical abuse, and social isolation. Two of the nationally publicized cases occurred in Topeka, Kansas, and Little Rock, Arkansas. Topeka operated eighteen public elementary schools for white children only and four schools for black children. The Reverend Oliver Brown, on behalf of his daughter Linda Carol Brown, and twelve other black plaintiffs, on behalf of their children, filed a lawsuit to protest this segregation. After much expert testimony, the U.S. Supreme Court in 1954 issued a landmark decision that ended segregation of children in public schools solely on the basis of race because segregation deprived minority children of equal educational opportunities. In 1957, nine black youths (known as "the Little Rock Nine"), led by Daisy Bates, desegregated Little Rock's Central High School. President Dwight D. Eisenhower had to use state troopers to protect the children from physical violence by armed white adults opposed to desegregation.

Bernice McNair Barnett

See also: *Brown v. Board of Education*; Civil Rights movement; Desegregation: public schools; Little Rock school desegregation; Segregation: de facto and de jure.

Church burnings

During the mid-1990's, specifically between January 1, 1995, and June 1, 1997, the southeastern United States experienced a rash of arsons, fire bombings, and attempted fire bombings of African American and multiracial houses of worship. Leaders in the African American communities targeted by the arsonists were quick to compare the activity to similar events

Agents of the federal Bureau of Alcohol, Tobacco and Firearms inspect a church burned in Mississippi during the summer of 1996. *(Reuters/Jeff Mitchell/Archive Photos)*

during the Civil Rights movement of the 1960's. Churches, they noted, had historically been the targets of hate groups because they were so closely associated with the black unity of the civil rights struggle. Several organizations, most notably the National Council of Churches, held press conferences calling on the Bureau of Alcohol, Tobacco, and Firearms (ATF), a section of the Treasury Department, and law enforcement agencies to be more aggressive in investigating the suspicious fires. President Bill Clinton responded to the public outcry with a call for federal oversight of the arson investigations.

Members of Congress unanimously passed legislation that expanded the circumstances under which the federal government could prosecute for damage to religious property. The measure extended the statute of limitations for prosecution of church arson cases from five to seven years and increased penalties for church arson from ten to twenty years. Despite criticism from many African American leaders that the Justice Department and the ATF were not moving quickly enough in their investigations, a special church arson task force arrested nearly two hundred suspects by mid-1997. More than one hundred of those arrested were eventually convicted in federal and state courts on charges related to the destruction of more than seventy churches. Those arrested were overwhelmingly white and nearly half were juveniles. Most of those found guilty of federal offenses were convicted of civil rights violations as a result of evidence that the crimes were racially motivated. Federal officials could find no evidence that the arson activity was coordinated or directed by a group of individuals or an organization. The response by the federal law enforcement agencies was particularly impressive in light of the fact that the church fire arrest and conviction rates were nearly twice the rate of more typical arson cases.

The national response in support of the victims of the church burnings was equally impressive. A joint effort by the U.S. Department of Housing and Urban Development, the National Council of Churches, Habitat for Humanity, and many other groups rebuilt most of the churches. The Congress of National Black Churches also established a fund to prevent future arsons and to rebuild churches that had been burned. The Eli Lilly Foundation contributed six million dollars to efforts to rebuild and repair the churches that had been destroyed. Even the sometimes controversial hotelier and philanthropist Leona Helmsley donated one million dollars to assist in the rebuilding effort.

Donald C. Simmons, Jr.

See also: Black church; Civil Rights movement; Racism: history of the concept.

Citizens' Councils

Citizens' Councils, prosegregation organizations of white southerners that flourished in the 1950's and 1960's, began with a single council in Indianola, Mississippi, in July, 1954. The council was created in reaction to the United States Supreme Court's ruling in *Brown v. Board of Education* in May, 1954, which found school segregation unconstitutional. During the next two years, as anger with the Court's decision mounted, Citizens' Councils appeared across the South from Virginia to Texas. The greatest concentrations of support appeared in the lower South. Membership, drawn primarily from the middle and upper classes of the region, reached 250,000 during the heyday of the Councils. The Councils' goal was to maintain white dominance through economic coercion and intimidation of blacks and political opposition to integration. The Councils were in the forefront of the growing resistance to the Civil Rights movement. In states such as Mississippi, they controlled the political agenda and sometimes even the machinery of government itself. The influence of the organization waned in the 1960's, but the Councils' legacy of bigotry and dislike for African American aspirations for justice remained strong. The Citizens' Councils represented the vehicle that many whites used to express southern unhappiness with the end of segregation.

Lewis L. Gould

See also: *Brown v. Board of Education*; Civil Rights movement; Segregation.

Civil disobedience

Civil disobedience is a form of political activism characterized by intentional violation of the law. Nonviolent disruptive actions, usually based on moral principles, are used to emphasize presumptive injustices.

Civil disobedience is a concept that encompasses a wide range of interpretations. The term frequently is used interchangeably with similar concepts, such as nonviolent resistance, nonviolent direct action, passive resistance, and pacifism, in discussions of structured opposition to laws or governmental policies that are perceived to be unjust or immoral. The fundamental tenet of civil disobedience is the purposeful, nonviolent opposition to laws or policies enacted by the state. In the United States, civil disobedience is associated with the intentional disregard for laws or policies enacted by the federal government, individual states, or local municipalities that individuals, groups, or specific populations find objectionable on moral or ethical grounds. Opposition to such laws is demonstrated in a variety of ways—from mainly verbal antagonism to outright disobedience. Some argue that civil disobedience must involve the willful resistance to laws, statutes, or social norms that are perceived to violate the ethical or moral ideals of certain segments of society. Others perceive civil disobedience to be the right of the individual or group to oppose the authority of the state when the state infringes upon civil liberties. Still others view civil disobedience and other forms of resistance merely as unlawful activity.

Definitions of Civil Disobedience   By most definitions, civil disobedience fulfills five conditions: the action taken by the protagonist is clearly illegal; it is done openly, rather than clandestinely; it is intended to call attention to a law, policy, or social condition; its intent is to improve the condition or change the law or policy; and the protagonist is willing to suffer the consequences for the act of defiance. Much attention has been given to the last condition. For some, civil disobedience requires the protagonist's willingness to endure whatever sanctions are forthcoming from the state for violating the law; any attempt on the part of the protagonist to avoid sanctions changes the violation from civil disobedience to merely breaking the law. Many people believe that if individuals or groups are found guilty of violating the law, they should suffer the consequence, regardless of their belief that the law is unfair. These people argue that illegal acts perpetrated during student rebellions, civil rights demonstrations, war protests, or antiabortion activities should culminate in the protagonists being prosecuted despite their claims that the law they broke or social policy they were protesting was unjust.

In some circumstances, the protagonist has no intention of avoiding the penalty for disobedience; in such instances, civil disobedience may be in consonance with nonviolent resistance and nonviolent direct action. In such cases, the goal may be to raise the level of consciousness regarding what the protagonist believes to be an immoral or unethical law. In other cases, the protagonist's intention is to fight the penalties for disobeying the law in the court system, with the aim of tying up the courts and judicial system, further dramatizing the initial concern. This strategy may be accompanied by the protagonist's insisting on a trial by jury, entailing lengthy litigation.

Civil disobedience also has been closely tied to the idea of nonviolence. While it has not been exclusively identified with nonviolent resistance, it has come to be seen as a nonviolent mode of protest. Relatively few would argue that social reform is undesirable; many citizens probably believe that reform would be beneficial in areas such as social welfare, health care, or the way political campaigns are financed. Many would insist, however, that reforms be pursued without violating the law, and particularly without the use of violence.

Proponents of the view that citizens have the right to disobey unjust laws or policies argue that it is good to disobey any law that encroaches upon human rights, particularly if, in the public's mind, it is always to be obeyed despite its unhealthy impact upon the growth of democracy. In such instances, civil disobedience is the organized expression of opposition to an existing evil (the law); civil disobedience did not create the evil, but directs resistance in a rationalized manner. Accordingly, civil disobedience may provide an organized outlet for opposition that is more acceptable than outright rebellion or some other form of unrestrained resistance.

Uses of Civil Disobedience   Civil disobedience is often used in issues involving the perception of what is just and moral. The issue of abortion, for example, has generated many debates over civil liberties and morality. Opposition to abortion has largely been predicated on certain moral views, for example: it is immoral to take any life; it is especially wrong to take the life of an unborn, defenseless human; abortion is cruel and painful; and the mother eventually will regret her decision to take her unborn child's life. This has prompted several forms of civil disobedience, and sometimes outright lawlessness, including passing out literature beyond boundaries established by the courts; picketing hospitals and clinics that perform abortions; blocking entrances to abortion clinics; harassing or attacking potential clients; destroying abortion clinics; and physically assaulting or killing medical personnel. The abortion controversy has often gone beyond the nonviolent posture that many believe to be an integral component of civil disobedience. There are many other issues where nonviolent civil disobedience has had a tremendous impact on society. The magnitude and consistency of civil disobedience sometimes have succeeded in changing laws that even the Supreme Court had at one time maintained were constitutional. It could be argued that without sustained civil disobedience, many of the unjust laws that existed in the South before the Civil Rights movement might not have been changed.

As a Weapon Against Segregation   During the legal segregation in the United States, from 1896 following the U.S. Supreme Court's *Plessy v. Ferguson* decision to *Brown v. Board of Education* in 1954, segregationists in many states had a legal right to discriminate against minorities. Viewed from a historical perspective, discrimination based on race was initially a moral issue because the "separate but equal" conclusion reached by the Supreme Court in *Plessy v. Ferguson* legally permitted it. It was later changed to a legal issue, following the reversal of that doctrine in *Brown v. Board of Education*. Consequently, the segregationist could no longer legally discriminate. The shift from segregation as a moral issue to one embroiled in legality was prompted in large part by civil disobedience, especially the sit-ins, jail-ins, and demonstrations subsequent to the *Brown* decision. While many would argue that laws that permit differential treatment based solely on race clearly should be illegal, for at least fifty-eight years segregation—along with all of its pernicious effects—was the law in much of the country.

Civil disobedience may involve the assertion of certain basic constitutional rights. Asserting the right to equal protection of the law may require denying the legitimacy of another law to some degree. For example, if some members of society are permitted to ride in the front of a bus, to deny the same right to others for some arbitrary reason, such as race—which was legal in some parts of the South into the 1960's—was a denial of the equal protection of the law. Consequently, denying the legitimacy of the law through civil disobedience was actually the exercise of a constitutional liberty.

Civil Disobedience in the Civil Rights Movement   Although the Montgomery, Alabama, bus boycott of 1955, in which Martin Luther King, Jr., first gained national prominence, is considered the catalyst for the Civil Rights movement, the initial act of civil disobedience was carried out by Rosa Parks when she disobeyed a local law by refusing to give up her bus seat to a white man when ordered by the driver. The subsequent boycott was not an act of civil disobedience, but an organized effort to force the white power structure in Montgomery to desegregate the local transit system. Although the boycott challenged a law, it fell within the limits of the law.

The student sit-ins of the 1960's, on the other hand, utilized civil disobedience to confront racial discrimination in the South. Three African American students from North Carolina Agricultural and Technical College in Greensboro, North Carolina, set in motion what is considered the modern "sit-in." On February 1, 1960, they quietly seated themselves at an F. W. Woolworth's lunch counter with the intent to draw attention to the practice of refusing to serve African Americans seated in public restaurants. Local custom dictated that African Americans must remain standing if they wished to be served. The three students were asked to leave because of their actions. When they refused to obey, they were summarily arrested. The sit-ins spread to stores that had similar segregation policies. By February 16, 1960, the sit-ins had spread to fifteen cities in five southern states. Sit-ins slowly moved beyond southern cities. At first the sit-ins were aimed at affiliates of F. W. Woolworth and S. H. Kress, but they soon targeted other variety stores.

The sit-ins began as a spontaneous act by three students, but by September, 1960, they involved nearly seventy thousand students, almost thirty-six hundred of whom were arrested at one time or another. Some sit-in demonstrators refused to post bail. This not only drew attention to the issue of racial discrimination, but caused financial and judicial problems for local municipalities. An unmistakable message was being sent by young civil rights activists: Civil disobedience would become a powerful tactic in the campaign against unjust laws based on race.

Civil disobedience in the form of sit-ins, demonstrations, and other modes of nonviolent direct action drew attention throughout the United States during the 1960's. As a result, the inequities of many southern practices came under scrutiny by many white citizens who had been oblivious to such practices. Drawing attention to perceived injustices has been a major goal behind many acts of civil disobedience.

Philosophical Underpinnings   Civil disobedience has a long and storied history in the development of American society. Credit for the birth of civil disobedience in the United States is often given to Henry David Thoreau, the nineteenth century American writer who wrote the essay "Civil Disobedience" after spending a night in jail in 1846 for refusing to pay the Massachusetts poll tax. Nevertheless, one of the best examples can be illustrated by the struggles of Mohandas K. Gandhi against the British imperial regimes in South Africa and India.

Gandhi studied Western philosophy and law in England, where he became familiar with Thoreau's views that later became the foundation on which he built his nonviolent strategies. From 1893 to 1914, Gandhi fought against oppressive legislation and the discriminatory treatment of Indians in South Africa. During this period he developed his moral doctrine of satyagraha and the nonviolent techniques that eventually were so successful in India. He was instrumental in getting the Indians' Relief Bill passed, which improved the political, social, and economic conditions of Indians in South Africa.

Following World War I, Gandhi returned to India where he began the struggle of seeking independence from Great Britain. He used civil disobedience as a nonviolent political tactic to challenge the legitimacy of the British sovereignty over India. He led strikes, boycotts, and nonviolent direct action strategies against the British. Gandhi encouraged Indians to discard their foreign clothing and to wear only garments made of Indian fabric. He was jailed on many occasions because of his actions. He always refused to eat when jailed, and because of his status, forced the British to capitulate to many of his demands; more important, he forced them to respond to Indian resistance with strategies other than violence. India was successful in winning its independence in 1947. Much of the credit is given to Gandhi and his insistence on nonviolent civil disobedience.

Civil disobedience and other forms of nonviolent resistance have proved to be effective tools for effecting social change. This is particularly critical when the protagonists are politically powerless and seek to bring about profound and systemic change. Regardless of the social arrangement in a society, whether the situation involves the suppression of a numerical minority, or a numerical majority, or marginalizing an ethnic or religious population, any attempt to effect change through force or physical violence typically results in the oppressed group being further oppressed. Civil disobedience allows the protagonist to challenge unjust laws or social conditions without experiencing the full might of the state. Public opinion serves to restrain the state from using undue physical force to terminate nonviolent opposition.

Charles C. Jackson

Core Resources

Nonviolence in America: A Documentary History (Indianapolis: Bobbs-Merrill, 1966), edited by Staughton Lynd, collects material on figures in American history who have advocated or used civil disobedience; the volume includes Martin Luther King, Jr.'s essay "Pilgrimage to Nonviolence." Gene Sharp's *The Politics of Nonviolent Action* (Boston: Porter Sargent, 1973) provides a

In 1930 Mohandas K. Gandhi (center front) led fellow Indian nationalists on the famous "Salt March to the Sea" to protest British restrictions on salt manufacture; a classic example of civil disobedience, the march helped to inspire similar protest marches in the U.S. Civil Rights movement. *(National Archives)*

penetrating analysis of the types of nonviolent resistance and the methods that have been used to bring about social and political change around the world. Written when the Civil Rights movement was at its peak, Martin Oppenheimer and George Lakey's *A Manual for Direct Action* (Chicago: Quadrangle Books, 1965) explains how to organize and carry out specific strategies and surveys the history of student nonviolent resistance activities. For an excellent collection of philosophical positions and personal reflections of historical figures who used civil disobedience in their struggles, see Michael P. Smith and Kenneth L. Deutsch, eds., *Political Obligation and Civil Disobedience: Readings* (New York: Thomas Y. Crowell, 1972). Burton Zwiebach's *Civility and Disobedience* (Cambridge, England: Cambridge University Press, 1975) is a scholarly but readable treatment of civility and disobedience that raises fundamental questions about whether individuals have the right to disobey certain laws.

See also: Civil Rights movement; Gandhi, Mohandas K.; Greensboro sit-ins; King, Martin Luther, Jr.; Southern Christian Leadership Conference.

Civil liberties

Civil liberties represent one of the most basic of all conceptions of individual human rights.

There is a critical distinction between civil liberties and civil rights. Civil liberties are seen as negative promises by (or negative commands to) the government not to do certain things. The U.S. Constitution's Article I, sections 9 and 10 (the prohibitions against the federal and the state governments respectively) and the entire Bill of Rights (the first ten amendments) are clearly lists of negative commands. The First Amendment, "Congress shall make no law respecting an establishment of religion," is only one of a long list. Other negative commands in the Bill of Rights include "No soldier . . . shall be quartered in any house. . . . No person shall be held to answer for a capital . . . crime, unless on indictment. . . . Excessive bail shall not be required."

Still, negative commands would not help much if a government did not also act positively to protect its citizens from improper acts by others. Purely negative commands need to be balanced with certain affirmative obligations, and these are properly known as civil rights. These become particularly important to members of groups that suffered discrimination in the past, such as African Americans, Asian Americans, Hispanic Americans, or women in the United States. Naturally, civil liberties and civil rights also overlap: A negative promise that the government will not interfere with free speech implies an affirmative promise that it will protect individuals who express their opinions, even in the face of majorities that wish to silence them. Still, distinguishing between the affirmative and the negative characteristics of two concepts is useful.

The Need for Negative Promises The best way to understand the distinction between negative promises and affirmative guarantees is to compare the mainly negative wording of the U.S. Constitution with the constitution written by Joseph Stalin for the Soviet Union in 1936. The Soviet constitution was revised a number of times before the collapse of the Communist regime in the early 1990's, but each version followed the general provisions of Stalin's 1936 draft. At the time of writing, Stalin had already defeated all rivals and stood at the height of his power. Apparently, he wanted a constitution for propaganda purposes. It would be easy to dismiss this document by saying that Stalin never intended to live up to it, but it is still instructive to see how its provisions were worded.

Stalin's constitution contained a "Bill of Rights and Duties"—affirmative promises of numerous material benefits not provided by the U.S. Constitution. Among these were "the right to work," or guaranteed full adult employment, and a "right to rest and leisure," including a maximum forty-hour workweek, lengthy paid vacations, and resorts for working people. Also guaranteed were rights to education, medical care, and maintenance in old age. Women were granted "equal rights"—a promise still not explicitly included in the U.S. Constitution.

Stalin's constitution also promised religious freedom and free expression, typically called "civil liberties." Unlike the U.S. Bill of Rights wording, "Congress shall make no law . . . ," Stalin's promise is affirmatively worded: "In conformity with the interests of the working people, and in order to strengthen the socialist system, the citizens of the Soviet Union are guaranteed by law: (a) freedom of speech; (b) freedom of the press; (c) freedom of assembly, including the holding of mass meetings; (d) freedom of street processions and demonstrations. These civil rights are ensured by placing at the disposal of the working people and their organizations printing presses, stocks of paper, public buildings, the streets, communications facilities, and other material requisites for the exercise of these rights."

Stalin's free-expression promise is remarkably generous, providing for an unrestrained right to "street processions and demonstrations," while the U.S. Constitution limits its protection only to those who "peaceably assemble." Still more generous is the promise to supply paper and printing presses. This is in stark contrast to the situation in the United States, where exercising "free" speech can cost considerable money for media advertising. Yet the extensive record of persecution of dissident Russian writers belies Stalin's promises. Why did Stalin's constitution not protect individuals? In fact, the innocent-sounding, presumably nonbinding introductory clause, "In conformity with the interests of the working people, and in order to strengthen the socialist system," acted as a limit on the promise of free expression that followed. Only press or speech that was in the "interests of the working people" or "strengthen[ed] the socialist system" was ever allowed in the Soviet Union.

Stalin's constitution promised a whole range of economic benefits, far beyond the financial ability of even the wealthiest government to provide for all citizens. Clearly, this document was a mere wish list for the future, not a constitution.

Although the U.S. Bill of Rights contains only negative promises, those promises are far more effective, for it costs nothing for Congress *not* to pass a law. Under Stalin, speech was declared "free," but one could not even buy it. In the United States, speech may cost money, but it is freely available in the marketplace. Starting with a broad affirmative promise, the Soviet Union ended with no free speech at all. The United States began with a limited, negatively worded promise of free speech and has found itself with an overwhelming flood of information.

Historical Trends in Court Cases   Originally, the most important purpose of the U.S. Bill of Rights was to protect the states from the danger of an overly powerful national government. The period from the adoption of the U.S. Constitution in 1789 to the Civil War (1861-1865) was devoted to protecting the state governments (and only indirectly the citizens) from the federal government. During this period, perhaps the most important of the entire Bill of Rights was the Tenth Amendment's promise that "the powers not delegated to the [national government] by the constitution, nor prohibited by it to the states are reserved for the states respectively, or to the people." The First Amendment begins with the phrase "Congress shall make no law," clearly making the federal government its only target; none of the other nine original amendments, however, includes this language. One might assume that the intention was for the entire Bill of Rights to apply to only the federal government, but, given the doubt, it was natural for someone to test this assumption.

Perhaps the most important test case to determine to which level of government the Bill of Rights applied was the case of *Barron v. Baltimore* (1833). The city of Baltimore paved a number of streets and dumped leftover construction materials into the water near a wharf that Barron owned. The floor of the bay was raised so high that ships could no longer use Barron's Wharf; thus he was deprived of his property interest in his livelihood without due process or just compensation. Barron decided to sue the city of Baltimore to recover damages. Baltimore was a subunit, however, under the "sovereign" state of Maryland, which did not provide the same guarantee against eminent domain actions which the federal constitution included. Because Barron could not succeed in the Maryland courts, he turned to the federal courts, only to discover upon reaching the Supreme Court that it regarded the Fifth Amendment as applying only to the federal government.

A fundamental civil liberty, the right to assemble peaceably has played an important role in the advancement of civil rights, as when this crowd gathered at the White House in 1933 to protest the unfair treatment accorded the African American men charged in the Scottsboro trials then underway in Alabama. *(National Archives)*

In effect, Barron was told that if the Maryland constitution did not offer him protection, he could not receive it from the federal government. With this decision, the Supreme Court declared that the first ten amendments to the Constitution applied only to the federal government and not to the states. This reflected the reality of the situation before the Civil War, especially with regard to the slavery of African Americans in southern states. No slave could claim the right of free speech by citing the First Amendment.

After the Civil War, Congress sought to reverse the *Barron* decision with the Fourteenth Amendment, which begins: "All persons born or naturalized in the United States, and subject to the jurisdiction thereof, are citizens of the United States and of the State wherein they reside." The point was to undo the notion of citizenship established in *Barron*. The language of this amendment certainly appears to mean that all persons, regardless of race, were to be citizens of both the United States and the state in which they lived and that citizenship could not be denied to African Americans as it had been in southern states. Thus the U.S. Constitution was to penetrate the boundaries of each state and extend to each individual citizen.

Then the Fourteenth Amendment, in negative language, states, "No State shall make or enforce any law which shall abridge the privileges or immunities of citizens of the United States; nor shall any State deprive any person of life, liberty, or property, without due process of law." Arguably, this section of the Fourteenth Amendment applies the negative commands contained in the Bill of Rights and elsewhere in the Constitution to the citizens of each state. Once the Fourteenth Amendment was ratified, it would appear that *Barron* had been overturned by an act of the American people.

The Changing Composition of the Supreme Court Though the Supreme Court did not initially interpret the Fourteenth Amendment in this way, it started to do so beginning in the 1920's. The Court has been guided by the so-called doctrine of selective incorporation, which holds that parts of the Bill of Rights are so basic to the notion of due process that the states cannot deny them to any persons residing within their borders. Thus, the words "Congress shall make no law" now mean that no government within the United States shall make any law that abridges the freedom of speech or of the press.

For most civil liberties, the process began in 1925 with the case of *Gitlow v. New York*, in which the Court applied the free-speech section of the First Amendment to the states. This act of selective incorporation set in motion a set of cases that applied most of the rest of the First Amendment to the states. In *Near v. Minnesota* (1931), the Court applied the free press section, and *Hague v. Congress of Industrial Organizations* (1939) applied the assembly section to the states. Free exercise of religion came partly in *Hamilton v. Regents of the University of California* (1934) and more completely in *Cantwell v. Connecticut* (1940). The nonestablishment of religion followed in *Everson v. Board of Education of Ewing Township* (1947). These cases maintained that the First Amendment (at least) had such a crucial relationship to due process that states could not deprive the citizens of its benefits without denying them due process.

The Court did not advance much toward incorporation until Earl Warren was named chief justice in 1953, for only portions of the First Amendment and a single clause of the Fifth Amendment had been applied to the states by then. Warren joined Associate Justices Hugo L. Black, William O. Douglas, and (partially) Tom C. Clark, who had long argued for a much fuller incorporation, in support of the application of more sections of the Bill of Rights. Later, the appointment of William J. Brennan (and others) made it possible for the Court to incorporate eventually nearly all of the Fourth, Fifth, Sixth, and Eighth Amendments—that is, nearly all the important sections of the Bill of Rights. Thus, the civil liberties familiar to U.S. citizens against the actions of both the federal and state governments are a rather recent addition to the understanding of civil liberties in the United States.

Richard L. Wilson

Core Resources

A general study of the subject, such as Henry J. Abraham and Barbara A. Perry's *Freedom and the Court* (6th ed., New York: Oxford University Press,

1994), is a good place to begin. For one view of incorporation, see Raoul Berger's *The Fourteenth Amendment and the Bill of Rights* (Oklahoma City: University of Oklahoma Press, 1989). *The Bill of Rights: Original Meaning and Current Understanding* (edited by Eugene W. Hickok, Jr., Charlottesville: University of Virginia Press, 1991) examines each element of the Bill of Rights. The 1936 Soviet constitution and Stalin's defense of it are found in *Readings in Russian Civilization* (edited by Thomas Riha, Chicago: University of Chicago Press, 1964).

See also: Civil rights; Fourteenth Amendment.

Civil rights

Civil rights are among the most basic of all conceptions of human individual rights, but they must be paired with civil liberties to be effective.

Civil rights are typically paired with civil liberties; together they constitute the realm of human individual rights. Civil liberties are negative limits on government's treatment of private citizens. In the United States, civil rights are affirmative obligations that various levels of government have to protect citizens from coercion (often called discrimination) by the government or by private citizens. In Canada, civil rights are exclusively defined as the government's obligation to protect one person from actions by another individual. Both are important parts of human rights, particularly for democratic governments, since how well a regime protects its citizens individually is of paramount concern.

Civil liberties have a longer, clearer relationship to U.S. government than do civil rights, given that U.S. history began with the Constitution's negative commands. From the nation's creation in the late eighteenth century to the Civil War (1861-1865), constitutional theory protected state governments (and only indirectly their citizens) from the federal government's power. During this period, the provision considered to be the most important of the Bill of Rights was the Tenth Amendment: "The powers not delegated to the United States by the constitution, nor prohibited by it to the states are reserved for the states respectively, or to the people."

The argument that the Bill of Rights restrained only the national government stemmed from the wording of the First Amendment, which begins: "Congress shall make no law." Although this phrase was omitted from the other nine amendments, the unwritten assumption was that the word "Congress" should be applied to all ten. It was natural for this assumption to be tested, as it was in *Barron v. Baltimore* (1833). Barron's livelihood came from a wharf that was rendered useless when the city of Baltimore dumped paving debris in the water, raising the bottom of the bay too high near the wharf. Barron decided to sue for money to recompense himself for his loss of livelihood. Baltimore was a subunit under Maryland State, whose constitution did not provide for the guarantee against such losses which the federal constitution's Fifth Amendment did. Thus, aware that he could not succeed in the Maryland courts, Barron turned to the federal courts; however, the Supreme Court regarded the Fifth Amendment as applying only to the federal government. The court told Barron that if the Maryland constitution did not offer him protection, he could not receive it from the federal government. This decision made it clear that the first ten amendments to the U.S. Constitution applied only to the federal government and not to the states.

The pre-Civil War conception of civil rights showed clearly in the case of *Scott v. Sandford* (1857). Dred Scott was an African American slave sold to a new owner who took him into a free state, into a free territory, and then back into a slave state. Since the U.S. Constitution's language did not include the word "slavery," it was not clear whether Scott's time in free areas meant that he had become free. In the highly politically charged pre-Civil War atmosphere, the Supreme Court might well have found that Scott was still a slave on narrow technical issues, but it went far beyond that by declaring unconstitutional the 1820 Missouri Compromise. This was the first congressional enactment to be invalidated since *Marbury v. Madison* (1803). Since the 1820 compromise had prevented a clash between North and South over slavery, the decision had explosive consequences leading to the Civil War. Another critical effect of the *Scott* decision was to reinforce the notion that one had citizenship in one's home state as well as another set of rights acquired only through that state in the national government, and that the limits on the national government did not necessarily apply to the state government.

The Fourteenth Amendment   After the Civil War, Congress sought to insert language into the Constitution that would at least potentially reverse both *Barron* and *Scott*. The Fourteenth Amendment's first section has four parts, the first of which reads, "All persons born or naturalized in the United States, and subject to the jurisdiction thereof, are citizens of the United States and of the State wherein they reside." This first statement seeks to undo the notion of citizenship established in *Barron*, whereby persons are primarily considered citizens of the state in which they reside and only secondarily, through that state, citizens of the United States. The Fourteenth Amendment's constitutional language certainly appears to mean that all persons, black or white, were to be citizens both of the United States and of the state in which they lived simultaneously, and that African Americans could not be denied citizenship as they had in southern states. This allowed the U.S. Constitution to reach through the boundaries of the state to reach each individual citizen.

The Fourteenth Amendment then states, "No State shall make or enforce any law which shall abridge the privileges or immunities of citizens of the United States; nor shall any State deprive any person of life, liberty, or property, without due process of law, nor deny to any person within its jurisdiction the equal protection of the laws." From a reading of the "plain meaning of the text," these words would seem to reverse the Court's decision in *Barron* by insisting that in subsequent comparable cases, those who found themselves in situations like Barron's could not be denied their property without "due process of law."

The Supreme Court's Response The Supreme Court, however, did not initially respond as if such were the case; instead, it seemed to resurrect the pre-Fourteenth Amendment constitutional understanding. In one important case, hundreds of butchers in New Orleans, operating as small individual businesses typical of nineteenth century America, were thrown out of business after what is widely regarded as the corrupt passage of a law in the Louisiana legislature granting a state franchise (monopoly) to one company. The butchers sued, arguing that they had been deprived of their property (their livelihood) by the state "without due process of law." In what seems a very curious decision today, the Supreme Court ruled (in what are known as the *Slaughterhouse* cases (1873) that the Fourteenth Amendment sought only to make African American citizens equal with white citizens and did not affect the relationships between white persons (that is, butchers as butchers).

A few years later, in the *Civil Rights* cases (1883), the Supreme Court invalidated the 1875 Civil Rights Act. This act had made it a federal crime for public conveyances, hotels, restaurants, or amusement halls to refuse admission to anyone because of race, color, or previous condition of servitude, but the Court found that the Fourteenth Amendment stopped only government discrimination, not that of individuals or businesses. The Court's outlook was even more damaging to civil rights when it confronted a case of governmental discrimination in *Plessy v. Ferguson* (1896). Homer Plessy, only one-eighth African American in descent, was classified as an African American and was denied the opportunity to ride in the segregated first-class sections of public transportation in Louisiana. He sued on grounds that segregation in public transportation denied him "equal protection of the laws" under the last clause in the first section of the Fourteenth Amendment. The Court ruled, however, that Plessy was provided "equal protection" as long as the state provided him with "equal" facilities, even if the facilities were separate. By this means, the doctrine of "separate but equal" came to be the binding interpretation of the equal protection clause. This seems even more curious (if not outrageous) in view of the Court's contention in the *Slaughterhouse* cases that the Fourteenth Amendment solely protected the rights of blacks.

The end result of these cases was that the late nineteenth century Supreme Court treated the Fourteenth Amendment as if it did not exist for ordinary citizens. If an individual was a white butcher in New Orleans, that person was not covered by the Fourteenth Amendment, because the Court said that the "original intent" of those who proposed the amendment was merely to bring blacks to the level of whites. If an individual was an African American citizen, that person could claim no protection from the amendment if a state provided any kind of remotely comparable separated facilities, even if they were quite unequal in fact. From a current perspective, the Fourteenth Amendment seems not to have provided much protection for U.S. citizens.

Applying the Equal Protection Clause   For nearly sixty years, the Court did not go very far toward reversing itself on civil rights, but it did chip away at *Plessy* around the edges. It had still not gone very far when Earl Warren was named chief justice in 1953, but his leadership made it possible for the Court to move toward protecting civil rights by applying the equal protection clause. The first decision in this direction was the famous *Brown v. Board of Education* (1954), which overturned the *Plessy* case by deciding that "separate but equal" was an impossibility because segregated schools were inherently unequal.

By overturning *Plessy*, the Court was announcing a new jurisprudence with revolutionary implications. Perceiving this, some legal scholars wrote searching challenges to *Brown*, but the Court won, not simply because it was the highest court in the land but because its interpretation of the Fourteenth Amendment rang truer to the original language than did the earlier view. In fact, segregated schools had not been equal to integrated schools, and the "separate but equal" doctrine had been used fundamentally to discriminate against African Americans by maintaining grossly unequal facilities.

State action was the principal focus toward which *Brown* was directed. Southern states had been taxing all of their citizens, black and white, but had been using that tax money to benefit whites far more than blacks. Since African American citizens had no effective way to vote in most southern states, they had no political remedy against discrimination. The states' abusive use of coercive power gave the Supreme Court its greatest moral justification for ending segregation in schools and other facilities.

The Supreme Court, the least powerful of American national institutions, must lead largely by persuading citizens that its decisions are correct. American courts do have sufficient legitimate strength so that the national and state executive branches will respond to court orders, and individuals who defy the courts will find themselves in great difficulty. In *Brown*, however, the Court was seeking not to influence an individual but to persuade large masses of people who had the force of the state on which to counterpoise their power against the courts. Many southern states responded to *Brown* by erecting legal and constitutional barriers against the Supreme Court decision, continuing to use their coercive power to deny African Americans "equal protection." At the same time, they failed to protect

African Americans from private racist groups such as the Ku Klux Klan.

Lacking support from the executive and legislative branches, the Court was unable on its own power to achieve the end of segregation. In the decade between the 1954 *Brown* decision and the passage of the 1964 Civil Rights Act, the courts decided case after case striking down discriminatory laws in southern states, a process that was so slow and tedious that only 1 percent of southern students were attending integrated schools by 1964. Only with the passage of the Civil Rights Act of 1964 and Voting Rights Act of 1965 did all three branches of the national government begin to act in concert for equal protection. Only when these acts were enforced by a sympathetic administration in the 1960's did the country begin to make real progress toward eliminating the improper use of southern state governmental power.

The problem was enormous because it was a question of striking down not only a handful of specific laws giving preference to whites over African Americans but also a whole fabric of law that protected privileges acquired over years of discrimination. The U.S. Constitution is designed to protect minorities that already have legal protections. Within the nation as a whole, white southerners became a minority who used the legal system to maintain their previous benefits. Although legislation should not be retroactive, the legal system should also benefit citizens equally, or the system's legal legitimacy will erode.

The attempt to redress all the problems caused by segregation was yet more difficult because many discriminatory acts were in the domain of activities long regarded as private and beyond the legitimate scope of government activity. Given their past benefits, citizens could rely on the constitutional and legal structure to resist integration. The Supreme Court could strike down statutes and state constitutional provisions one after the other, but once it had rendered the legal system presumably neutral, schools would still be largely segregated because of private decisions made by citizens without any overt governmental support. This became especially clear in the pattern of segregation in northern schools, which proved to be based on residential housing patterns. When the Court could find deliberate decisions made by local authorities to bring about the segregation of schools, it could strike them down; it could do far less, however, when discrimination was not the result of deliberate governmental action.

However, the notion of civil rights entails affirmative guarantees that the government will act to provide fairness for all individuals. Moreover, other groups besides African Americans claim to have suffered discrimination in the past (no group more obviously so than women) and were not granted equal protection of the laws in the late 1800's, despite their pressing claims at that time. For some such groups the case for relief from past discrimination is not so clear. They will need to advance their claims carefully and persuasively if they are to win the support of a broad segment of fellow Americans.

Richard L. Wilson

Core Resources

An excellent book of general scholarship in this field is Henry J. Abraham and Barbara A. Perry's *Freedom and the Court* (6th ed., New York: Oxford University Press, 1994). A cogent statement of the case against the Court's current understanding of civil rights is made by Raoul Berger in *The Fourteenth Amendment and the Bill of Rights* (Oklahoma City: University of Oklahoma Press, 1989). Ronald J. Fiscus's *The Constitutional Logic of Affirmative Action* (Durham, N.C.: Duke University Press, 1992), presents a tightly logical argument in support of the concept of affirmative action as a part of the package of rights known as "civil rights." An opposing view can be found in Kent Greenwalt's *Discrimination and Reverse Discrimination* (New York: Alfred A. Knopf, 1983).

See also: Affirmative action; *Brown v. Board of Education*; Civil liberties; Civil Rights Act of 1960; Civil Rights Act of 1964; *Civil Rights* cases; Civil Rights movement; Discrimination: racial and ethnic; Fourteenth Amendment; Missouri Compromise; *Plessy v. Ferguson*; *Scott v. Sandford*; Segregation: de facto and de jure; Voting Rights Act of 1965.

Civil Rights Act of 1957

During the mid-1950's, the Civil Rights movement gathered momentum as it challenged racial segregation and discrimination in many areas of southern life. One area where progress proved slow was voting rights. Intimidation and irregular registration procedures limited electoral participation by African Americans. By 1957, support for legislation to protect voting rights was growing among Northern Republicans and Democrats in Congress. Yet Congress had not passed a civil rights bill since 1875, and there was strong southern opposition to any change in the status quo. It was, however, Senator Lyndon B. Johnson of Texas, the Senate majority leader, who took the lead. Not known at this point in his career as an advocate of civil rights, Johnson used his considerable legislative ability to shepherd the new bill through Congress. It passed just as the Little Rock school integration crisis was breaking.

The bill had several major provisions. It created a new body, the Civil Rights Commission, to investigate complaints of violations of civil rights. It raised the Civil Rights Section of the Department of Justice to the status of a division, to be headed by an assistant attorney general. It also made it a federal crime to harass those attempting to vote and allowed the attorney general to initiate proceedings against those violating the law.

The law's short-term effects were modest. Though the number of African American voters did grow, many impediments to voting remained, especially in the rural South. Many criticized the act's weak enforcement procedures: The Civil Rights Commission could gather information and investigate complaints, but it could take no action to protect those trying to vote. Not until the Voting Rights Act of 1965 would effective machinery for ensuring voting rights be established.

On the other hand, in the early 1960's, the administration of President John F. Kennedy did use the act's provisions (which were strengthened by the 1960 Civil Rights Act) to proceed against some of the worst cases of harassment. Also the act broke a psychological barrier by putting the first national civil rights law in eighty-two years on the books. It also highlighted the importance of voting rights to the overall civil rights struggle.

William C. Lowe

See also: Civil rights; Civil Rights Act of 1960; Civil Rights Act of 1964; Civil Rights Act of 1968; Civil Rights Act of 1991; Civil Rights Acts of 1866-1875; *Civil Rights* cases; Little Rock school desegregation.

Civil Rights Act of 1960

As the Civil Rights movement progressed in the 1950's, efforts to desegregate led to a backlash in the form of bombings and burnings of black churches, homes, and other property. African Americans, otherwise fully qualified, were still denied the right to vote by many local officials, often under implicit threat of violent reprisals.

During 1959, the Civil Rights Commission made its first report, minutely documenting a massive denial of the right to vote in the South and recommending that the president appoint federal voting registrars in response to citizen complaints. Attorney General William P. Rogers proposed instead that complaints should be filed with federal courts, which would appoint voting referees. In the House, a bill favoring the referee plan passed. Majority Leader Lyndon B. Johnson and Minority Leader Everett Dirksen then maneuvered passage of the bill in the Senate. Southern conservatives were pleased that the bill was so weak that no major change occurred; civil rights proponents had to accept half-a-loaf in order to advance their cause.

According to section 6 of the act, the procedure for those deprived of the right to register or to vote is to complain to the U.S. attorney general to file suit in a federal court, which has ten days to respond. If the court finds that a pattern or practice of exclusion has existed in a voting jurisdiction for at least one year, the judge appoints one or more voting referees. Within a second ten-day period, the voting referees then screen applicants to determine whether they meet statutory requirements for voting; if an applicant is found qualified to vote, the judge then issues a voting certificate to the

President Dwight D. Eisenhower signing the Civil Rights Act of 1960. *(Library of Congress)*

applicant, who can vote in the next election, provided that the initial application was filed twenty days before the election.

To ensure enforcement of the right to vote, section 6 provides that election officials who refuse to honor the federal voting certificate can be found in contempt of court. The U.S. attorney general, in filing a motion to find an election official in contempt of court, can also sue the state in which the voter resides in case the voting official is later fired.

Since voting records were often destroyed in cases of this sort, section 3 requires all election officials to keep records of votes cast in federal elections for twenty-two months.

The law did not challenge voting requirements, such as the literacy test, only the unequal application of voting requirements to blacks and whites. Later voting rights acts repealed various artificial voting requirements. Other provisions of the 1960 Civil Rights Act empower the Civil Rights Commission to administer oaths and permit U.S. government property to be used for desegregated schools when facilities for locally desegregated schools are unavailable.

Michael Haas

See also: Civil rights; Civil Rights Act of 1957; Civil Rights Act of 1964; Civil Rights Act of 1968; Civil Rights Act of 1991; Civil Rights Acts of 1866-1875; Voting Rights Act of 1965.

Civil Rights Act of 1964

The Civil Rights Act of 1964 outlawed the exclusion of African Americans from hotels, theaters, restaurants, and other public accommodations; barred federal funds to any activity that involved racial discrimination; warranted the Justice Department to initiate school desegregation suits; and forbade racial discrimination in employment and union membership policies.

The legislation that became the Civil Rights Act of 1964 was originally proposed by President John F. Kennedy on June 19, 1963, following a confrontation with Alabama governor George Wallace over the admission of black students to the University of Alabama. Kennedy declared that the bill should be passed "not merely for reasons of economic efficiency, world diplomacy and domestic tranquility—but above all because it is right." The act was forcefully advocated by President Lyndon B. Johnson after Kennedy's assassination. Its passage was facilitated both by pressure from civil rights advocates and by segregationist responses to those pressures. Events that helped rouse the public to support civil rights included the March on Washington in August, 1963, the bombing of black churches, the "battle of Oxford" that ensued when James Meredith sought to enter the University of Mississippi, the mistreatment of freedom marchers and freedom riders, and the murder in Mississippi of three civil rights workers.

Passage of the act came only after senators voted to end a filibuster on June 19, 1964, exactly one year after Kennedy had proposed the bill. Republican senator Everett Dirksen, the Senate minority leader, shared credit for passage of the act. Traditionally an opponent of civil rights legislation, Dirksen implored Republicans to support the bill as "an idea whose time has come."

Major Provisions of the Act   Unlike the first two civil rights acts of the modern period—those of 1957 and 1960, which were limited principally to ensuring the right to vote—the 1964 act attacked segregation on a broad front. The final bill was stronger than Kennedy's proposal to Congress. Its main provisions are found in the first seven of the act's ten titles. Title I, concerned with voting, was intended to create more effective enforcement of the right to vote in federal elections without consideration of color or race. It expedites the procedure for settling voting rights suits and mandates that uniform standards be applied to all individuals seeking to register and vote. To diminish the discriminatory use of literacy and comprehension tests, it equates completion of the sixth grade with literacy. Finally, it empowers the U.S. attorney general to bring suit if there is a "pattern or practice" of voting discrimination.

Title II forbids discrimination on the basis of race, color, religion, or national origin in places of public accommodation. Privately owned or operated facilities, such as country clubs, are exempted from the Title II prohibition. Title III deals with public facilities such as municipally owned or state-owned or operated hospitals, libraries, and parks. It authorizes the attorney general to bring a civil suit to order desegregation of any such facility whenever the attorney general receives a written complaint of discrimination from an individual or individuals unable to take the necessary legal actions themselves.

Title IV's concern is public education. Its main provision authorizes the U.S. Office of Education to organize training institutes to prepare school personnel to deal with desegregation; to assist school districts, states, and other political subdivisions in implementing school desegregation plans; and to offer financial assistance to school boards to facilitate their hiring of specialists for in-service training.

Title V reauthorized the U.S. Commission on Civil Rights, created by the Civil Rights Act of 1957, for four years and gave it the additional responsibilities of serving as a national clearinghouse for civil rights information and investigating allegations of fraud in voting. Under Title VI, any federal body that offers contracts, grants, or loans is required to bar discrimination on the grounds of race, color, or national origin from programs it supports financially.

Title VII established a federal right to equal opportunity in employment and created the Equal Employment Opportunity Commission (EEOC) to assist in implementing this right. Under Title VII, employers, employment agencies, and labor unions are required to treat all persons without regard to their color, race, religion, sex, or national origin. Equality or nondiscrimination was mandated in all phases of employment, including hiring, firing, promotion, job assignments, and apprenticeship and training. Gender was inserted into the bill at the insistence of Senator James Eastland, a Democrat from Mississippi, in the vain hope that its inclusion would weaken support

President Lyndon B. Johnson signs the Civil Rights Act of 1964, as other government and civil rights leaders look on. *(Library of Congress)*

for the entire bill. The final three sections of the act confer no rights. They provide structures for federal authorities to operate while mitigating possible conflicts with communities under pressure to comply with other provisions of the act.

Subjected to judicial scrutiny, the 1964 legislation survived several challenges to each of its main sections. Many of its provisions were later strengthened by subsequent legislation, including the Voting Rights Act of 1965 and the Civil Rights Act of 1968.

Ashton Wesley Welch

Core Resources

Among the many fine sources for information on the Civil Rights movement and the 1964 Civil Rights Act are Derrick A. Bell, Jr.'s *Race, Racism, and American Law* (2d ed., Boston: Little, Brown, 1980), Charles S. Bullock III and Charles M. Lamb's *Implementation of Civil Rights Policy* (Monterey, Calif.: Brooks-Cole, 1984), Anthony Lewis's *Portrait of a Decade* (New York: Bantam Books, 1965), and Sig Synnestvedt's *The White Response to Black Emancipation* (New York: Macmillan, 1972).

See also: Civil rights; Civil Rights Act of 1957; Civil Rights Act of 1960; Civil Rights Act of 1968; Civil Rights Act of 1991; Civil Rights Acts of 1866-1875; Civil Rights movement; Equal Employment Opportunity Commission; Voting Rights Act of 1965.

Civil Rights Act of 1968

The Civil Rights Act of 1968 banned racial discrimination in the sale or rental of most types of housing; it also extended most of the protections of the Bill of Rights to Native Americans.

After 1965, the Civil Rights movement devoted increasing attention to conditions in the North. It found much segregation there, a condition that was rooted in residential patterns rather than in Jim Crow laws. The prevalence of segregated housing determined the composition of schools and other aspects of urban life. Martin Luther King, Jr.'s Chicago campaign in 1966 focused national attention on the housing issue. His lack of success showed that white resistance to opening neighborhoods to minority residents was strong and would be difficult to overcome. Urban riots in northern and western cities provoked a "white backlash," as many northern whites ceased their support for further civil rights reform. In 1966 and 1967, President Lyndon B. Johnson tried and failed to persuade Congress to pass civil rights bills outlawing discrimination in housing.

Passing the Act   In 1968, liberal Democrats in the Senate brought forward a new civil rights bill containing a fair housing provision. Heavy lobbying by Clarence Mitchell, of the National Association for the Advancement of Colored People (NAACP), helped to marshal a majority of senators in support of the bill. As with earlier civil rights measures, southern senators attempted to talk the bill to death with a filibuster. However, in return for some relatively minor modifications in the bill, the leader of the Republican minority, Senator Everett Dirksen of Illinois, agreed to support an attempt to cut off the filibuster. This succeeded, and the bill passed the Senate on March 11, 1968.

In the House of Representatives, passage was far from sure. The assassination of Martin Luther King, Jr., on April 4, however, shocked the country and dramatically altered the political landscape. Support for the bill grew; it passed easily and was signed by President Johnson on April 11.

Fair Housing   The main thrust of the 1968 Civil Rights Act was to outlaw discrimination on the basis of race, religion, or national origin in the sale and rental of most forms of housing in the United States, as well as in the advertising, listing, and financing of housing. Exempted from the act's coverage were single-family houses not listed with real estate agents and small apartment buildings lived in by the owner. (About a month after the act became law, the Supreme Court ruled, in the case of *Jones v. Alfred H. Mayer Company*, that the Civil Rights Act of 1866 prohibited racial discrimination in housing and other property transactions.) Two other provisions of the act also grew out of the racial turmoil of the 1960's. One enumerated specific civil rights whose violations were punishable under federal law. Another sought to make the act more acceptable to the growing number of Americans concerned about urban riots by specifying stiff penalties for inciting or engaging in riots.

As a housing measure, the act proved disappointing. Its enforcement provisions were weak. Those with complaints of discrimination were directed to file them with the Department of Housing and Urban Development (HUD), which would then attempt to negotiate a voluntary settlement. If this failed, complainants would have to file their own lawsuits; the federal government would intervene only in cases where there was a clear pattern of past discrimination. In addition, white resentment at attempts to integrate neighborhoods remained high. Banks often found ways to avoid the law's provisions, making it difficult for many African American families to secure necessary financing. By the late twentieth century, it was clear that the act had not ended the country's dominant pattern of racial segregation in housing.

The Indian Bill of Rights

The Civil Rights Act of 1968 contained another provision unrelated to concerns over fair housing: the Indian Bill of Rights. This was grounded in the fact that Indians on reservations, as members of tribal communities, were not considered to be covered by the Bill of Rights. In 1896, the Supreme Court had ruled, in the case of *Talton v. Mayes,* that the Bill of Rights did not apply to Indian tribes or to their courts. In 1961, Senator Sam Ervin, a North Carolina Democrat, was surprised to discover the fact. Over the next several years, he held hearings on the subject. In 1968, he was able to amend the civil rights bill moving through the Senate to include coverage of Indian rights.

The Indian Bill of Rights extended a variety of constitutional protections to Native Americans with regard to the authority of their tribal governments. Among these were freedom of speech and religion, as well as protections for those suspected or accused of crimes. In fact, all or part of the First, Fourth, Fifth, Six, and Eighth Amendments were held to apply to reservation Indians, as was the Fourteenth Amendment's guarantee of due process. Some parts of the Bill of Rights were not included, however; the First Amendment's ban of religious establishments was not included, in deference to tribal customs, nor were the Second Amendment's right to bear arms or the Third's prohibition against the quartering of troops. Most important to most Indians was a provision that required tribal permission before states could further extend jurisdiction over tribal land.

William C. Lowe

Core Resources

Useful views of the 1968 Civil Rights Act may be found in James A. Kushner's *Fair Housing: Discrimination in Real Estate, Community Development, and Revitalization* (New York: McGraw-Hill, 1983), Lyndon B. Johnson's *The Vantage Point: Perspectives of the Presidency 1963-1969* (New York: Holt, Rinehart and Winston, 1971), Donald G. Nieman's *Promises to Keep: African-Americans and the Constitutional Order, 1776 to the Present* (New York: Oxford University Press, 1991), and John R. Wunder's *"Retained by the People": A History of the American Indians and the Bill of Rights* (New York: Oxford University Press, 1994).

See also: Civil rights; Civil Rights Act of 1957; Civil Rights Act of 1960; Civil Rights Act of 1964; Civil Rights Act of 1991; Civil Rights Acts of 1866-1875; Civil Rights movement; *Jones v. Alfred H. Mayer Company.*

Civil Rights Act of 1991

To many supporters of the Civil Rights movement, the 1980's was a decade of disappointment, when earlier gains seemed threatened by unsympathetic presidents and a conservative political atmosphere. Especially troubling from this viewpoint was the direction taken by the U.S. Supreme Court. In 1989, the Court issued a number of decisions that seemed to endanger past protections against employment discrimination by making the position of voluntary affirmative action programs less secure (*Richmond v. J. A. Croson Company*), making it more difficult for women and minorities to sue for job discrimination (*Wards Cove Packing Company v. Atonio*), and reducing protection against racial harassment on the job (*Patterson v. McLean Credit Union*).

Reaction against these decisions, especially the last two, made it easier for liberal Democrats to create a bipartisan coalition in Congress in support of an effort to pass a new civil rights bill. Though the administration of President George Bush did not initially support the bill, the president did sign the bill when it finally passed after two years of congressional consideration and debate.

The Civil Rights Act of 1991 took the form of a series of amendments to Title VII of the Civil Rights Act of 1964. Among its many sections were three important provisions. One sought to overturn the *Wards Cove* decision, which had required those claiming employment discrimination to prove that a specific employer practice had created a discriminatory effect and allowed employers to justify such a practice as a "business necessity." The act eliminated the latter claim as a defense against a charge of intentional discrimination. Another provision counteracted the *Patterson* decision by extending the 1875 Civil Rights Act's ban on racial discrimination in contracts to cover protection from harassment on the job. Finally, the act allowed victims of discrimination to sue for larger monetary damages in cases brought under the 1964 Civil Rights Act and the 1990 Americans with Disabilities Act.

Though rather technical and legalistic in character, the 1991 Civil Rights Act did make it easier for those who considered themselves victims of various types of discrimination to bring their cases to court.

William C. Lowe

See also: Civil rights; Civil Rights Act of 1957; Civil Rights Act of 1960; Civil Rights Act of 1964; Civil Rights Act of 1968; Civil Rights Acts of 1866-1875; *Richmond v. J. A. Croson Company*.

Civil Rights Acts of 1866-1875

After the Thirteenth Amendment abolished slavery throughout the United States in 1865, almost all freed blacks were without property or education, and most white southerners bitterly opposed any fundamental improvement in their political and social status. In 1865-1866, southern legislatures enacted the highly discriminatory black codes, and proponents of racial equality responded by calling for new federal laws.

Congress, using its new authority under the Thirteenth Amendment, overrode President Andrew Johnson's veto to pass the first Civil Rights Act on April 9, 1866. This law conferred citizenship on African Americans, a measure necessitated by the Supreme Court's Dred Scott decision (*Scott v. Sandford*, 1857). The law included a list of enumerated rights, including the right to make and enforce contracts, to sue and give evidence in court, and to purchase and inherit all forms of property. It also punished public officials if they used their legal powers to deny equality to blacks. Since the law's constitutionality was questionable, many of its major provisions were incorporated into the Fourteenth Amendment.

NEGRO EXPULSION FROM RAILWAY CAR, PHILADELPHIA.

The Civil Rights Act of 1875 was designed to ban such forms of racial discrimination as preventing members of minorities from using public transportation, but it was overturned by the Supreme Court eight years later. *(Library of Congress)*

On July 16, 1866, Congress again overrode President Johnson's veto, this time to enlarge the scope of the Freedmen's Bureau. Among other items, this law authorized the bureau to use military commissions to try persons accused of violating the civil rights of freedmen.

Again voting to override a presidential veto on March 2, 1867, Congress passed the First Reconstruction Act. Dividing the South into five military districts, the act required southern states to call new constitutional conventions elected by universal manhood suffrage and to ratify the Fourteenth Amendment. Under the act, 703,000 blacks and 627,000 whites were registered as voters, with black majorities in five states.

As the Ku Klux Klan conducted a wave of terrorism against African Americans and Republicans in the South, Congress responded with the Ku Klux Klan Acts of 1870 and 1871, which provided police protection to enforce the rights guaranteed in the Fourteenth and Fifteenth Amendments. In several decisions, such as *United States v. Cruikshank* (1876), the Supreme Court ruled that key parts of the statutes exceeded the constitutional powers of Congress.

Finally, on March 1, 1875, President Ulysses S. Grant signed into law the Civil Rights Act of 1875. This far-reaching act, largely the work of Senator Charles Sumner, outlawed discrimination based on race in public accommodations (inns, businesses, theaters, and the like) and made it illegal to exclude blacks from jury trials. In the *Civil Rights* cases (1883), however, the Supreme Court struck down most of the 1875 law, holding that the Fourteenth Amendment did not authorize Congress to prohibit discrimination by private individuals. This decision ended almost all federal attempts to protect African Americans from private discrimination until the passage of the Civil Rights Act of 1964.

Although the Civil Rights Acts of the Reconstruction era failed to guarantee any long-lasting equality for blacks, they did provide points of reference for the Civil Rights movement of the 1950's and 1960's. The Civil Rights Act of 1866 was resurrected in *Jones v. Alfred H. Mayer Company* (1968), when the Supreme Court upheld its use to outlaw private racial discrimination in economic transactions as a "badge of slavery."

Thomas T. Lewis

See also: Black codes; Civil rights; Civil Rights Act of 1964; Civil Rights Act of 1968; *Civil Rights* cases; Fourteenth Amendment; Freedmen's Bureau; *Jones v. Alfred H. Mayer Company*; Ku Klux Klan; Reconstruction; *Scott v. Sandford*; Thirteenth Amendment; *United States v. Cruikshank*.

Civil Rights cases

In the aftermath of the Civil War, the U.S. Constitution was amended three times in five years. The three amendments, taken as a whole, were designed not only to end slavery but also to eliminate its "badges and incidents." Each of the amendments contained a clause empowering Congress to pass implementing legislation. In 1875, Congress passed a Civil Rights Act that made it illegal for anyone to deny access to places of public accommodation— including inns, public transportation, and theaters—on account of race, color, or previous condition of servitude. Five cases claiming violations of the public accommodations provisions were consolidated for decision by the Supreme Court.

The Court ruled that Congress did not have the authority to prohibit discrimination by private individuals. Justice Joseph P. Bradley's majority opinion analyzed the congressional authority granted by two of the Civil War Amendments. The Fourteenth Amendment, he said, gave Congress authority to provide relief from state action which interfered with a person's rights to due process of law and to equal protection of the laws. The amendment did not allow Congress to legislate against an invasion of rights by private individuals. Such power belonged to the state alone. Since the Civil Rights Act purported to provide a remedy for private discrimination, it exercised a congressional power not granted by the Constitution.

In regard to the Thirteenth Amendment, the Supreme Court conceded that Congress had been empowered to abolish "all badges and incidents of slavery"; however, the "badges and incidents" included only legal disabilities, such as the inability to make contracts, hold property, and have standing in court. They did not include the "social rights of men and races in the community." The Court concluded that it was time for the former slave to "take the rank of a mere citizen, and cease to be the special favorite of the laws."

In his dissent, Justice John Marshall Harlan argued that since state governments established and maintained the roads, highways, and harbors used by public conveyances, and since the states licensed theaters, inns, and other places of public accommodation, state tolerance of discrimination amounted to state action that furthered discrimination in violation of the Fourteenth Amendment.

The significance of the *Civil Rights* cases is twofold. First, the Court ruled that Congress could not outlaw discrimination by private parties under the authority of the Civil War Amendments. Therefore, the victims of racial discrimination could expect relief only from state governments, which, in the South, had by 1883 reverted to the control of white supremacists. Second, the *Civil Rights* cases prevented Congress from legislating against private discrimination in public accommodations for nearly one hundred years. In 1964, Congress passed a Civil Rights Act that drew its authority not from the Civil War Amendments but from the "commerce clause" in the U.S. Constitution.

William H. Coogan

See also: Civil rights; Civil Rights Acts of 1866-1875; Fourteenth Amendment; Thirteenth Amendment.

Civil Rights movement

The quest for political equality in the second half of the twentieth century transformed the face of American politics; the pursuit of economic equality has met with greater opposition and has had less success.

Although the modern Civil Rights movement began with the Montgomery bus boycott in 1955, the struggle for civil rights has been an ongoing battle. The founding of the National Association for the Advancement of Colored People (NAACP) in 1909 was one of the first attempts to organize in the pursuit of civil rights. With the exception of some legal victories under the leadership of the NAACP, there was little progress in the field of civil rights until the end of World War II.

Voting Rights   With the end of Reconstruction after the Civil War, all the southern states developed devices to eliminate black voters. Each of the southern states adopted new state constitutions between 1890 and 1910 and employed devices such as the grandfather clause, the white primary, the poll tax, and the literacy test to strip blacks of their right to vote. These devices were enormously successful. There were more than 130,000 black voters in Louisiana in 1896. By 1900, only two years after Louisiana adopted a new constitution containing many discriminating features, there were only 5,320 black voters left on the rolls.

For several reasons, African Americans made securing the right to vote their number-one objective. First, the U.S. Constitution, particularly the Fifteenth Amendment, contains specific guarantees against voter discrimination. Second, blacks believed there was less social stigma involved in granting the right to vote than in integration. Integration meant race mixing, which was feared by white southerners. Giving blacks the right to vote did not mean that whites would have to intermingle with blacks. Finally, African Americans believed that securing the right to vote would bring about other changes. Black voting would result in the election of black politicians, and it would force white politicians to moderate their racial views.

The grandfather clause was the first major barrier to fall. Grandfather clauses said that if a person had a relative who voted before the Civil War began in 1861, then the person was exempt from other voter qualifications. Because blacks were not allowed to vote before the Civil War, they had to meet voter qualifications such as poll taxes and literacy tests. The U.S. Supreme Court unanimously struck down grandfather clauses in *Guinn v. United States* (1915).

The next major barrier to fall was the white primary election. As the term implies, only whites were permitted to vote in primaries. Since southern politics was dominated by the Democratic Party, whoever won the Democratic primary would win the general election. If blacks could not participate in the primary selection process, then they had no real input into the selection of political candidates.

In 1924, the Texas legislature passed a law prohibiting blacks from participating in that state's primary election. A unanimous U.S. Supreme Court struck down the Texas law in *Nixon v. Herndon* (1927). Immediately, the Texas legislature passed another law delegating authority to the executive committee of each party to determine who could participate in the primaries. As expected, they excluded blacks from participation. In a 5 to 4 decision, the U.S. Supreme Court once again threw out Texas' white primary in *Nixon v. Condon* (1932). Undaunted, Texas made a third effort to ban blacks from the primaries. In 1932, the state convention of the Texas

Democratic Party, without any authorization from the state legislature, limited primaries to white voters. A unanimous U.S. Supreme Court, in *Grovey v. Townsend* (1935), upheld the action of the state convention, concluding that there was no state discrimination involved. Political parties were voluntary associations that had the right to determine their membership. It was not until *Smith v. Allwright* (1944), some twenty years after the first Texas white primary law was passed, that the U.S. Supreme Court finally declared white primaries to be unconstitutional. The NAACP had brought most of the white primary cases, including the *Smith* case, to the U.S. Supreme Court.

The third major voting barrier to fall was the poll tax, which was the payment of a fee in order to vote. Blacks were less able to afford the tax, and poor whites could always find someone to pay or waive their tax. Opponents of the poll tax tried to get Congress to abolish the fee. Five times the House of Representatives passed legislation to ban poll taxes, but each time the legislation was filibustered by southern senators. In 1964, the Twenty-fourth Amendment, which eliminated poll taxes in federal elections, was approved. Two years later, in *Harper v. Virginia Board of Elections*, the U.S. Supreme Court abolished poll taxes in state and local elections.

The last barrier to fall was also the most significant barrier in keeping blacks from voting: the literacy test. Most literacy tests required the voter to be able to read, write, and understand sections of the state or federal constitution. Although many blacks could pass the reading and writing portion of the test, almost all failed the understanding portion, primarily because white voter registrars had the sole authority to determine if a person understood a section of the constitution.

Attempts to get the courts to ban literacy tests were unsuccessful. The U.S. Congress passed the Voting Rights Act of 1965, which prohibited literacy tests in areas that were covered by the law. In 1970, an amendment to the Voting Rights Act banned literacy tests in all fifty states, and another amendment in 1975 permanently banned literacy tests.

School Desegregation

Before the Civil War, most states prohibited blacks from getting an education. After the Civil War, schools were established for black education, but on a segregated basis. In many areas, education for blacks ended at the sixth grade. High schools, vocational schools, and colleges and universities were often unavailable for black students.

In 1890, the Louisiana legislature passed a Jim Crow law requiring "separate but equal" accommodations for white and black passengers on the railroads. The railroads backed a challenge to the law because of the additional expense they would encounter. Homer Plessy, one-eighth black, was selected to test the law; he sat in the whites-only coach and was arrested. In *Plessy v. Ferguson* (1896), in a 7 to 1 decision, the U.S. Supreme Court upheld the Louisiana law. The Court found no violation of the "equal protection clause" of the Fourteenth Amendment because whites were as separated from blacks as blacks were from whites. Although the *Plessy* decision had nothing to do with education, the doctrine of "separate but equal" was quickly adopted to justify segregated schools.

The NAACP led the legal attack against segregated schools. The first strategy of the organization was not to seek to overturn *Plessy* but, on the contrary, to seek enforcement of *Plessy*. African American schools were indeed "separate," but were they "equal"? Black schools received far fewer dollars per student to operate, and black teachers were paid a fraction of what white teachers received. Black schools had a limited curriculum, few textbooks, no transportation for students, and often the buildings were no more than one-room shacks. In a series of Supreme Court cases involving higher education in the South, the NAACP time and again demonstrated that black schools were not equal. In fact, in many of the cases, there were no law schools or professional schools available to blacks. The Supreme Court consistently ordered the enrollment of black students where "separate but equal" was not being met.

By the late 1940's, the NAACP was ready to mount a direct challenge to *Plessy v. Ferguson*. Cases were brought in South Carolina, Delaware, Virginia, Kansas, and the District of Columbia. In 1954 the U.S. Supreme Court overturned *Plessy* and the "separate but equal" doctrine in *Brown v. Board of Education*. Chief Justice Earl Warren, speaking for a unanimous Court, wrote: "We conclude that in the field of public education the doctrine of 'separate but equal' has no place. Separate educational facilities are inherently unequal."

Black churches, such as Birmingham's Sixteenth Street Baptist Church, were major centers of Civil Rights movement organizing. *(Library of Congress)*

Many southern states invoked the doctrine of states' rights and argued that the federal government was usurping the power of states to control education. Massive resistance to the court's decision became the standard policy throughout the South. Some school districts closed their schools rather than integrate, while other communities exploded in violence. When a large, unruly mob prevented the integration of Central High School in Little Rock, Arkansas, President Dwight D. Eisenhower was forced to send in federal troops to protect the nine black students.

Token integration was the policy during the 1960's, but in 1969 the U.S. Supreme Court finally declared that the time for delay was over. Fifteen years after *Brown*, the Court declared that school districts were ordered to comply "at once" with the *Brown* decision. School districts increasingly relied upon busing as the means to desegregate the schools, and opponents of busing in both the north and south argued that it was leading to the destruction of neighborhood schools.

Public Accommodations   On December 1, 1955, a racial incident in Montgomery, Alabama, transformed the face of the Civil Rights movement. On that day, Rosa Parks, a black seamstress, refused to give up her seat on a Montgomery bus to a white passenger. Parks was arrested, and her arrest ushered in the Civil Rights movement. Blacks, led by a new resident to the community, the Reverend Martin Luther King, Jr., organized one of the most effective mass movements and boycotts in the nation's history, a boycott of the city's bus system. Almost a year after the boycott began, Montgomery officials reluctantly desegregated the bus system after a decision from the Supreme Court.

King emerged from the bus boycott as a national political figure, and in 1957, he and his supporters established the Southern Christian Leadership Conference (SCLC). Combining his Christian beliefs with the precepts of nonviolent resistance, King led several mass protest movements against what he perceived to be the moral injustices of a segregated society. In 1963, King wrote his famous "Letter from Birmingham Jail," in which he outlined his views on just and unjust laws. That same year, King led more than 200,000 civil rights supporters on a March on Washington, D.C. In 1965, King led one of the last major protests of the Civil Rights movement when he and his supporters marched from Selma to Montgomery, Alabama, to pressure Congress to pass a voting rights bill.

Another significant phase of the Civil Rights movement was characterized by "sit-ins." Triggered by four black college students seeking service at the "white" lunch counter of the local Woolworth's in Greensboro, North Carolina, within days similar sit-ins took place in more than sixty communities. Two months after the sit-in started in Greensboro, the lunch counters were integrated.

Many of the student leaders in the sit-in movement came together in 1960 and established the Student Nonviolent Coordinating Committee (SNCC).

SNCC played a major role in voter registration drives throughout the South. By the mid-1960's, tired of the violence against them and the slow pace of change, SNCC became one of the most militant of the civil rights organizations and a key exponent of "black power."

In 1960, the Congress of Racial Equality (CORE) initiated the "Freedom Rides." Thirteen riders—some white, some black—boarded buses in Washington, D.C., on a trip through the heart of the deep South. Attacked and viciously beaten by white mobs outside Anniston, Alabama, and in Birmingham, the Freedom Riders focused the attention of the nation on the failure of southern states to protect passengers in interstate travel.

Realizing the difficulties blacks experienced in seeking service in public accommodations such as hotels, restaurants, and theaters, Congress passed the landmark Civil Rights Act of 1964, which made it illegal to discriminate in public accommodations on grounds of "race, color, religion or national origin." Another section of the law banned discrimination in employment and established the Equal Employment Opportunity Commission (EEOC) to enforce the law. The section on employment discrimination established "affirmative action," an approach that has been blamed by some for eroding white support for the Civil Rights movement.

The Collapse of the Civil Rights Movement   After 1965, the Civil Rights movement fell into disarray and decline. There were numerous reasons for the decline of the movement. To begin with, the broad base of public support for civil rights began to erode. Many Americans believed that Congress had passed enough legislation to deal with the problem of discrimination (most notably the sweeping 1964 Civil Rights Act) and that now it was time to let those laws work. Another factor was the nationalization of the push for civil rights. Until the mid-1960's the civil rights issue was widely viewed as a southern problem. When the movement moved northward, some white northerners withdrew their support. With the institution of busing for school desegregation and the attempt to integrate housing, many white Americans felt threatened.

The controversy over affirmative action policies also divided support for the movement. To many Americans, affirmative action meant quotas and programs that unfairly threatened their own job security. Another factor was the diffusion of the movement as it was broadened to include discrimination based on age, gender, physical disability, and sexual orientation. Fewer Americans were willing to support what they viewed as special privileges for women, the disabled, and homosexuals than to support civil rights, particularly voting rights, for African Americans.

The urban riots of the 1960's shattered white support for civil rights. White voters and politicians—President Lyndon B. Johnson among them—felt betrayed by the riots. They thought that the nation was trying to deal with the problems of racism and discrimination. Congress had passed three civil rights laws and one voting rights law within an eight-year period. When the

Watts riot in Los Angeles broke out within a week after passage of the Voting Rights Act of 1965, the "white backlash" against civil rights essentially brought the movement to a halt. The riots represented the chasm that still existed between black and white, and they frightened many whites into thinking of "law and order" first and civil rights gains second. On the national scene, the escalating war in Vietnam drew attention away from the Civil Rights movement. When Martin Luther King, Jr., openly opposed the war, he was widely criticized by many civil rights leaders, as well as by President Johnson. In the late 1960's, the Vietnam War displaced the issue of civil rights.

Ideological disputes among black leaders of the movement also led to its collapse. Major disputes arose among civil rights organizations such as the NAACP, SCLC, CORE, and SNCC with respect to tactics and objectives. Younger blacks, particularly those in SNCC, were dismayed by the slow pace of change and, as a result, favored more militant tactics. The emergence of the Black Power movement in 1966, led by young leaders such as Stokely Carmichael of SNCC, was a direct assault on the approach of King and other moderates.

Accomplishments   The Civil Rights movement forever altered the political landscape of the United States. Perhaps the greatest accomplishment of the movement can be seen in the thousands of African Americans who hold elective office. The number of black members of Congress was at a record high in the mid-1990's. African Americans have been elected to virtually every political office in all areas of the country. The Civil Rights movement also ended the humiliating practice of segregation and abolished the laws which attempted to create two classes of citizens. Finally, the Civil Rights movement created a sense of pride and self-esteem among those who participated in the movement.

Darryl Paulson

Core Resources

Good overviews of the Civil Rights movement include Fred Powledge's *Free at Last? The Civil Rights Movement and the People Who Made It* (Boston: Little, Brown, 1991) and Robert Weisbrot's *Freedom Bound: A History of America's Civil Rights Movement* (New York: Plume, 1991). An excellent source on the major barriers to black voting and the struggle to overturn those barriers is Steven Lawson's *Black Ballots: Voting Rights in the South, 1944-1969* (New York: Columbia University Press, 1976). On school desegregation, the best single source is Richard Kluger's *Simple Justice: The History of Brown v. Board of Education and Black America's Struggle for Equality* (New York: Alfred A. Knopf, 1976). The legislative battle over the Civil Rights Act of 1964 is splendidly told by Charles and Barbara Whalen's *The Longest Debate* (Washington, D.C.: Seven Locks Press, 1985). The major civil rights organizations are described in Clayborne Carson's *In Struggle: SNCC and the Black Awakening of the 1960's*

(Cambridge, Mass.: Harvard University Press, 1981) and Taylor Branch's *Parting the Waters: America in the King Years, 1954-63* (New York: Simon & Schuster, 1988).

See also: Affirmative action; Black Power movement; Busing and integration; Children in the Civil Rights movement; Civil Rights Act of 1964; Congress of Racial Equality; Freedom Riders; Jim Crow laws; Little Rock school desegregation; Montgomery bus boycott; National Association for the Advancement of Colored People; *Nixon v. Herndon*; *Plessy v. Ferguson*; Race riots of the twentieth century; Segregation: de facto and de jure; Southern Christian Leadership Conference; Student Nonviolent Coordinating Committee; Voting Rights Act of 1965.

Civil Rights Restoration Act

In 1987, Congress required recipients of federal financial assistance to uphold nondiscriminatory requirements of the 1964 and subsequent civil rights legislation in all respects, not merely in activity aided by federal funds.

Title VI of the Civil Rights Act of 1964 mandated that federal funds could not be used to support segregation or discrimination based on race, color, or national origin. The law did not affect a number of other civil rights problems, however. At Cornell University's School of Agriculture, for example, women could not gain admission unless their entrance exam scores were 30 percent to 40 percent higher than those of male applicants. Epileptics were often barred from employment, and persons in their fifties were often told that they were qualified for a job but too old. To rectify these problems, Congress extended the scope of unlawful discrimination in federally assisted schools in Title IX of the Education Amendments Act of 1972 to cover gender; the Rehabilitation Act of 1973 expanded the same coverage to the disabled; and the Age Discrimination Act of 1975 added age as a protected class.

Enforcement of the statute regarding education was initially assigned to the Office for Civil Rights (OCR) of the U.S. Department of Health, Education, and Welfare, which later became the U.S. Department of Education. OCR ruled that the statute outlawed not only discrimination in the particular program supported by federal funds but also discrimination in programs supported by nonfederal funds. All recipients of federal financial assistance were asked to sign an assurance of compliance with OCR as a condition of receiving a federal grant.

Grove City College   From 1974 to 1984, Grove City College in western Pennsylvania received $1.8 million in tuition grants and guaranteed student loans but refused to sign an assurance of compliance. The college argued that the funds were for students, not the college, but OCR insisted that the financial aid was administered as a part of the college's financial aid program and, therefore, the college must pledge as a whole not to discriminate on the basis of race, color, national origin, or gender. OCR instituted enforcement proceedings against Grove City College, and an administrative law judge ruled in 1978 that the college could no longer receive federal student loan moneys.

Grove City College and four students desiring financial aid then sued. In 1980, when the case was first tried, the federal district court ruled in favor of Grove City College on the grounds that no sex discrimination had actually occurred. On appeal, the court of appeals reversed the lower court's decision, and the matter was taken up by the Supreme Court of the United States, this time with Terrel H. Bell, head of the newly created federal Department of Education, as the defendant.

In *Grove City College v. Bell* (1984), Justice Byron R. White delivered the majority opinion of the Court, which held that OCR did not have sufficient congressional authority to withhold funds from Grove City College for failure to sign the assurance of compliance. Moreover, according to the Court, violations of Title VI could occur only in the specific program or activity supported directly with federal funds, a judgment that went beyond the question raised by the case. Justices William J. Brennan, Jr., and Thurgood Marshall dissented.

A New Bill   Shortly after the Supreme Court ruling, OCR dropped some seven hundred pending enforcement actions, resulting in an outcry from civil rights groups over the decision. Representative Augustus F. Hawkins authored the Civil Rights Restoration Act in the House, and Senator Edward "Ted" Kennedy sponsored the bill in the Senate. Their aim was to amend all the affected statutes—Title VI of the Civil Rights Act of 1964, Title IX of the Education Amendments Act of 1972, the Rehabilitation Act of 1973, and the Age Discrimination Act of 1975. According to the bill, any agency or private firm that wanted to receive federal financial assistance would have to comply with the nondiscrimination requirement as a whole, even if the aid went to only one subunit of that agency or firm.

Although Hawkins's version quickly passed in the House of Representatives, the measure was caught up in the politics of abortion, and the bill died in the Senate. Opponents advanced more than one thousand amendments over a period of four years, and representatives of the administration of President Ronald Reagan testified against passage of the law. A group known as the Moral Majority broadcast the fear that the bill would protect alcoholics, drug addicts, and homosexuals from discrimination, although there were no such provisions in the proposal.

More crucially, the Catholic Conference of Bishops, which was traditionally aligned with the Civil Rights movement, wanted two amendments to the bill. One proposed amendment, which was unsuccessful, would have exempted institutions affiliated with religious institutions from complying with the law if religious views would be compromised thereby. The other proposed amendment, which was opposed by the National Organization for Women, was an assurance that no federal funds would be spent on abortion. Congress delayed finding a compromise.

In 1987, leaving out references to abortion, Congress finally adopted the Civil Rights Restoration Act. By vetoing the measure, Reagan became the first president to veto a civil rights bill since Andrew Johnson. Supporters of the act sought to override the presidential veto. Opponents in the Senate tried to destroy the bill by various amendments in debate on the floor of the Senate on January 28, 1988. Senator John C. Danforth proposed an amendment that would disallow federal payments for abortion. This amendment passed. With the passage of the act by the Senate on March 22, 1988, Congress overrode Reagan's veto, and the law went into effect immediately.

Michael Haas

Core Resources

The law is explained and analyzed in Veronica M. Gillespie and Gregory L. McClinton's "The Civil Rights Restoration Act of 1987: A Defeat for Judicial Conservatism" in *National Black Law Journal* (12, Spring, 1990), Robert K. Robinson, Billie Morgan Allen, and Geralyn McClure Franklin's "The Civil Rights Restoration Act of 1987: Broadening the Scope of Civil Rights Legislation" in *Labor Law Journal* (40, January, 1989), and Robert Watson's "Effects of the Civil Rights Restoration Act of 1987 upon Private Organizations and Religious Institutions" in *Capital University Law Review* (18, Spring, 1989). Mark Willen's "Congress Overrides Reagan's Grove City Veto" in *Congressional Quarterly Weekly Review* (46, March 26, 1988) explains the parliamentary maneuvers required to get the law passed.

See also: Affirmative Action; Civil Rights Act of 1964; Civil Rights Act of 1991.

Civil War and African Americans

Both the North and the South relied upon African Americans to support the war effort. In the South, African American service raised doubts concerning the role of blacks in Southern society, especially when many Southerners recommended the use of slaves as soldiers. In the North, blacks pointed to their military service as proof that they deserved equal treatment under the law.

Members of the 4th U.S. Colored Troops at Fort Lincoln in 1865. *(Library of Congress)*

President Abraham Lincoln initially regarded the Civil War (1861-1865) as a means to preserve the Union, so he rejected calls for African American military service. He feared that black troops would alienate the border states and harden the Southern commitment to the war. However, the advancing Union armies were magnets for escaped slaves, and officers soon used African Americans as laborers. In 1862, some officers began recruiting former slaves as soldiers without government permission. In July, 1862, Congress authorized the president to use black troops, but it was not until the release of the Emancipation Proclamation in January, 1863, that Lincoln allowed for the enlistment of African American soldiers.

Military Service   Approximately 180,000 African Americans served in the Union army during the war, with an estimated 37,000 losing their lives in combat or to disease. Another 29,000 African Americans served as seamen, making up a quarter of the Union navy. Because of Northern discriminatory attitudes, black soldiers and sailors often performed manual labor, releasing white soldiers for combat duty. Given the opportunity, however, African Americans fought valiantly. Black Union soldiers met the enemy in 449 separate engagements. They faced great risks from Confederate soldiers who were outraged at the sight of an African American in uniform. At Fort Pillow, Tennessee, and Poison Spring, Arkansas, rebel troops murdered African Americans who were attempting to surrender. At war's end, sixteen soldiers and four seamen had been awarded the Congressional Medal of Honor. Many black soldiers remained in the military, serving in western units. Native Americans soon dubbed them "Buffalo soldiers" because their hair resembled that of the buffalo.

Although the navy was integrated, African Americans who enlisted in the army served in segregated units, often under white officers who had little respect for them. African Americans were not permitted to become officers until 1865, and only about one hundred of them obtained commissions. Because they were regarded as laborers, African Americans received less pay than white soldiers. They received ten dollars per month minus three dollars for clothing, while whites earned thirteen dollars a month plus a clothing allowance. This situation led to increasing resentment in the later years of the war as blacks saw more combat. When William Walker refused to report for duty until his pay was equal to that of white soldiers, he was court-martialed. Found guilty of mutiny, he was executed by a firing squad in March, 1864. Three months later, Congress approved the equalization of pay rates with retroactive pay through the beginning of 1864. Soldiers who could prove they were free as of April 19, 1861, were permitted retroactive pay for service in 1862 and 1863, which meant that many former slaves were not eligible for the back pay. Shrewd officers got around this unfair provision by having black soldiers swear that they did not owe anyone labor on that day, an oath that former slaves could honestly take.

In addition to military service, African Americans assisted the Union war effort by performing many other duties. Approximately 200,000 African Americans served as nurses, cooks, teamsters, or laborers. Slaves fleeing to the Union forces often provided valuable information regarding troop movement and terrain.

After the Union army abandoned its opposition to using black troops in combat, the 54th Massachusetts Colored Regiment became one of the most distinguished fighting units of the Civil War. *(Library of Congress)*

The Confederacy When war broke out in 1861, a small number of free African Americans in the South, motivated by a sense of regional loyalty, volunteered to enlist in the Confederate army. Some of these men served in military units during the war. Although they never saw combat, two Louisiana regiments of African Americans called the Native Guards drilled with the state militia. However, the notion of African Americans serving in the military contradicted the belief in white superiority, and the Confederate government officially prohibited African Americans from military service until March, 1865. At that time, desperation prompted the government to approve the enlistment of 300,000 slaves in the army. Because the war ended only a month later, very few African Americans actually served in the Confederate army.

Despite the ban on military service, African Americans played a crucial role in the Southern war effort. They provided support for the military, cooking food, working in field hospitals, and performing manual labor such as digging trenches and building roads. Because African Americans completed these essential tasks, white soldiers were not diverted from combat duty. The Confederate navy also made use of African Americans, usually as firemen, cooks, and laborers. Moses Dallas, an inland pilot, guided a Confederate force in a successful attack on a Union gunboat in 1864. Robert Smalls, a slave who worked on an armed ship, the *Planter*, brought his family on board and sailed the vessel out of port while the officers were ashore. Smalls surrendered the ship to the Union navy and became a hero for his efforts.

African Americans also worked in the industries that supplied the army. They worked alongside whites in the iron mines, composing approximately half the labor force at the Tredegar Iron Works in Richmond, Virginia, and an estimated 20 percent of the workers in the Confederate Ordnance Department were black. Perhaps the most important role that African Americans played during the war was on the home front. As whites left the farms and plantations to fight in battle, the Confederacy became dependent upon African Americans for the production of agricultural products.

Thomas Clarkin

Core Resources

Benjamin Quarles's *The Negro in the Civil War* (Boston: Little, Brown, 1953) provides an overview of African American experiences during the war. Noah Andre Trudeau's *Like Men of War: Black Troops in the Civil War, 1862-1865* (Boston: Little, Brown, 1998), examines African American actions in specific battles. James M. McPherson's *The Negro in the Civil War* (New York: Vintage Books, 1965) includes documents and statements from the Civil War era.

See also: Emancipation Proclamation; Military and racial/ethnic relations; Military desegregation.

Class theories of racial/ethnic relations

Class theories of racial and ethnic relations argue that prejudice and racism are inextricably linked with economic exploitation in a capitalist society.

Oliver C. Cox, an African American sociologist, described one of the earliest class-based theories of intergroup relations in *Caste, Class, and Race: A Study in Social Dynamics* (1948). Cox argued that African American workers in the United States were in the same position as exploited workers in any capitalist system. They were underpaid, abused, and exploited by employers who made huge profits. In Cox's view, exploitation of African Americans in the Old South had begun during slavery, but it persisted even after the death of slavery in 1865. Racial prejudice and discrimination were very advantageous in terms of money and wealth to the ruling white community. White workers, although they also received low wages, were not in the same position as African American workers because they had the advantage of being members of what they believed was the superior race. Cox's central point was that capitalist exploitation led to the subordination of Africans and that racism was used to justify the inferior status of black workers.

Exploitation as a Method of Control   Relations between whites and blacks have been based on a totally unequal exchange virtually from the time of the first contacts between Europeans and Africans. The nature of the relationship changed over time, from master and slave to capitalist and wage earner, but the motive remained the same, to make as much money as possible for the dominant white class. Economic exploitation, accomplished first through the use of force and enslavement, created a new underclass. As slaves, the Africans were controlled completely and for their entire lives by their masters. They were without power to control their own development, education, or working conditions. Those who exploited the Africans came to believe that only a backward and inferior people would allow themselves to become slaves, and they rationalized their acts by saying that the Africans were meant to become slaves. Although the slaves gained their freedom in the 1800's, the economic exploitation of African Americans did not end.

The earliest advocate of the class theory of race relations was W. E. B. Du Bois, the great African American educator, historian, and sociologist. Beginning with a series of essays published in 1903 as *The Souls of Black Folk*, Du Bois presented his view that economic exploitation was at the root of white American prejudice. According to Du Bois, whites had held on to their view of African inferiority for so long because they benefitted financially from it. White American workers and business executives prospered because blacks were forced into low-wage, low-prestige jobs. African Americans worked for less than half the wages of white workers because low-paying jobs were all that was available to them. Du Bois argued that the stability of the economic system was based on keeping African Americans badly paid, badly educated, and living in a state of almost constant fear through actual and threatened beatings and lynchings. The exploitative nature of American race relations was also shown by the many laws passed in states throughout the country, but especially in the South, that separated people by skin color in every area of life, from education to housing to employment opportunities.

Class and the Colonial Model of Race Relations   Advocates of the class model, such as sociologist Robert Blauner, distinguish between "external" and "internal" colonialism. As occupants of an internal colony, African Americans find themselves in the same position as people in a country subjected to a long period of imperial domination by an outside group (traditional, or external, colonialism). In both cases, the ruling class dominates, exploits, and degrades the people it has conquered economically, socially, and politically. It destroys the culture of its victims, leaving nothing except despair and degradation. All power transfers to a small economic elite of wealthy landowners and businesspeople from the dominant class. In the internal model, exploited people, excluded from full participation in the new economy, form a "colony" within the dominant society.

Members of the excluded population have little wealth, health, or happiness; however, their exclusion enables them to create a separate history and culture, sometimes based on memories of what it was like before "colonization." According to proponents of the colonial model of race relations, this culture of opposition, sometimes called the culture "behind the veil," was developed in slave quarters in the American South and still exists in American inner cities. Members of the oppressed class hate and despise the ruling class so much that they want to avoid contact with it at all costs.

The dominant and subordinate classes conflict with each other on many issues, not only economic questions such as wages and jobs. Generations of exploitation and second-class treatment create vastly differing views of everything from education to religion and crime control to politics. Conflicting worldviews are a basic characteristic of exploitative systems of racial and ethnic relations including colonialism. Capitalism divides society into social classes, and if that society is not homogeneous, it also divides the working class along racial and ethnic lines that prevent workers from seeing themselves as a unified class of exploited people. A working class divided by racial and ethnic hostilities cannot come together to push for economic justice for its members. In this way, the major beneficiary of a racially divided lower economic class is the dominant wealthy class. Marxist theories of race relations make exactly this point.

A newer Marxist perspective described in historian Eugene Genovese's *Roll, Jordan, Roll: The World the Slaves Made* (1974) incorporates earlier Marxist theories but adds another factor. Genovese notes that a racial consciousness

develops among the exploited class and enables it to challenge the supremacist views of the ruling class. This spirit of nationalism helps the underclass
develop a sense of purpose and dignity that enables the group to challenge
the economic and political power of the dominating elite.

Impact on Public Policy   Under the class theory of race relations,
exploitation can have two different results. Because conflict between the
oppressor and oppressed involves more than just economic issues, it can lead
to violence and revolution or to an extreme degree of separation between
the classes, a separation so great that one group can barely understand the
thinking, customs, and morality of the other. Anthropologist Oscar Lewis
found evidence of this separation among minority groups in the United
States in the 1960's. Lewis called the separate culture developed by the
underclass the "culture of poverty." Many minority groups had experienced
poverty and prejudice for so long that they had come to think differently
than the white majority about the meaning of their lives and their futures.
Work, love, survival, crime, happiness, and contentment meant different
things to the poor from what they meant to middle-class Americans. Lewis
argued that because of years of discrimination and abuse, African Americans,
Latinos, and Native Americans had become so different from whites that
only an act of violent revolt could restore them to lives of dignity and value.

Sociologist William J. Wilson shares some of the views held by advocates
of class theories of racial/ethnic relations, although he disagrees with the
more revolutionary implications of the "culture of poverty" concept. In *The
Declining Significance of Race* (1978) and several other works, Wilson argues
that something similar to a culture of poverty does exist. He also notes that
white workers and business leaders benefited economically from racial
exploitation, for a long time using U.S. inner cities as a source of cheap labor.
Problems began, however, when low-skilled jobs began to disappear from
urban communities in the 1960's and 1970's as corporations began to move
their manufacturing facilities to the suburbs where land was plentiful and
inexpensive or to Asia and Latin America where labor was cheaper. Unemployment increased because many of the poor had no way to get to jobs in
the suburbs. The loss of industry led to lower city tax bases and a subsequent
decline in the city's schools. Those African American families who had
become middle class, often through education, abandoned the old neighborhoods and headed for the suburbs. The most exploited class, the poorly
educated, underskilled, low-wage earning, sometimes welfarereceiving inner-city poor, were left behind. The culture of what Wilson termed the
"truly disadvantaged" stressed violence, escape, pessimism, and a lack of
value for life.

Wilson's solutions—to improve schools and encourage corporations to
return to inner cities—seemed rather meager, but they had a major impact
on social policies adopted in the 1980's and the 1990's. The concept of
"enterprise zones," aimed at encouraging businesses to relocate in inner

cities, and the campaign to improve the quality of education found in inner-city schools are both in line with Wilson's ideas. However, these reforms do not address the question of economic exploitation nor do they consider the problem of how racial prejudice has been used to justify economic inequality. Those problems, which theories of the class origins of racial and ethnic relations seek to address, remain unresolved.

Leslie V. Tischauser

Core Resources
    Robert Blauner's *Racial Oppression in America* (New York: Harper & Row, 1972) provides an overview and detailed analysis of the social class model. Oliver Cox's *Race Relations: Elements and Social Dynamics* (Detroit, Mich.: Wayne State University Press, 1976) presents the basics of class theories of racial/ethnic relations, as does Cox's older survey, *Caste, Class, and Race: A Study in Social Dynamics* (Garden City, N.Y.: Doubleday, 1948). William J. Wilson's views are found in *The Declining Significance of Race: Blacks and Changing American Institutions* (Chicago: University of Chicago Press, 1978). For an interesting critique of the view offered by Wilson, see sociologist Charles Vert Willie's *Oreo: On Race and Marginal Men and Women* (Wakefield, Mass.: Parameter Press, 1985).

    See also: Black flight; Internal colonialism; Wilson-Willie debate.

Clinton massacre

In 1875, widespread resentment of Congressional Reconstruction (the effort to rebuild and rehabilitate the South after the Civil War) mounted among whites in Mississippi. White Democrats began coordinating efforts to carry the fall statewide elections. The dominant issue for Democrats in the 1875 electoral campaign was the threat or fear of race war. Several race riots had already occurred throughout Mississippi during the summer. Democratic political solidarity was still in question, however, until the Clinton massacre of September 4. Clinton, a town in Hinds County, was the site of a political rally to which both Democratic and Republican speakers were invited. The rally was disrupted by gunfire, and both blacks and whites were killed and wounded. Confusion followed. News of the Clinton massacre, as it is now known, quickly spread throughout the state. Bands of armed whites converged on Clinton, and a reign of terror followed. Officials estimated that twenty to fifty blacks were killed by the angry white mobs. Many blacks fled to other towns, and some sought refuge in the woods. The Republican governor of Mississippi, unable to convince the president to send troops, watched helplessly as an undeclared race war waged throughout the state.

Freedmen were denied access to the polls or were forced to vote for Democratic candidates. The Clinton massacre had served as the spark that inspired white Mississippi "redeemers," as they were called, to do whatever necessary to take control away from the Republicans and force black submission.

Donald C. Simmons, Jr.

See also: Disfranchisement laws in Mississippi; Race riots of 1866; Race riots of 1943; Race riots of the twentieth century; Reconstruction.

Clinton's Initiative on Race

On June 14, 1997, President Bill Clinton unveiled the Initiative on Race in his "One America" speech, delivered at the University of California at San Diego's commencement ceremony. The Initiative on Race promoted a national dialogue on race relations in the United States. This dialogue was to take place largely through open meetings around the country and was designed to produce a plan to calm racial tensions and promote economic opportunities for all Americans.

By executive order, Clinton created an advisory board of seven persons representing diverse perspectives on the race issue: historian John Hope Franklin (chair); Linda Chavez-Thompson, executive vice president of the AFL-CIO; the Reverend Susan Johnson Cook; former New Jersey governor Thomas Kean; Los Angeles attorney Angela Oh; Robert Thomas, chief executive officer of Nissan, USA; and former Mississippi governor William Winter. The board was charged with promoting a constructive national dialogue to confront and work through concerns on race, increasing understanding of both the history and course of the country with respect to race relations, encouraging community leaders across the nation to develop initiatives to soothe racial tensions, and producing solutions to racial problems. The Department of Justice was to provide financial and administrative support, and the board was to disband on September 30, 1998, unless extended by presidential authorization.

In his speech, President Clinton called race relations the nation's "greatest challenge" and "greatest opportunity." He spoke of the United States' complicated history of race relations, which has been marked by both progress and division. The challenge, he said, was to "break down the barriers in our lives, our minds and our hearts." For this to happen, the country had to engage in "a candid conversation on the state of race relations today." Clinton promised to help lead the American people "in a great and unprecedented conversation about race." In addition to the dialogue on

race, Clinton's speech focused
on expanding opportunities to
all people—which included using affirmative action "in the
right way" and ensuring educational opportunities—and
demanding that each individual as well as the justice system
take responsibility for respecting the rights of all citizens
and enforcing each person's
civil rights. Clinton also called
on the advisory board to examine problem areas of "substantial impact," including
education, economic opportunity, housing, health care, and
administration of justice.

The Initiative on Race was
not meant to seek a quick or
easy fix. The multicultural democracy envisioned by Presi-

President Bill Clinton *(Library of Congress)*

dent Clinton would require commitments from government, businesses,
communities, and individuals. In his speech, Clinton suggested that the
ultimate solution must come from the human spirit.

Robert P. Watson and Claudia A. Pavone Watson

See also: Constitutional racism; Institutional racism; Racism: changing
nature of; Racism: history of the concept.

Colegrove v. Green

Three voters who resided in Illinois districts with much larger populations
than other congressional districts in the state filed an action to challenge the
unequal sizes of Illinois legislative districts. In Illinois and other states, state
legislatures had marked out legislative districts of unequal size or else had
failed to draw new district boundaries when population patterns changed.
One congressional district in Illinois, for example, contained 914,000 people
while another district contained only 112,000. The effect of such maldistribu-
tion was to dilute the voting strength of voters in larger districts and enhance
the power of voters in smaller districts. In Congress, two representatives
from districts containing fewer than 150,000 people could outvote a repre-

sentative from a district containing more than 900,000. Thus government was more responsive to and controlled by people from smaller districts rather than representative of the wishes of the majority of voters, whose votes would be diluted in larger districts. Rural interests in many states controlled political power and the development of public policy, despite the fact that a majority of citizens lived in urban and suburban areas.

In an opinion by Justice Felix Frankfurter, the Supreme Court on June 10, 1946, declined to decide whether unequal legislative districts violated the equal protection rights of voters in larger districts. On behalf of a five-member majority, Frankfurter declared that issues concerning legislative districting were "beyond [the] competence" of courts because such issues were "of a peculiarly political nature and therefore not meant for judicial determination." By labeling legislative districting a "political question" unsuited for judicial resolution, the majority of justices avoided any examination of questions about discrimination and voting rights that were raised by the existence of unequal districts.

Three dissenting justices, Hugo L. Black, William O. Douglas, and Frank Murphy, complained that the Court was improperly permitting state legislatures to violate the rights of voters in larger districts. One justice, Robert H. Jackson, did not take part in the case.

The Court's decision left districting temporarily in the hands of state legislatures. Justices Black and Douglas were still on the Court two decades later, however, when a new set of justices revisited the issue and decided that districts must be designed with comparable populations in order to avoid violating citizens' equal protection rights. In *Baker v. Carr* (1962), the Supreme Court decided that such legislative districting questions were not reserved for the legislative branch alone but could also be examined by the judiciary. In the subsequent cases of *Wesberry v. Sanders* (1964) and *Reynolds v. Sims*, the *Colegrove* precedent was completely eliminated when the Court mandated that federal and state legislative districts be of equivalent sizes.

Christopher E. Smith

See also: Redistricting; Representation: gerrymandering, malapportionment, and reapportionment; *Reynolds v. Sims.*

Coleman Report

The *Equality of Educational Opportunity* study, known as the Coleman Report, was released in 1966. This study, conducted by James S. Coleman, focused on the effect that school desegregation had on the academic attainment of black and white students. After controlling for students' family background characteristics, the report concluded that the strongest influence on the individual achievement of both black and white students was the educational proficiency of their peers. In upper grades, this influence was found to be two to three times greater for black students than for white students.

Increased diversity in the racial composition of schools was also found to have a positive effect on the achievement of African American students, decreasing the achievement gap between African American students and white students by nearly half, despite findings of lower self-esteem among African American students in racially diverse classrooms than among racially isolated African American students. For white students, increased racial diversity in the classroom, especially during the first three grades, was found to decrease their preference for white peers. Data provided by the Coleman Report were analyzed in 1967 by the U.S. Commission on Civil Rights and again in the 1969 McPartland study to provide a more comprehensive analysis of the effects of desegregation.

Terri L. Canaday

See also: Desegregation: public schools; Education and African Americans; Education and racial/ethnic relations; Integration.

Colfax massacre

The terrorist group known as the White League formed across Louisiana during the Reconstruction (1863-1877) to keep African Americans out of the political arena. The league's activities led to the Colfax massacre, the bloodiest single instance of racial violence in the Reconstruction period in all the United States. Disputes over the 1872 election results had produced dual governments at all levels of politics in Louisiana. Fearful that local Democrats would seize power, former slaves under the command of African American Civil War veterans and militia officers took over Colfax, the seat of Grant Parish, Louisiana.

On Easter Sunday, April 13, 1873, a series of brutal acts were carried out by the White League in Colfax, resulting in the deaths of more than sixty African Americans. After the African American men had laid down their weapons and surrendered, many were flogged, mutilated, and murdered, and African American women were also raped and murdered. A pile of more than twenty bodies was found half-buried in the woods. Monroe Lewis, an elderly black gentleman, was dragged from his bed, forced to say his prayers, and then shot. After being forced to cook food for a party of more than ninety white men, Charles Green was executed. Petitions to President Ulysses S. Grant requesting that justice be rendered were ignored.

Alvin K. Benson

See also: Charleston race riots; Reconstruction.

College admissions

In North America, a degree from a college or university has long been viewed as an important means of attaining a measure of financial and social success. For a combination of reasons, however, certain ethnic and racial groups matriculate at considerably lower rates than whites and Asian Americans. Certain minority groups are even more underrepresented among graduating students. This phenomenon is commonly viewed as one reason that certain minority groups experience higher levels of poverty and lower social standing.

In the 1960's and 1970's, many colleges and universities implemented affirmative action components in their admissions processes. Such programs frequently included provisions that allowed applicants from targeted minority groups to be admitted with lower test scores than those in nontargeted groups. Some programs set quotas for certain categories of students, essentially dividing the available slots into blocks defined by race, gender, or ethnicity. Such outright quota setting was ruled unconstitutional by the U.S. Supreme Court in its 1978 *Regents of the University of California v. Bakke* decision.

For the next two decades, race and ethnicity continued to influence college admissions decisions, albeit not as the sole criterion. The practice became increasingly controversial, however. Many whites, like Allan Bakke, believed that affirmative action discriminated against them. Affirmative action was attacked on other grounds as well. Some minority students resented the fact that, irrespective of their actual abilities, it was assumed that they were accepted to college under a lower standard. Other minority leaders chafed

The phasing out of affirmative action in several major universities' admission policies during the mid-1990's appeared to threaten a return to the racially imbalanced student bodies of earlier eras. *(National Archives)*

at the very notion that certain groups of people, by simple virtue of their skin color, required special accommodations to enter college. Also some qualified nontargeted minority applicants, such as some Asian Americans, were denied admission to make way for targeted minority applicants.

Another controversial effect of affirmative action in college admissions was the presence of large numbers of minority students who, being admitted under lower standards, were underprepared for the rigors of college. As a result, many minority groups have experienced disproportionately high failure and dropout rates. Some see such failures as evidence of curricula and standards biased against minorities. Others have charged that under-prepared students do not belong in college and that efforts to retain these at-risk students have essentially lowered standards in curricula and graduation requirements.

As the academic and social consequences of affirmative action in college admissions became more openly debated in the 1990's, efforts to end the practice became more vigorous. Affirmative action suffered a number of blows in the late 1990's, including a 1995 decision by the Regents of the University of California to end affirmative action in admissions and hiring. The following year, the state's voters passed Proposition 209, the California Civil Rights Initiative, which placed the Regents' ban on affirmative action in state law and extended it to all public hiring and admissions. Similar actions were taken in other states, notably Texas. The immediate effects were mixed, with some of the more prestigious universities experiencing sharp drops in minority admissions. Conservatives have viewed these results as proof that racial preferences had been allowing unqualified applicants to be admitted simply on the basis of skin color or ethnicity. Liberals decry the resultant lack of racial and ethnic diversity on some campuses. By the end of the 1990's, efforts were under way at some campuses to reintroduce diversity by using a different criterion, such as socioeconomic status, in processing admissions.

Steve D. Boilard

See also: Affirmative action; *Bakke* case; College entrance examinations; Intelligence and race.

College entrance examinations

College entrance examinations are one of several measures used by U.S. colleges and universities to select candidates for admission. Criticism of these tests revolves around possible bias in the tests and how they are used.

American colleges and universities consider a variety of factors when selecting students for admission. These factors may include, but are not necessarily limited to, high school grades, class rank, difficulty of courses taken, personal interviews, letters of reference, and samples of students' written works. In addition, most colleges and universities require students to submit test scores from one or more of several nationally administered standardized tests. Known collectively as college entrance examinations, the most commonly used tests in the United States are the American College Test (ACT) and the Scholastic Aptitude Test (SAT). Some students also may take Achievement Tests (ATs) and the Preliminary Scholastic Aptitude Test/National Merit Scholarship Qualifying Test (PSAT/NMSQT).

The Tests According to the American College Testing Assessment Program (ACTAP), which created and administers the ACT, the test does not ask students to recall specific information learned in high school but rather asks students to demonstrate their reasoning ability in four fields: English, mathematics, reading, and scientific reasoning. Students receive scores on a scale of 1 (low) to 36 (high) for each of the four skill areas, and a composite score. In addition, students receive scores on a scale of 1 (low) to 18 (high) for each of the seven subsections of the test. Student scores are also presented as percentiles.

The SAT, created and developed by Educational Testing Service (ETS), is administered in cooperation with the College Entrance Examination Board. Like the ACT, the SAT is designed to measure skills necessary for college-level work. The SAT tests two basic skill areas, verbal ability and mathematical reasoning, using a multiple-choice format.

The version of the SAT in use until the mid-1990's had two verbal sections containing questions involving antonyms, analogies, sentence completion, and reading comprehension. It also had two mathematical reasoning sections containing questions involving problem solving and quantitative comparisons. Each of these skill areas (verbal ability and mathematical reasoning) was scored on a scale of 200 (low) to 800 (high). Composite and percentile scores were provided. This version of the SAT also contained a fifty-question test of standard written English and a series of experimental questions. The experimental questions are not included in the student's score but are used in the development of future test questions.

ATs, administered by the College Board, were examinations based on specific knowledge of subjects including American history, European history, French, German, Hebrew, Latin, Spanish, mathematics, biology, chemistry, physics, English composition, and English literature. Some colleges required students to take these tests in addition to the SAT.

In the 1990's, Educational Testing Service developed new tests, the SAT I and SAT II, to replace the SAT. Like the SAT, the SAT I tests two basic skill areas: verbal and mathematical reasoning and is scored similarly. The SAT I verbal reasoning section focuses on analogies, sentence completion, and critical reasoning and contains a new critical reading section that tests vocabulary in context, analysis and synthesis, interpretation, and evaluation.

The mathematical reasoning section allows the use of calculators, and a proportion of examination questions require students to enter the answer they calculate.

The SAT II was designed to replace the ATs and the test of standard written English. Content areas are expanded, and the test of standard written English is combined with the English composition test (an AT). The new writing test of the SAT II contains a series of multiple-choice questions testing grammar and usage and an essay section.

The Preliminary Scholastic Aptitude Test/National Merit Scholarship Qualifying Test, administered primarily during the junior year in high school, contains two sections testing verbal skills and mathematical reasoning in a multiple-choice format. Test scores are used to award National Merit Scholarships, National Achievement Scholarships, and Achievement Scholarships.

Criticisms of the Tests   Despite their importance and wide use, college entrance examinations are not without their flaws or their critics. The two main organizations that create college entrance examinations, Educational Testing Service and the American College Testing Assessment Program, work to maintain and improve the validity and reliability of the tests and to avoid bias. Nevertheless, the tests have been subjected to some serious criticisms, and it is because of the tests' importance that such criticism must be considered. Criticisms focus on the existence of bias and flawed questions, testing procedures, and accusations of lack of due process, violation of privacy, and misuse of test results. Critics have argued that standardized college entrance examinations are biased against women, the poor, minorities, students from rural areas, and students whose first or primary language is not English.

Other things being equal, high test scorers should perform better in college than low test scorers. National SAT test score averages have consistently showed that men perform better on the test than women. The gender gap in test scores varies by year but is generally 50 to 60 points. Gender differences on the SAT are greater on the mathematical reasoning section than on the verbal ability section. A similar pattern exists regarding PSAT/NMSQT scores. Men also score higher on the mathematics, reading, and scientific reasoning sections of the ACT. If standardized college entrance examinations accurately predict future academic success, men should have higher average grades in college than women. Yet, at least during the first year of college, women have higher average grades than men.

Educational Testing Service states that women's scores are lower because greater numbers of women have been taking the test since 1970 than took it in previous decades. Consequently, the test pool for women is increasingly less selective and includes a greater number of low scorers, reducing the overall average. Ruth Ekstrom, Marilane Lockheed, and Thomas Donlon, however, have found that the structure of test questions influences gender performance. Women are less likely to answer a test item correctly if the question contains only, or refers primarily to, male characters. A survey of the reading comprehension passages contained in SAT examinations showed that 93 percent of the characters to which the passages refer are male. In addition, evidence indicates that college entrance examinations place more emphasis on subject areas such as science and mathematics in which men have traditionally outperformed women. Accordingly, test content selection may account for some of the gender differences in test scores.

Students from wealthier families score higher on college entrance examinations. In the case of the SAT, students whose family income is more than $70,000 a year have test-score averages of 996. Students whose family income is under $10,000 a year have test-score averages of 780. ACT test scores and family income show a similar correlation. These patterns may stem from differences in educational opportunities rather than differences in aptitude. Additionally, less affluent students may be unable to afford test preparation courses.

Minority students score lower on college entrance examinations than whites. Differences vary by group and over time. For example, 1989 SAT scores show that average combined test scores for African Americans were 200 points lower than those of whites. Of all minority groups, Asian Americans performed the best. The 1989 SAT average combined score for Asian Americans was 934, compared to 937 for whites. ACT average composite scores follow similar patterns.

There is also evidence that college entrance examinations may contain bias against students from rural areas and students whose first or primary language is not English. James Loewen found that incoming University of Vermont students from rural areas have SAT scores that average 100 points lower than those of students from urban areas; however, the actual academic performance of the two groups is similar. Alicia Schmitt found that Hispanic students who take the SAT are much more likely to answer incorrectly questions that contain cognates and/or homographs. Consequently, differences in test scores between Latinos and whites may be partially the result of language differences, not differences in aptitude for college work.

In addition to bias, critics have charged that college entrance examinations contain flawed questions (questions that have more than one meaning or more than one answer), which may unfairly penalize test takers. Critics have also charged ETS with using unethical testing procedures, lack of due process protection, and invasion of privacy. John Weiss, Barbara Beckwith, and Bob Schaeffer claim the experimental questions on the SAT are fundamentally unfair because they violate the principle of informed consent and are flawed. In addition, no due process protection exists for students who are accused of cheating on the examination. Students may appeal to ETS, but ETS has sole discretion in determining guilt or innocence in cases of suspected cheating.

Finally, college entrance examinations have been criticized for being misused by scholarship agencies and colleges and universities. Many scholarships are awarded primarily on the basis of PSAT/NMSQT, SAT, or ACT scores, though college entrance examinations are not specifically designed for this purpose. The National Merit Scholarships, awarded by the National Merit Scholarship Corporation, are given on the basis of PSAT/NMSQT scores. Roughly 62 percent of National Merit Scholarship are awarded to men. Critics claim that gender, economic, racial, geographic, and language biases in the PSAT/NMSQT place women, the poor, minorities, rural Americans, and individuals whose first or primary language is not English at a competitive disadvantage for these awards.

Standardized testing has become an established feature of American life. More than 100 million standardized tests are administered each year. Despite their flaws, college entrance examinations provide a systematic and relatively objective means to select candidates for admission. For schools that receive large numbers of applications for admission each year, test scores provide a relatively inexpensive and time-effective way to screen candidates. Realizing the flaws in standardized testing and the danger of overreliance on test scores, some institutions have developed alternatives to the traditional selection process.

Charles V. Smedley

Core Resources

The Uses and Misuses of Tests (San Francisco: Jossey-Bass, 1984), edited by Charles W. Daves, provides a good discussion of critical issues regarding the use of standardized tests. Books that criticize standardized tests include James Crouse and Dale Trusheim's *The Case Against the SAT* (Chicago: University of Chicago Press, 1988), Banesh Hoffmann's *The Tyranny of Testing* (New York: Crowell-Collier, 1962), John G. Weiss, Barbara Beckwith, and Bob Schaeffer's *Standing Up to the SAT* (New York: Arco, 1989), and Phyllis Rosser's *Sex Bias in College Admissions Tests: Why Women Lose Out* (3d ed., Cambridge, Mass.: The Center, 1989).

See also: College admissions; Education and African Americans; Intelligence and race.

Color coding

Color coding is social stratification based on skin color. Under this system, skin color and other physical characteristics as well as behaviors associated with particular racial groups are used to place people in specific social classes.

Most color coding is based on stereotypes of racial phenotypes. As Michael Omi and Howard Winant suggest in *Racial Formation in the United States* (1986), the concept of "race" in contemporary American life—whether a person is black, white, or Asian—is based largely on phenotypical, and therefore readily observable, characteristics such as skin color, hair color and texture, and body shape and size. Secondarily, color coding draws on stereotypical behaviors and characteristics associated with a particular race.

In the United States, color coding involves using a set of physical and social attributes associated with "whiteness" and white people to which all other nonwhite groups are compared. Light-skinned people are generally given higher social status, largely because of the privileges attendant on Caucasian heritage—to being and to appearing white. Both literary and social science sources indicate that social and economic access and mobility are strongly influenced by whether or not a nonwhite person is able to "pass" for white. The ease with which a person passes for white depends not only on the individual's physical appearance—the lightness of the skin—but also on whether that person possesses certain mannerisms and character traits associated with being white. These include the person's manner of speech, circle of friends and associates, educational status, occupation, and culture. Social status and privilege are accorded to those who are able to "pass" for white or to associate themselves with whiteness through social networks, occupations, or educational achievements that are typical of white people.

Valli Kanuha

See also: Discrimination: racial and ethnic; Passing; Race as a concept; Racial formation theory.

Color of law

An action performed under color of law has the appearance of authority and legality but is actually unauthorized and illegal. The color of law provision in the U.S. Code has been important in civil rights cases, particularly in enforcement of the rights guaranteed by the Fourteenth Amendment.

"Color," in the phrase "color of law," means having the appearance but not the reality; it means pretense, semblance, or disguise. Acting under color of law therefore means maintaining a position of legal authority when in fact a person, usually a government official, does not have that authority (for example, performing an illegal act as though it were legal). Acting under color of law is an abuse of power.

Color of law is a powerful civil rights provision in the U.S. Code. Section 1983, Title 42, grants a cause of action to every person who, "under color of any statute," is deprived of any rights, privileges, or immunities guaranteed by the Constitution or by law. Section 1983 has been called the Fourteenth Amendment's legislative "sword": It provides that state law cannot be enforced to work against the privileges and immunities provided by the Fourteenth Amendment.

Two notable civil rights cases that involved the color of law provision were *Monroe v. Pape* (1961) and *United States v. Price* (1966). In *Monroe*, thirteen police officers were accused of misusing their authority by entering a home without warning, ransacking it, and using their authority in a manner inconsistent with state law. Justice William O. Douglas held that the alleged action occurred under color of law and that the victim had recourse to the courts. Color of law was held to apply to all rights guaranteed by the Fourteenth Amendment. In *Price*, eighteen people were implicated in the Mississippi murder of three civil rights workers. Justice Abe Fortas's opinion stated that even private citizens (as opposed to state officials) can be said to be acting under color of law when they are working in concert with state officials.

Glenn Canyon

See also: Civil rights; Fourteenth Amendment.

Colored Women's League

The Colored Women's League (CWL), also known as National League of Colored Women and Washington Colored Woman's League, emerged in Washington, D.C., when black women active in education, benevolent, and literary societies joined together in June, 1892, in an effort to improve conditions for African Americans. Helen A. Cook, wife of the Honorable John T. Cook, served as president, and the recording secretary was Charlotte Forten Grimké, a teacher from Port Royal, South Carolina. Other founders included Coralie Franklin Cook, wife of a Howard University administrator; teachers Anna J. Cooper, Mary Jane Patterson, Mary Church Terrell, and Anna E. Murray from M Street School; and Josephine B. Bruce, the first black teacher in the Cleveland schools, who later married Senator Blanche K. Bruce.

As Chicago prepared to host the World Columbian Exposition of 1893, the Board of Lady Managers rejected the petitions of these Washington women to participate in the planning process because they did not represent a national organization. In response, the Washington Colored Woman's League issued an invitation to black women throughout the country to affiliate as a national league. Women's clubs responded from the state of South Carolina and from the cities of Philadelphia, Kansas City, Denver, and Norfolk, Virginia. In January, 1894, they incorporated, becoming the Colored Women's League. In October, the CWL received an invitation for membership in the National Council of Women (NCW). Its members accepted and sought to expand representation for the NCW convention in the spring of 1895. Instead, the competition between women's clubs in New York and in Boston resulted in the creation of a second national organization, the

National Federation of Afro-American Women. The two national organizations merged in July, 1896, to form the National Association of Colored Women (NACW) to promote for self-protection, self-advancement, and social interaction. In 1896, Terrell became the first president of the NACW.

Dorothy C. Salem

See also: African American women; National Association of Colored Women; National Black Women's Political Leadership Caucus; National Council of Negro Women.

Commission on Civil Rights, U.S.

The reports and studies of the Commission on Civil Rights have been an important factor in the passage of major civil rights legislation.

The U.S. Commission on Civil Rights was created in 1957 by Congress as part of the Civil Rights Act of 1957. It consisted of six members, appointed by the president and approved by Congress. The original purpose of the agency was to monitor civil rights (particularly violations of voting rights in the South), issue reports, and then disband, but Congress has continuously renewed its mandate. The Commission on Civil Rights (abbreviated as CRC, for Civil Rights Commission) was created in the wake of the 1954 Supreme Court decision in *Brown v. Board of Education*. In this case, the Court decided that separate facilities for black and white students in public education were unconstitutional. A year later, in *Brown II*, the Court ruled that schools must integrate with "all deliberate speed." No specific timetable was given, however, for fear of further alienating southern whites.

The CRC helped lay the foundation for the civil rights legislation of the 1960's. The commission's mandate involved investigating voting rights violations, collecting and studying voting data related to denials of equal protection under the law, and appraising federal laws and policies as they related to equal protection. In addition to creating the CRC, the 1957 Civil Rights Act made the civil rights component in the Justice Department a division, and empowered the U.S. attorney general to initiate civil court proceedings to enforce voting rights. The 1957 statute gave the attorney general the power to intervene only on a case-by-case basis, which was tedious, as there were thousands of cases of voting rights violations.

Civil Rights Legislation During Dwight D. Eisenhower's administration, the Commission on Civil Rights investigated voting rights violations in eight southern states and found no fewer than a hundred counties using discriminatory measures against African Americans. The Civil Rights Act of 1960 was passed as a result of the CRC's 1959 report. Although the CRC had recommended that Congress pass legislation authorizing federal registrars in obstructionist districts, the act only provided court-appointed referees to oversee and resolve alleged voting rights abuses. Continuing studies by the CRC would assist in more powerful legislation in 1964 and 1965.

The 1964 Civil Rights Act was instrumental in the desegregation of public facilities in a still-segregated South. Based on ongoing concerns and studies by the CRC in education, voting, and employment, and influenced by the intensifying Civil Rights movement and the March on Washington in 1963, the 1964 act forbade racial discrimination in public facilities, voting registration procedures, and employment. The act empowered the attorney general to intervene and take civil action in cases of racial discrimination in public accommodations. It also cut federal funds to school districts that discriminated and created the Equal Employment Opportunity Commission to oversee discrimination complaints in the workplace.

The 1965 Voting Rights Act is the most powerful legislation in the area of suffrage, and it eliminated virtually all remaining loopholes. The act effectively took the process of voter registration out of the hands of states and localities, providing federal machinery for this process. The legislation also forbade literacy tests in most instances. In addition, a preclearance mechanism (often called Section 5) was put in place that required political districts to submit proposed changes in elections or districts to the federal government for approval. A "clean record" provision was instituted, allowing political districts to be removed from coverage of the preclearance provision if no discrimination or voting irregularities have been found for the previous ten years.

The CRC has played a vital role in the extension of the 1965 Voting Rights Act and thus in continued suffrage among African Americans in the Deep South. One of the most controversial areas of the act, the preclearance provision, was challenged by southerners. Testimony by the CRC revealed that southern states, and particularly Mississippi, were seeking to subvert the intent of the act and dilute the black vote and black political victories. Legislatures did this by racial gerrymandering of political districts, going to at-large systems of municipal elections, developing multimember districts, and consolidating black and white counties. The CRC was instrumental in the extension of Section 5 and the drafting of other provisions of the 1970 Voting Rights Act. Reports by the commission would play an important role in the 1975 and 1982 extensions of the act as well.

Challenges and Impact   A major challenge to the commission came in the early 1980's, after it issued a 1981 statement entitled *Affirmative Action in the 1980's*, which advocated quotas to ensure the hiring of minorities. President Ronald Reagan strongly opposed the recommendations and re-

162 Compromise of 1850

moved three of the CRC's commissioners, appointing more conservative commissioners. A lawsuit ensued, and in 1983 **Reagan** was ordered by the courts to reinstate the commissioners he had fired. Also in 1983, the commission was reorganized by a compromise congressional act (Reagan had vowed to veto an act routinely renewing the commission) to consist of eight members chosen by the president and Congress. The commission was criticized from many quarters in the 1980's, partly for appearing to succumb to various political pressures, and many of its leaders, including Clarence Pendleton, were controversial. In the early 1990's, it began to resume the more active role it had played in the past.

Originally intended as a watchdog agency, the Commission on Civil Rights has been essential as a bipartisan fact-finding body and a resource for both Congress and the president in developing legislation. While its early charge was in the area of voting rights, it has conducted numerous studies and provided congressional testimony in education, housing, racial segregation, employment discrimination, and denial of civil rights on the basis of race, creed, color, religion, national origin, sex, age, or disability.

Mfanya D. Tryman

Core Resources

Among the best sources for information on the CRC are Gerald David Jaynes and Robin M. Williams, Jr., eds., *A Common Destiny: Blacks and American Society* (Washington, D.C.: National Academy Press, 1989); Theodore Eisenberg's article "Civil Rights Commission," in *Civil Rights and Equality: Selections from the Encyclopedia of the American Constitution* (New York: Macmillan, 1989); Frank R. Parker, *Black Votes Count* (Chapel Hill: University of North Carolina Press, 1990); Steven F. Lawson, *Running for Freedom* (New York: McGraw-Hill, 1991); Hugh Davis Graham, *Civil Rights and the Presidency* (New York: Oxford University Press, 1992); Charles S. Bullock III and Charles M. Lamb, *Implementation of Civil Rights Policy* (Monterey, Calif.: Brooks/Cole, 1984); and Gertrude Ezorsky, *Racism and Justice* (Ithaca, N.Y.: Cornell University Press, 1991).

See also: *Brown v. Board of Education*; Civil Rights Act of 1957; Civil Rights Act of 1960; Civil Rights Act of 1964; Civil Rights Act of 1968; Civil Rights Act of 1991; Civil Rights Acts of 1866-1875; Civil Rights movement; Voting Rights Act of 1965.

Compromise of 1850

A last national attempt to resolve the question of slavery in the territories brought the nation closer to civil war.

The U.S. Constitution, while creating a mechanism for the addition of states and acknowledging the right of each state to permit and even encourage slavery within its boundaries, made no mention of slavery's status in future states. Congress, when it admitted a state, could impose any condition it wished. The national government had first addressed the issue of slavery in territories and new states when the Confederation Congress passed the Northwest Ordinance of 1787. This ordinance excluded slavery from the unsettled area north of the Ohio River to the Mississippi River's eastern bank, the edge of the United States' holdings.

The Missouri Question   The issue reemerged in 1817, when Missouri, where between two thousand and three thousand slaves lived, applied to join the United States as a slave state. The question came before the Congress in 1819, and sectional tensions erupted. The U.S. Senate had eleven states each from the free North and the slave-owning South, but the North's growing population gave it a decisive advantage in the House of Representatives, so proslave forces committed themselves, at the minimum, to maintaining a balance between the regions in the Senate.

A temporary solution emerged in 1820, when Senator Henry Clay of Kentucky brokered a solution to the crisis. The Missouri Compromise stipulated that Missouri would be admitted to the Union as a slave state, while Maine, which had petitioned for statehood in late 1819, was admitted as a free state. The compromise also prohibited slavery from the remainder of the Louisiana Purchase in the area north of 36°30′ north latitude, while permitting it south of that line. Between 1820 and 1848, this solution maintained national peace, and the Senate remained balanced.

The Southwest and California   The Mexican-American War disrupted the relative peace. The United States received millions of acres of land spanning the area from the Continental Divide west to the Pacific Ocean and south from the forty-ninth parallel to Mexico. Before the war ended, David Wilmot, a member of the House of Representatives from Pennsylvania, attached an amendment to an appropriations bill stipulating that any territory acquired from Mexico must exclude slavery in perpetuity. Although the bill failed to win passage, the Wilmot Proviso fueled the smoldering fires of sectionalism, as many assumed that any additional western lands would be governed by the Missouri Compromise.

In 1849, just a year after the discovery of gold in California, the young California Republic petitioned the Senate for admission to the Union. Besides disrupting the balance between slave and free states, California straddled the 1820 compromise's line and threw the prior agreements into chaos. In both houses of Congress, the question of slavery became paramount: Southerners rejected any attempt to exclude the practice from the West by nearly unanimous margins, while Free-Soilers from the North rejected the possibility of losing equal economic competition by similar percentages. Left in the middle were some elements of the national Whig Party, which struggled to preserve the Union while remaining a national party. The idea of disunion grew. Senator John C. Calhoun of South Carolina, long a firebrand for states' rights, proposed the formation of a sectional party to guarantee the practice of slavery. William Seward, an abolitionist representative from New York, also rejected the possibility of a compromise, citing the immorality of slavery. President Zachary Taylor, a hero of the Mexican-American War and a southerner, supported California's admission as a free state while rejecting the extreme position of persons such as Calhoun.

Five Resolutions   The first concrete proposal for compromise came from Senator Clay on January 29, 1850. Clay proposed a series of five resolutions: that the California Republic join the United States as a free state; that the rest of the territory acquired in the Mexican Cession be organized without any decision on slavery; that Texas receive monetary compensation in exchange for giving up its claims to parts of contemporary New Mexico; that the slave trade within the District of Columbia be abolished (although the actual practice of slavery would not be affected); and that a more rigorous fugitive slave law be enacted.

On February 5 and 6, Clay presented his resolutions and spoke for the Union's preservation. One week later, Mississippi senator Jefferson Davis rejected Clay's proposals, using bitter language that also attacked northern intentions. On March 4, the ailing Calhoun, in a speech delivered by Virginia's James Mason, rejected compromise on the principle of slavery in the territories. On March 7, Daniel Webster acknowledged that both sides had just grievances and urged support for Clay's whole plan, calming some tensions with his eloquent plea that the Union be preserved. On March 11, Seward stated the abolitionist's opposition to the compromise because of the immorality of slavery.

In April, the Senate referred Clay's resolutions to a select committee. The committee reported back to the full Senate an omnibus bill that contained the substance of the five original resolutions and sparked another four months of debate. Two major stumbling blocks to the compromise disappeared in July, when President Taylor and Calhoun both died. Millard Fillmore, who supported the compromise's ideas, replaced Taylor, who had bitterly opposed the omnibus bill. While Clay was vacationing, Stephen A. Douglas broke the omnibus bill into five parts and steered them through the Senate, and the House of Representatives followed suit. By September 20, Congress had adopted the five bills that made up the Compromise of 1850.

In 1854, the attempts at balancing the competing interests of the Free-Soil North with the proslave South ended when Senator Douglas proposed that the Kansas and Nebraska areas be organized using the concept of popular sovereignty. Congress adopted the Kansas-Nebraska Act that year, triggering the formation of a national political party dedicated to the idea of an exclusively free-soil policy in the West. The new Republican Party immediately became a force on the national political landscape, and its candidate, John C. Frémont, came within four states of being elected president in 1856. Ultimately, the election of Abraham Lincoln in 1860, a man committed to both the preservation of the Union and the free-soil doctrine, drove the South to secession.

John G. Clark, updated by E. A. Reed

Core Resources

Works that examine the forces and events preceding the Civil War include Bruce Collins's *The Origins of America's Civil War* (New York: Holmes & Meier, 1981), editor Eric Foner's *Politics and Ideology in the Age of the Civil War* (New York: Oxford University Press, 1980), Hamilton Holman's *Prologue to Conflict: The Crisis and Compromise of 1850* (New York: W. W. Norton, 1966), David Potter's *The Impending Crisis, 1848-1861* (New York: Harper & Row, 1976), and editor Kenneth Stampp's *The Causes of the Civil War* (rev. ed., Englewood Cliffs, N.J.: Prentice-Hall, 1974).

See also: Bleeding Kansas; Fugitive slave laws; Kansas-Nebraska Act; Missouri Compromise; Proslavery argument.

Compromise of 1877

The Compromise of 1877 represents the attempt toward equality that failed during Reconstruction (1863-1877) when newly elected President Rutherford B. Hayes ended efforts to establish a biracial democracy in the South. During his presidential campaign, Hayes favored "home rule" for the South as he campaigned against New York governor Samuel J. Tilden, a Democratic reformer. Although Tilden won the popular vote, Hayes claimed victory in South Carolina, Florida, and Louisiana. Republican Reconstruction governments still con-

After ending Reconstruction in the southern states, newly elected president Rutherford B. Hayes forgot his pledge to protect the rights of former slaves. *(Library of Congress)*

trolled these states, and it was doubtful that a former Union general could carry them by any other means than fraud.

Many southern Democrats, particularly scalawags, accepted Hayes's election, particularly if he would leave the South alone after taking office. Ohio Republicans and southern Democrats met in a Washington, D.C., hotel and reached an agreement that if Hayes could assume the presidency, he would remove federal troops from South Carolina and Louisiana so that Democrats could regain control. Hayes consented after being sworn in. Race relations worsened because the Democrats ignored their promises to treat southern blacks fairly and Hayes forgot his pledge to ensure the rights of freedmen. Reconstruction had allowed African Americans to reconstitute their families, participate in government, and enjoy equality in dealing with whites, but the 1877 Compromise engendered a hatred of reform throughout the South for nearly one hundred years. African Americans would suffer social restrictions until the 1960's.

Douglas W. Richmond

See also: Freedmen's Bureau; Reconstruction.

Confiscation Acts of 1861 and 1862

In August, 1861, the United States Congress passed a law confiscating all property, including slaves, used in the Confederate war effort. The law required judicial proceedings before any property could be appropriated, and it left unclear whether any confiscated slaves would be freed. The following July, Congress passed the Second Confiscation Act. The 1862 law, which also required a judicial hearing, declared that rebels were traitors whose property could be seized for the lifetime of the owner. The only property that would not be returned to the rebels' heirs was slaves, who were regarded as captives of war and set free after a period of sixty days. President Abraham Lincoln doubted that Congress possessed the constitutional authority to free slaves in the states. When he signed the bill into law, he included a statement of objections to its provisions. Although the power to confiscate rebel property was rarely used during or after the war, the difference between the first and second acts revealed the growing determination in the Union to end slavery and set the stage for the Emancipation Proclamation, which Lincoln issued in January, 1863.

Thomas Clarkin

See also: Emancipation Proclamation; Slavery: history.

Congress of Racial Equality

The Congress of Racial Equality (CORE) helped to eliminate discrimination in interstate travel on buses and trains and to end discrimination in both the public and private sectors of society, especially in housing and employment. CORE was founded in Chicago in the spring of 1942 by fifty young people who were committed to nonviolent direct action in their opposition to segregation and racial discrimination. Although James Farmer, the first national director of CORE, is often given credit for the founding of CORE, George Houser, Bernice Fisher, Homer Jack, Joe Guinn, and James Robinson also played substantial roles.

Initially, CORE was a volunteer organization. Along with the Fellowship of Reconciliation, CORE began the Freedom Rides in 1947. These early rides were called "journeys of reconciliation." They consisted of integrated teams of young adults traveling throughout the upper South on interstate buses testing the 1946 Supreme Court ruling that outlawed segregation in interstate travel.

CORE gained much of its reputation for its participation in the student sit-ins and the Freedom Rides of the early 1960's. The Freedom Rides were a response to the 1960 Supreme Court ruling expanding its 1946 decision. The Court decreed that train and bus terminals used by passengers engaged in interstate travel must also be desegregated. Arrests and violence followed the two integrated CORE teams in 1960 as they sought to force the hand of the federal government. With the assistance of the Student Nonviolent Coordinating Committee (SNCC) and the Southern Christian Leadership Conference (SCLC), they were successful in forcing the Interstate Commerce Commission to institute new penalties for noncompliance with the decreed desegregation.

During the first half of the 1960's, CORE carried on a number of concurrent campaigns around the country. While the national office focused on voter registration, local CORE chapters concentrated on desegregating lunch counters and roadside restaurants and fighting for fair housing practices, equal employment opportunities, and school integration. CORE participated in demonstrations, boycotts, and marches with the SCLC, SNCC, and the National Association for the Advancement of Colored People (NAACP). CORE took a leadership role in the 1963 March on Washington and was one of the ten civil rights organizations that met with President John F. Kennedy before the march.

In 1964, CORE began to move away from nonviolent direct action and political neutrality, and by 1966, it had developed a political action program and was active in community organizing. CORE eventually broke with the nonviolent integrationist philosophy and joined the ranks of the more radical activist groups. CORE embraced "black power" and replaced James Farmer with Floyd B. McKissick as its national director.

Elected national director of CORE in 1968, Royal Innis served until 1970, by which time the organization's effectiveness was essentially over. *(Library of Congress)*

The anti-integration posture assumed by CORE tended to push it more and more to the fringe of the Civil Rights movement. Membership in CORE dwindled during the 1970's and 1980's, and by the 1990's, it had experienced such a drop in membership and support that it was only a shell of its former self. Many attribute its decline to a change in philosophy and to the black nationalist position it took in the 1960's.

Charles C. Jackson

See also: Civil Rights movement; Freedom Riders; National Association for the Advancement of Colored People; Southern Christian Leadership Conference; Student Nonviolent Coordinating Committee.

Congressional Black Caucus

The Congressional Black Caucus, a group comprising African American members of the U.S. Congress, was established in 1970 by thirteen members of the House of Representatives who joined together "to promote the public welfare through legislation designed to meet the needs of millions of neglected citizens." Before that year, the House had never had so many African Americans among its 435 members, yet thirteen was still a small minority. The founders of the Congressional Black Caucus hoped that they could gain more visibility and power working together than they could acting alone.

In 1971, the Congressional Black Caucus was granted a meeting with President Richard M. Nixon, during which its members presented a document describing sixty actions the government should take on domestic and international issues. The president promised to promote desegregation by seeing that civil rights laws were more stringently enforced (later, caucus members came to believe that he did not work hard enough to fulfill his promise). Media coverage of the meeting helped the group gain recognition. Over the next quarter-century, members of the caucus built and strengthened ties with other influential members of the black community, including educators, community and religious leaders, and local and state legislators, which enabled the group to influence public policy at all levels of government.

Although originally formed to promote the concerns of African Americans and other members of minority groups, the caucus also worked to ensure that the government assisted others in need, including children, the elderly, and the physically and mentally ill. The group asserts that it is possible and desirable to develop a national African American position on matters of federal policy, and it has sought to direct that effort. Since its founding, the group has introduced and supported legislation concerning domestic issues such as employment, welfare and health care reform, education reform, small business development, urban revitalization, and federal disaster relief. In 1981, members of the caucus spoke out against the budget proposed by President Jimmy Carter, believing that it devoted too much funding to the military and too little to social programs.

At House Judiciary Committee hearings in 1996, following a rash of firebombings of black churches across the South, the caucus criticized the federal government's apparent failure to prosecute those guilty of the crimes. Many of the group's positions have been unpopular, even among some African Americans; in the late 1990's, for example, the caucus strongly endorsed the work of the controversial leader of the Nation of Islam Louis Farrakhan, who was accused by many of teaching anti-Semitism.

As the visibility and influence of the caucus increased, the group called for action on international issues of special concern to African Americans, including human rights. It was one of the earliest and strongest voices urging

Members of the Congressional Black Caucus seen during a meeting with President Richard M. Nixon in 1971. *(Library of Congress)*

that the United States use pressure against apartheid in South Africa and to call for increased attention and aid to other African nations.

Cynthia A. Bily

See also: Black nationalism; Church burnings.

Conservative theorists

The subject of race relations is one of the primary axes whereby American conservatism and liberalism are distinguished. Conservative theorists frequently downplay the significance of race in determining an individual's opportunities in life. They tend to view racial tensions as a product of misunderstandings or cynical manipulation by self-appointed minority leaders.

The terms "conservative" and "liberal" in U.S. political ideology are some-what ambiguous, having changed over time. This is especially true with regard to racial issues. Early in the country's history, "conservatism," which tends to oppose radical change, could be used in defense of slavery. After the abolition of slavery, some conservatives defended segregation and other racist institutions. Therefore, it should not be surprising that conservatives traditionally have resisted programs to further advance the interests of minorities, such as affirmative action and racial quotas. By the 1990's, however, a combination of societal and cultural changes had brought about a situation in which conservatism was strongly associated with positions once championed by civil rights leaders such as the Reverend Martin Luther King, Jr.

Conservative Philosophy Modern conservatism, sometimes called "neoconservatism," emphasizes the rights and interests of individuals over the interests of groups. This fundamental principle was at the center of King's calls for a "color-blind society." King sought the elimination of racial discrimi-nation, which was prevalent in the 1950's and 1960's. Conservatism in the late twentieth century embraced that same notion and used it against some of the governmental programs created to advance minority rights. The premier example of this is affirmative action. Although the term applies to a range of programs, in principle, affirmative action targets underrepre-sented minority groups for jobs, promotions, college admissions, political office, and other social goods. Affirmative action's goals are advanced through quotas, preferences, set-asides, and special outreach. Conservatism opposes most of these manifestations of affirmative action because they treat individuals according to their race or ethnicity. Although proponents of affirmative action claim that this "reverse" discrimination is necessary to compensate for the legacy of past discrimination, conservatives counter that this is still a form of discrimination and thus is harmful.

The conservatives' argument against affirmative action presumes that racial discrimination is not a significant factor in contemporary society. It implies that a level playing field has been achieved in economic and social relations. Such beliefs are vigorously challenged by advocates of affirmative action.

Individualism   Conservatives' attitudes toward discrimination stem in part from conservatism's philosophy of individualism. Conservatism holds that the interests of the individual should be the most important target of government policy. This contrasts with modern American liberalism, which allows for a greater emphasis on group interests. In other words, conservatives reject the idea of African American interests or Latino interests and, in fact, may reject the popular notion of African American or Latino communities. They believe that all of these are reducible to individuals, each of whom is unique and possesses his or her own set of interests.

Conservatism's emphasis on individual interests depoliticizes the issue of race. Although certain minority populations experience a higher degree of poverty, drug addiction, homelessness, incarceration, out-of-wedlock births, or other social and economic ills, conservatism prescribes actions that focus on root causes and do not specifically use race as a criteria for assistance. For example, conservatives believe that programs to create job opportunities for minorities living in depressed areas should be available to all unemployed persons in depressed areas, regardless of race. Similarly, policies that happen to affect one minority group more than others—for instance, imposing higher penalties for possession of illegal drugs that are preferred by a particular minority group—should be evaluated on their merits and not according to their relative impact on racial groups.

Overall, conservatism has come to take a rather academic and idealistic view of race. It has largely embraced the principles advocated by the Civil Rights movement of the 1950's and 1960's.

Conservatism and Race   Although earlier conservative views on race— such as those that defended slavery and segregation—were unlikely to be held by racial minorities, modern conservatism has been espoused by a growing number of African Americans, Latinos, and other minority members. Politically, this fact has been used by white conservatives to defend themselves against charges of racism.

One of the better-known black conservatives is Shelby Steele, of the Hoover Institute at Stanford University. Steele has written extensively about affirmative action, charging that it has the effect of reinforcing blacks' exclusion from the American mainstream. He has repeatedly argued that African Americans need to let go of the culture of "racial victimization," which he views as a self-defeating strategy. He also has decried the "divisive politics" of most of the liberal minority-advocacy groups who claim to speak for African Americans. Steele refers to the leadership of such groups as "the anointed" and argues that they are out of touch with the actual interests and desires of African Americans.

A number of other African American conservatives became highly visible in the late 1980's and 1990's. Among these was Stanley Crouch, who began as a writer on jazz and culture, then increasingly turned to matters of race and politics. Crouch's views are eclectic, and more than anything, he has earned a reputation as an iconoclast. However, he shares many of modern conservatism's views about race, especially its skepticism about liberal prescriptions on the subject. Thomas Sowell, an African American economist at Stanford University, takes a conservative view on racial issues, especially as they relate to welfare and economics. Sowell's work in the mid-1990's sought to explain the importance of ethnicity to socioeconomic outcomes. By using case studies from around the world, Sowell drew distinctions between culture (which is malleable) and race.

The linkage between race and conservatism took another interesting turn in the 1990's with the election of J. C. Watts, Jr., to the U.S. Congress. As an African American Republican, Watts was something of an anomaly, and his outspoken conservatism on matters of race earned him considerable publicity. For conservatives, the presence of Watts on their side helps to weaken their opponents' claims that conservative views on race are racist, or at least ethnocentric. Interestingly, Watts, like many of the conservative theorists listed above, has been criticized by some other African Americans as being somehow untrue to his race. For example, in 1990, the executive director of the National Association for the Advancement of Colored People (NAACP), Benjamin Hooks, said that "these people have nothing to offer except a conservative viewpoint in black skin." The notion that the color of one's skin should be relevant to one's political ideology riles black conservatives. As Watts has stated, "My father raised me to be a man, not a black man."

Steve D. Boilard

Core Resources

More and more conservative theorists are writing books on race. Shelby Steele's books include *The Content of Our Character: A New Vision of Race in America* (New York: HarperPerennial, 1991); *The Vision of the Anointed: Self-Congratulation as a Basis for Social Policy* (New York: Basic Books, 1995); and *A Dream Deferred: The Second Betrayal of Black Freedom in America* (New York: HarperCollins, 1998). Steele also helped produce a Public Broadcasting Service (PBS) television special about the racially motivated murder in Bensonhurst in 1990, "Seven Days in Bensonhurst." William Julius Wilson's *When Work Disappears: The World of the New Urban Poor* (New York: Random House, 1996) offers a black conservative's view of the problems facing inner-city African Americans and others. The range of Stanley Crouch's writings on race is illustrated in his early and recent works. See his *Ain't No*

Ambulances for No Nigguhs Tonight (New York: R.W. Baron, 1972) and *The All-American Skin Game: Or, The Decoy of Race* (New York: Pantheon, 1995). Amy Waldman has written a somewhat critical overview of J. C. Watts's relationship with the Republican Party in "The GOP's Great Black Hope," in *Washington Monthly* (vol. 28, no. 10, October, 1996).

See also: Affirmative action; Civil Rights movement; Discrimination: racial and ethnic; Quotas; "Reverse" racism; Set-asides; Wilson-Willie debate.

Constitutional racism

Three provisions of the Constitution of the United States, as adopted at Philadelphia in 1787, legalized slavery. These provisions, which provided a constitutional basis for treating those descended from Africans as inferior to those descended from Europeans, form the basis of what has come to be known as constitutional racism.

Some delegates at the constitutional convention wanted to abolish slavery, but the southern states, driven by economic dependency on the institution, insisted on retaining it. To ensure that the newly drafted constitution would be adopted by both northern and southern states, a compromise emerged between proslavery and antislavery delegates, and three specific clauses were included.

One provision, Article I, section 9(1), allowed the slave trade to continue until 1808. The part of the Constitution dealing with amendments, Article V, stipulated that this provision could not be amended.

Another compromise involved the status of slaves. Because the number of seats allocated in the House of Representatives for each state were to be apportioned on the basis of population, southern states might have considerable power in the new national legislature. However, a segment of the southern states' population was made up of slaves, who were not considered to have any civil rights and therefore could not vote. The compromise, provided for in Article I, section 2(3), was to calculate the number of persons in each state based on the decennial census, with each slave equal to three-fifths of a white person. Native Americans, who were not considered American citizens, were counted in the census, but their numbers were not used in calculating how many congressional seats were to be apportioned to the states.

A third provision, Article III, section 2(3), enabled slave owners to retrieve runaway slaves even from states that had abolished slavery. Congress later implemented this provision by passing the Fugitive slave laws (1793, 1850), which in turn were held to be constitutional by the U.S. Supreme Court in *Scott v. Sandford* (1857). In this case, a slave owner moved from Missouri to

Illinois, taking along his property and his slaves. Because Illinois law prohibited slavery, Dred Scott, one of the slaves, sued to gain his freedom. The court ruled, however, that descendants of Africans, even those who obtained freedom from their former masters, were not citizens of the United States, had no civil rights, and therefore could not file a lawsuit or vote in an election. *Scott v. Sandford* provoked a constitutional crisis because laws in northern states that disallowed slavery and granted some civil rights to descendants of Africans were in effect nullified. The court's decision did much to infuriate opponents of slavery and sowed the seeds for the Civil War.

With the adoption of the Thirteenth Amendment to the Constitution in 1865, slavery was abolished. The Fugitive slave laws, accordingly, were nullified. Southern states obtained additional seats in the House of Representatives, as they could count every former slave as one person instead of three-fifths of a person. Reapportionment based on the 1870 census gave equal weight to black and white citizens but still excluded Native Americans.

The doctrine of "reason of state" has been used to discriminate against various minorities on several occasions. Under this doctrine, the preservation of the state is held to have priority over constitutional rights. Recent instances are associated with World War II, when the U.S. Supreme Court upheld the constitutionality of military rule of Hawaii and the incarceration of Japanese Americans.

Michael Haas

See also: Censuses, U.S.; Fugitive slave laws; *Scott v. Sandford*; Slavery: history; Thirteenth Amendment; Three-fifths compromise.

Cooper v. Aaron

In *Brown v. Board of Education* (1954) the Supreme Court ordered an end to segregated schools and overturned the "separate but equal" doctrine established in *Plessy v. Ferguson* (1896). The ambiguity about how to implement school desegregation, however, created the opportunity for school boards to delay and defy the court's order.

After the *Brown* decision, the Little Rock, Arkansas, school board approved a plan calling for the desegregation of grades ten through twelve in 1957, to be followed by the desegregation of junior high schools and, finally, the elementary schools. The plan was to be completed by the 1963 school year.

Nine black students, carefully selected by the National Association for the Advancement of Colored People (NAACP), were to begin integration of Central High School on September 3, 1957. The day before desegregation was to begin, Governor Orval Faubus ordered the Arkansas National Guard to prevent the black students from enrolling. Governor Faubus claimed that he acted to prevent violence from occurring. After three weeks, a federal court injunction forced the National Guard to withdraw. On September 23, the nine black students entered Central High School and were met by an unruly mob. President Dwight D. Eisenhower was forced to dispatch federal troops to Little Rock to enforce the Court's desegregation order. In the face of the civil unrest, the school board asked for and received a two-and-a-half-year delay in their desegregation plan. The NAACP appealed the delay in *Cooper v. Aaron.*

Two primary issues confronted the U.S. Supreme Court. First, could the desegregation plan be postponed because of the fear of civil unrest? On September 12, 1958, a unanimous Supreme Court emphatically said no: "The law and order are not here to be preserved by depriving the Negro children of their constitutional rights." Second, were the governor and legislature bound by decisions of the federal court? Invoking the supremacy clause of the Constitution, the Court said: "No state legislative, executive or judicial officer can War against the Constitution without violating his under-taking to support it."

Although Governor Faubus lost the legal battle, he became a political folk hero in Arkansas and was elected to six consecutive terms (1955-1967). President Eisenhower was both praised and condemned for his actions. He was praised for sending in federal troops to enforce the Court's decision and condemned for failing to endorse personally the *Brown* decision and lend the weight and prestige of the White House to the Court's ruling. The *Cooper* case was the first legal confrontation over the enforcement of *Brown v. Board of Education.* The courts stood alone in this enforcement effort until Congress passed the 1964 Civil Rights Act. The Civil Rights Act endorsed the *Brown* decision and cut off federal funds to school districts refusing to comply with the Court's desegregation decision.

Darryl Paulson

See also: *Brown v. Board of Education;* Civil Rights Act of 1964; Discrimination: racial and ethnic; Little Rock school desegregation; *Plessy v. Ferguson;* Segregation: de facto and de jure.

Council of Federated Organizations

The Council of Federated Organizations (COFO) was developed in 1962 as a coalition of civil rights groups to coordinate voter registration in the southern regions of the United States. The COFO's president was Aaron

Henry and its director was Robert Moses. More than 90 percent of COFO funding was provided by the Student Nonviolent Coordinating Committee (SNCC), which received money from the Voter Education Project. The COFO worked closely with SNCC and other civil rights organizations on its projects. Though the organization lost its funding in 1963, its most significant endeavor was the 1964 Freedom Summer project in Mississippi. This project arose from a mock election held in Mississippi in 1963 that showed that African Americans would vote if given the opportunity. Moses devised a new strategy of bringing white college students to Mississippi over the summer break to work on the voter registration project along with black activists. COFO workers were beaten and arrested, and some were shot at and even killed for assisting in registering black voters. They also operated freedom schools for African American children and helped organize the Mississippi Freedom Democratic Party. The COFO made Americans aware of the discrimination that African Americans experienced in Mississippi at the hands of its white residents.

Jennifer Lynn Gossett

See also: Civil Rights movement; Freedom Summer; Mississippi Freedom Democratic Party; Student Nonviolent Coordinating Committee.

Crime and race/ethnicity

One of the major issues associated with criminal justice in the United States is the relationship between race and crime. A large disparity exists between the numbers of African Americans, Hispanics, and other minorities in the general population and their numbers among those incarcerated in jails and prisons.

Although approximately 12 percent of the population of the United States is African American, blacks represent more than half of those imprisoned. In the mid-1990's, the Bureau of Justice Statistics of the U.S. Department of Justice reported that blacks were incarcerated at a rate six times that of the white population. In addition, four in ten of those on death row are black, and young black men are far more likely than whites to be the victims of police brutality. Blacks are also disproportionately represented among victims of crime. African Americans are three times more likely than whites and others to be victims of robbery and more than twice as likely to be victims of aggravated assault.

Data on Hispanics are often unreliable because many criminal justice agencies use only the classifications white and black. When Hispanics are included as white, statistics for both non-Hispanic whites and Hispanics are questionable. The practice inflates the number of whites in the system and creates the impression of fewer disparities than actually exist. Bureau of Justice Statistics reports on incarceration, however, indicate that in the mid-1990's, Hispanics accounted for 17 percent of prisoners, while they made up approximately 9 percent of the general population.

Statistics indicate that Asian Americans are underrepresented in both federal and state prisons. Although they constitute about 4 percent of the U.S. population, they are only 1 percent of those incarcerated. The majority of Asian American offenders are associated with nonviolent crimes such as gambling or prostitution.

Reliable Native American crime statistics are virtually nonexistent because such data are not gathered consistently in Indian country. Different tribes have different relationships with U.S. government agencies, contributing to problems both in defining and in reporting crimes among Native Americans.

Regardless of differences of experience among minority groups, it is impossible to examine crime and punishment in the United States without addressing whether these disparities are the result of discrimination, and whether such discrimination is a feature of the criminal justice system or if criminal justice simply mirrors the racism and inequality that exist in the larger society.

Stereotyping Crime   For many white Americans, "crime" means violent crime and the typical offender is young, black, and male, and the typical victim is white. In some communities, the image of the criminal is the Latino "gangbanger" or the violent "drunken Indian." In fact, based on arrest statistics collected by the Federal Bureau of Investigation (FBI) in the Uniform Crime Reports, for all crimes except murder and robbery, the typical offender is white. As the National Crime Victimization Survey repeatedly confirms, the majority of crimes are intraracial, involving offenders and victims of the same race. However, politicians and the mass media have used sensationalism and misinformation to intensify the public's fears and to lead to policies that promise to be "tough" on crime but that tend to ensnare poor, minority youths in the criminal justice system.

Popular policies, such as three-strikes-and-you're-out laws that mandate life sentences for three-time offenders, the abolition of parole, and mandatory sentences for relatively minor drug crimes, help account for the disparities between the percentage of minorities in the population and their percentage among prisoners. Although such policies may not have overt racist intentions, they result in perpetuating inequality based on race. Most of the three-strikes laws allow prosecutors to exercise tremendous discretion in determining which offenses qualify as a strike. Although many citizens may imagine that such policies will catch violent career criminals, they have often been used against small-time criminals who are arrested on property crimes and drug offenses. Rand Corporation research and 1994 data from the Los Angeles Public Defender's office suggest that blacks were being charged under the law at a rate seventeen times that of whites.

Law Enforcement   Discussions of race and criminal justice often focus on confrontations between police and members of minority groups. Incidents such as the 1991 beating of Rodney King and its aftermath or the assault on Alfred Louima in a New York City police station in 1997 seem to represent entrenched prejudice in the criminal justice system. Historically, the poor and minorities have commonly been victims of "curbside justice" at the hands of law enforcement officers, and until the 1980's, when in *Tennessee v. Garner* the Supreme Court ruled the fleeing-felon rule unconstitutional, they were likely to be shot by the police as "fleeing felons." Studies published in the 1994 edition of the *Sourcebook of Criminal Justice Statistics* show that African Americans and Hispanics consistently have less favorable attitudes toward the police than do white Americans. These negative perceptions are based not only on incidents of police brutality or misconduct but also on a belief that police departments will not discipline the officers who are guilty but will instead form a wall of silence to protect them. Thus, for many minorities, misconduct goes beyond the actions of individual racist police officers and extends to the institutional policies that refuse to make such officers accountable for their actions.

Many cities have adopted community policing strategies to address hostile relations between law enforcement officers and citizens, particularly those who reside in minority neighborhoods. Such programs use foot patrols to place police officers closer to the citizens in nonconfrontational situations. Officers work with community groups to deal with neighborhood problems and to reduce victimization. In some cases, minority police officers are assigned to minority neighborhoods.

Nationwide, the number of minority police officers has increased since the early 1970's when the 1972 amendments to the Civil Rights Act of 1964 prohibited racial or gender employment discrimination by state or local governments. The 1990 census indicated that 10 percent of police in the United States were African Americans and 5.2 percent were Hispanic. The percentages are far higher in cities such as Cleveland and Miami, where aggressive efforts have been made to recruit minority officers.

Race Issues in the Courts   In the courts, the connection between race and bail decisions, charges, jury selection, legal representation, and juvenile processing is ambiguous. Overt discrimination is seldom seen in most U.S. courtrooms, partly because in the 1960's, the Supreme Court repeatedly ruled that the constitutional rights of the accused must be respected by the state courts. On the other hand, such factors as the economic status of defendants and the quality of legal representation are indisputably linked. Research published in the *Journal of Quantitative Criminology* demonstrates that factors such as unemployment, a prior criminal record, and pretrial detention (the inability to make bail) have an impact on the probability of conviction. Members of minority groups, who are also more likely to be poor, suffer double disadvantages in the court system.

In the film *To Kill a Mockingbird* (1962), based on Harper Lee's novel, a southern lawyer (Gregory Peck, front left) defends a poor African American (Brock Peters, front right) falsely accused of rape. Its depiction of the justice system is considered so authentic that it is used in the training of lawyers. *(Museum of Modern Art, Film Stills Archive)*

Race and Sentencing   Many observers of the U.S. criminal justice system have claimed that racial discrimination is clearly observable in sentencing. They charge specifically that African Americans are liable to receive harsher sentences than whites who are convicted of similar crimes. Others argue that blacks receive heavier sentences because they commit more and graver crimes. Mandatory federal sentences that impose penalties that are fifty times heavier for distribution of crack cocaine (used mostly by African Americans) than for powdered cocaine (used mostly by whites) seem to symbolize the disparity.

Studies of sentencing discrepancies such those conducted by Cassia Spohn, John Gruhl, and Susan Welch (1982) and Joan Petersilia (1983) reveal a complex situation in which blatant racism is seldom a factor but some judges take race into account by imposing harsher sentences on African Americans and other minorities who commit violent crimes against whites and more lenient sentences when victims are members of minority groups. In some jurisdictions, in marginal cases, whites are more likely to get probation, and blacks are more likely to be sent to prison. With respect to juvenile processing, white youths are more apt to be released to their parents, while a juvenile facility is a more probable destination for minority youths.

Examinations of the correlation of race with the death penalty show one consistent pattern. As the widely respected and frequently quoted studies done by David Baldus, George Woodworth, and Charles Pulaski, Jr., in 1990 showed, those who murder whites are more likely to receive a capital sentence than those who murder African Americans. On several occasions, the Supreme Court has been asked to rule on the constitutionality of the death penalty given the racial disparity in its use. Although the Court acknowledged in *McCleskey v. Kemp* (1987) that there was statistical evidence of race as a factor in the application of capital punishment, it refused to find the discrimination unconstitutional.

Implications   The United States has one of the highest rates of incarceration in the world, and minorities are disproportionately included among those confined. Although minorities have always been overrepresented in U.S. prisons, the disparity has increased dramatically since the 1980's. During the 1990's, more African Americans were under the supervision of the correctional system (in jail or prison, on probation or parole) than were enrolled in college. Hispanics were imprisoned at twice their representation in the general population. It is impossible to ignore the implications for the future, if sizable numbers of young people receive their higher education in a correctional institution rather than on a college campus.

Most observers attribute this growth in incarceration to the war on drugs. Law enforcement agencies at both the federal and state levels have focused their efforts on visible and open drug trafficking, the sort that occurs in poor, minority neighborhoods. They make more arrests in such communities than in affluent or suburban areas, where drug use is likely to be less obvious. The numbers of arrests, coupled with mandatory sentences for drug offenses, help to account for the expanded minority populations in prisons.

In examining the issues of race and criminal justice, many scholars have concluded that less overt racial discrimination occurs in the system than did in the past. Changes in the legal status of minority groups, Supreme Court decisions protecting the rights of the accused, and political action by African American, Hispanic, and other ethnic groups have helped to reduce discrimination. However, discrimination remains a factor in accounting for the disparate experiences of whites and minorities at all stages of the criminal justice system, from encounters with the police to charging to sentencing. Coupled with the economic biases inherent in the system, race and color continue to influence Americans' experiences of crime and punishment.

Mary Welek Atwell

Core Resources

The Color of Justice: Race, Ethnicity, and Crime in America, by Samuel Walker, Cassia Spohn, and Miriam DeLeone (Belmont, Calif.: Wadsworth, 1996), is an excellent introduction to contextual discrimination in the criminal justice system. Jerome G. Miller's *Search and Destroy* (New York: Cambridge, 1996) finds systematic discrimination in all facets of criminal justice. In *Unequal Justice: A Question of Color* (Bloomington: University of Indiana, 1988), Coramae Richey Mann focuses on how minorities experience the criminal justice system. She maintains that the system reflects the racism prevalent in American society. In *The Myth of a Racist Criminal Justice System* (Monterey, Calif.: Brooks/Cole, 1987), William Wilbanks reviewed literature on the system and concluded that charges of racism within criminal justice are false. Andrew Hacker's *Two Nations: Black and White, Separate, Hostile, Unequal* (New York: Ballantine, 1992) examines inequality throughout American society and looks especially at the relationship between interracial crime and inequality. Studies of sentencing patterns include Cassia Spohn, John Gruhl, and Susan Welch's "The Effect of Race on Sentencing: A Re-examination of an Unsettled Question," in *Law & Society Review* (vol. 16, 1981-1982), Joan Petersilia's *Racial Disparities in the Criminal Justice System* (Santa Monica, Calif.: Rand Corporation, 1983), and David C. Baldus, George Woodworth, and Charles A. Pulaska, Jr.'s *Equal Justice and the Death Penalty* (Boston: Northeastern University Press, 1990).

See also: Criminal justice system; Discrimination: racial and ethnic; Drugs and racial/ethnic relations; Jury selection; King, Rodney, case; *McCleskey v. Kemp*; Police brutality.

Critical race theory

Critical race theory was a response to the mid-1970's conservative, reactionary attack on the achievements of the civil rights struggle and the failure of liberalism to stave off this attack, both ideologically and in public policy. This response was initially led by scholars of color such as Derrick Bell, Mari Matsuda, Charles Lawrence, and Kimberle Crenshaw, as well as white theorist Alan David Freeman.

Critical race theory argues that white racism is a hegemonic, socially and historically constructed cultural force in American society. This racism expresses itself in popular culture by believed myths, stories, legal rules, and the institutional disposition of prestige and power via the concept of whiteness. Critical race theorists use popular culture to deconstruct this hegemony (ideological, cultural, and political domination) by developing a broader, alternate reality through writing fiction and nonfiction. They also combine critical legal theory with an analysis of how law constructs race and gender and thus reveal how liberal legalism (rule of law/equal protection) advances white domination and interests at the same time that it purports to advance the civil rights of minorities and women. In fact, Bell and Freeman argue that white power is solidified by the narrow constraints of civil rights law as it has been interpreted by the courts. According to critical legal theory, too many justices in black robes, either consciously or unconsciously, subscribe to myths of white supremacy, and in this context fact-sensitive evidence makes formal equality a mask that hides how "whiteness," both unintentional and intentional, contours legal doctrine.

Critical race theory's major goal is to be antithetical to both liberal and conservative scholarly assumptions about neutral and objective, discursive, detached intellectual inquiry. Critical race theorists reject these values and see themselves as politicized, counterinsurgent scholars who create oppositional worldviews aimed at the liberation of all oppressed societal groups. For example, these "race crits" argue that the concept of meritocracy is fallacious—that whether discrimination is intentional or unintentional is immaterial in a society in which wealth, education, and power are distributed and affirmed by the workings of a hierarchy of white over black. By revealing, through a process called "internal critique," the internal contradictions of the concept of meritocracy, race crits hope that this clarification will create a "crisis of logic," or demonstrate the lack of logic in treating rich and poor alike, as both can be potentially prosecuted for violating a neutral/objective law against begging for bread in the streets.

In demonstrating the intersectional contexts of race, class, and gender, race crits seek to challenge the legitimacy of white supremacy and its most potent tactic of using the powerful ideology of "color blindness." This idea is powerful because of its varied sources, one of which is Justice John M. Harlan's dissent in the 1896 *Plessy v. Ferguson* case (in which Harlan touted the ideal of a color-blind society) and the other being the Reverend Martin Luther King, Jr.'s often-quoted clarion that one should be judged by the content of one's character and not by the color of one's skin. Race crits argue that race consciousness is so hegemonic that to ignore what one's optic processes immediately perceive and automatically connect to value judgments is actually to perpetuate white supremacy. The perpetuation of this myth is effected by ignoring the fact that every minority individual is forced by whiteness into a dual consciousness. The social and historical context of this duality is faced every day by blacks and other racial and ethnic minorities, such as when a person of color must decide whether to buy "flesh-colored" bandages or when he or she is recognized as the "first" black, Chicano, or female judge, lawyer, or prosecutor. The falsity of color blindness is exposed in such situations.

The development of critical race theory has experienced some major turning points: In 1980, students of color at Harvard University confronted the administration over the teaching of an alternative course on race and law; future race crits, including Lawrence, Matsuda, Crenshaw, and others, were involved in this incident. Another turning point was the rise of critical legal studies conferences and the insurgency by feminist crits and race crits within this movement by the 1986 and 1987 conferences. The 1987 conference, coordinated by a consortium of Los Angeles area law schools, was entitled "The Sounds of Silence." The unsilenced voices of the race crits were heard in a plethora of workshops at this conference, and selected papers presented were published in a special edition of the *Harvard Civil Rights and Civil Liberties Review* (spring, 1987). Another major event was a critical race theory conference at Mills College in Oakland, California, 1993, where various scholars met to discuss critical race theory. Out of this conference two different volumes on critical race theory were produced: *Critical Race Theory: The Cutting Edge* (1995), edited by Richard Delgado, and *Critical Race Theory: The Key Writings That Formed the Movement* (1995), edited by Kimberle Crenshaw, Neil Gotanda, Gary Peller, and Kendall Thomas.

Malik Simba

See also: Color coding; Ideological racism; Institutional racism; Naïveté explanation of racism; *Plessy v. Ferguson*; Psychology of racism; Racism as an ideology; Racism: history of the concept.

Culture of poverty

The term "culture of poverty" has been used to describe the values, principles, and lifestyles associated with people living at the lowest economic levels of society. Because many minorities and immigrants grow up in a culture of poverty, it has profound implications for intergroup relations.

"Culture of poverty" is a term that refers to the pattern of life, the set of beliefs, and the typical behavior found among people who live in an environment dominated by economic deprivation. Culture is the way in which people live their lives and includes all the habits learned by an individual from other members of the community. In its broadest sense, a culture contains the essential information one needs to live in a given environment. Because the environment found in impoverished communities is built upon deprivation, isolation, discrimination, poor education, lack of jobs, crime, drugs, alcohol abuse, and welfare dependence, these negative forces shape the attitudes, expectations, and behavior of residents.

Oscar Lewis, an American anthropologist famous for his description of the effects of poverty on human lives in *La Vida: A Puerto Rican Family in the Culture of Poverty—San Juan and New York* (1966), believed that the values children learn from their parents about how to survive in such desperate circumstances make them less able to move out of poverty. Lewis suggested that only a violent revolution overturning capitalist society would enable the poor to find dignity and equality. Working within the system would not solve any problems because the values poor people learn include hatred for education (which rarely helps to get a person out of the slums), self-indulgence (since alcohol and drugs offer a quick way out of misery), and unwillingness to save or sacrifice for the future well-being of one's self or family (since the future offers little hope for improving one's economic circumstances). None of these values leads to educational or occupational advancement. The culture learned by the poor works against their ever getting out of poverty. For things to change, according to Lewis, the environmental conditions need to change.

Defining Poverty   Poverty takes three forms: social poverty, which is defined as economic inequality, or the lack of means to provide a minimally adequate standard of living; pauperism, a word that signifies an inability of individuals to take care of themselves; and voluntary poverty, which includes those who for religious and philosophical reasons give up material possessions to pursue prayer, meditation, or art. In the United States, most of the poor fall into the first two categories and include the unskilled, the uneducated, and a large number of children. As of 1993, the government defined as poor nonfarm families of four with incomes under $12,500, about half the income of an average American family of four. Farm families qualify as poor with slightly less income.

According to government figures, in 1992, about 32 million Americans, or 13 percent of the population, lived below the poverty level. That figure represented an increase of almost 4 million people since 1984, the largest proportion reported by the U.S. Bureau of the Census since the 1950's, when 22.4 percent of the nation lived in officially declared poverty. In 1988, the bureau issued a report on the American poor that showed that 10 percent of whites, 31.6 percent of blacks, and 26.8 percent of Hispanics were impoverished; 20 percent of American children lived in poverty. More than half the families labeled poor were headed by single mothers, and those numbers were growing. Many of the poor, almost 45 percent, worked full-time but in jobs that required few skills, offered no opportunities for advancement, and generally had no benefits such as health insurance. For the "working poor," jobs themselves seemed to offer no opportunity for moving up the economic ladder. Working hard for forty hours a week or longer did not guarantee success.

Sources of Poverty   Race itself is not a cause of poverty; however, the American tradition of racial segregation and discrimination has guaranteed that large numbers of African Americans—almost two out of every five—live under the poverty line. The major causes of poverty in the United States include chronic unemployment resulting from low levels of education and lack of skills; low wages in unskilled entry-level occupations as well as in agricultural labor; old age; and catastrophes such as floods, fires, or large medical bills.

Poverty is seen by many as a sign of wickedness and moral degeneracy: People are poor because they are lazy and corrupt. These attitudes must be faced and absorbed into a poor person's consciousness every day, and they only increase a sense of frustration and hopelessness. In a society that exalts the work ethic such as the United States, not working becomes a sign of individual worthlessness and insignificance. This attitude represents one of the most devastating nonmaterial effects of being poor.

According to the culture of poverty thesis, ending employment discrimination, raising wages, and increasing employment opportunities through job training programs would all help to reduce poverty, but the attitudes of the poor would change only very slowly because a whole way of life would need to be transformed. Education is the key to changing attitudes, especially by reducing the sense of despair frequently experienced by poor people. Yet dropout rates approach 45 percent in high schools in slum districts, and a majority of impoverished adults are functionally illiterate; a major change in educational outcomes thus would be required before schools could be accepted as a way out of poverty.

In American society, more than 71 percent of the African American poor live in large cities or surrounding suburbs, while most poor whites (almost 68 percent) are found in small towns, suburbs, and rural areas. In his book *The Truly Disadvantaged: The Inner City, the Underclass, and Public Policy* (1987), University of Chicago sociologist William J. Wilson observes that many African Americans live in neighborhoods with high concentrations of people in similarly desperate economic circumstances, with average incomes of less than $5,000 a year. Poor black people, especially, tend to live in areas surrounded by other poor blacks and thus have little opportunity to meet or learn from individuals with more secure economic futures. These are the truly disadvantaged members of American society, the people who feel most cut off from the American mainstream, and the people most influenced by the culture of poverty.

Tough Environments   In the environment of the slum, cultural patterns emerge that promote survival in the midst of dangerous and violent conditions. Crime rates, murder rates, and levels of drug addiction, alcoholism, mental illness, hypertension, and other measures of social disintegration, including divorce, child abuse, and spouse abuse, are far higher in inner cities than in any other parts of the United States. Survival in these circumstances requires a toughness of spirit and a distrust of others. Because slum residents usually do not get adequate city services such as garbage collection and police protection, distrust of government grows, leading to increased levels of hopelessness and helplessness. Not even the schools, historically the institutions most used by immigrant and minority groups as the path to success, typically offer the type of skills and training necessary to make it out of the ghetto. The dream of college seems very distant to people without enough money to buy food.

The goals of the poor may be similar to those of the more well-to-do in terms of better jobs, improved educational opportunities, and a more pleasant future for their children, but the experience of the poor does not provide evidence that such dreams will ever come true. In many impoverished and racially segregated neighborhoods, crime, usually involving drug sales, offers a far quicker route to material success. Welfare payments, whether through Aid to Families with Dependent Children (AFDC), general assistance, or other aid programs, are another source of survival for the truly poor, although the welfare reforms of the late 1990's significantly curtailed these resources as long-term options. Such help, inadequate as it usually is, increases dependency and tends to reduce self-respect, as it is considered a sign of personal weakness to receive welfare.

Leslie V. Tischauser

Core Resources

Andrew Hacker's *Two Nations: Black and White, Separate, Hostile, Unequal* (New York: Charles Scribner's Sons, 1992) is a thorough analysis of racial issues in the United States. *A Common Destiny: Blacks and American Society*, edited by Gerald D. Jaynes and Robin M. Williams (Washington, D.C.: National Academy Press, 1988) attempts to refute the idea of a distinct culture of poverty, seeing discrimination and racism as the only impediments to full equality. William J. Wilson's *The Truly Disadvantaged: The Inner City, the Underclass, and Public Policy* (Chicago: University of Chicago Press, 1987) shows the devastating impact of poverty and the culture of poverty on millions of Americans. Charles Murray's *Losing Ground: American Social Policy, 1950-1980* (New York: Basic Books, 1984) saw a culture of poverty developing from American welfare programs and called for eliminating welfare and increasing incentives to work.

See also: Economics and race; Poverty and race; Welfare's impact on racial/ethnic relations.

Desegregation: defense

The 1941 desegregation of the U.S. defense industry was a major step in the advancement of African American civil rights and black-white relations.

Ever since the Revolutionary War, the United States had experienced difficulty in bringing African Americans into its military. Although one of the victims of the Boston massacre, Crispus Attucks, was an African American, and black soldiers were with George Washington when he made his famous 1776 Christmas crossing of the Delaware River to attack the Hessians at Trenton and Princeton, it was not until the Civil War (1861-1865) that African American troops were recruited officially into the United States Army. Even then, however, a rigid policy of segregation was maintained. In the two wars that followed, the Spanish-American War (1898) and World War I

(1917-1919), both the Army and Navy had black troops, but largely in supporting roles, and always as separate, segregated units. In addition, black troop strength was kept deliberately low, partly to avoid offending white soldiers and partly because the military establishment had a low opinion of the abilities of African American troops.

Roosevelt's Role   During the 1930's, however, under the presidency of Franklin D. Roosevelt, these prejudiced traditions began to change. Roosevelt's New Deal, which had been put into place to fight the ravages of the Great Depression, also addressed a number of social conditions, including civil rights. Although civil rights were never at the forefront of Roosevelt's agenda, his administration was more committed to them than any previous presidency had been, and his wife, the redoubtable Eleanor Roosevelt, was an especially strong and capable advocate for racial equality and justice. In addition, the shrewdly realistic president, who foresaw the coming struggle with Nazi Germany, realized that the U.S. military needed every capable citizen, of whatever color or background. The policy of "Jim Crowism," or rigid segregation of blacks and whites, remained largely in place, however.

Correctly estimating the extent and depth of prejudice against African American participation in the military, especially in positions of responsibility, Roosevelt moved cautiously. He had been assistant secretary of the Navy under President Woodrow Wilson during World War I; now, Roosevelt prodded and encouraged the Navy high command to enlist additional African Americans and to place them in positions of greater responsibility than stewards or mess servers. Gradually and slowly, the Navy responded. A similar broadening took place in the Army in 1935, when the president insisted that African American medical officers and chaplains be called up from the reserves. On October 9, 1940, Roosevelt announced a revised racial policy for the armed forces; its intent was to bring more African Americans into the military and to place them in positions of trust and responsibility. At a glacial but perceptible pace, the United States military was becoming more receptive to African Americans.

The progress was not sufficiently rapid for many African Americans, among them A. Philip Randolph, president of the Brotherhood of Sleeping Car Porters, one of the strongest and most effective African American unions in the country. Randolph, who well understood that black voters had become an essential part of the Democratic Party's electoral base, calculated that Roosevelt would need to respond to African American demands, especially as the 1940 presidential elections approached. Randolph's logic and timing were correct.

In 1940, Roosevelt ran for an unprecedented third term as president. Randolph, along with former Republican city councilman Grant Reynolds of New York City, began a campaign against the Jim Crow practices still prevalent in the United States military. Randolph and Reynolds also called for greater opportunities for African American workers in the rapidly growing defense industries, which had arisen as the United States rearmed against the threat from Nazi Germany and imperialist Japan. As the campaign intensified, Roosevelt faced a difficult situation that threatened his southern, conservative support at the same time that it endangered his urban, liberal allies. When Randolph announced plans for a march on Washington, scheduled for July 1, 1941, Roosevelt knew he must act. His determination was steeled by the resolve of his wife, Eleanor, who had long been a champion of equal rights for African Americans, and whose contacts with the black community were strong and deep.

On June 25, 1941, Roosevelt issued Executive Order 8802, which enunciated a broad policy of racial equality in the armed forces and the defense industry. The order was clear and sweeping in its intent:

> In offering the policy of full participation in the defense program by all persons regardless of color, race, creed, or national origin, and directing certain action in furtherance of said policy . . . all departments of the government, including the Armed Forces, shall lead the way in erasing discrimination over color or race.

President Roosevelt backed up the policy by establishing the Fair Employment Practices Committee, which was charged with monitoring and enforcing compliance among civilian contractors. It is estimated that Roosevelt's executive order, combined with the work of the commission, helped to bring fifty-three thousand African American civilians into defense industry jobs they otherwise would not have held.

The timing of the policy was impeccable. Randolph and the other campaign leaders, satisfied that the Roosevelt administration was sincere in its commitment to civil rights, called off the march on Washington. Political conservatives, who otherwise might have challenged the president's order, had to admit that it would not be proper to expect African Americans to serve in the military without allowing them to hold responsible positions and achieve corresponding rank. Black voters responded enthusiastically to the Roosevelt reelection campaign, helping him to sweep to victory in the November balloting.

Inevitably, there were racial tensions and outbreaks of violence, especially in lower- and middle-class northern neighborhoods. In 1943, for example, tension between black and white workers led to open violence at a park on Belle Isle near Detroit; in the end, federal troops had to be called in to restore order, and twenty-five African Americans and nine whites had been killed. Similar, if less bloody, events took place in other cities. Still, the transition to a more equitable situation continued in both civilian and military life.

However, the traditional segregation remained. During World War II, black units still were kept separate and apart from white troops, and were generally reserved for support and logistical duties rather than combat. When the difficulties and emergencies of battle required it, African American units were brought into the fighting line; generally, they acquitted

African American women were not permitted to serve in the Navy's Women Accepted for Voluntary Emergency Service (WAVES) until 1944. *(National Archives)*

themselves well. By the end of the war, African Americans had distinguished themselves as ground soldiers, sailors, and pilots in both combat and non-combat situations. After the surrender of the Axis powers in 1945, there was a sense of inevitable change ahead for the United States military. The question of whether it would be a peaceful, productive change remained.

Post-World War II Harry S Truman, who assumed the presidency in 1945 after the death of Franklin D. Roosevelt, was determined to make the change in a proper fashion. He assembled a special Civil Rights Committee which, on October 30, 1947, issued its report, *To Secure These Rights.* Clearly and unhesitatingly, the report called for the elimination of segregation in the United States military.

As the 1948 presidential elections approached, the issue of African Americans in the military affected the political atmosphere. Truman and the national Democratic Party, as heirs of the Roosevelt New Deal, had strong connections with the Civil Rights movement and its leaders; at the same time, much of the traditional Democratic strength was in the South, where civil rights issues were strongly opposed by the entrenched establishment. Southern politicians, such as Strom Thurmond of South Carolina, threatened to bolt the party if the Democrats adopted a strong civil rights platform at their convention; however, inspired by the passionate appeal of Mayor Hubert H. Humphrey of Minneapolis, the Democrats did indeed adopt a positive plank on civil rights. The southerners stormed out, nominating Thurmond to run on the "Dixiecrat" ticket, and Truman went on to win a come-from-behind victory in November.

One element of that victory was his own Executive Order 9981, issued on July 26, 1948, just after the Democratic Party convention. Truman's order was similar to but stronger than Roosevelt's: It required equal opportunity in the armed forces of the United States, regardless of race, and called upon the military services to move immediately to implement the directive. The Air Force reacted promptly and soon achieved remarkable integration of black and white troops; the Navy and Marines were more hesitant in their acceptance. In the end, however, all branches of the armed forces responded, making them among the most egalitarian and equitable of U.S. institutions.

Michael Witkoski

Core Resources

Richard Dalifiume's *Desegregation of the U.S. Armed Forces: Fighting on Two Fronts, 1939-1953* (Columbia: University of Missouri Press, 1969) emphasizes the role of African Americans as soldiers, sailors, and airmen and sheds additional light on Roosevelt's order and its impact. Bernard C. Nalty's *Strength for the Fight: A History of Black Americans in the Military* (New York: Free Press, 1986) provides a comprehensive narrative of the relationship between African Americans and the U.S. armed forces. Richard Stillman's *Integration of the Negro in the U.S. Armed Forces* (New York: Frederick A. Praeger, 1968) provides an especially good discussion of the Roosevelt and Truman policies regarding blacks in the military. The U.S. Department of Defense's *Black Americans in Defense of Our Nation* (Washington, D.C.: Government Printing Office, 1991) is a pictorial documentary that covers all branches of the armed forces and include defense- and military-related occupations as well. C. Vann Woodward's *The Strange Career of Jim Crow* (2d rev. ed., New York: Oxford University Press, 1966) has remained a definitive work on legal and official segregation in American life.

See also: Civil War and African Americans; Military and racial/ethnic relations; Military desegregation; Race riots of 1943.

Desegregation: public schools

School desegregation, mandated by the Supreme Court's 1954 Brown v. Board of Education *decision, involved first the dismantling of legally required separate schools for whites and blacks and later "affirmative action" to produce genuine integration.*

School desegregation refers, in the narrowest sense, to the policy of dismantling the legally enforceable system of separate schools for black and white

Americans that prevailed in southern and border states from the late nineteenth to the mid-twentieth century. The Fourteenth Amendment to the Constitution of the United States, ratified in 1868, proclaimed the "equal protection of the law" for all citizens of the United States. In 1896, the Supreme Court held in the case of *Plessy v. Ferguson* that separate public facilities for African Americans were legal as long as they were "equal." Since that time, black plaintiffs had sometimes won cases by arguing that inadequate schools for blacks were unequal in public funding or physical facilities with the corresponding schools for whites. In the landmark *Brown v. Board of Education* decision in 1954, however, the doctrine of "separate but equal" was itself challenged. The African American plaintiffs argued, and the Supreme Court agreed, that such a legally mandated, separate school system for blacks was inherently unequal and hence denied African American citizens the equal protection of the law.

Brown's Impact   The logic of this decision assumed a crucial importance. Written by Chief Justice Earl Warren and unanimously endorsed by the nine justices, it established the framework for a chain of later decisions. The Court maintained, first, that education had become essential to the exercise of citizenship and was entitled to such equal protection. Second, it maintained that intangible factors must be considered in the assessment of equality. A lack of opportunity to interact in discussions and exchange views with those of the majority culture might itself handicap a minority. Among these intangible factors, the court borrowed heavily from a brief submitted by social scientists as "friends of the court." Segregation, this brief maintained, was construed by both whites and blacks to imply black inferiority. This feeling of inferiority had depressed the motivation of black children to learn and hence depressed their educational progress. Implied by the decision was a third strand of the social science argument: that stereotyping by whites in their views of blacks (and hence, prejudice) was promoted by racial segregation.

For a decade following this decision, the courts were lenient, white resistance was high, and only token desegregation occurred in most southern states. While it was held that school districts should proceed to desegregate "with all deliberate speed," the truly operative principle was "freedom of choice." No black child who wished to attend a previously white school could be refused, but blacks were inhibited by custom and by social and economic pressures, and only a small number chose to go to traditionally white schools. Many whites opposed any desegregation whatsoever. An influx of black students, they argued, would "ruin" the public schools by flooding them with students who were functioning at a level behind that of their white age-mates. Various strategies were employed to avoid large-scale integration. New private academies for whites were constructed, and states provided tuition grants to assist students to attend such academies; in a few locations, public schools were closed. In 1964, a decade after the *Brown v. Board of*

Education decision, fewer than 2 percent of all southern black students were attending integrated schools.

Push for Integration   In the mid-1960's, however, an era of federal activism began. The Civil Rights Act of 1964 provided for the mandatory suspension of federal aid to school districts shown to be practicing racial discrimination. In 1966, this antidiscrimination clause was invoked, and federal funds were withdrawn from some of the more resistant school districts. In 1968, the Supreme Court in *Green v. County School Board of New Kent County* reinterpreted the *Brown* mandate to require whatever "affirmative action" was necessary to achieve an integrated school system. In later cases such as *Swann v. Charlotte-Mecklenburg Board of Education* (1971), the court elaborated that such affirmative action could require the transportation of students between schools, the reassignment of teachers, and a consideration of the white-black student ratio in evaluating the success of such affirmative action. Although controversial, the activist approach obtained results. By 1975, 44 percent of the black students in southern states were in schools with a white majority.

By the late 1970's, however, patterns of social separation became more complex. Many cases of racial segregation that attracted the attention of the courts were in northern cities. Racial separation was imposed not by the law but by economic and social factors such as housing patterns. Much of the middle class, including most whites, either moved to suburban communities

The federally ordered desegregation of Central High School in Little Rock, Arkansas, in 1957 produced a confrontation that focused national attention on school desegregation. *(Library of Congress)*

or placed their children in private schools. Court orders to desegregate seemed only to encourage "white flight" and resegregation. Public opinion also became more complex. While the public continued to support racial integration, it became strongly opposed to the use of forced busing to achieve integration. Some former supporters of integration now championed the alternative of black separation and empowerment. Political leadership and the Supreme Court grew more conservative. In a series of legal challenges, the courts held that remedies such as busing between school districts could not be prescribed unless each of these school districts was guilty of deliberate segregation. Prosecutions by the Justice Department for violations of Title VI of the Civil Rights Act slowed to a trickle. Although blacks continued to become part of an increasing variety of society's institutions, legal and political pressures to desegregate diminished greatly.

Sociological Support   The jurists who decided *Brown v. Board of Education* were informed by social science findings that were both critical of the present and optimistic about the future. Sociologist Gunnar Myrdal, in his influential *An American Dilemma* (1944), interpreted the incompatibility between the American ideal of equality of opportunity and the continuing presence of a legally sanctioned, race-based caste system as a chronic source of embarrassment to the national psyche. The research that was presented to the Court in *Brown v. Board of Education* suggested that the isolation of one group from another in a competing environment could breed mutual antagonisms and unflattering stereotypes. Once formed, such stereotypes become self-fulfilling prophecies influencing both the responses of others and one's perception of oneself. A famous study by psychologist Kenneth Clark showing that black children select white dolls as prettier was submitted as evidence that black children often adopt a negative, prejudiced view of themselves. This thesis—that segregation breeds prejudice, which in turn breeds mutual hostility, self-hate, and failure—was explicitly cited in Chief Justice Warren's opinion. It could be inferred that Warren also agreed that closer contact between blacks and whites would result in more equal opportunity by reducing prejudices, raising black self-esteem, and increasing academic success by African Americans.

Studies of the short-term effects of desegregation in schools have concentrated on changes in academic performance, changes in black and white attitudes toward each other, and changes in black self-esteem. More often than not, black academic achievement tends to be modestly improved after desegregation, and white academic achievement is not adversely affected. Attitudes of whites about blacks sometimes become more positive, sometimes become more negative, and sometimes change not at all. A crucial factor in increased positive attitudes is the existence of relationships that are both equal-status and cooperative in the pursuit of common goals. Black self-esteem has shown little change. Four decades later, at least 65 percent of black children still preferred white dolls, just as in Clark's pre-1954 studies.

An examination of the broader, long-term social and economic effects of desegregation also suggests a mixed picture. The resegregation of cities offers to inner-city black children opportunities that are dramatically unequal. Fear of changes in the quality of education following desegregation has in urban areas exacerbated white flight and the flight of middle-class blacks from urban areas. Indeed, many minority children of the inner city seem trapped in areas of crime, drugs, and violence in schools that are underfunded, underheated, undertaught, and overcrowded; the students have few middle-class black role models. These children seem to have little more opportunity than segregated black children did in 1954. For them, the net effect of the many social changes has been, at best, to break even.

There are, however, winners. Many graduates of the more successfully desegregated schools report cross-racial friendships of a quality that would have been rare before 1954. The highest-ranking black graduates of southern high schools are admitted to highly selective colleges with a regularity that would once have been astounding. The bottom line is that the *Brown v. Board of Education* decision was historically inevitable. That a constitutional democracy such as the United States would have approached the twenty-first century with a legally mandated caste system is almost unthinkable.

Thomas E. DeWolfe

Core Resources

Gordon W. Allport's *The Nature of Prejudice* (abridged ed., Garden City, N.Y.: Doubleday, 1958) describes much of the theory and research included in the social science brief in the *Brown* decision. Harold B. Gerard's "School Desegregation: The Social Science Role" (*American Psychologist*, August, 1983) reconsiders predictions made by psychologists in *Brown*, arguing that they were too optimistic. Jennifer L. Hochschild's *The New American Dilemma: Liberal Democracy and School Desegregation* (New Haven, Conn.: Yale University Press, 1984) argues that desegregation is resisted because racism is as firmly rooted in the United States as is the ideal of equality. Jonathan Kozol's *Savage Inequalities* (New York: Crown, 1991) is an impassioned account of underclass children in large U.S. cities and of the underfunded, overcrowded schools they attend. George R. Metcalf's *From Little Rock to Boston: The History of School Desegregation* (Westport, Conn.: Greenwood Press, 1983) is a detailed history of the federal government's efforts to desegregate schools. Gunnar Myrdal's *An American Dilemma: The Negro Problem and Modern Democracy* (New York: Harper, 1944) highlights the incompatibility between core American ideals and the treatment and segregation of blacks. Raymond Wolters' *The Burden of Brown: Thirty Years of School Desegregation* (Knoxville: University of Tennessee Press, 1984) gives a detailed account of how five communities responded to the necessity of desegregating schools between 1954 and 1984. *Desegregation and the Supreme Court* (Boston: D. C. Heath, 1958), edited by Benjamin Ziegler, contains the text of the *Brown* decision and other related decisions.

See also: Affirmative action; *Alexander v. Holmes County Board of Education*; Black colleges and universities; *Brown v. Board of Education*; Civil Rights Act of 1964; Education and African Americans; Education and racial/ethnic relations; Equal educational opportunity; Jim Crow laws; Ole Miss desegregation; *Plessy v. Ferguson.*

Detroit riot

The Detroit riot of 1967 was among the costliest race riots in U.S. history. Forty-one people died, nearly two thousand were injured, and damage estimates ranged from a quarter to a half billion dollars.

Urban race riots, which had taken place in Harlem in New York City in 1964 and 1967 and Watts in Los Angeles in 1965, had become part of the social upheaval of the decade. The urban unrest peaked during the summer of 1967. From Omaha, Nebraska, to Washington, D.C., riots took place in nearly 150 U.S. cities. In a July 12-16 riot in Newark, New Jersey, twenty-seven people died, more than eleven hundred were injured, and property damage reached fifteen million dollars.

The Riot Detroit, Michigan, was a curious place for violence to erupt. Many African Americans commanded high wages in the automobile factories and high positions in the liberal United Automobile Workers union. About 40 percent of Detroit's 550,000 African Americans owned or were buying their own homes. Community leaders, both black and white, had made a civics lesson of the city's bloody race riot of 1943, which had left thirty-four dead and moved President Franklin D. Roosevelt to send in federal troops. Detroit's mayor, Jerome Cavanagh, had been elected with the support of the African American community.

However, a minor police incident on July 23, 1967, provided the spark that ignited the Detroit ghetto. An early-morning raid of a speakeasy on a run-down street resulted in knots of African American onlookers taunting the police. A brick crashed through the window of a police cruiser. At this point, the police could have either pulled out or used force to break up the crowd. They did neither. They dispatched cruisers but did nothing else; consequently, mobs gathered and started fires, then looting began. As the fires spread, so did the looting, creating a carnival atmosphere in the ghetto. Children joined adults in racing from stores with their arms full of groceries, liquor, or jewelry. Cars pulled up to businesses and their occupants filled them with appliances and other goods.

Both the mayor and the governor seemed paralyzed. Mayor Cavanagh ordered more swimming pools opened, and Governor George Romney suggested seeding rain clouds above the ghetto. Neither police nor peacemakers could stop the riot.

In order to quell the riot, Governor Romney deployed the National Guard, and President Lyndon B. Johnson sent in U.S. Army paratroopers. Although the Army troops were able to secure their sector of the ghetto, events went badly elsewhere. The National Guard and the police seemed to assume a license to kill. A subsequent investigation by the *Detroit Free Press* found that most of the official reports about the forty-three riot-related deaths (all but eight of them African Americans) had been pure fabrications. Three African Americans were shot as they sat in a car. A deaf man was killed because he couldn't hear a warning. A child holding a broom was gunned down. Finally, on the sixth day, July 28, the riot just burned itself out.

Impact President Johnson moved quickly to appoint a commission to study the roots of urban racial unrest. The Kerner Commission, named for its chairman, Governor Otto Kerner of Illinois, operated on the twin premises that the nation must ensure the safety of its people and that the nation must get at the root causes of racial strife.

The commission, which released its report in 1968, determined that the riots were not directed at white Americans but instead at their property and authority. It described a causal chain of "discrimination, prejudice, disadvantaged conditions, . . . all culminating in the eruption of disorder at the hands of youthful, politically aware activists." The frustration experienced by African Americans living in the ghetto was found to have long historical roots. The commission noted that the historical pattern of black-white relations had been "pervasive discrimination and segregation," which had resulted in whites leaving the inner cities and thus creating black ghettos. Young African Americans, alienated by the conditions produced by discrimination and segregation, had flocked to the banner of black power.

The commission concluded that the United States was moving toward separate and unequal societies, white and black. It called for increased national communication among races in order to end stereotypes and hostility.

Brian G. Tobin

Core Resources

Richard N. Goodwin, a former speechwriter for President Johnson, fits the 1967 Detroit riot into the context of the times in *Remembering America: A Voice from the Sixties.* Journalist William Serrin's article "The Crucible," in the January/February, 1991, issue of the *Columbia Journalism Review,* is a firsthand account of the riot.

See also: Kerner Report; Newark race riots; Race riots of 1943; Race riots of the twentieth century; Watts riot.

Discrimination

Discrimination in one form or another appears to be endemic to all societies. In the United States, various groups have experienced various forms of discrimination, including racial discrimination, sexual discrimination (denial of certain rights to women), religious discrimination, cultural discrimination, age discrimination, discrimination against the disabled (both physically and mentally), and discrimination on the basis of sexual orientation.

Discrimination is the unequal treatment, whether intentional or unintentional, of individuals or groups on the basis of group membership that is unrelated to merit, ability, or past performance. The two most pervasive types of discrimination are legal discrimination and institutional discrimination. Legal discrimination is unequal treatment that is sustained by law. Institutional discrimination is a subtle form of unequal treatment based on race or ethnicity that is entrenched in social custom (that is, social institutions). Institutional discrimination may include segregated housing patterns, redlining by financial institutions, and the practice of minority group members being forced continually into low-paying jobs. Prejudice, which is often confused with discrimination, is the prejudgment of people, objects, or even situations on the basis of stereotypes or generalizations that persist even when facts demonstrate otherwise (for example, the majority of women on welfare are white, yet the stereotype of a female welfare recipient is that of a black woman with a brood of children).

The most pernicious acts of discrimination in the United States have been directed against racial and ethnic minorities. The history of racial and ethnic relations in the United States demonstrates that differential treatment has been accorded to all minority groups. A minority group is sometimes defined any group in a disadvantaged or subordinate position (in this sense, a minority may actually constitute a numerical majority; for example, blacks in South Africa). Minority populations have experienced the entire range of race relations, including assimilation, pluralism, legal protection, population transfer, continued subjugation, and extermination. While all minority populations have experienced some degree of discrimination, perhaps the most cruel and enduring discrimination has been experienced by those of African descent.

Africans were first brought to North America in 1619, and they proved to be an excellent source of inexpensive labor for the developing European colonies. In its early development, slavery was not rationalized by attitudes of racial superiority but simply by the need for cheap labor. Racial justification for slavery came later, as a strategy for maintaining the continued subjugation of blacks. Depicting blacks as subhuman, irresponsible, promiscuous, and lazy helped to stave off, for many years, groups (for example, abolitionists) bent upon ending slavery. The development of racist ideology during slavery has—over the years—continued to influence the relationship between blacks and whites in the United States.

The end of slavery in the United States did not, and could not, bring an end to discrimination. Discrimination had become institutionalized; it was embedded in social custom and in the very institutions of society. Initially, the Thirteenth, Fourteenth, and Fifteenth Amendments to the Constitution, along with the Civil Rights Acts of 1866 and 1867, did much to eliminate legal discrimination against the newly freed slaves. Yet many of those gains were abrogated by state legislatures in the South following the abrupt end of Reconstruction in 1877. The states of the Old Confederacy were able to circumvent much of the legislation passed during the Reconstruction period. They were able to sanction discrimination and deny civil rights by means of a set of laws called the black codes. The black codes virtually reintroduced many of the conditions that existed during slavery. Although the Fourteenth and Fifteenth Amendments guaranteed citizenship and the right to vote, these rights were abridged through intimidation, the poll tax, the grandfather clause, and literacy tests. Beginning in the 1880's, a more comprehensive set of laws—referred to as Jim Crow—gave rise to a system of legal segregation in South. This system of legal segregation was sanctioned by the "separate but equal" doctrine established in the *Plessy v. Ferguson* decision of 1896.

Legal Remedies Substantial progress against Jim Crow did not occur until fifty-eight years later, with the *Brown v. Board of Education* decision (1954). In the *Brown* decision, the Supreme Court overturned *Plessy*, arguing that the concept of "separate but equal" was "inherently unequal." The *Brown* decision spurred many African Americans to exercise the rights and privileges guaranteed to all citizens under the Constitution. Beginning in the 1960's, the underlying legal, political, and economic context of race relations changed in the United States. Demonstrations, sit-ins, and marches by African Americans and their supporters caused America to begin addressing the second-class citizenship of minority groups. As a consequence, epoch-making legislation was passed in the form of the 1964 Civil Rights Act, affirmative action (in employment and education) was introduced, and governmental agencies actively tried to stamp out discrimination against minorities.

Yet riot after riot erupted across the nation in the 1960's. A combination of economic frustration, police brutality, resistance to desegregation, and assassinations of such leaders as the Reverend Martin Luther King, Jr., contributed to the eruptions. The Kerner Commission, which was commissioned to study the conditions leading up to the riots, concluded that "white racism" and discrimination were responsible for the outbreak of violence. Joseph S. Hines suggests in *Politics of Race* (1975) that African Americans have operated in a caste-like racial structure in the United States that has relegated them to inferior status, relative powerlessness, material deprivation, and

Discrimination has historically taken many forms, as when Birmingham police halted a peaceful march of African Americans protesting segregation in 1963 for parading without a permit—a charge unlikely to have been brought against whites marching to protest integration. *(Library of Congress)*

socio-psychic resentment. Segregation and discrimination have been used as mechanisms for maintaining the sociopolitical structure (status quo). Within this structure, African Americans are members of a racial category for life; they are generally consigned to marry within their group; they are often avoided, both as ritual and as custom; and they experience limited opportunities.

Discrimination remains embedded in the social, political, and economic fabric of the United States. Employment and promotional opportunities are still strongly influenced by race. Consequently, minorities typically earn only a fraction of what white males earn, they tend to hold political office far less often than their numbers in the general population should warrant, and they are still excluded from membership in certain elite clubs because of their race.

Charles C. Jackson

Core Resources

Hernan S. Cruz's *Racial Discrimination* (rev. ed., New York: United Nations, 1977), Joe R. Feagin and Clairece B. Feagin's *Discrimination American Style* (Englewood Cliffs, N.J.: Prentice-Hall, 1978), and Vernon Van Dyke's *Human Rights, Ethnicity, and Discrimination* (Westport, Conn.: Greenwood Press, 1985) survey various aspects of discrimination. Richard Kluger's *Simple*

Justice: The History of Brown v. Board of Education and Black America's Struggle for Equality (New York: Alfred A. Knopf, 1976) focuses on one of the central episodes in the history of American discrimination.

See also: Bigotry; Civil Rights movement; Discrimination: behaviors; Discrimination: racial and ethnic.

Discrimination: behaviors

Discrimination is perpetrated in many ways, including negative self-fulfilling prophecies, selective perception, avoidance of specific groups, denial of access (to jobs, housing, and the voting booth), tokenism, harassment, and violence. Many groups have been discriminated against in the United States, including women, Jews, Catholics, African Americans, Native Americans, Latinos, Asian Americans, Arab Americans, homosexuals, people with disabilities, people with mental illnesses, and the elderly.

Self-fulfilling prophecies are expectations that evoke behavior that makes the originally false conception true. Under this insidious process, the person who is the target of prejudice and therefore is expected to act or to be a certain way, responds to the prejudice by beginning to behave in a way that confirms the prejudice. For example, if an individual believes that all women are delicate and vulnerable, that person will tend to treat women this way, and women in turn will tend to act more helpless when interacting with that individual.

Selective perception, in which people's perceptions of the same incident differ, is another type of discriminatory behavior. For example, in one classic study, white college students watched a videotape of an argument between a white and black student. The argument grew heated, and in one version, the white student shoved the black student; in another version, the black student shoved the white student. White students described the white student who shoved as "playing around" or "dramatizing," but they described the black student who shoved as "violent."

Avoiding members of minority groups, even minor interactions such as making eye contact, is a passive form of discriminatory behavior that typically occurs in work, business, or recreational settings. It produces a subtle harmful effect by overlooking or minimizing the contributions of minority groups.

Another form of discriminatory behavior is denying equal access. For example, historically in the United States, fewer job opportunities have been available to women than men, especially at higher levels of government, business, and academics. Related to job discrimination is pay discrimination—women continue to receive lower pay for work similar or equal to that of men.

In tokenism, prejudiced people engage in positive but trivial or relatively insignificant actions toward members of a group they dislike. For example, a manager may make a token kindly gesture toward a minority member on staff (buying the person lunch at an expensive restaurant) or hire a minority member into a predominantly white work environment. Through this positive but insignificant gesture, the manager intends to avoid or at least delay more important actions such as promoting the individual or integrating the workplace. Having made this gesture, the manager feels that he or she has done something for the minority group. Tokenism has negative consequences for the minority member and perpetuates discrimination.

Discrimination can also take the form of overt actions such as harassment. For example, about 20 percent of women report that they have been sexually harassed on the job. In 1986, the U.S. Supreme Court ruled that sexual harassment violates civil rights, giving women a legal way to fight this behavior.

Aggressive behavior, which includes verbal abuse, vandalism, and crimes of violence, is another way in which discrimination is practiced. When taken to an extreme, this kind of behavior leads to intergroup warfare. It can also undermine the ability of members in diverse groups to interact positively and productively in their daily lives.

Lillian M. Range

See also: Discrimination: racial and ethnic; Tokenism.

Discrimination: racial and ethnic

Responding to racial and ethnic discrimination and conflict has been particularly challenging for the U.S. government, given the immigrant nature of American society and the long-standing commitment to the principle of equality before the law in the country's political culture.

Within the founding documents of the United States are contradictory statements on equality and freedom—and hence on people's right not to be discriminated against. The Declaration of Independence calls it self-evident that "all men are created equal" and have "unalienable rights." Yet prior to the Thirteenth Amendment (1865) the Constitution upheld the institution of slavery, notably in a provision that fugitive slaves must be returned to their owners. Any new country proclaiming equality while allowing slavery and thinking of an entire race as inferior is founded on an impossible contradiction, one that many of the founders undoubtedly realized would have to be faced in the future. Until the mid-twentieth century, however, the federal government generally avoided becoming involved in attempts to legislate against discrimination, allowing the states to establish their own policies. Many of the states, being closer to the people and their prejudices than the federal government was, were inclined to condone discrimination and even actively encourage it through legislation.

Discrimination existed in many different areas of life, including education, employment, housing, and voting rights. Two major pieces of legislation of the 1960's were designed to attack discrimination in these areas: the Civil Rights Act of 1964 and the Voting Rights Act of 1965. The primary avenue for fighting discrimination is through the courts, a fact which causes problems of its own. The Equal Employment Opportunity Commission (EEOC), for example, has the power to bring lawsuits involving employment discrimination; however, a huge number of charges of discrimination are brought before the agency. For that reason, as of the mid-1990's it had a backlog of many thousands of cases awaiting its attention. In discrimination cases the courts have sometimes applied a standard of discriminatory intent and sometimes relied on a standard of discriminatory impact.

Some types of discrimination are easier to see and to rectify than others. A number of activists and legal experts had shifted their attention by the 1980's to a type of discrimination generally known as "institutional discrimination." Institutional discrimination refers to discrimination that is built into social or political institutions, frequently in nearly invisible ways. Institutional discrimination is sometimes not even intentional.

Development of the American Nation   The framework for the development of the United States and its treatment of ethnic minorities was established during the first half century of the nation's history. When the American Revolution ended in 1783, there were few people in the thirteen colonies who considered themselves "Americans," as opposed to Virginians, Pennsylvanians, New Yorkers, and so on. Nevertheless, the people who joined under the Articles of Confederation had much in common. They shared a common language, ethnic stock, and history as well as a philosophy of government that stressed individual rights over group rights. Given time and interaction, one would expect these former colonials to develop a common sense of national identity.

To a substantial extent, that integration occurred during the nineteenth century via such common endeavors as the successful wars against the Spanish in Florida, against Britain in 1812, and against various Indian tribes. As people moved westward to the frontier, the conquest of the continent itself also became a unifying national purpose.

Yet a major challenge to the development of this emerging sense of national identity also arose during the nineteenth century. Between 1830 and 1910, while the country was absorbing new territory, approximately forty-four million immigrants entered the United States, mostly Europeans with backgrounds differing from the white Anglo-Saxon prototype of the founders. Moreover, the Civil War resulted in the freeing of millions of African American slaves, who suddenly became American citizens. There was also a trickle of immigrants arriving from Asia. Finally, there were Jewish immigrants, primarily in the Northeast, and Hispanics, primarily in the Southwest. The country's citizenry was becoming multiethnic and multiracial.

Native Americans   Adopted in 1789, the U.S. Constitution made Native Americans wards of the federal government. Treaties with the tribes, like all treaties, were to be federal affairs, and the Supreme Court has repeatedly affirmed the exclusive nature of this power of Congress (*Cherokee Nation v. Georgia*, 1831; *The New York Indians v. United States*, 1898). The Supreme Court has also repeatedly upheld the federal government's right to rescind—by ordinary legislation or the admission of new states to the union—those rights accorded the tribes by prior treaties (the *Cherokee Tobacco* case, 1871; *United States v. Winans*, 1905). Even the rationale for the guardian-ward relationship existing between the federal government and the tribes has been elucidated in the opinions of the Court. Essentially, it involves three elements: the weakness and helplessness of Native Americans, the degree to which their condition can be traced to their prior dealings with the federal government, and the government's resultant obligation to protect them. Few of the federal policies adopted before World War II, however, can be described as protective or even benign toward Native Americans.

Policies toward Native Americans traditionally built on the pattern of relations with the tribes established by Europeans prior to the ratification of the Constitution. For hundreds of years, the French, Portuguese, Spanish, English, and Dutch subdued the tribes they encountered, denigrated their cultures, and confiscated their lands and wealth. Early U.S. actions continued the pattern, especially where tribes physically hindered western expansion. During the 1830's, the concept of Indian Territory (land for the Native Americans territorially removed from European settlers) gained favor among European Americans.

When even the most remote of areas were eventually opened to European immigrants, the Indian Territory policy was abandoned in favor of a reservation policy: relocating and settling tribes within contained borders. Meanwhile, contact with European diseases, combined with the increasingly harsh life forced on Native Americans, had devastating effects on the tribes in terms of disrupting their societies and dramatically reducing their numbers. Beginning in the 1880's, reservation policies were frequently augmented by forced assimilation policies: Many young Native Americans were taken from their reservations and sent to distant boarding schools. There, tribal wear and ways were ridiculed, and speaking native languages in class could mean beatings. Only with World War I did these policies soften.

Significant changes in government attitudes toward Native Americans did not come until the Indian New Deal was instituted by reform-minded commissioner of Indian affairs John Collier in the 1930's. In the late 1960's, another chapter opened as Indians began to demand their own civil rights in the wake of the predominantly African American Civil Rights movement. More enlightened federal policies toward Native Americans began to emerge, and since the 1960's considerable legislation has appeared, including the 1968 American Indian Civil Rights Act and the 1975 Indian Self-Determination and Education Assistance Act. A number of factors have worked against Native Americans in advancing their own cause, among them the small number of Native Americans (less than 1 percent of the American population), the assimilation of their most educated members into the general population, and the fact that Native Americans generally think of themselves not as "Indians" or "Native Americans" but as members of a specific tribe.

Discrimination in Immigration Policy Fulfillment of the United States' self-determined manifest destiny to spread from the Atlantic to the Pacific Ocean required people, and early in the nineteenth century the government opened its doors wide to immigrants from Europe.

Yet even during this period, the door was open to few beyond Europe. Hispanic immigrants could enter the country fairly easily across its southern border, but American memories of Texas's war with Mexico made the country inhospitable toward them. More conspicuously, immigration policy was anti-Asian by design. The Chinese Exclusion Act, for example, passed in 1882, prohibited unskilled Chinese laborers from entering the country. Later amendments made it even more restrictive and forced Chinese people living in the United States to carry identification papers. The law was not repealed until 1943. Beginning with the exclusion laws of the 1880's, quotas, literacy tests, and ancestry requirements were used individually and in combination to exclude Asian groups. Indeed, even after the efforts during the 1950's to make the immigration process less overtly discriminatory, preferences accorded to the kin of existing citizens continued to skew the system in favor of European and—to a lesser extent—African immigrants.

Meanwhile, Asians who succeeded in entering the country often became the targets of such discriminatory state legislation as California's 1913 Alien Land Bill, which responded to the influx of Japanese in California by limiting their right to lease land and denying them the right to leave any land already owned to the next generation. The most overtly discriminatory act against Asian immigrants or Asian Americans was perpetrated by the federal government, however, which under the color of wartime exigencies relocated tens of thousands of U.S.-born Japanese Americans living on the West Coast to detention camps during World War II. The Supreme Court upheld the relocation program in *Korematsu v. United States* (1944).

It was not until the 1960's and 1970's, during and following the Vietnam War and the collapse of a series of United States-supported governments and revolutionary movements in Asia and Latin America, that the United States opened its doors to large numbers of immigrants and refugees from Asia and the Hispanic world. The government went so far as to accord citizenship to children born of foreigners illegally living in the country.

African Americans   Nineteenth century European immigrants generally were able to make the transition to American citizenship effectively. The urban political machines found jobs for them and recruited them into the political process as voters who, in turn, supported the machines. The prosperity of the country, manifested in the land rushes of the nineteenth century, the industrial revolution, and the postwar economic booms of the twentieth century, enabled the vast majority of these immigrants to achieve upward mobility and a share of the good life.

The citizens who were unable to fit into this pattern, apart from the reservation-bound American Indian tribes, were the African Americans. Enslaved in thirteen states prior to the Civil War (1861-1865) and kept in subservience by state laws and various extralegal arrangements for generations afterward, African Americans remained a social, economic, and political underclass with little expectation of progress until nearly eighty years after the Civil War Amendments were added to the Constitution to free and empower them.

The Thirteenth Amendment (1865) abolished slavery, the Fourteenth Amendment (1868) was designed to prevent states from interfering with the

Signs such as this were common before the Civil Rights Act of 1964 began to turn the tide against government-sanctioned racial discrimination. *(Library of Congress)*

rights of former slaves, and the Fifteenth Amendment (1870) constitutionally enfranchised African Americans. By the end of the nineteenth century,
however, Supreme Court opinions and state action had combined to mini-
mize the impact of these amendments. In the *Slaughterhouse* cases (1873),
the Supreme Court crippled the Fourteenth Amendment. The Court's
decision limited the amendment's privileges and immunities clause only to
those rights a citizen has by virtue of national citizenship, not state citizenship. Second, it interpreted the due process clause as a restraint only on how
a state may act, not on what it can do. Only the equal protection clause of
the Fourteenth Amendment, which the Court limited to issues of race,
continued to offer protection to the newly freed slaves, and in two subsequent cases even that protection was substantially reduced.

First, in the *Civil Rights* cases of 1883, the Supreme Court ruled that the
equal protection clause applies only to state action, not to private discrimination. Then, in the pivotal case *Plessy v. Ferguson* (1896), the Court held that
states could satisfy the requirements of the equal protection clause by
providing "separate-but-equal" facilities for blacks and whites. In the mean-
time, the states began to employ literacy tests, poll taxes, and other devices
and arrangements to restrict the ability of African Americans to vote.

Inclusion Policies   Between 1896 and 1936, not only did the separate-
but-equal doctrine legitimize racial discrimination, but also the Supreme
Court persistently sustained separation schemes as long as facilities of some
kind were provided to a state's black citizens—even if the facilities were
woefully inferior to those provided to the white community. In the mid-
1930's, however, responding to cases being appealed by the National Association for the Advancement of Colored People (NAACP), the Supreme
Court began to shift direction. Between 1936 and 1954, it began to demand
that states provide equal facilities to both races and to adopt more demanding tests for measuring the equality of segregated facilities. A Texas system
providing separate law schools for blacks and whites, for example, was ruled
unconstitutional in 1950 in *Sweatt v. Painter* because the black law school
lacked the "intangibles" (such as reputation and successful alumni) that
confer "greatness" on a law school and hence was unequal to the long-
established school of law for white students at the University of Texas.
Likewise, during the same period the Supreme Court began to remove some
of the state-imposed obstacles to African Americans voting in the South and
to limit the use of state machinery to enforce private acts of discrimination.
The separate-but-equal test itself was finally abandoned in 1954, when, in the
landmark case *Brown v. Board of Education*, the Supreme Court ruled that
segregated facilities are inherently unequal in public education.

The *Brown* decision led to a decade-long effort by southern states to avoid
compliance with desegregation orders. With the Supreme Court providing
a moral voice against segregated public facilities, however, these state efforts
failed when challenged in court. Moreover, a powerful multiracial Civil

Rights movement emerged to demand justice for African Americans in other areas as well. In response, Congress enacted such landmark legislation as the 1964 Civil Rights Act (outlawing discrimination in employment and in places of private accommodation), the 1965 Voting Rights Act, and a series of affirmative action laws designed to benefit groups traditionally discriminated against in American society.

As a result of these laws, the profile of the United States as a multiracial society was irrevocably altered. This change occurred almost entirely as a result of action within the country's legal and constitutional channels. To be sure, prejudice cannot be legislated away even though discrimination can be made illegal. In the mid-1990's, most American cities continued to possess a large African American underclass even as affirmative action and Head Start programs were becoming controversial and being canceled. On the other hand, the policies that had been adopted during the 1950's and 1960's enabled a sizable African American middle and professional class to develop, and many American cities had elected African Americans to govern them by the 1990's. It has been argued that the growing prosperity of a subgroup of the African American community undercut the power of the Civil Rights movement. By the 1990's, a number of successful and affluent African American leaders, such as Supreme Court justice Clarence Thomas, were themselves opposing further affirmative action plans as well as further efforts to finance welfare programs perceived as primarily benefiting a heavily minority urban underclass.

Joseph R. Rudolph, Jr., and McCrea Adams

Core Resources

For good short discussions of government policies toward Native Americans, see Edward H. Spicer, *The American Indians* (Cambridge, Mass.: Belknap Press of Harvard University Press, 1980), and Francis Paul Prucha, *Indian Policy in the United States: Historical Essays* (Lincoln: University of Nebraska Press, 1981). Immigration and discrimination is well treated in Nathan Glazer, ed., *Clamor at the Gates: The New American Immigration* (San Francisco: Institute for Contemporary Studies, 1985); Ronald Takaki, ed., *From Different Shores: Perspectives on Race and Ethnicity in America* (2d ed., New York: Oxford University Press, 1994); and Nathan Glazer and Daniel Patrick Moynihan's classic, *Beyond the Melting Pot: The Negroes, Puerto Ricans, Jews, Italians, and Irish of New York City* (2d ed., Cambridge, Mass.: MIT Press, 1970). Interesting works within the vast literature on the Civil Rights movement include Leon Friedman, *The Civil Rights Reader: Basic Documents of the Civil Rights Movement* (New York: Walker, 1968); Anna Kosof, *The Civil Rights Movement and Its Legacy* (New York: Watts, 1989); and Dennis Chong, *Collective Action and the Civil Rights Movement* (Chicago: University of Chicago Press, 1991).

See also: Affirmative action; Black Power movement; *Brown v. Board of Education*; *Civil Rights* cases; Civil Rights movement; *Griggs v. Duke Power*

Company; Heart of Atlanta Motel v. United States; Jim Crow laws; *Jones v. Alfred H. Mayer Company; Plessy v. Ferguson;* Race riots of the twentieth century; *Swann v. Charlotte-Mecklenburg Board of Education; Sweatt v. Painter.*

Disfranchisement laws in Mississippi

In August, 1890, the Mississippi legislature passed laws that effectively eliminated the black vote in the state.

At the end of the nineteenth century, Mississippi and South Carolina had the largest black populations in the United States. In 1890, fifty-seven of every hundred Mississippians were black. The Fifteenth Amendment to the U.S. Constitution (ratified in 1870) provided that no state could deny the right to vote on account of race; thus, Mississippi had a large black electorate. During the early 1870's, Mississippi voters elected hundreds of black office-holders, including members of Congress, state legislators, sheriffs, county clerks, and justices of the peace. In the mid-1870's, white Democrats launched a counteroffensive, using threats, violence, and fraud to neutralize the African American vote. After 1875, very few blacks held office in Mississippi.

By 1890, many politicians in Mississippi were calling for a convention to write a new constitution for the state. They complained that although only a small number of African Americans were voting, this small number could prove decisive in close elections. Many white leaders feared that black votes could decide close elections and worked toward a new constitution with provisions that effectively would disfranchise black voters. It would be difficult to draft such provisions, however, without running afoul of the Fifteenth Amendment.

The state's two senators illustrated the divisions of opinion that were so widespread among white Mississippians. Senator Edward C. Walthall argued against a constitutional convention, warning that it would only excite political passions for no good purpose. He felt certain there was no way to eliminate black political participation without violating the Fifteenth Amendment, and that if Mississippi made such an attempt, the U.S. government would show new interest in enforcing African American voting rights. On the other hand, Senator James George attacked the old constitution, claiming that it had been drafted by carpetbaggers and ignorant former slaves. George urged that the "best citizens" should now take the opportunity to draft a new state constitution. He warned that black voting could revive unless the state took measures to reduce the black electorate by provisions of the state's highest law.

A bill calling a constitutional convention passed both houses of the state legislature in 1888, but Governor Robert Lowry vetoed it, warning that it was better to accept the state's existing problems than to run the risk of creating new ones by tampering with the state's constitution. Two years later, a similar bill passed both houses of the legislature, and the new governor, John M. Stone, signed the law. Election for delegates was set for July 29, 1890. The voters would elect 134 delegates, 14 of them from the state at large and the rest apportioned among the counties.

The state's weak Republican Party (to which many African Americans adhered as the party that had freed them from slavery) decided not to field a slate of candidates for at-large delegates. In heavily black Bolivar County, Republicans did offer a local delegate slate with one black and one white candidate. In Jasper County, the white Republican candidate for delegate, F. M. B. "Marsh" Cook, was assassinated while riding alone on a country road. In two black-majority counties, the Democrats allowed white conservative Republicans onto their candidate slates. In several counties, Democrats split into two factions and offered the voters a choice of two Democratic tickets. As it turned out, the constitutional convention was made up almost exclusively of white Democrats. The membership included only three Republicans, three delegates elected as independents, and one member of an agrarian third party. Only one of the 134 delegates was black: Isaiah T. Montgomery of Bolivar County.

The Mississippi Plan   Delegates elected the conservative lawyer Solomon S. Calhoon as president of the convention and immediately set about their work. Convention members had no shortage of ideas on how to limit the suffrage almost exclusively to whites without violating the Fifteenth Amendment. Some suggested that voters must own land, which few African Americans in Mississippi did. Others favored educational tests, since African Americans, only a generation removed from slavery, had had fewer educational opportunities than whites and therefore were often illiterate.

As finally devised, the Mississippi plan for disfranchisement had a number of parts, the most important of which were a literacy test and a poll tax. Under the literacy test, the would-be voter must either be able to read or to explain a part of the state constitution when it was read to him. This latter provision, the so-called "understanding clause," was included as a loophole for illiterate whites. Delegates knew that voting registrars could give easy questions to white applicants and exceedingly difficult ones to African Americans. The poll tax provision stated that a person must pay a poll tax of at least two dollars per year, for at least two years in succession, in order to qualify to vote. The voter would have to pay these taxes well in advance of the election and keep the receipt. The tax was quite burdensome in a state where tenant farmers often earned less than fifty dollars in cash per year. Because Mississippi's African Americans were often tenant farmers, poorer than their white counterparts, it was thought they would give up the right to vote rather than pay this new tax.

The Effect   In a notable speech, the black Republican delegate, Isaiah T. Montgomery, announced that he would vote for these new suffrage provisions. He noted that race relations in the state had grown tense and that black political participation in the state had often led whites to react violently. His hope now, Montgomery explained, was that black disfranchisement would improve race relations and as the years passed, perhaps more African Americans would be permitted to vote. The new constitution passed the convention with only eight dissenting votes; it was not submitted to the voters for their ratification.

The new suffrage provisions went into effect just before the 1892 elections. The new voter registration requirements disfranchised the great majority of African Americans in the state; they also resulted in the disfranchisement of about fifty-two thousand whites. The new registration resulted in a list of seventy thousand white voters and only nine thousand African American voters. The predominantly black state Republican Party had won 26 percent of the vote for its presidential candidate in 1888; after the new registration, in 1892, the Republican standard-bearer won less than 3 percent.

Under the Constitution of 1890, Mississippi had an almost exclusively white electorate for three-quarters of a century. This constitution served as a model for other Southern states, which eagerly copied the literacy test, the understanding clause, and the poll tax into their state constitutions. Only after passage of new laws by the U.S. Congress in 1964 and 1965 would African American voters again make their strength felt in southern elections.

Stephen Cresswell

Core Resources

Stephen Cresswell's *Multiparty Politics in Mississippi, 1877-1902* (Jackson: University Press of Mississippi, 1995) discusses the drafting of the 1890 constitution and its role in limiting the success of the Republican and Populist Parties. Albert D. Kirwan's *Revolt of the Rednecks: Mississippi Politics, 1876-1925* (Lexington: University Press of Kentucky, 1951) remains the basic political history for the period before, during, and after the state's 1890 constitutional convention. J. Morgan Kousser's *The Shaping of Southern Politics: Suffrage Restriction and the Establishment of the One-Party South, 1880-1910* (New Haven, Conn.: Yale University Press, 1974) is a detailed explanation of how new constitutions in Mississippi and other southern states led to a homogeneous electorate, essentially a small clique of middle-class whites.

See also: Black codes; Civil Rights Acts of 1866-1875; *Civil Rights* cases; Fourteenth Amendment; Freedmen's Bureau; Ku Klux Klan; *Plessy v. Ferguson*; Reconstruction; Thirteenth Amendment.

Drugs and racial/ethnic relations

Because much of the drug trafficking and use in the United States involves ethnic gangs and communities and because the criminal justice system has been accused of disproportionately targeting certain ethnic groups and neighborhoods, the relationship between illegal drugs and ethnic background will remain an impassioned political topic.

Some of the groups involved in drug trafficking and consumption include majority (Italian American and Irish American) and minority (Latino and Asian American) ethnic groups, native-born (African American) groups and foreign-born (Russian) groups, and largely foreign-born minority groups such as Jamaicans. Nonethnic groups include motorcycle gangs and white Americans. Patterns of use and trade differ in the various ethnic and nonethnic communities. For example, white Americans tend to use powder cocaine whereas African Americans commonly prefer crack cocaine; Asian Americans typically prefer to trade in opium and heroin while whites usually deal in marijuana and amphetamines. Although these generalizations are essentially valid, exceptions of course exist. All of these trafficking and consumption patterns constitute illegal behavior, which inevitably results in the prosecution of many offenders. From the start of the war on drugs in the early 1970's, questions began to arise regarding possible civil liberties violations that occurred in the criminal justice system's zeal to win the war.

Caucasians and Drugs   No single ethnic or racial group completely monopolizes any particular aspect of the illegal drug trade; however, it is possible to draw broad boundaries within which particular groups specialize and control "market share." Caucasian traffickers can be divided into three major categories: La Cosa Nostra (commonly known as the Italian Mafia), found in all major metropolitan areas; the Irish mafia, especially the Winter Hill gang in the Boston/New England area; and the Russian mafia, which is most prominent in New York City (Brighton Beach) and Los Angeles (the Fairfax district). All deal chiefly in heroin, although cocaine, marijuana, and other illicit drugs make up an important part of their business. The Italian and Irish gangsters have been around for decades, the former being identified with organized crime to the point of stereotyping. The Russian mafia became a larger factor in the late 1980's after the collapse of the Soviet Union, which resulted in widespread open corruption in that nation and abundant migration from its former republics to the United States. Many of these migrants were members of, or drawn to, Russian organized crime.

The Russians, like the Soviets before them, obtain illegal drugs from the opium-producing nations of the Golden Crescent (Iran, Afghanistan, and

Pakistan) and have strong connections in the Muslim areas through which much of the opium and heroin pass on their way to Russia, from where the drugs are transported to Western Europe and North America, usually to New York City. Italian traffickers, who controlled the trade in opiates until the 1970's, also use Golden Crescent sources as well as those in the Golden Triangle (Myanmar, Laos, and Thailand). By the late twentieth century, Nigerian smugglers moved much of the opium from Asia and the Middle East to Europe, where Sicilian and Corsican traffickers shipped the drugs, usually from Marseilles or Amsterdam to New York City.

The majority of marijuana is planted by individual whites, principally in the rural parts of the American West or South and often on public land, largely owing to marginal incomes derived from the growing of traditional crops. A considerable part of methamphetamine production occurs in private white residences, though this enterprise is truly a cottage industry that knows no ethnic or racial boundaries. Street and motorcycle gangs distribute methamphetamines and other drugs.

Latinos and Drugs   Most of the world's cocaine is produced in Peru, Bolivia, Ecuador, Chile, and Colombia, and control of the drug's shipment to the United States is usually in the hands of cartels, either Colombian (Cali or Medellin) or Mexican (Tijuana, Sinaloa, Ciudad Juarez, and Gulf). The Mexican traffickers, who account for approximately three-fourths of all cocaine sold in the United States, became major factors in cocaine distribution when the U.S. government began to close off traditional points of entry for the drug in south Florida and the Caribbean in the late 1980's. The Colombian cartels farmed out distribution to the Mexicans, who moved the drug up the Pacific corridor. The Mexican cartels also funneled opium, obtained from Asian traffickers, from Mexico to the United States, where the illegal drugs were distributed by the Mexican mafia (composed of Mexican Americans and Mexican nationals), other ethnic gangs, and street dealers of all backgrounds.

Asians and Drugs   Asian gangs became major players in the drug trade during the last three decades of the twentieth century. Like Russian organized crime, Asian criminal activity grew along with migration generated by politics and poverty and tended to victimize members of the Asian American community. Asian organized crime became heavily involved in drug traffic by the 1980's, challenging Italian predominance. Of the numerous Asian gangs (Chinese secret societies, Vietnamese or Vietnamese-Chinese gangs, the Japanese yakuza) the ethnic Chinese groups control the lion's share of the drug enterprise, largely because they have connections throughout the world, particularly in Southeast Asia, where Golden Triangle opium is produced and shipped to Bangkok, where it awaits shipment to North America. Opiates are smuggled into the United States either from the south by ethnic Chinese gangs in cooperation with the Mexican mafia or from the north by Vietnamese-Chinese gangs in Vancouver, Canada, who carry contraband across the border into Montana and North Dakota.

African Americans and Drugs   African American participation in drug dealing tends to involve crack cocaine and street gangs, including the rival Bloods and Crips, which originated in Los Angeles and had established branches in many major urban centers west of Chicago by the mid-1980's. Jamaican gangs (also known as posses) originated along the East Coast and moved west, introducing crack cocaine to Kansas City, St. Louis, Dallas, and Houston by the mid-1980's. All of these gangs have been linked to extremely violent behavior, stemming partly from turf wars. The U.S. Attorney General's office has compared their paroxysms of brutality to the battles between legendary gangsters Frank Nitti and Al Capone. The office found that in contrast to these violent and visible gangs, many drug enterprises in African American communities involved "men and women who operated like successful business people with small or no criminal records."

Ethnic Groups and Drug Consumption   By the early 1990's, the war on drugs, especially the Just Say No campaign, had succeeded in making drugs less appealing, and drug use declined from the levels reached during the 1960's and 1970's but hardly disappeared. Among ethnic groups, Latinos in Los Angeles dipped cigarettes in PCP (phencyclidine, or angel dust), Iranian Americans smoked heroin, African Americans favored crack cocaine, and many ethnic groups consumed marijuana, which was gradually becoming more potent. White Americans also continued to use marijuana and other drugs, and LSD (lysergic acid diethylamide) enjoyed a resurgence among college students. By the late twentieth century, people were beginning to use drugs at a younger age, and the array of available drugs had grown significantly.

A December, 1994, *Los Angeles Times* series on crack cocaine focused on the drug's destructive impact on the city's minority communities. However, drug problems were hardly limited to poor, ethnic communities, as was pointed out in a late 1990's antidrug commercial. The spot began with the statistic "Forty-six percent of minors using marijuana are found in the inner city," then asks the question "Do you know where the other 54 percent reside?" as a young white in the suburbs skateboards up to a friend, who hands him a joint. In short, drugs cut across all racial, ethnic, income, and neighborhood barriers. One drug treatment executive put it this way: "When it comes to drugs, there is a complete democracy." Some communities and ethnic groups are clearly more negatively affected than others by drugs, which give rise to gangs, violence, illnesses, family ruptures, and job losses. However, the 1998 arrest, conviction, and lenient sentence given a Newport Beach, California, socialite for cocaine possession, the arrests of such movie stars as Charlie Sheen and Robert Downey, Jr., and the gang-related killings of musician Tupac Shakur and an undercover teenage drug informant for the Brea, California, police department demonstrate that drug usage and violence cut across racial, ethnic, and class lines.

Ethnic Groups and the Criminal Justice System   The question of whether the state and federal governments' antidrug activities violate people's civil rights finds citizens from all backgrounds—liberal and conservative, black and white, rich and poor—responding affirmatively and negatively. Those who believe that violations have occurred claim that the war on drugs gives government more power than is prudent, resulting in invasions of privacy (such as drug testing), needless confiscations of property, and misuse of the military to enforce drug laws (such as assigning military personnel to border patrol duty). Those who believe that civil rights have not been violated assert that these antidrug actions are both necessary and proper. In either case, the laws designed to stamp out illegal production, distribution, and consumption of illicit drugs need to be applied fairly, and many people maintain that a disproportionate number of minorities end up in the criminal justice system and, once there, are more likely to be convicted and more likely to receive harsher sentences. Critics note that under federal law, the possession of one gram of crack cocaine (favored mainly by African Americans) involves the same penalties as possession of one hundred grams of powder cocaine (the type used primarily by whites). They assert that this, along with the fact that since 1986 more than 97 percent of crack cocaine defendants in federal court are minority members, represents discrimination. The counterargument is that the wealthy can afford the legal advice that minimizes or eliminates encounters with the criminal justice system. A 1996 U.S. Supreme Court decision decreed that such disparities did not constitute unequal treatment. However, a *Los Angeles Times* editorial took issue, arguing, "These federal drug laws are not only unfair on their face but pernicious in their application."

Thomas D. Reins

Core Resources

The best introduction to debates surrounding late twentieth century drug problems in the United States is found in Neal Bernards's *War on Drugs: Opposing Viewpoints* (San Diego: Greenhaven Press, 1990), which devotes considerable attention to the connection between ethnicity and drugs. Physician David F. Musto provides the historical background to the War on Drugs in *The American Disease: Origins of Narcotic Control* (New York: Oxford University Press, 1987), which discusses racial minorities and drugs. Psychiatrist Thomas Szasz's *Ceremonial Chemistry* (New York: Doubleday, 1974) explores the drug issue as it relates to Asian Americans and to Malcolm X. Daniel K. Benjamin and Roger L. Miller recommend how to deal with users, dealers, and the criminal justice system in *Undoing Drugs: Beyond Legalization* (New York: Basic Books, 1991). Ronald Hamowy's *Dealing with Drugs: Consequences of Government Control* (San Francisco: Pacific Research Institute for

Public Policy, 1987) contains articles that scrutinize the nature of addiction, drug-related crime, and government antidrug activities. For a good picture of Asian drug activities, consult *Asian Organized Crime*, by the U.S. Senate Committee on Governmental Affairs (Washington, D.C.: Government Printing Office, 1991).

See also: Crime and race/ethnicity; Criminal justice system.

Dyer antilynching bill

After World War I, the National Association for the Advancement of Colored People (NAACP) sought congressional sponsors for federal antilynching legislation. More than three thousand people, mostly African Americans, had been lynched between 1889 and 1918. Of sixty-nine lynchings in 1921, 92 percent involved African Americans. In April, 1921, President Warren Harding requested that Congress pass antilynching legislation. Representative L. C. Dyer of Missouri introduced a bill that made lynching a national crime subject to federal prosecution and penalty. The House in January, 1929, easily adopted the Dyer bill, 220 to 119.

The Dyer bill languished in the Senate Judiciary Committee. Southern senators opposed the federal government's interference with the police powers of the states. The Dyer bill finally reached the Senate floor at a special session on the ship subsidy bill in November, 1922. The NAACP intensified its efforts to secure passage of the Dyer measure, sending senators a memo, signed by numerous professionals, urging adoption. Southern and border senators, led by Oscar Underwood of Alabama and Pat Harrison of Mississippi, filibustered the Dyer bill for a week. Republican senators at a December caucus abandoned their efforts to secure approval of the Dyer bill, clearing the way for Senate consideration of the ship subsidy bill. Other antilynching bills, including the Costigan-Wagner bill of 1935 and the Wagner-Gavagan bill of 1940, likewise failed.

David L. Porter

See also: Lynchings; *United States v. Cruikshank*.

Ebonics

On December 18, 1996, the Oakland School Board unanimously passed a resolution declaring black English, or African American English, to be "the genetically based" language of African American students. Public reaction was swift and remarkably explosive. *The New York Times* (December 24, 1996) declared that "black slang is a distinct language." The news media were filled with stories and editorials, and black English was the topic on numerous talk shows, serious and entertainment-oriented. However, the media largely ignored the findings of at least two or three decades of research done by sociolinguists about the structure of black English vernaculars and the learning difficulties experienced by children who speak black English, or Ebonics. This research was employed in the historic 1974 *Lau v. Nichols* U.S. Supreme court ruling, the passing of the Equal Educational Opportunities Act (1974), and the 1979 Supreme Court case involving black-English-speaking students at Ann Arbor, Michigan's Martin Luther King, Jr., Elementary School.

The Oakland board members used several terms for the language spoken by African Americans; however, "Ebonics" was the term adopted by the media and the public. The term "Ebonics" was introduced by Robert Williams in 1957 and is based on the blending of "ebony" (black) and "phonics" (sounds). Other terms such as "African American English" and "black English," which are used in linguistic studies, better capture the characteristics of this distinct American speech variety and its users.

There is some question as to whether Ebonics is a separate language or a dialect of English. Because the term "dialect" can be viewed as derisive, linguists prefer to use the neutral term "variety." Ebonics is a variety of English that is as distinct and as colorful as Irish English or Australian English. Ebonics has its own complex rules. For instance, an Ebonics speaker might say "She hungry" for the standard English "She's hungry," deleting the present tense of the verb "to be." The Ebonics speaker might substitute "Not no more" for the standard "Not any more," using multiple negation. Ebonics uses the word "be" to mean "sometimes" or "often," as in the sentence "She be tired," which in standard English is rendered "She is tired sometimes."

The rules that govern Ebonics are commonly found in many languages of the world. Therefore, characterizing Ebonics as structurally weak, somehow defective, or ungrammatical, or labeling it as slang is incorrect and reflects deeper social and racial problems in U.S. society. The Linguistic Society of America passed a resolution in January, 1997, stating that the variety of English known as Ebonics is "systematic and rule-governed like all natural speech varieties."

Ebonics is not a separate language, as first was claimed by the Oakland School Board and others. Proponents of Ebonics as a separate language claim that it has the vocabulary of English, but a grammar based on Niger-Congo or West African languages; however, this is incorrect. In spite of some structural differences, Ebonics much more closely approximates the structure and the lexicon of standard English than that of the West African languages.

Tej K. Bhatia

See also: Education and African Americans; Education and racial/ethnic relations; Equal educational opportunity.

Economics and race

Racial differences, especially in earnings and employment, are of ongoing empirical and theoretical interest to economists. Racial differences in labor markets are caused by demand-side factors, such as discrimination in hiring and pay, by supply-side factors, such as different levels of education and work experience, or by a combination of supply and demand factors.

There are many differences between members of various races in the sphere of economic activity. Differences appear in earnings, wealth, and income; employment patterns within and across occupations, industries, and geographical regions; unemployment rates; educational and job experience attainment; and socioeconomic factors such as family structure, crime rates, and life expectancy. In the United States, non-Hispanic whites have the most favorable economic status by all the measures listed above, while blacks generally have the least favorable status; Asians, Hispanics, and Native Americans fall in between on most economic measures. Unemployment rates are higher among nonwhites than whites, especially for the young. Whites generally earn higher wages and salaries and, therefore, generally have higher family incomes than nonwhites. Additionally, whites command a larger than proportionate percentage of national wealth, which includes investment income as well as earnings; they are disproportionately represented in the more desirable jobs such as the managerial and professional occupations.

Socioeconomic factors tend to compound the relatively unfavorable economic status of nonwhites. Nonwhites have higher average household and family sizes, so their smaller family income is divided among more people than is the family income of whites. Nonwhites are more likely to reside in female-headed households, which have lower incomes than do male-headed households.

Race and Income   The study of the role of race in determining income is a topic which can be approached from both the demand and supply sides of the market for labor. For example, measurement of earnings differentials by race falls under the areas of human capital theory and discrimination theory. Human capital theory, a supply-side argument, argues that a person's wages are determined in large part by his or her productivity, and that an individual's productivity can be increased by investment in education or on-the-job training; therefore, differences in earnings by race can be linked to differences in human capital attainment. Discrimination theory, a demand-side theory, says that the wages paid to workers reflect the preferences of employers, employees, or customers as to the race of the worker. In any of these three cases, the workers in the preferred group or groups receive higher wages than equally productive workers receive in the other, disliked groups. Discrimination may affect the acquisition of human capital as well as its effective utilization on the job. If nonwhites are denied full access to educational opportunities, then they will enter the workforce possessing fewer marketable skills than whites and will command a lower wage. Also, if a worker believes he or she is likely to encounter discrimination in the workplace, he or she may invest less in human capital than otherwise and earn even less than he or she would in the absence of labor market discrimination.

There are many other possible sources of racial differences relating to differential labor productivity and differential access to productive assets. Acquisition of English is a crucial step in achieving higher earnings for immigrants. Additionally, nonwhites who have strong networks of members of their racial group to tap for job opportunities will prosper relative to isolated nonwhites. Nonwhites may have imperfect access to capital markets because of discrimination by lenders and a lack of accumulated family assets.

A more controversial source of racial earnings differences is different valuations of labor relative to leisure for different racial groups. If one group has a relatively high valuation of leisure, this is reflected both in a high reservation wage and a lower probability of being employed and in a lower number of hours worked by those members of the group who are employed.

Programs and Effects Various policies have been enacted which attempt to influence either supply-or demand-side forces in order to lessen racial economic differences. The civil rights legislation passed in the United States in the 1960's attacked many forms of discrimination, such as segre-

In 1900 Booker T. Washington (seated, second from left) and T. Thomas Fortune founded the National Negro Business League to promote black enterprise. *(Library of Congress)*

gated schools. In such systems, white and nonwhite schools were separate but not equal, and the goal was to make a quality public education available to all races. Legislation attacking discrimination in hiring has been passed in an attempt to ensure that jobs are open to all qualified applicants regardless of racial origin. Job training programs targeted at nonwhites have been set up by private and public groups. Finally, affirmative action policies have attempted to counter years of hiring discrimination by setting formal hiring quotas for nonwhites in large firms and governmental units.

Much research has focused on measuring the effects of antipoverty and antidiscrimination programs. There has been an increase in the non-white/white earnings differential. Data from 1960 show an earnings differential for workers employed full-time (thirty-five or more hours per week, at least forty weeks per year) of 0.66, or 66 cents earned by a nonwhite male to every dollar earned by a white male; this ratio had risen to 0.80 by 1980. How much of this earnings increase can be attributed to the civil rights legislation passed in the 1960's and how much is attributable to independent societal forces is a hard question to answer, especially since discrimination can affect both investment in productive skills and the return obtained on those skills.

Another topic of continuing interest to economists is the effect of the minimum wage on minority employment. Black youth unemployment hit record levels in the 1970's and 1980's; if discouraged workers are included, then nonworking rates for black males can be as high as 75 or 80 percent in many urban locales. A question that arises is whether the minimum wage keeps employers from hiring some of these youths. It appears that rises in the minimum wage affect black workers, especially the young, disproportionately. If young blacks experience difficulty in their initial entry into the labor force, their subsequent work history may be altered unfavorably relative to a situation where they can enter a job which is low-paying but may lead to more lucrative subsequent employment.

Interest also focuses on assessing the success of various microeconomic policies, such as job training initiatives, which disproportionately serve nonwhites. Concern with the high nonwhite unemployment rates led to the use of job creation programs at the federal and local government levels in the 1970's. Researchers have attempted to determine if enrollment in a job training program improves earnings for participants relative to those not enrolled (or relative to what they would have earned without receiving the training). Generally, gains in earnings appear to be modest for participants.

Controversial Programs The extent of poverty among different races and the effects of welfare programs on racial groups have also been studied. One controversial topic is whether the Aid to Families with Dependent Children (AFDC) program created more poor black female-headed households than would have existed otherwise. Critics of AFDC argue that it encouraged poor young females to have more children out of wedlock than they would otherwise have had and to remain out of the labor force while receiving support in the form of AFDC benefits.

Another controversial topic is the effect of affirmative action policies on racial earnings and employment differences. While workplace race segregation has been declining over time, it continues to persist. Using the Duncan index to measure race segregation by occupation, researchers showed that in 1960, 45 percent of nonwhite men and 50 percent of nonwhite women would have had to move into white-dominated occupations in order to achieve workforce desegregation for each sex. By 1986, only 29 percent of nonwhite men and 26 percent of nonwhite women would have had to change jobs in order to achieve complete racial desegregation. While affirmative action programs combined with antidiscrimination laws appear to have increased hiring and promotion rates for minorities, critics argue that there may be costs in decreased productivity if less qualified minority applicants are hired instead of more qualified white applicants.

Comparative Studies   Government, through legislation and implementation of programs, has had a large influence on racial differences, and government agencies hire large numbers of minorities. Nonwhites tend to make higher hourly earnings relative to whites in the public sector: In 1960, the earnings differential in the public sector for nonwhite versus white males was 0.64; the private-sector differential was 0.79. This trend continued, although the difference narrowed: By 1980, the public and private sector differentials were 0.79 and 0.86, respectively. It is unclear whether these differences are the result of less discrimination in hiring and pay in government than in the private sector.

Another use of economic concepts in studying racial issues is to compare economic variables, mainly earnings, for different immigrant groups. The United States has experienced many waves of immigrants. While nineteenth century and early twentieth century waves of immigration were from Europe, immigration in the 1970's and 1980's consisted primarily of an influx of Southeast Asians and a mass of mostly illegal immigrants from Mexico and Central America. It is interesting to examine earnings differences for immigrant groups over time: A general pattern is that immigrants make low earnings relative to natives when they first arrive, and subsequently improve their earnings status; their descendants then make even higher earnings than did their parents. Whether newer waves of immigrants will experience this same pattern of steady improvement in economic status or will constitute a permanent underclass in American society is debatable.

Another puzzle for economists is why some immigrant groups prosper in the labor market relative to others. Asian immigrants, especially Chinese and Japanese, have higher earnings and employment rates than do other immigrant groups. An interesting pattern is that immigrant black groups, such as West Indians, have higher earnings than do native blacks. A large part of these differences appear to be attributable to the higher education of the successful groups.

U.S. Historical Patterns Interest in racial differences in the United States stems from two historical phenomena: the forcible introduction of a large number of blacks into the country through the institution of slavery, and the basic fact that the U.S. population has been fed throughout American history by large waves of immigrants.

The main focus on racial differences in the United States has been on black-white differences. Blacks comprise the largest racial minority in the United States and occupy a unique position in the historical legacy of the country as the only racial group to have been forced to enter the country in large numbers through the institution of slavery. Their pattern of assimilation into the economic mainstream appears to differ substantially from those of all other groups of immigrants.

There has been much debate about whether this unique historical position is responsible for the subsequent lack of success on the part of blacks to improve their socioeconomic status as rapidly as other racial groups, such as the Chinese and Japanese, have done. In the 1980's, several "neoconservative" economists, including George Gilder and Thomas Sowell, argued that social class is a more important determinant of racial differences than is discrimination. Other economists, however, including Thomas Boston, argue that class is the product of racial discrimination and, therefore, it is not useful to draw a distinction between class and discrimination as possible causes of blacks' low socioeconomic status.

While much research has focused on identifying the sources of economic differences between racial groups, many economic researchers are more interested in evaluating and improving social programs aimed at narrowing these differences. There are many issues revolving around use of appropriate methodology for achieving both research agendas. One basic problem is how to measure the relative contributions of labor supply and demand factors to an individual's wage rate. Another problem is how to evaluate a program by comparing participants to a control group's experiences: If the participants are not carefully matched to appropriate controls, results may be attributed to differences in the groups rather than the program's effects. Also, the widespread use of nonexperimental data to evaluate program effects is inherently problematic because so many influences occur simultaneously: Changes in the nonwhite/white earnings differential between 1960 and 1980 may have been caused by increased governmental antidiscrimination efforts, by erosion of prejudice in society regardless of governmental actions, or by increased productivity of minority workers. Ongoing debates over appropriate use of research tools ensure the continuing role of economists in the discussion of societal racial differences.

Joyce P. Jacobsen

Core Resources

Thomas D. Boston's *Race, Class, and Conservatism* (Winchester, Mass.: Unwin Hyman, 1988) aims to rebut the central propositions of neoconservative economists on the role of racial discrimination in black economic advancement. Robert Cherry's *Discrimination: Its Economic Impact on Blacks, Women, and Jews* (Lexington, Mass.: Lexington Books, 1989) covers black youth employment problems, black-Jewish relations, and the impact of social welfare programs. Ronald G. Ehrenberg and Robert S. Smith's *Modern Labor Economics: Theory and Public Policy* (3d ed., Glenview, Ill.: Scott, Foresman, 1988) contains an excellent chapter on the economics of discrimination. *A Common Destiny: Blacks and American Society* (Washington, D.C.: National Academy Press, 1989), edited by Gerald David Jaynes and Robin M. Williams, Jr., provides a comprehensive report on the socioeconomic status of blacks in the United States since 1940. Sar A. Levitan, Garth L. Mangum, and Ray Marshall's *Human Resources and Labor Markets* (2d ed., New York: Harper & Row, 1976) includes a clear description of the main economic theories of racial discrimination. Thomas Sowell's *Markets and Minorities* (New York: Basic Books, 1981) covers the experience of racial and ethnic minorities in America in various economic settings.

See also: Employment among African Americans; Labor movement; Poverty and race.

Edmonson v. Leesville Concrete Company

Thaddeus Edmonson, an African American construction worker, sued his employer, the Leesville Concrete Company, in 1988, claiming compensation for injuries suffered in a workplace accident. Edmonson invoked his right to a trial by jury. During the pretrial examination of potential jurors, the company's lawyers used their peremptory challenges to excuse two of the three black members of the panel. Edmonson asked the district court to require the company to provide a race-neutral explanation of the dismissals of the black panelists. Under *Batson v. Kentucky* (1986), racial motivation for juror challenges was held unconstitutional in criminal cases. In *Batson*, the U.S. Supreme Court had reasoned that the use of race as a criterion in jury challenges by the prosecution violates the equal protection clause of the U.S. Constitution. Edmonson's case presented the issue of whether such dismissals are improper in civil cases. The trial court denied Edmonson's request and, after conflicting decisions in the court of appeals, he appealed to the Supreme Court.

In 1991, Justice Anthony Kennedy wrote for the Court in a 6-3 decision holding that racially based juror challenges are unconstitutional even in civil cases. Because the juror challenges use the power of the government to select jury members, the discrimination becomes "state action" even though invoked by a private litigant. All state action must be consistent with constitutional rules forbidding racial discrimination.

Justice Sandra Day O'Connor dissented, arguing that only governmental discrimination is forbidden by the equal protection clause and that the act of Leesville Concrete's counsel was not state action.

Robert Jacobs

See also: *Batson v. Kentucky*; Jury selection.

Education and African Americans

Since the emancipation of the slaves in 1863, the debate has raged over the role of education and educational institutions in the African American community in the United States. After the Civil Rights movement of the 1950's and 1960's, the importance of an equal education and performance on standardized testing led the educational community to reevaluate the impact of education and its significance for African American students.

The Civil War (1861-1865), Reconstruction (1863-1877), and the Thirteenth Amendment (1865) ended slavery. Although free African Americans had attended schools in some northern states long before the Civil War, southern states had prohibited the teaching of either slave or free African American children. Emancipation in 1863 brought with it the challenge of providing educational opportunities for the freed men and women and their children, particularly in the former Confederate states.

In 1865, Congress created the Freedmen's Bureau to help former slaves adjust to freedom. The bureau continued to function until 1872 and, under the leadership of General O. O. Howard, established schools throughout the South. At their peak in 1869, these schools had about 114,000 students enrolled. The schools taught reading, writing, grammar, geography, arithmetic, and music through a curriculum based on the New England school model. A small number of African American teachers were trained in these schools, but the schools were usually staffed by northern schoolteachers, who brought with them their values, their educational ideas, and their methods. These white educators from northern states promoted the stereotypical idea of the kind of education African Americans should receive. Samuel C. Armstrong and many like-minded educators stressed industrial training and social control over self-determination. Many believe this philosophy was designed to keep African Americans in a subordinate position.

Washington to Du Bois   Booker T. Washington was the leading educational spokesperson for African Americans after the Civil War. Washington, who was born a slave, experienced the hectic years of Reconstruction and, in a speech delivered at the Atlanta Exposition in 1895, painfully articulated the outlines of a compromise with the white power structure, a policy later known as accommodationism. A student of Armstrong, Washington believed that industrial education was an important force in building character and economic competence for African Americans. He believed in moral "uplift" through hard work. At the Tuskegee Institute, which he helped establish in 1881, Washington shaped his ideas into a curriculum that focused on basic academic, agricultural, and occupational skills and emphasized the values of hard work and the dignity of labor. He encouraged his students to become elementary schoolteachers, farmers, and artisans, emphasizing these occupations over the professions of medicine, law, and politics.

Although revered initially, Washington has become an increasingly controversial figure. Some people say he made the best of a bad situation and

Facilities such as this southern schoolhouse for African Americans in 1939 made a mockery of the "separate-but-equal" doctrine in education. *(Library of Congress)*

that, although he compromised on racial issues, he can be viewed as a leader who preserved and slowly advanced the educational opportunities of African Americans. Critics of Washington see him as an opportunist whose compromises restricted African American progress.

W. E. B. Du Bois was a sociological and educational pioneer who challenged the established system of education. Du Bois, an opponent of Washington's educational philosophies, believed the African American community needed more determined and activist leadership. He helped organize the Niagara Movement in 1905, which led to the founding in 1909 of the National Association for the Advancement of Colored People (NAACP). Du Bois was a strong opponent of racial segregation in the schools. Unlike Washington, Du Bois did not believe in slow, evolutionary change; he instead demanded immediate change. Du Bois supported the NAACP position that all American children, including African American children, should be granted an equal educational opportunity. It was through the efforts of the NAACP that the monumental U.S. Supreme Court case *Brown v. Board of Education* (1954) outlawed segregation in U.S. public schools. Du Bois believed in educated leadership for the African American community and developed the concept of the Talented Tenth, the notion that 10 percent of the African American population would receive a traditional college education in preparation for leadership.

Post-Civil Rights Era   Du Bois's educational and political philosophies had a significant influence on the Civil Rights movement of the 1950's and 1960's. Out of the effects of public school desegregation during the 1950's and 1960's and the Black Power movement of the 1970's grew a new perspective on the education of African Americans. Inspired by historians such as Cheikh Anta Diop and Basil Davidson, educational philosophers such as Molefi Kete Asante formed the Afrocentric school of education. Asante and his followers maintain that a curriculum centered on the perspective of African Americans is more effective in reaching African American youth than the Eurocentric curriculum to which most students are exposed. Low test scores and historically poor academic records could be the result, according to Afrocentrists, of a curriculum that does not apply to African American students.

Statistics   According to *The African American Education Data Book* (published in 1997 by the Research Institute of the College Fund/United Negro College Fund), in 1994, approximately 43.5 million students were enrolled in public elementary and secondary schools, and nearly 5 million students were enrolled in private elementary and secondary schools. African Americans represented 16.5 percent of all public school enrollments. African Americans were underrepresented at private elementary and secondary schools, where they constituted only 9.3 percent of all enrollments. The number of African Americans enrolled in public schools declined as grade level increased, a finding that supports the evidence that African Americans leave school at higher rates than children of the same age in other racial groups. African Americans represented only 12.5 percent of those who received regular high school diplomas in 1994.

In schools made up primarily of African American students and located mainly in economically depressed urban centers, nearly a quarter of all students participated in remedial reading programs, and 22 percent participated in remedial math. By comparison, schools with less than 50 percent African American students had 14.8 percent of students enrolled in remedial reading and 12 percent enrolled in remedial math. Furthermore, only 87 percent of African American high school seniors graduate on time compared with 93 percent of non-African American seniors.

Test Scores   African American students have historically scored far below whites in geography, writing, reading, and math. The National Educational Longitudinal Study of 1988 reported that the average seventeen-year-old African American student had a reading score only slightly higher than that of the average white thirteen-year-old. Compared with whites, African American Scholastic Aptitude Test (SAT) takers had lower high school grade-point averages, fewer years of academic study, and fewer honors courses. Data collected by the National Assessment of Educational Progress, however, reveal that African Americans had registered gains in reading, math, and other subjects between the 1970's and the 1990's. Despite these gains, African Americans are underrepresented among high school seniors applying for college and represented only 9 percent of the college population in the 1990's (a decrease from 10 percent in the 1970's).

It is not surprising that many African Americans see no value in postsecondary education. Regardless of socioeconomic status or whether they had received a high school diploma, a higher percentage of African Americans who were eighth-graders in 1988 were unemployed and not in college than their white counterparts in 1993, a year after their scheduled high school graduation. Despite affirmative action legislation, African Americans still are less likely to be hired for a job when competing against equally qualified white applicants.

Socioeconomic Status   In both 1980 and 1990, African American high school sophomores were concentrated in the lowest two socioeconomic status quartiles. The proportion of African Americans in the lowest socioeconomic status quartile declined from 48 percent in 1980 to 39 percent in 1990. In both 1980 and 1990, African Americans were underrepresented in the upper two socioeconomic status quartiles. In addition, African Americans often attend schools with fewer resources in poorer neighborhoods of large, urban areas. Fifteen percent of schools that have primarily African American students have no magnet or honors programming, as opposed to only 1.6 percent of schools with a majority of white students. Also, a higher percentage of schools with a majority of African American students participated in the National School Lunch Program. The poverty level in the African American community is one of the factors believed to be responsible for consistently low scores on standardized testing. Along with poverty, the African American community has also experienced a greater amount of violence and delinquency among high-school-age youths. The homicide rate among African American men increased by more than two-thirds in the late 1980's, according to a study by Joe Schwartz and Thomas Exter (1990).

Parental Attitudes   Although much of the effort of public policymakers goes into integrating schools and creating more diversity in inner-city schools, African American parents seem more interested in developing a stronger academic program in their children's schools. A survey taken in 1998 by Public Agenda, a nonpartisan public-opinion research firm, showed that 80 percent of African American parents favored raising academic standards and achievement levels in primarily African American schools over emphasizing integration. Eleven percent of the parents polled said they would like to see the schools both integrated and improved. Of the white parents polled, 60 percent expressed a fear that discipline and safety problems, low reading scores, and social problems would result if African American students were transferred to a mostly white school. The Public Agenda survey demonstrates the differences in opinions on education based on racial background. For example, nearly 50 percent of African American parents felt that teachers demanded too little of their children because of the children's race. Despite the difference in opinion on these public issues, both African American and white parents expressed a great interest in their children's school success and the quality of their children's education.

Jason Pasch

Core Resources

A good introduction to the topic can be found in *The Encyclopedia of African American Education* (Westport, Conn.: Greenwood Press, 1996), edited by Faustine C. Jones-Wilson. *Issues in African American Education* (Nashville, Tenn.: One Horn Press, 1991), by Walter Gill, provides good background on the issues surrounding education. Booker T. Washington's *Up from Slavery* (New York: Doubleday, 1938) is a classic text on Washington's educational philosophy and life story. W. E. B. Du Bois's ideas can be found in *The Philadelphia Negro: A Social Study* (Philadelphia: University of Pennsylvania Press, 1899) and *Dusk of Dawn: An Essay Toward an Autobiography of a Race Concept* (New York: Harcourt, Brace & World, 1940). The Afrocentric philosophy is described in Molefi Kete Asante's *Kemet, Afrocentricity, and Knowledge* (Trenton, N.J.: Africa World Press, 1990). Statistics covering every aspect of African American education can be found in *The African American Education Data Book* (Research Institute of the College Fund/UNCF, 1997), by Frederick D. Patterson, Michael T. Nettles, and Laura W. Perna.

See also: Accommodationism; Afrocentrism; Atlanta Compromise; *Brown v. Board of Education*; College admissions; College entrance examinations; Employment among African Americans; Freedmen's Bureau; National Association for the Advancement of Colored People; Niagara Movement; Talented Tenth.

Education and racial/ethnic relations

Educational reform has been a focal point for improvement of racial and ethnic relations since 1954. This movement began with attempts to integrate the public schools and has since extended to the expansion of the school curriculum.

The purpose of educational reform is to improve the educational status quo. In the area of race relations, it has involved the push to integrate public schools. Some education experts suggest that integrated educational facilities are far more advantageous than segregated ones. In 1954, segregated educational facilities—historically associated with discrimination and racism in the United States, as made official with the U.S. Supreme Court's decision in *Plessy v. Ferguson* (1896) that "separate but equal" facilities were permissible—were challenged by the Supreme Court's decision in *Brown v. Board of Education* (1954). In the latter case, the Supreme Court determined that segregated educational facilities for African Americans were "inherently" unequal, placing black students at an educational disadvantage that they were unlikely ever to overcome. Although racial and ethnic relations were a major focus of educational reform even before the *Brown* litigation, the real push for school integration began only after *Brown*.

School Integration The 1950's witnessed massive social changes; chief among these was a renewed consciousness among people of color in general, and African Americans in particular, of their second-class place in society. Nowhere was this discrimination more evident than in racially segregated facilities, from public restrooms and restaurants to public schools. That segregation only echoed the deeper social and economic divisions between the races. In the wake of the *Brown* decision, however, the latter part of the decade began to witness a push for integrated schools.

Segregationists, particularly in the South, fought school integration at every step with a campaign of intimidation and delays called "massive resistance." At the same time, Cold War fears of Soviet technological superiority—which came to a head with the 1957 launching of the first artificial satellite to orbit Earth, the Soviets' *Sputnik*—spurred a drive toward the production of new math and science curricula in the schools. The goal was to produce more mathematicians, scientists, and engineers to combat the perceived Soviet threat. Conservative pressures to maintain the status quo therefore joined with postwar fears of a Communist takeover to mitigate against social equality in the classroom. At the same time, in the wake of *Brown*'s official denunciation of segregation, African Americans began taking bold steps to secure their civil rights: In December, 1955, Rosa Parks refused to sit at the back of a Montgomery, Alabama, bus and spawned the Montgomery bus boycott; in September, 1957, a plan to integrate a high school in Little Rock, Arkansas, was met by white resistance that extended to the level of Governor Orval E. Faubus, who resisted the entry of nine African American students with the National Guard. Racial strife would increase over the next years as the Civil Rights movement bloomed and liberal politicians stepped up their efforts to desegregate public schools.

Reform in the 1970's proved to be both prescriptive and reactionary. It was prescriptive in its call for more "effective schools" and reactionary as a strategy for helping to quell student activism during the period. Busing also emerged during this period as a controversial measure to integrate schools. Busing actually predates the effort to desegregate the public schools. For many years in the South, busing was used to facilitate segregation by transporting black youth to segregated black schools and transporting white students to segregated white schools. It became controversial when the federal courts decided that buses could be used for the opposite end—to bring black youth into white communities. Part of the controversy concerned objections that busing required extended periods of time traveling to and from school; however, given that such objections were rarely voiced when busing was used for purposes of segregation, many civil rights activists saw these objections as a smokescreen masking resistance to integration. Busing was the most feasible strategy for transporting large numbers of students and would remain the primary method for implementing mandatory pupil reassignment for purposes of desegregation.

A Nation at Risk?   The 1980's and 1990's witnessed a renewed call for the production of more mathematicians, scientists, and engineers. Much of this reform was initiated by the 1983 report *A Nation at Risk*. The report focused on what was seen as the failure of the public schools, the failure of public schoolteachers in their professional preparation and in their classroom instruction, and a prescription for strengthening the public school curriculum. In many school districts, many of the reform measures proffered by *A Nation at Risk* have been implemented. The number of academic core courses has been increased in high schools, teacher preparation programs at most of the major institutions of higher education have undergone restructuring, assessment tests at grades four, eight, and twelve have been implemented, and most public high schools have introduced requirements for computer literacy.

However, desegregation has not fared as well. Many school districts still remain segregated. Strategies such as schools of choice, magnet schools, and mandatory busing have all had varying degrees of success in the desegregation effort. Some school districts have been released from their obligation to enforce desegregation, a few because they had achieved a degree of "racial balance," particularly via magnet schools. The release for some, however, was not a function of successful desegregation but rather an artifact of white flight to the suburbs and to private schools.

White Flight School desegregation has therefore never been fully achieved. As the mandate to desegregate was issued by the federal courts, the incidence of white flight increased. Initially a movement of middle-class whites to escape the decay and dangers of life in the city, white flight turned into a flight to avoid desegregation. As a result, many inner-city white schools initially forced to desegregate became predominantly black and Latino over time. In some large urban districts, desegregation became a feeble attempt to reshuffle the remaining white students into predominantly black and Latino schools. In the late 1990's, more than one-third of the states had African American and Latino students attending schools with minority populations exceeding 65 percent. In Illinois, New York, and Michigan, more than 80 percent of the African American student population attended segregated schools; in New York, Illinois, Texas, and New Jersey, more than 80 percent of the Latino student population attended segregated schools. A number of school districts once considered desegregated have become resegregated. Additionally, some have developed "second-generation segregation," which involves the sorting of students into academic tracks based on ability grouping. Disproportionately, African American and Latino students are placed into the lower academic tracks (especially in special education programs) while whites and Asian Americans are placed in the higher tracks. This phenomenon occurs even in schools said to be racially balanced.

Curriculum Reform and Multicultural Education Beginning in the late 1960's and early 1970's, educational reform began to address racial and cultural differences not only through school integration but also through the curriculum. Much of this reformation emerged in the form of three new curriculum approaches: multicultural education, bicultural education, and centric education. Innovative and revolutionary, these new approaches have generated substantial controversies. Much of the debate stems from the fact that each approach makes race or ethnicity a focal point of the curriculum.

Multicultural education has been by far the most sweeping educational reform designed to deal with the issues of racism and discrimination. In the broadest sense, multicultural education is an extension of the Civil Rights movement, for the elimination of discrimination is not merely an issue of school attendance—of a black or Latino or Asian youth's right to sit next to white youth—but, more important, a struggle for equity in the pursuit of equality of opportunity.

Joel Spring argues that multicultural education programs have four primary goals: to build tolerance of other cultures, to eliminate racism, to include curricular content on other cultures, and to enable students to perceive the world from more than one cultural perspective. In their book *Multicultural Education: Issues and Perspectives* (1998), James A. Banks and Cherry A. McGee Banks suggest that multicultural education is not merely an idea but also an educational reform movement and a process. Its primary goal is to change the structure of educational institutions so that racial and cultural makeup, gender, and exceptionalities do not influence the opportunity to achieve academically.

In practice, multicultural education has taken a variety of forms, from the early grades to higher education, manifesting itself not only in choices to teach the culture and history of nondominant peoples such as African Americans, American indigenous populations, and Latino peoples but also to consider different interpretations of the causes of historical events and different evaluations of their outcomes. Even in science—and particularly with advances in the discipline of genetics—advances have radically altered nineteenth and early twentieth century explanations of racial and ethnic differences: Where once these were seen as a product of heredity, it is now known, for example, that variations in DNA (the genetic material that determines human traits, from eye and skin color to intelligence) are virtually identical across all groups of human beings and thus have no impact on their social, economic, and other potentials.

Bicultural Education "Biculturalism" literally means operating in two different cultures simultaneously. The premise of bicultural education is to implement educational strategies that help members of subcultures—such as African Americans, Asian Americans, Native Americans, and Latinos—to function in the dominant (Eurocentric) culture without having to forsake their own cultures. All too often, individuals from subcultures have been expected to give up their native cultures if they were to experience a measure of success in the dominant culture. Many successful members of subcultures have articulated resultant feelings of alienation—both from the dominant culture and from their own native culture. A bicultural curriculum is structured in ways to help subcultures deal with the effects of racism and discrimination. Learning styles associated with particular subcultures are integrated into the curriculum. In addition, the teachers and other personnel are recruited from educators possessing a certain attitudinal posture that helps rather than hinders learning among subcultures. Some researchers suggest that the bicultural education environment should be warm, should employ a greater latitude of interpretation with respect to written material, and should use the child's own language for initial instruction to achieve the most positive results—for example, Spanish for Latino students, native tongues for American Indians, and even Ebonics for African Americans when such an approach proves to facilitate learning.

Centric Education   Centric education is often also referred to as ethno-centric education. Supporters of centric education take a more radical position relative to Eurocentric education than either multicultural or bicultural educators. In predominantly Latino schools that focus on Latino culture, centric teachers often use Spanish during informal interaction with students. This has proven to ease the acculturation process. Latino-centered education has gained a tentative foothold in the southwestern United States, although by far the most controversial centric approach has been Afrocentric education.

Afrocentrists (advocates of Afrocentricity) argue that an Afrocentric education has major implications for both the lifestyle that many African Americans have chosen to pursue and the type of education that they desire for their children. Although Afrocentric education is considerably more radical than multicultural education, some educational scholars actually view it as a single-group study under the broad rubric of multicultural education. Single-group studies are said to provide students from subcultures with a sense of their history and identity and, more important, with a sense of direction and purpose in their lives. An Afrocentric curriculum includes units or courses about the history and culture of African Americans, focusing particularly on how African Americans (and other subcultures) have been victimized and on their social, political, and cultural struggles for liberation. Pedagogy is also predicated on the ways that African American youth learn best.

Impact on School Curriculum   Multicultural, bicultural, and centric education do not merely advocate for the addition or deletion of certain types of material but also challenge the very existence of the curriculum that has historically been used in the public school—and therein lies much of the controversy over these various modes of educational reform. Longstand-ing distortions about European American traditions, heroic figures, and culture are often exposed and open to criticism under the multicultural, bicultural, and centric traditions. Hence, these approaches, while valuing the cultures and contributions of people of color, have been perceived by some whites as concomitantly devaluing European contributions. Such a perception is generally false; most efforts at educational reform have as their goal the amelioration, not the aggravation, of intergroup relations.

Charles C. Jackson

Core Resources

James A. Banks and Cherry A. McGee Banks's *Multicultural Education: Issues and Perspectives* (Boston: Allyn & Bacon, 1998) provides an excellent description of the nature of multicultural education and the types of curricula that can be found under the multicultural rubric. Molefi Kete Asante introduced the term "Afrocentric" in his classic *Afrocentricity* (Trenton, N.J.: Africa World Press, 1988) and laid the foundation for the discussion of the centric perspective in education. Joel Spring's *American Education: An Introduction to Social and Political Aspects* (4th ed., New York: Longman, 1989) and *Deculturalization and the Struggle for Equality* (Boston: McGraw-Hill, 1998) provide an intriguing discussion of the educational struggles of dominated subcultures in American society, focusing on the historical struggles of African Americans, Asian Americans, Mexican Americans, Native Americans, and Puerto Ricans.

See also: Afrocentrism; *Alexander v. Holmes County Board of Education*; *Brown v. Board of Education*; Busing and integration; College admissions; College entrance examinations; Desegregation: public schools; Education and African Americans; Equal educational opportunity; *Plessy v. Ferguson*; *Swann v. Charlotte-Mecklenburg Board of Education.*

Emancipation Proclamation

The Emancipation Proclamation of January 1, 1863, extended the legal state of freedom to most American slaves.

Although the American Civil War (1861-1865) was the result of sectional conflict regarding the issue of slavery, both the Union and the Confederate governments initially denied that slavery was a war issue. The Confederate government claimed that it was fighting only to defend the principle of states' rights. The Union government claimed that it was fighting to preserve the Union of states against Confederate efforts to destroy it.

Lincoln's Cautious Approach to Emancipation   From the very beginning of the war, abolitionists, Radical Republicans, and black activists urged President Abraham Lincoln to use the war as an opportunity to strike down slavery. Lincoln, though, acted in a cautious manner in the early months of the war. Until September, 1862, Lincoln refused to include the abolition of slavery as one of the Union's war aims. Furthermore, when radical commanders in the Union Army ordered the emancipation of slaves in parts of the occupied South in 1861-1862, Lincoln countermanded the orders.

These actions caused reformers to question the depth of Lincoln's own commitment to antislavery. In Lincoln's defense, it must be noted that Lincoln both publicly and privately often expressed a heartfelt abhorrence of slavery. Yet Lincoln knew that a premature effort to turn the war into a

Decorated text of the Emancipation Proclamation. *(Library of Congress)*

crusade for emancipation would be counterproductive to the cause of freedom. An early act of emancipation would prompt loyal slave states such as Kentucky, Maryland, and Missouri to join the Confederacy and probably cause the defeat of the Union. From a practical point of view, the Union government could not abolish slavery in the South if it lost the war.

The Origins of Lincoln's Emancipation Policy

Lincoln was finally encouraged to seek emancipation because of the actions of the slaves themselves. During the war, some 600,000 slaves—about 15 percent of the total—escaped from their masters. Slaves understood that the advance of the Union army through the South presented them with an unprecedented opportunity for escape. Most escaped slaves sought shelter with the Union army.

The presence of large numbers of slaves within Union army lines presented Union commanders with the question of whether the slaves should be returned to their rebellious masters or allowed to stay with the army and use up its scarce resources. Most Union commanders allowed the slaves to remain with the army, justifying this decision out of military necessity. Pointing to the right of armies under international law to seize or destroy enemy property being used to sustain the war effort, Union commanders claimed the right to seize the Confederacy's slave laborers as contraband of war.

The actions of Union commanders shifted the focus of emancipation from human rights to military necessity, thereby encouraging Lincoln to adopt a general policy of emancipation and giving Lincoln an argument with which to win public support for this policy.

The Proclamation and Its Limits   Lincoln's Emancipation Proclamation, which was issued January 1, 1863, declared that slaves in areas in rebellion against the United States were free. Slaves in the loyal slave states and slaves in areas of the Confederacy already under Union control were not freed by the proclamation. Because of this fact, some commentators have criticized the proclamation, claiming that the proclamation had little impact because it sought to free the Confederate slaves who were beyond Lincoln's control and neglected to free the slaves within his control. This criticism ignores several facts regarding Lincoln's action. The Emancipation Proclamation amounted to an announcement that henceforward, the Union army would become an army of liberation. Whenever the Union army captured an area of the Confederacy, it would automatically free the slaves in that region.

President Abraham Lincoln *(Library of Congress)*

Additionally, the limited scope of Lincoln's proclamation was prompted by the limited powers of the president under the Constitution. Lincoln pointed out that, as president, his only constitutional power to emancipate slaves was derived from his power as commander in chief to order the military destruction of property that supported the enemy's war effort. Slaves belonging to masters in states loyal to the Union and slaves belonging to masters in areas of the Confederacy previously captured were not currently being used to support the enemy's war effort. In making this argument, Lincoln was not being evasive or cautious in seeking the emancipation of all American slaves. One month before he issued the Emancipation Proclamation, Lincoln proposed to Congress the passage of a constitutional amendment that would have freed all slaves living in the loyal border states and in currently occupied portions of the Confederacy.

The Effects of the Proclamation   In the end, perhaps two-thirds of American slaves were freed by the Emancipation Proclamation. The remainder of American slaves were freed by the laws of state governments in loyal slave states and by the Thirteenth Amendment (1865), which abolished slavery in the United States.

Harold D. Tallant

Core Resources

Slaves No More: Three Essays on Emancipation and the Civil War (Cambridge, England: Cambridge University Press, 1992), by Ira Berlin et al., LaWanda Cox's *Lincoln and Black Freedom: A Study in Presidential Leadership* (Columbia: University of South Carolina Press, 1981), Eric Foner's *Nothing But Freedom: Emancipation and Its Legacy* (Baton Rouge: Louisiana State University Press, 1983), John Hope Franklin's *The Emancipation Proclamation* (Garden City, N.Y.: Doubleday, 1963), and James M. McPherson's *Ordeal by Fire: The Civil War and Reconstruction* (2d ed., New York: McGraw-Hill, 1992) discuss the proclamation and its effects from a variety of viewpoints.

See also: Abolition; Civil Rights Acts of 1866-1875; Civil War and African Americans; Reconstruction; Slavery: history.

Employment among African Americans

African Americans have historically been discriminated against in both hiring and promotion. Race relations will improve as African Americans become more prominent in positions of high responsibility.

African Americans continue to be confronted with the historical factors that produce racial discrimination in employment. Three salient factors contributing to racial discrimination in employment are trends in historical antecedents, educational level attainment, and employment and unemployment rates. Much excellent scholarly research provides data on these factors. In James Blackwell's *The Black Community: Diversity and Unity* (1975) and Talmadge Anderson's *Introduction to African American Studies* (1994), the authors provide historical and empirical data that more fully explain these areas.

Historical Antecedents   The first African American laborers were indentured servants who were brought to Jamestown, Virginia, in 1619. From the beginning, African Americans were not afforded a level playing field in employment. The seminal work by John Blassingame, *The Slave Community* (1972), offers a very good account of this period. Because the contemporary notion of rates of employment and unemployment is not relevant for slave labor, it is not possible to compare the work of African Americans and that of whites during the period of institutional slavery in America, which lasted from the mid-seventeenth century through 1865, more than two centuries.

Following slavery, most African Americans were involved in farm labor at very low wages. The majority lived in the South and often worked as sharecroppers or day laborers. In the first quarter of the twentieth century, in an effort to escape the rigid de jure (legal) segregation that restricted their opportunities for employment in the South, African Americans began moving to the North in search of better jobs in record numbers. Finding themselves in the midst of the rapidly growing Industrial Revolution, African Americans began to acquire jobs that paid wages that far exceeded those they could receive as farm hands in the South.

After World War II, more African Americans acquired skilled and professional jobs. Although in the 1990's, the wages earned by African Americans are still below those of white workers, they have slowly but steadily increased relative to those of whites. According to the U.S. census, the African American median family income was 72 percent of that of whites in 1969. By 1993, that percentage had increased only to 81 percent. For female-headed households, the median family income has remained unchanged, at about 81 percent that of whites. It is this trend that best reflects an important relationship between the races in the area of employment.

Educational Attainment Levels   The most pervasive trend in African American and white employment is that the former has always lagged behind the latter. In both percentage of employed and earnings, African Americans compare poorly with whites. Analysis of employment data from the 1960's into the 1990's shows that African American unemployment rates were double those of whites. As reported by Claudette E. Bennett in *The Black Population in the United States*, the unemployment rate for African American men in 1994 was 14 percent; the rate for white men was 6.7 percent. In that same year, African American women were unemployed at 12.1 percent while white women had an unemployment rate of 5.5 percent. Two factors substantially contribute to this disparity: educational differences and discrimination in hiring and promotions.

Educational attainment is perhaps the highest social goal among Americans. It is generally believed that success in life, especially employment, is directly correlated to the level of education a person obtains. Since 1940, the disparity between African Americans and whites in educational attainment for grades K-12 has narrowed greatly. By 1990, the median years of education among the two groups was about equal. Although the percentage of whites having some high school (30 percent) far exceeded that of African Americans (19 percent), the percentage having completed high school for both groups in 1990 was 36 percent.

However, the percentage of whites with advanced degrees is nearly three times that of African Americans. The educational inequality at the post-high-school level places African Americans at a disadvantage when attempting to qualify for professional jobs. The World Future Society predicts that the average job in the United States in the year 2000 will require about fourteen years of education, and African Americans are predicted to remain behind. Some of the needed improvements in the educational system that will better prepare African Americans are offered by Charles V. Willie and Inabeth Miller in their book *Social Goals and Educational Reform* (1988). Additional proposals are made in the book edited by Gerald David Jaynes and Robin M. Williams, Jr., *A Common Destiny: Blacks and American Society* (1989). Some of the proposed remedies include improving physical facilities in urban and rural schools, providing equivalent educational resources for all students, improving teacher quality and teacher training, enhancing school-community relations, and hiring and promoting substantially more African American faculty and administrators.

Unemployment Rates   Two factors stand out in any description of the African American experience in hiring and promotion in the United States. The unusually high rates of unemployment (official and hidden) and a modest presence in senior management positions point to major disparities between blacks and whites. Hidden unemployment refers to those persons discouraged in seeking employment and those who are involuntary part-time workers. The National Urban League estimates that the hidden unemployment rate for African Americans may be nearly double that of the official reported rate.

Independent of gender, the unemployment rate for African Americans has continued to be more than double that of whites. This reality has held despite affirmative action, set-asides, and minority hiring policy programs. Similarly, the median per capita income for African American households and families has remained greatly below that of whites. Wealth owned by African Americans is less than 1 percent of that owned by whites. In the area of median worth of household, the U.S. Bureau of the Census reported in 1988 that African American worth was only 23 percent that of whites for families consisting of married couples. For female-headed families, African American families' worth was only 3 percent that of whites. Three times as many African American female-headed households live in poverty as those headed by white women.

Even within the corporate structure, African Americans have faired poorly. The federal Glass Ceiling Commission reported in 1995 that African Americans experienced disproportionately high resistance to advancement to high-level decision-making positions when compared with whites with similar education and training. Many of the experiences faced by African Americans in the corporate business environment are presented by George Davis and Glegg Watson in *Black Life in Corporate America: Swimming in the Mainstream* (1985). In a capitalist system in which employment and maximum fulfillment of human potential are vital to the accumulation of wealth, unfair employment practices have denied African Americans full opportunity to develop and maintain favorable conditions of wealth when compared with whites. With increasing national public policy that severely dampens affirmative efforts to level the playing field in hiring and promotion, the need for better education and employment seems less likely to be met.

Joe R. Feagin and Melvin P. Sikes argue in their book *Living with Racism: The Black Middle-Class Experience* (1994) that African Americans have been adversely affected by the racist hiring and promotion practices in the area of employment. However, most critical has been a failure of the nation to capitalize on an opportunity for a productive investment in African American human capital.

William M. Harris, Sr.

Core Resources

James Blackwell's *The Black Community: Diversity and Unity* (New York: Harper & Row, 1975), Talmadge Anderson's *Introduction to African American Studies* (Dubuque, Iowa: Kendall/Hunt, 1994), and John Blassingame's *The Slave Community* (New York: Oxford University Press, 1972) examine slavery and various historical factors that contribute to workplace discrimination against African Americans. Statistics on African Americans and employment are found in *The Black Population in the United States* (Upland, Pa.: Diane Publishing, 1995). Two books dealing with African Americans in the workplace are George Davis and Glegg Watson's *Black Life in Corporate America: Swimming in the Mainstream* (New York: Doubleday, 1985) and Joe R. Feagin and Melvin P. Sikes's *Living with Racism: The Black Middle-Class Experience* (Boston: Beacon Press, 1994). *Social Goals and Educational Reform* (Westport, Conn.: Greenwood Press, 1988), edited by Charles V. Willie and Inabeth Miller, and *A Common Destiny: Blacks and American Society* (Washington, D.C.: National Academy Press, 1989), edited by Gerald David Jaynes and Robin M. Williams, Jr., suggest education reforms.

See also: Affirmative action; Discrimination: racial and ethnic; Economics and race; Education and African Americans; Great Migration; Poverty and race; Quotas; Set-asides; Sharecropping.

Entitlement programs

In the United States, entitlement programs such as Old-Age, Survivors, and Disability Insurance (OASDI), Medicare, Supplemental Security Income (SSI), Unemployment Compensation (UC), and Temporary Assistance for Needy Families (TANF) embody the idea of the right to a minimum level of economic welfare and security according to standards prevailing in society. A question of fairness arises since contributors to and beneficiaries of such programs vary in race and ethnicity.

The Social Security Act of 1935 established a two-tiered system primarily of cash benefits. The higher-benefit tier comprised old-age insurance, more commonly known today as the Old-Age, Survivors, and Disability (OASDI) program, and unemployment compensation for the industrial labor force. The lower-benefit tier included two income- or means-tested assistance programs, Aid to Dependent Children (which became Aid to Families with Dependent Children, or AFDC) and Old-Age Assistance (later incorporated into the Supplemental Security Insurance, or SSI, program), which provided minimal support to those poor considered to be outside the wage labor pool. An examination of two programs, OASDI, commonly known as Social Security, and Temporary Assistance for Needy Families (TANF), the successor to AFDC, illustrates the relationship between race and ethnicity and entitlements; these programs challenge prevalent notions of fairness and, thereby, work against harmonious racial and ethnic relationships.

Old-Age, Survivors, and Disability Insurance   The Social Security Act of 1935 excluded agricultural workers and domestic servants—who were mostly African Americans—from both old-age insurance and unemployment compensation. More than three-quarters of African Americans, many of whom were sharecroppers, lived in the South in 1935, and the federal old-age insurance benefit of fifteen dollars per month would have provided more cash than a cropper family would typically see in a year. Because of southern opposition, the act was written so that agricultural workers and domestic servants were eligible only for means-tested assistance programs.

Although coverage was expanded to most of the workforce by 1960 and benefits were indexed to inflation and maximum taxable wages were indexed to future wages in 1972, pockets of old-age poverty remained, primarily among minorities and women. Although poverty rates among white males over age sixty-five dropped from 10.4 percent in 1972 to 5.7 percent in 1996 and among elderly women from 16.5 percent to 12.1 percent, the decline among African Americans, from 39.9 percent to 25.3 percent, still left significant numbers of poor black people.

Social Security also distributes costs and benefits unevenly. African American women are less likely than white women to qualify for a spouse benefit because only women who have been married for at least ten years are eligible. In 1970, 73.5 percent of white women aged forty-five to sixty-four were married, compared with 54.1 percent of black women; 20.4 percent of black women were separated, divorced, or had an absent husband, compared with only 7.3 percent of white women. Moreover, in 1970, only 39.5 percent of all married white women with a husband present were in the labor force, compared with 50 percent of married, nonwhite women with a husband present. Thus, Social Security taxes of black working women have historically subsidized the spouse benefits of white housewives.

Issues regarding the fairness of Social Security also extend to ethnic groups with high concentrations of working legal immigrants. Such immigrants contribute to the payroll tax that supports the present generation of retirees, but they are ineligible for future Social Security benefits (unless they become citizens) even though they might have the requisite earnings history. The Immigration Reform and Control Act of 1986 promoted family reunification. As a result, many Latinos and Asian Americans encouraged their able-bodied relatives to come to the United States from such countries as Cuba, the Dominican Republic, Mexico, Peru, Cambodia, Korea, Laos, Japan, and Vietnam. These ethnic Americans may be denied the economic protections of Social Security in the event their working immigrant relatives retire in the United States with little or no savings.

Temporary Assistance for Needy Families Temporary Assistance for Needy Families (TANF), formerly Aid to Families with Dependent Children (AFDC), was nearly federalized in the early 1970's and turned over to the states in 1996. In both instances, race and ethnicity played pivotal roles. Coming off the Civil Rights movement and related urban riots in the late 1960's, President Richard M. Nixon's proposed Family Assistance Plan (FAP) would have provided a federally guaranteed income for the working and nonworking poor. FAP sought to quell urban disturbances and decrease welfare dependency by providing incentives for African American men to become family breadwinners and for African American women to stay home with their children, while also paradoxically promising to encourage women on welfare to work more.

In effect, however, FAP would have nearly tripled the welfare rolls and would have had its greatest impact on the South. In 1971, about ten million people were AFDC recipients; FAP would have made twenty-eight million people eligible for assistance. Overall, 52 percent of those covered by FAP would have been southerners and two-thirds of poor African Americans in the South would have received some payment. Because family size determined benefit levels, FAP would have doubled or tripled household incomes. It would also have increased wage levels to nearly triple a farm laborer's income. Southerners joined members of organized labor, who opposed the FAP requirement of working at jobs paying the prevailing rather than the minimum wage, and welfare mothers, who thought the FAP benefit too low, to defeat the measure in the Senate in 1972.

Between the 1970's and 1990's, an increasing proportion of welfare benefits went to young, single mothers. Trends in out-of-wedlock births were such that in 1993, white illegitimacy rates approached 24 percent, close to the rate that led many in the 1960's to believe that the black family was near collapse, and the black illegitimacy rate was 69 percent. In addition, by the early 1990's, immigrant welfare participation was, on average, higher than that of native-born Americans—9.1 percent versus 7.4 percent respectively. Some Latino and Asian immigrant groups used welfare at a rate far above that of American-born blacks (13.5 percent). Dominican and Cuban immigrants had welfare rates of 27.9 percent and 16.0 percent respectively, and Cambodian and Laotian immigrants had rates of 48.8 and 46.3 percent respectively.

Most white Americans came to see welfare recipients not as equal citizens with justifiable needs but increasingly as the undeserving poor and began to view welfare not as deserved support for the needy but as handouts for shirkers. By the mid-1990's, the political climate regarding the role of government had changed so that increased reliance on market forces eclipsed income maintenance and other interventionist strategies designed to ensure a modicum of income equality and economic well-being. Over the objection of many African American and ethnic congressional leaders, the Personal Responsibility and Work Opportunity Reconciliation Act of 1996 ended the federal mandate for welfare and set a five-year outside limit on the amount of time a family could receive cash assistance. In addition, the law barred future legal immigrants from receiving food stamps, Medicaid, disability benefits, and most other forms of federally funded social services for the first five years they were in the country. Because of their disproportionate participation in these programs, poor African American, Latino, and Asian American women and their children were thought to be most adversely affected by the legislation.

Richard K. Caputo

Core Resources

Increased racial tensions associated with the politics of entitlement programs are addressed in Richard K. Caputo's *Welfare and Freedom American Style II: The Role of the Federal Government, 1941-1980* (Lanham, Md.: University Press of America, 1994), Jill Quadagno's *The Color of Welfare: How Racism Undermined the War on Poverty* (New York: Oxford University Press, 1994), and Linda Faye Williams's "Race and the Politics of Social Policy" in *The Social Divide: Political Parties and the Future of Activist Government*, edited by Margaret Weir (Washington, D.C.: Russell Sage Foundation, 1998). Ethnicity and entitlements are discussed in Peter Brimelow's *Alien Nation* (New York: Random House, 1995) and Robert Suro's *Strangers Among Us* (New York: Alfred A. Knopf, 1998). William Julius Wilson's *The Truly Disadvantaged: The Inner City, the Underclass, and Public Policy* (Chicago: University of Chicago Press, 1987) is a benchmark study in the relationship between race and public policy. The Urban League Web site, which follows social policy legislation bearing on race relations, can be found on the Internet at www.urban.org.

See also: Aid to Families with Dependent Children; Poverty and race; Welfare reform: impact on racial/ethnic relations; Welfare's impact on racial/ethnic relations.

Environmental racism

Environmental racism is the disproportionately high allocation of environmental disease factors to underprivileged racial and ethnic groups through biased public policy and industrial practices associated with urban and regional planning or environmental design.

Activist Benjamin Chavis is credited with coining the phrase "environmental racism" in 1987 during a demonstration against the placing of a toxic-waste landfill in an African American community in Warren County, North Carolina. The systematic segregation of neighborhoods by race and ethnicity enables governments and other agencies to practice environmental racism. The economic and political inequalities that arise from such segregation create impoverished regions with lower environmental awareness and little political power. This makes it easy for governments and businesses to choose these regions as places to locate externalities of industrial development that are likely to have a harmful effect on the environment. Three specific biases—remediation, situational, and judicial—are evident in environmental racism.

Remediation bias leads to the preferential cleanup of pollutants from an area inhabited by white Americans while polluted areas in minority communities are left untouched. An often-cited example of remediation bias is the case involving the Anacostia and Potomac Rivers in the Washington, D.C., region. More than one billion dollars was spent to clean the Potomac, which travels along white neighborhoods, but no efforts were made to clean the equally polluted Anacostia, which flows through African American neighborhoods.

Situational bias is the location of industries known to produce hazardous environmental pollutants, such as incinerators and landfills, in neighborhoods inhabited by minority races and ethnic groups. For example, Kettleman City, California, a community that is 95 percent Latino, is home to the largest toxic-waste dump in the western United States. Despite the already heavy burden of environmental pollution from agricultural chemicals and toxic industrial waste, Chemical Waste Management proposed building a new toxic waste incinerator in the city in 1988. The local county government approved the plan on the basis of a 1,000-page environmental impact report that was not accessible to the general population and without direct consultation with any of the area's residents until a lawsuit was filed to remedy the situation.

Judicial bias causes polluters of environments occupied by white Americans to suffer significant punitive repercussions, while those who pollute areas occupied by racial minorities and ethnic groups receive no punishment or only minor penalties. Studies have found that companies found guilty under existing hazardous-waste laws suffer 500 percent more severe penalties at sites populated by white Americans than at sites populated by minority groups. This leads to the perception that the threat of punitive action deters polluters only in predominantly white neighborhoods, leading to further resistance against integration of residential areas. Another form of judicial bias affects Native American communities. In 1986, the Western Shoshone National Council began to contest the authority of the United States to use the Nevada test site, which includes the southern Newah homelands, for explosion of nuclear weapons and other hazardous bombs. The U.S. Department of Energy sponsored proposals to build nuclear waste dumps within Shoshone lands without Newah permission. Cases involving Native Americans are often complication by the question of who has jurisdiction over the affected regions.

Environmental racism can be reduced or eliminated through political empowerment of minority communities and vigilant activism by community organizations. The establishment of a national center to approve proposed sites for pollution-prone industries would nullify tendencies toward environmental racism fostered by biases in regional politics.

Oladele A. Ogunseitan

See also: Criminal justice system; Discrimination: racial and ethnic; Racism: changing nature of.

Equal educational opportunity

"Equal educational opportunity" refers to the right of everyone to receive an equal chance for access to a good education, not to an "equal" education. The latter is impracticable; the former, if not completely achievable, can be approximated and, to the extent it is achieved, can ameliorate intergroup relations.

Americans have long believed that schools could solve most social problems. Schools were used to Americanize immigrants during the latter part of the nineteenth century and the early part of the twentieth century. They were viewed as the most appropriate institution for fighting childhood diseases and combating the advantage that the Soviets had in aerospace technology during the 1950's. During the 1960's, schools were the point of entry into fighting the War on Poverty. In the 1970's, schools were seen as instruments in solving the problem of unemployment. Schools, in the 1980's, were perceived as instruments to help the United States increase its competitiveness in global markets. Essentially, in each decade since World War II the schools have been expected to solve one or more social problems. Above all, schools have been expected to provide equal educational opportunity.

Definitions   "Equal educational opportunity" has been assigned a variety of meanings by a number of educational scholars. It is complex; its meaning often shifts, depending on the context in which it is used. According to Charles A. Tesconi, Jr., and Emanuel Hurwitz, Jr., in their book *Education for Whom? The Question of Equal Educational Opportunity* (1974), "equal educational opportunity" does not describe a state of affairs but suggests what ought to be—what should be, or what is desirable. Joel Spring, in *American Education: An Introduction to Social and Political Aspects* (1989), contends that equal educational opportunity cannot be achieved. The best that can be offered is the opportunity to an education. Factors such as intellectual ability, social class, and property value within specific school districts all affect access to education and the quality of education received. Consequently, the argument persists that the only way to approximate equal educational opportunity is to equalize educational "input": Equalization in access, curricula, facilities, staff, administration, and management must be approximated across schools. Conversely, if some schools provide significantly less in terms of facilities, staff, or curricular offerings, students attending such schools do not receive equal educational opportunity. These issues have prompted litigation, by poor school districts in many areas of the United States, which challenges traditional methods of financing schools. The assumption is that equalizing funding will help foster greater equal educational opportunity.

A different approach emphasizes educational "output," which is at odds with educational "input." Proponents of this approach hold that equal educational opportunity must be measured by how well students demonstrate achievement in school. Such a position maintains that whatever mechanisms (resources, staffs, or facilities) are necessary to assist primarily lowerincome and minority students to achieve should be utilized in the effort to equalize educational opportunity. There is a prescriptive function to the notion of educational output. Educational output arguably could be viewed as the approach upon which the compensatory programs and legislation of the 1960's and 1970's were premised, including the Vocational Education Act of 1963, the Civil Rights Act of 1964, the Economic Opportunity Act of

Resolving the question of what constitutes equality of educational opportunity was a major stumbling block in the drive to desegregate schools and colleges. *(Library of Congress)*

1964, the 1965 revision of the National Defense Education Act, the Elementary and Secondary Education Act of 1965, Public Law 93-380 of 1974, and Public Law 94-142 of 1975.

School Desegregation   The concept of equal educational opportunity was the basis upon which African Americans, through the National Association for the Advancement of Colored People (NAACP), were able to argue successfully before the Supreme Court (*Brown v. Board of Education of Topeka, Kansas,* 1954) to end the system of segregated schools in the South. The Supreme Court affirmed that racially identifiable African American schools did not provide equal educational opportunity. Chief Justice Earl Warren argued in the unanimous opinion of the Supreme Court that to separate black children from white children solely on the basis of race not only was unconstitutional discrimination but could generate a feeling of inferiority as well—one that might affect the hearts and minds of black children in ways unlikely ever to be undone. While the implementation of the mandate to desegregate the public schools in the South was delayed (in some instances by more than sixteen years), de jure segregation was constitutionally ended with the *Brown* decision. Still, desegregation of the public schools was only the first step in the effort to achieve equal educational opportunity for all.

Segregated schools were viewed as responsible not only for the disparity in facilities, the lower level of curricular offerings, and the overall lower qualifications of school personnel which were characteristic of black schools but also for the disparities in academic achievement between black and white students. Such beliefs contributed to an already growing body of research suggesting that minority students were culturally disadvantaged, or culturally deprived. Investigation into the beliefs and causes of the lower academic achievement of minorities (especially on standardized and IQ tests) became known as "deficit theory" research and functioned as the driving force behind many of the compensatory education programs of the 1960's and 1970's.

Many of the strategies suggested for remedying low academic achievement by African Americans (and poor students in general) were premised on deficit theory. Deficit theory inferred that the child, the family, or the culture of the child (which was much more palatable) made that child socially and intellectually unprepared for success in school. Arthur K. Spears, in "Institutionalized Racism and the Education of Blacks" (in *Readings on Equal Education*, 1984), later suggested that deficit theory was, in practice, more damaging than helpful because it failed to focus attention on the structural problems in public education. Nevertheless, much of the educational and social policy during the 1960's and 1970's looked to deficit theory to help explain educational, social, economic, and even political inequality. Beginning in the 1960's, educational policy began to address the perceived deficiencies of specific populations through compensatory education and early intervention programs.

The Coleman Report   One of the principal components of the 1964 Civil Rights Act was a call for the investigation into the suspected racial inequalities in educational opportunities. Researchers led by James Coleman collected data from approximately 60,000 teachers and approximately 570,000 students. The research findings suggested that social class background accounted for the variation in black and white academic achievement. Given that a significantly greater proportion of African Americans come from lower-class backgrounds than do whites, this fact was proposed as the rationale for their lower academic achievement. Based on this research, many social scientists and educators began to suggest that the minorities themselves were not intellectually deficient, as some earlier scientists had argued, but that these groups suffered from "cultural deprivation." Their homes, families, neighborhoods, and in general their culture made them disadvantaged. The solution proffered by some social reformers was early intervention programs and compensatory education. Early intervention programs, it was argued, would give disadvantaged youth a "head start" in preparation to enter school. Such programs would provide the proper cultural exposure and the intellectual stimulation missing from the child's normal environment. Compensatory education would provide the remediation (of skills and knowledge) for students already in school.

The War on Poverty   The Coleman Report (*Equality of Educational Opportunity*, 1966), along with liberal advocates (in and out of education), had a tremendous impact on U.S. education policy. President Lyndon B. Johnson initiated one of the most comprehensive domestic campaigns in U.S. history to eradicate poverty. Referred to as the War on Poverty, it was proclaimed to end poverty and inequality by destroying the "cycle of poverty" that tended to entrap the poor, generation after generation. Poor housing, inadequate health care, poor diet, and inequality of educational opportunity were thought to contribute to the cycle of poverty. Education was, by far it was thought, the most critical component in the cycle. If a link in the cycle were ever to be broken, it would best be accomplished through education.

Most of the educational programs created as a result of the War on Poverty were unsuccessful. Some proponents argued that inadequate funding and mismanagement were the reasons the programs failed to live up to expectations. A number of opponents argued that the programs were ill-conceived and were doomed to failure because they could not change the home environment of the child. One program, however—Head Start—did prove to be somewhat successful and has continued to assist low-income, pre-elementary youth in preparation for school.

Charles C. Jackson

Core Resources

Equality of Educational Opportunity (Washington, D.C.: U.S. Government Printing Office, 1966), by James S. Coleman et al. (the Coleman Report), had far-reaching ramifications regarding public opinion and government policy. John U. Ogbu's "Class Stratification, Racial Stratification, and Schooling," in *Class, Race, and Gender in American Education*, edited by Lois Weis (Albany: State University of New York Press, 1988), demonstrates the relationship between race and class stratification in schooling in America. Myra P. Sadker and David M. Sadker's *Teachers, Schools, and Society* (2d ed., New York: McGraw-Hill, 1991) details the barriers that minorities have encountered in attempting to achieve equal educational opportunity. Joel Spring's *American Education: An Introduction to Social and Political Aspects* (4th ed., New York: Longman, 1989) gives an excellent overview of the forces that affect equal educational opportunity. Charles A. Tesconi, Jr., and Emanuel Hurwitz, Jr.'s *Education for Whom? The Question of Equal Educational Opportunity* (New York: Dodd, Mead, 1974) takes a dialectical approach to the issue.

See also: *Brown v. Board of Education*; Education and African Americans; Education and racial/ethnic relations; Equality of opportunity; *Plessy v. Ferguson*.

Equal Employment Opportunity Act

The Equal Employment Opportunity Act, which became law March 24, 1972, stipulated that government agencies and educational institutions could not discriminate in hiring, firing, promotion, compensation, and admission to training programs; it also allowed the Equal Employment Opportunity Commission (EEOC) to bring discrimination lawsuits directly rather than referring them to the attorney general.

Equal employment opportunity issues emerged in the 1960's as a result of changes in societal values, the changing economic status of women and minorities, and the emerging role of government regulation in the area of civil rights. The enactment of the 1964 Civil Rights Act occurred at a time when African Americans were fighting for equal treatment and protection under the law with respect to voting rights, employment, fair housing, and better educational facilities. A provision of this act was the prohibition of discriminatory hiring practices on the basis of race, color, religion, sex, or national origin. The 1964 act, however, lacked major enforcement and punishment provisions. It also failed to include all aspects of employment within government, labor, and the private sector. Almost ten years after the passage of the Civil Rights Act of 1964, Congress was lobbied to provide amendments to the act which would enhance employment opportunities for minorities.

The passage of the Equal Employment Opportunity (EEO) Act of 1972 amended Title VII of the Civil Rights Act of 1964 by expanding the protection of individuals with regard to hiring, firing, promoting, and other human resource functions to all persons without regard to race, color, religion, sex, or national origin. The EEO Act strengthened the enforcement powers of the 1964 Civil Rights Act by allowing individuals who believed that they were being discriminated against to file suit in court for legal recourse to remedy the discriminatory employment practices.

The EEO Act of 1972 tied previous employment legislation (the Civil Rights Act of 1964, Executive Order 11246 of 1964, and the Intergovernmental Personnel Act of 1970) together and required federal and state agencies, government subcontractors, small businesses with more than fifteen employees, and labor organizations to establish affirmative action programs to remedy past discriminatory practices and to prevent future discriminatory employment problems.

Donna Echols Mabus

See also: Affirmative action; Civil Rights Act of 1964; Equal Employment Opportunity Commission; Equality of opportunity; *Griggs v. Duke Power Company.*

Equal Employment Opportunity Commission

Created by the Civil Rights Act of 1964, the Equal Employment Opportunity Commission (EEOC) takes an active role in monitoring workplace compliance with civil rights legislation; it investigates complaints of discrimination based on race, ethnicity, sex, age, religion, national origin, or disability. The increasing numbers of cases being brought under the Civil Rights Acts of 1866 and 1871 and the Fourteenth Amendment in the 1950's and 1960's encouraged passage of the Civil Rights Act of 1964 to provide protection for workers against discrimination in the workplace. The Equal Employment Opportunity Commission (EEOC) was created to investigate complaints and to provide legal remedy to those victimized.

Initially, the EEOC focused on cases of racial discrimination in the private sector. The landmark Supreme Court decision in *Griggs v. Duke Power Company* forced employers to show the job-relatedness of employment requirements. In 1972, the Civil Rights Act of 1964 was amended to include the public sector as well as the private. Affirmative action programs were created during the 1960's and 1970's, and the EEOC monitored their implementation and operation. EEOC regulatory efforts were very broadly focused and, through consolidation of complaints into class actions, the agency was able to address broad categories of discrimination.

Judicial interpretation of the Civil Rights Act of 1964 expanded the focus of the commission to include sex discrimination and sexual harassment cases. EEOC guidelines addressed issues such as sex-based job classifications ("pink collar" occupations) that limited employment opportunities for women. The concept of comparable worth was addressed by the EEOC in the 1970's. A lack of presidential support for equal employment opportunity during the 1980's, however, slowed the process of reducing sex discrimination and addressing issues of sexual harassment. In 1978, the *Regents of the University of California v. Bakke* case challenged the validity of affirmative action programs, and the status of such programs was being hotly debated as the decade ended.

Under Presidents Ronald Reagan and George Bush, the EEOC was much less active than it had been during the 1960's and 1970's. Under the direction of Clarence Thomas, who was appointed chairman by President Reagan, the commission was much less aggressive in investigating complaints and declined to pursue sex discrimination complaints based on the concept of comparable worth. The imposition of quotas to rectify cases of long-term discrimination and the consolidation of broad classes of discrimination were effectively ended. The handling of cases one by one severely limited the effectiveness of the EEOC. The Civil Rights Act of 1991 reaffirmed the principles of equal employment opportunity and affirmative action, although the use of quotas was discontinued.

William L. Waugh, Jr.

See also: Affirmative action; *Bakke* case; Civil rights; Civil Rights Act of 1964; Civil Rights Act of 1991; Equal Employment Opportunity Act; Equality of opportunity; *Griggs v. Duke Power Company.*

Equality

Equality is the balanced or equal distribution of resources, opportunities, and rewards provided by a society, regardless of an individual's race, color, gender, age, sexual orientation, religion, or previous condition of servitude.

Historically, Karl Marx and Friedrich Engels, in *The Communist Manifesto* (1848), argued that the most important source of inequality within a society relates to the control or ownership of the means of production. They believed that after a prolonged struggle between two social classes they termed the bourgeoisie (the merchant class) and the proletariat (the worker class), a classless society and equality would emerge. The primary characteristic of this society would be the distribution of resources based on an individual's needs. Because some individuals will need more and therefore receive more, this proposed method of distribution does not develop perfect equality within a society. However, Marx and Engels contended that resources would be in abundance, and all individuals within the society would have their needs met, so the slight inequality that would exist would be acceptable.

However, Kingsley Davis and Wilbert Moore, in their article "Some Principles of Stratification" (*American Sociological Review*, 1945), argued that inequality is necessary. They contended that certain positions within society are of greater importance than others to the well-being of society. If all individuals received equal shares of societal resources regardless of their position, there would be no motivation for an individual to attempt to achieve the rigorous training necessary to fill the important positions. Consequently, important activities might not be completed, resulting in damage to or the demise of society. Theorists such as Gerhard Lenski, Max Weber, and Talcott Parsons viewed stratification of society as inevitable and equality as potentially counter to the social forces at work within society.

Legally, equality has been an evasive goal for racial and ethnic minorities throughout the history of the United States. In an effort to acquire equal access to societal resources, minority group members have appealed to the Supreme Court of the United States on several occasions. In *Brown v. Board of Education* (1954), the Supreme Court rejected the argument of *Plessy v.*

Ferguson (1896) and several lower courts that equality could be measured by such tangibles as condition of buildings, transportation, curricula, educational qualifications of teachers, quality and extent of teacher training, pupil-teacher ratio, extracurricular activities, and time and distance involved in travel to school. The Court ruled that equality involves qualities that are intangible and incapable of being measured. In addition, the Court stated that separate educational facilities were inherently unequal because of these intangible qualities. Through court cases such as *Brown*, the Supreme Court attempted to lend its power to minorities, thereby making it possible for them to become more successful in their efforts to acquire valuable resources and gain equality with the majority white group. However, these Supreme Court rulings, while being of assistance, have not completely alleviated social inequality in the United States.

Ione Y. DeOllos

See also: *Brown v. Board of Education*; Equality of opportunity; Inequality; *Plessy v. Ferguson*.

Equality of opportunity

Minimally, equality of opportunity involves a situation in which individuals are not excluded from competing for desirable positions because of their race, sex, or class background. More broadly, this ideal of justice requires that race, sex, and socioeconomic background do not negatively influence one's chances for economic success. Thus equality of opportunity calls for hiring processes, including recruitment and screening practices, free of discrimination against minorities and women. To make the competitive race for desirable positions fair, it is also necessary that men and women, people of different races, and the economically advantaged and disadvantaged all have equal educational opportunities for developing their abilities. The same applies to groups such as visually impaired individuals and people with physical disabilities.

During the 1950's and 1960's it became widely acknowledged that American society did not offer equal opportunity to all its citizens, and judicial and legislative action was undertaken to correct this situation. In *Brown v. Board of Education* (1954), the Supreme Court mandated racial integration in public schools, arguing that segregated schools deprive minority children of equal educational opportunity. Title VII of the Civil Rights Act of 1964 prohibits discrimination in employment. During the 1970's the federal government initiated affirmative action programs, requiring that employers not only refrain from intentional discrimination but also actively recruit women and minorities for underrepresented positions and eliminate bias in job criteria. These programs might involve that qualified minorities or women are hired or promoted instead of equally or seemingly more qualified white males. Critics view these programs as violating the equality of opportunity of white males, and of the population in general; their defenders maintain that such programs only eliminate the undeserved competitive advantage that white males have acquired because they are not subject to institutional discrimination, as minorities and women are. Critics succeeded during the 1980's in curtailing but not eliminating affirmative action programs. Since the 1960's, various laws have been adopted that improve the educational and job opportunities of individuals who are physically impaired. Much less political attention has been given to addressing inequality of opportunity caused by economic poverty as such.

Harry van der Linden

See also: Affirmative action; *Bakke* case; *Brown v. Board of Education*; Civil Rights Act of 1964; Equal Employment Opportunity Act; Equal Employment Opportunity Commission.

Fair Employment Practices Committee

In the spring of 1941, as the United States prepared to enter World War II, African American leaders pressured the administration of Franklin D. Roosevelt to eliminate segregation in the armed forces and discriminatory hiring practices in the booming war industries. A. Philip Randolph, president of the Brotherhood of Sleeping Car Porters, the largest black labor union, threatened a massive march on Washington, D.C., by a hundred thousand demonstrators under the banner Democracy Not Hypocrisy—Jobs Not Alms. Roosevelt, hoping to avoid an embarrassing racial protest that might divide the Democratic Party and his administration at a time when he needed unity for his war-preparedness program, moved to head off the March on Washington movement by meeting with Randolph and Walter White, president of the National Association for the Advancement of Colored People (NAACP). On June 25, 1941, a week before the planned march, Roosevelt issued Executive Order 8802. It prohibited discrimination by employers, unions, and government agencies involved in defense work on the basis of race, creed, color, or national origin but made no mention of desegregating the armed forces. Roosevelt established the Fair Employment Practices Committee (FEPC) to investigate complaints and redress grievances stemming from the order. Randolph and White accepted the compromise arrangement and called off the march.

Although African Americans hailed the FEPC as the greatest step forward in race relations since the Civil War, Roosevelt initially gave the agency little authority. Underfunded and understaffed, the FEPC at first could do little more than conduct investigations into complaints received and make recommendations, relying on the powers of publicity and persuasion to achieve change. In mid-1943, however, amid mounting concern that manpower shortages were hurting the war effort, Roosevelt beefed up the agency by giving it the authority to conduct hearings, make findings, issue directives to war industries, and make recommendations to the War Manpower Commission to curb discrimination.

The FEPC had a mixed record of accomplishment in eliminating racial discrimination in the war industries and government agencies. It resolved less than half of the eight thousand complaints received, and employers and unions often ignored its compliance orders with impunity. Although African American employment in the war industries increased from 3 percent in 1942 to 8 percent in 1945 and the federal government more than tripled its number of black employees, such changes had more to do with wartime labor shortages than FEPC actions. Nevertheless, the FEPC scored some significant successes. In 1944, federal troops broke up a strike by white Philadelphia transit workers and enforced an FEPC directive that blacks be upgraded to positions as streetcar operators. At war's end, despite the FEPC's shortcomings, African American leaders and white liberals hoped to transform the committee into a permanent agency. In 1946, however, southern Democrats in the Senate filibustered a bill to extend the FEPC and killed the agency. Although several northern states passed their own Fair Employment Practices acts, the Senate again blocked bills to create a permanent FEPC in 1950 and 1952. Not until the Civil Rights Act of 1964 did the federal government establish another agency devoted to eliminating racial discrimination in employment practices.

Richard V. Damms

See also: Brotherhood of Sleeping Car Porters; Civil Rights Act of 1964; Desegregation: defense; Discrimination: racial and ethnic; Employment among African Americans; Labor movement; Military desegregation; National Association for the Advancement of Colored People.

Fair Housing Act

The Fair Housing Act, which became law April 11, 1968, prohibited discrimination in housing, helping to break racial enclaves in residential neighborhoods and promoting upward mobility for minorities.

The Civil Rights Act of 1866 provided that all citizens should have the same rights "to inherit, purchase, lease, sell, hold, and convey real and personal property," but the law was never enforced. Instead, such federal agencies as the Farmers Home Administration, the Federal Housing Administration, and the Veterans Administration financially supported segregated housing until 1962, when President John F. Kennedy issued Executive Order 11063 to stop the practice.

California passed a general nondiscrimination law in 1959 and an explicit fair housing law in 1963. In 1964, voters enacted Proposition 14, an initiative to repeal the 1963 statute and the applicability of the 1959 law to housing. When a landlord in Santa Ana refused to rent to an African American in 1963, the latter sued, thus challenging Proposition 14. The California Supreme Court, which heard the case in 1966, ruled that Proposition 14 was contrary to the Fourteenth Amendment to the U.S. Constitution, because it was not neutral on the matter of housing discrimination; instead, based on the context in which it was adopted, Proposition 14 served to legitimate and promote discrimination. On appeal, the U.S. Supreme Court let the California Supreme Court decision stand in *Reitman v. Mulkey* (1967).

Johnson's Efforts   President Lyndon B. Johnson had hoped to include housing discrimination as a provision in the comprehensive Civil Rights Act of 1964, but he demurred when southern senators threatened to block the nomination of Robert Weaver as the first African American cabinet appointee. After 1964, southern members of Congress were adamantly opposed to any expansion of civil rights. Although Johnson urged passage of a federal law against housing discrimination in requests to Congress in 1966 and 1967, there was no mention of the idea during his State of the Union address in 1968. Liberal members of Congress pressed the issue regardless, and southern senators responded by threatening a filibuster. This threat emboldened Senators Edward W. Brooke and Walter F. Mondale, a moderate Republican and a liberal Democrat, respectively, to cosponsor fair housing legislation, but they needed the support of conservative midwestern Republicans to break a filibuster. Illinois Republican senator Everett Dirksen arranged a compromise whereby housing discrimination would be declared illegal, but federal enforcement power would be minimal.

In the wake of *Reitman v. Mulkey*, the assassination of Martin Luther King, Jr., on April 4, 1968, and subsequent urban riots, Congress established fair housing as a national priority on April 10 by adopting Titles VIII and IX of the Civil Rights Act of 1968, also known as the Fair Housing Act or Open Housing Act. Signed by Johnson on the following day, the law originally prohibited discrimination in housing on the basis of race, color, religion, or national origin. In 1974, an amendment expanded the coverage to include sex (gender) discrimination; in 1988, the law was extended to protect persons with disabilities and families with children younger than eighteen years of age.

Title VIII prohibits discrimination in the sale or rental of dwellings, in the financing of housing, in advertising, in the use of a multiple listing service, and in practices that "otherwise make unavailable or deny" housing, a phrase that some courts have interpreted to outlaw exclusionary zoning, mortgage redlining, and racial steering. Blockbusting, the practice of inducing a white homeowner to sell to a minority buyer in order to frighten others on the block to sell their houses at a loss, is also prohibited. It is not necessary to show intent in order to prove discrimination; policies, practices, and procedures that have the effect of excluding minorities, women, handicapped persons, and children are illegal, unless otherwise deemed reasonable. Title VIII, as amended in 1988, covers persons who believe that they are adversely affected by a discriminatory policy, practice, or procedure, even before they incur damages.

The law applies to about 80 percent of all housing in the United States. One exception to the statute is a single-family house sold or rented without the use of a broker and without discriminatory advertising, when the owner owns no more than three such houses and sells only one house in a two-year period. Neither does the statute apply to a four-unit dwelling if the owner lives in one of the units, the so-called Mrs.-Murphy's-rooming-house exception. Dwellings owned by private clubs or religious organizations that rent to their own members on a noncommercial basis are also exempt.

Enforcement   Enforcement of the statute was left to the secretary of the Department of Housing and Urban Development (HUD). Complaints originally had to be filed within 180 days of the offending act, but in 1988, this period was amended to one year. HUD has estimated that there are about two million instances of housing discrimination each year, although formal complaints have averaged only forty thousand per year. The U.S. attorney general can bring a civil suit against a flagrant violator of the law.

According to the law, HUD automatically refers complaints to local agencies that administer "substantially equivalent" fair housing laws. HUD can act if the local agencies fail to do so, but initially was expected only to use conference, conciliation, and persuasion to bring about voluntary compliance. The Fair Housing Amendments Act of 1988 authorized an administrative law tribunal to hear cases that cannot be settled by persuasion. The administrative law judges have the power to issue cease and desist orders to offending parties.

HUD has used "testers" to show discrimination. For example, a team of blacks and whites might arrange to have an African American apply for a rental; if turned down, the black tester would contact a white tester to ascertain whether the landlord were willing to rent to a white instead. That testers have standing to sue was established by the U.S. Supreme Court in *Havens v. Coleman* (1982).

Under the administrative law procedure, penalties are up to $10,000 for the first offense, $25,000 for the second offense, and $50,000 for each offense thereafter. Attorneys' fees and court costs can be recovered by the prevailing party. In 1988, civil penalties in a suit filed by the U.S. attorney general were established as up to $50,000 for the first offense and $100,000 for each offense thereafter.

Title IX of the law prohibits intimidation or attempted injury of anyone filing a housing discrimination complaint. A violator can be assessed a criminal penalty of $1,000 and/or sentenced to one year in jail. If a complainant is actually injured, the penalty can increase to $10,000 and/or ten years of imprisonment. If a complainant is killed, the penalty is life imprisonment.

Under the laws of some states, a complainant filing with a state agency must waive the right to pursue a remedy under federal law. In 1965, a couple sought to purchase a home in a St. Louis suburban housing development, only to be told by the realtor that the home was not available because one of the spouses was African American. Invoking the Civil Rights Act of 1866, the couple sued the real estate developer, and the case went to the Supreme Court. In *Jones v. Alfred H. Mayer Company* (1968), the Court decided that the Civil Rights Act of 1866 did permit a remedy against housing discrimination by private parties.

The effect of the 1968 Fair Housing Act, however, has been minimal. Without a larger supply of affordable housing, many African Americans in particular have nowhere to move in order to enjoy integrated housing. Federal subsidies for low-cost housing, under such legislation as the Housing and Urban Development Act of 1968 and the Housing and Community Development Act of 1974, have declined significantly since the 1980's. Conscientious private developers are confronted with the text of a law that aims to provide integrated housing but proscribes achieving integration by establishing quotas to ensure a mixed racial composition among those who seek to buy or rent dwelling units.

Michael Haas

Core Resources

James A. Kushner's *Fair Housing: Discrimination in Real Estate, Community Development, and Revitalization* (Colorado Springs, Colo.: McGraw-Hill, 1983) is a compendium of legislation and litigation. George R. Metcalf's *Fair Housing Comes of Age* (New York: Greenwood Press, 1988) is a comprehensive evaluation of the precedent, purposes, and problems of enacting, implementing, and enforcing fair housing legislation. *The Fair Housing Act After Twenty Years* (New Haven, Conn.: Yale Law School, 1989), edited by Robert G. Schwemm, evaluates the political and social impediments to achieving nondiscrimination in housing.

See also: Civil Rights Act of 1964; Civil Rights Restoration Act; Housing.

Fifteenth Amendment

The Fifteenth Amendment to the U.S. Constitution, adopted in 1869 and ratified in 1870, stated that the right to vote could not be denied to any citizen "on account of race, color, or previous condition of servitude." The purpose of the amendment was to extend the franchise to the African American men who had been freed from slavery as a result of the Civil War. At the time, women were not regarded as citizens and were therefore not covered by the measure. The amendment marked a continuation of the program of the Republican Party to provide political rights for black men after the defeat of the Confederacy. The Thirteenth Amendment had ended slavery, and the Fourteenth Amendment had provided civil rights to all citizens born or naturalized in the United States. These amendments, however, had not ensured that black men could vote throughout the United States. To accomplish that end, the Republicans in Congress, in a lame-duck Congress that met in early 1869, decided that ensuring the right to vote would both carry on the moral impetus of Reconstruction (1863-1877) and act to offset any political comeback of the antiblack Democratic Party.

A constitutional amendment would have the additional benefit, as the Republicans saw it, of providing a clear legal basis for enforcement of voting rights in the South. In its language, the amendment did not ensure that blacks could hold public positions nor did it rule out such barriers to voting

African Americans marching in New York City to celebrate the ratification of the Fifteenth Amendment in April, 1870.

as literacy tests or property requirements. Nonetheless, it represented a clear forward step for African Americans and offered the promise of greater participation in elections and the operations of government.

The ratification process broke down along the existing party alignments of the Reconstruction era. Republicans favored the measure and Democrats resisted it in the state legislatures that addressed ratification. It required vigorous campaigning, especially in such key states as Ohio, to achieve approval from the requisite number of states by March, 1870.

Despite its place in the U.S. Constitution, the Fifteenth Amendment did not prevent southerners from excluding African Americans from the political process at the end of the nineteenth century. With a political stalemate between Republicans and Democrats in Washington, enforcement of the amendment proved difficult. Federal courts did not encourage a broad interpretation of the amendment. In 1889-1890, the Republicans endeavored to strengthen federal legislation to ensure fair elections in the South, but Democrats defeated their efforts. When the Democrats regained control of the White House and both branches of Congress in 1893-1895, they repealed the existing legislation that gave the government authority over elections. As a result, discriminatory practices kept African Americans from voting in many parts of the South for three-quarters of a century.

In the middle of the twentieth century with the rise of the Civil Rights movement, efforts resumed to revive the Fifteenth Amendment. The Voting Rights Act of 1965 enabled blacks to enter the political process in large numbers and, in so doing, to redeem the unfulfilled promise that the framers of the Fifteenth Amendment had originally envisioned.

Lewis L. Gould

See also: Civil Rights movement; Fourteenth Amendment; Grandfather clauses; Jim Crow laws; Literacy tests; Poll tax; Thirteenth Amendment; Voting Rights Act of 1965.

Fourteenth Amendment

A definition of citizenship designed for former slaves, the Fourteenth Amendment provides protection against state violations of civil rights that has become crucial to all citizens of the United States.

The Fourteenth Amendment to the U.S. Constitution, ratified by Congress in 1868, was part of the plan for Reconstruction following the Civil War (1861-1865) and was formulated by the Republican majority in the Thirty-ninth Congress. Before Congress met in December, 1865, President Andrew Johnson had authorized the restoration of white self-government in the former Confederate states, and the congressmen and senators from those states waited in Washington to be seated in Congress. The abolition of slavery had destroyed the old compromise under which five slaves counted as three free persons in apportioning representation in the House and the electoral college, and the Republicans wanted to make sure that the South did not add to its numbers in the House and thus profit from rebellion.

Between December, 1865, and May, 1866, the Republicans attempted to hammer out a program that would accomplish their purposes in the South, unite members of their party in Congress, and appeal to northern voters. Given the diversity of opinion within the party, this undertaking proved to be difficult. Radical Republicans wanted African American suffrage, permanent political proscription, and confiscation of the property of ex-Confederates. Some maintained they were authorized in these actions by the Thirteenth Amendment, which, they believed, gave Congress the power to abolish the "vestiges of slavery." Moderate Republicans, on the other hand, feared political repercussions from African American suffrage, as such a requirement would result in beginning the Reconstruction process over again. Many moderates also believed that an additional amendment to the Constitution was needed to provide precise authority for Congress to enact civil rights legislation.

From deliberations of the joint committee and debate on the floor of the House came the Fourteenth Amendment. Many Republicans believed that the proposal was in the nature of a peace treaty, although this view was not explicitly stated. If the South accepted the amendment, the southern states were to be readmitted and their senators and representatives seated in Congress; in other words, Reconstruction would end. Republicans presented a united front during the final vote as a matter of party policy. Because the amendment was an obvious compromise between radicals and moderates, it was too strong for some and too weak for others.

The Amendment   The Fourteenth Amendment became the most important addition to the Constitution since the Bill of Rights had been adopted in 1791. It contains five sections:

Section 1, the first constitutional definition of citizenship, states that all persons born or naturalized in the United States are citizens of the United States and of the state in which they reside. It includes limits on the power of states, by providing that no state may abridge the privileges and immunities of citizens, deprive any person of life, liberty, or property without due process of law, or deny to any person within its jurisdiction the equal protection of law. This section was intended to guarantee African Americans the rights of citizenship, although the amendment's framers did not define exactly which rights were included. Nor did they define "state action" to specify whether the term meant only official acts of state government or the actions of individuals functioning privately with state approval.

The courts later interpreted the due process clause to extend the rights of the accused listed in the Bill of Rights, which had applied only to the federal government, to the states. They expanded the notion of equal protection to include other categories, such as sex and disability, as well as race. They also interpreted the word "person" to include corporations as legal persons; under this interpretation, corporations found protection from much state regulation.

Section 2 gives a new formula of representation in place of the old three-fifths compromise of the Constitution, under which five slaves were counted as equal to three free persons in determining a state's representation in the House of Representatives and the electoral college. All persons in a state were to be counted for representation, but if a state should disfranchise any of its adult male citizens, except for participation in rebellion or any other crime, the basis of its representation would be reduced proportionately. While not guaranteeing suffrage to African Americans, this provision threatened the South with a loss of representation should black males be denied the vote.

Section 3 declares that no person who has ever taken an oath to support the Constitution (which included all who had been in the military service or held state or national office before 1860) and has then participated in the rebellion can be a senator or representative or hold any civil or military office, national or state. This disability could be removed only by a two-thirds vote of both houses of Congress. This section took away the pardoning power of the president, which congressional Republicans believed Andrew Johnson used too generously.

Section 4 validates the debt of the United States, voids all debts incurred to support rebellion, and invalidates all claims for compensation for emancipated slaves.

Section 5 gives Congress authority to pass legislation to enforce the provisions of the Fourteenth Amendment.

The correspondence and speeches of those who framed the Fourteenth Amendment do not support any theories of economic conspiracy or ulterior motives. The framers desired to protect the former slaves and boost Republicanism in the South by barring old Confederates from returning to Congress and the electoral college with increased voting strength. They hoped to do this without threatening the federal system or unduly upsetting the relationship between the central government and the states. At the same time, Republicans wanted to unify their party and project a popular issue for the approaching electoral contest against Andrew Johnson.

William J. Cooper, Jr., updated by Mary Welek Atwell

Core Resources

Michael Les Benedict's *A Compromise of Principle: Congressional Republicans and Reconstruction, 1863-1869* (New York: W. W. Norton, 1974) emphasizes the Republicans' concern that the Fourteenth Amendment maintain the role of the states in the federal system. LaWanda Cox and John H. Cox's

Politics, Principle, and Prejudice: Dilemma of Reconstruction America, 1865-1866 (New York: Free Press, 1963) posits that civil rights, rather than merely partisan politics, was the central issue during Reconstruction. Harold M. Hyman and William Wiecek's *Equal Justice Under Law: Constitutional Development, 1835-1875* (New York: Harper & Row, 1982) includes a thorough discussion of the Fourteenth Amendment as a logical and necessary extension of the Thirteenth Amendment. Donald E. Lively's *The Constitution and Race* (New York: Praeger, 1992) focuses on the association of attitudes toward race and constitutional interpretation.

See also: Civil Rights Acts of 1866-1875; Emancipation Proclamation; Freedmen's Bureau; Reconstruction; Thirteenth Amendment.

Free African Society

The Free African Society was the first major secular institution with a mission to aid African Americans.

Both the origins of the Free African Society and the long-term repercussions of its founding form an essential part of the religious history of African Americans. The original organization itself was of short duration: About seven years after it was organized in 1787, it disappeared as a formal body. In its immediate wake, however, closely related institutions emerged that tried to take over its proclaimed mission.

Generally speaking, prior to the 1790's people of African slave origins who managed to obtain their individual freedom had only one option if they wished to practice Christianity: association, as subordinate parishioners, in an existing white-run church. Several churches in the American colonies before independence, including the Quakers and Methodists, had tried to identify their religious cause with that of the black victims of slavery.

Richard Allen   Richard Allen, born in 1760 as a slave whose family belonged to Pennsylvania's then attorney general, Benjamin Chew, was destined to become one of the earliest religious leaders of the black segment of the American Methodist Church. As a youth, Allen gained extensive experience with Methodist teachings after his family was separated on the auction block in Dover, Delaware. Allen was encouraged by his second owner, Master Stokeley, to espouse the religious teachings of the itinerant American Methodist preacher Freeborn Garrettson. Allen's conversion to Methodism was rewarded when Stokeley freed him at age twenty to follow the calling of religion. His freedom came just as the Revolutionary War ended.

For six years, Allen worked under the influence of Methodist evangelist Benjamin Abbott and the Reverend (later Bishop) Richard Whatcoat, with whom he traveled on an extensive preaching circuit. Allen's writings refer to Whatcoat as his "father in Israel." With Whatcoat's encouragement, Allen accepted an invitation from the Methodist elder in Philadelphia to return to his birthplace to become a preacher. At that time, Philadelphia's religious environment seemed to be dominated by the Episcopal Church. This church had been active since 1758 in extending its ministry to African Americans. It was St. George's Methodist Episcopal Church, however, that, in the 1780's, had drawn the largest number of former slaves to its rolls. Once the circumstances of blacks' second-class status became clear to Allen, he decided that his leadership mission should be specifically dedicated to the needs of his people. Within a short time, he joined another African American, Absalom Jones, in founding what was originally intended to be more of a secular movement than a formal denominational movement: the Free African Society.

Absalom Jones   Absalom Jones was older than Allen and had a different set of life experiences. Born a slave in Delaware in 1746, Jones served for more than twenty years in his master's store in Philadelphia. He earned enough money to purchase his wife's freedom, to build his own home, and finally, in 1784, to purchase his own freedom. He continued to work for his former master for wages and bought and managed two houses for additional income. His success earned for him great respect among other free blacks and opened the way for him to serve as lay leader representing the African American membership of St. George's Methodist Episcopal Church.

Traditional accounts of Jones's role in the founding of the Free African Society assert that, when Jones refused to comply with the announcement of St. George's sexton that African American parishioners should give up their usual seats among the white congregation and move to the upper gallery, he was supported by Richard Allen, in particular. The two then agreed that the only way African Americans could worship in an environment that responded to their social, as well as religious, needs would be to found an all-black congregation. Some sources suggest that Jones's reaction to the reseating order was the crowning blow, and that Allen previously had tried to organize several fellow black parishioners, including Doras Giddings, William White, and Jones, to support his idea of a separate congregation, only to have the idea rejected by the church elders.

Organization Goals   Whatever the specific stimulus for Allen's and Jones's actions in 1787, they announced publicly that their newly declared movement would not only serve the black community's religious needs as a nondenominational congregation but also function as a benevolent mutual aid organization. The latter goal involved plans to collect funds (through membership fees) to assist the sick, orphans, and widows in the African

American community. Other secular social assistance aims included enforcement of a code of temperance, propriety, and fidelity in marriage. It is significant that a number of the early members of the Free African Society came to it from the rolls of other Protestant churches, not only St. George's Methodist Episcopal congregation.

The dual nature of the organization's goals soon led to divisions in the politics of leadership. Apparently, it was Allen who wanted to use the breakaway from St. George's as a first step in founding a specifically black Methodist church. Others wished to emphasize the Free African Society's nondenominational character and pursue mainly social and moral aid services. Within two years, therefore, Allen resigned his membership, going on to found, in July, 1794, the Bethel African Methodist Episcopal Church. Although this move clearly marked the beginnings of a specifically African American church with a defined denominational status, Allen's efforts for many years continued to be directed at social and economic self-help projects for African Americans, irrespective of their formal religious orientation.

By 1804, Allen was involved in founding a group whose name reflected its basic social reform goals: the Society of Free People of Color for Promoting the Instruction and School Education of Children of African Descent. Another of Allen's efforts came in 1830, when Allen, then seventy years of age, involved his church in the Free Produce Society in Philadelphia. This group raised money to buy goods grown only by nonslave labor to redistribute to poor African Americans. It also tried to organize active boycotts against the marketing and purchase of goods produced by slave-owning farmers, thus providing an early model for the grassroots organizations aimed at social and political goals that would become familiar to African Americans in the mid-twentieth century.

The Free African Society passed through several short but key stages both before and after Richard Allen's decision to remove himself from active membership. One focal point was the group's early association with the prominent medical doctor and philanthropist Benjamin Rush. Rush helped the Free African Society to draft a document involving articles of faith that were meant to be general enough to include the essential religious principles of any Christian church. When the organization adopted these tenets, in 1791, its status as a religious congregation generally was recognized by members and outsiders alike. More and more, its close relationship with the Episcopal Church (first demonstrated by its "friendly adoption" by the Reverend Joseph Pilmore and the white membership of St. Paul's Church in Philadelphia) determined its future denominational status. After 1795, the Free African Society per se had been superseded by a new church built by a committee sparked by Absalom Jones: the African Methodist Episcopal Church. This fact did not, however, prevent those who had been associated with the Free African Society's origins from integrating its strong social and moral reform program with the religious principles that marked the emer-

gence of the first all-black Christian congregations in the United States by
the end of the 1790's.

Byron D. Cannon

Core Resources

Carol V. R. George's *Segregated Sabbaths: Richard Allen and the Emergence of
Independent Black Churches, 1760-1840* (New York: Oxford University Press,
1973) includes discussion of the African American churches' eventual abolitionist activities. Mwalimi I. Mwadilitu's *Richard Allen: The First Exemplar of
African American Education* (New York: ECA Associates, 1985) focuses on the
career of Richard Allen, including his functions after 1816 as the first bishop
of the African Methodist Episcopal Church.

See also: African American Baptist Church; AME Church; AME Zion
Churches; American Anti-Slavery Society; Black church; Black codes; *Liberator, The*; Pennsylvania Society for the Abolition of Slavery.

Free blacks

In 1860, an estimated 500,000 free people of African ancestry resided in the
United States; of these, approximately half lived in the slaveholding South.
Most of these free blacks were former slaves who had purchased their
freedom or were freed in their masters' wills, but a significant minority were
freeborn. Their experiences varied by region; those in the northern states,
although limited in economic opportunity, enjoyed greater political and
social freedom than their counterparts in the South, where demand for black
labor was greater but free blacks were regarded with suspicion. The majority
of free blacks lived in extreme poverty; however, a small but significant
number achieved modest prosperity and a few attained substantial wealth,
in some instances purchasing plantations and becoming slaveholders.

Free African Americans of the antebellum period exerted profound
influence upon black society in the post-slavery United States. The abolitionist rhetoric of former slaves such as Frederick Douglass and Samuel Ringgold
Ward influenced later generations of black activists, and the activities of free
southern blacks set precedents for race relations and relations among African
Americans after emancipation. The political and legal restrictions placed on
free blacks by fearful southern whites in the antebellum period provided a
blueprint for racial oppression in the South during the era of segregation.

Michael H. Burchett

See also: Abolition; Civil War and African Americans; Freedmen's Bureau;
Slavery: history.

Free-Soil Party

As the Whig Party disintegrated, the Free-Soil Party was one of the factions that filled the political vacuum; in time Free-Soil Party members helped to form the Republican Party. In 1846, Representative David Wilmot introduced a measure to prohibit slavery in territories obtained as a result of the Mexican-American War, and almost immediately the political parties divided on the matter. Uniting with the Liberty Party and antislavery Whigs, the antislavery "barnburners" formed the Free-Soil Party, which nominated Martin Van Buren for the presidency in 1848. He did not obtain a single electoral vote, but he won 291,000 popular votes in the North and Midwest. The election was won by Zachary Taylor, a hero of the Mexican-American War, who refused to state his political positions.

The Free-Soilers next formed the "Free Democracy of the United States," which held a convention in 1852 during which it nominated John Hale for the presidency on the platform of "Free Soil, Free Speech, Free Labor, and Free Men." The Democratic nominee, Franklin Pierce, who favored the Compromise of 1850, won the election.

The nation seemed to want compromise and avoidance of war. This time the Free-Soil candidate received only 156,000 presidential votes, and the party seemed to have lost influence.

Even so, the antislavery forces recovered, as antagonisms between the sections intensified. War actually erupted in Kansas, as the two groups contested for control of the territory. In July, 1854, antislavery elements came together to form the Republican Party. Free-Soilers filtered into the Republican ranks and were very much in evidence at the party's 1856 convention, which nominated John C. Frémont for the presidency. With this, the Free-Soil Party dissolved.

Robert Sobel

See also: Abolition; Compromise of 1850; Slavery: history.

Freedmen's Bureau

The Freedmen's Bureau was established by the federal government to assist newly freed African Americans in making the transition from slavery to freedom.

On March 3, 1865, Congress created the Freedmen's Bureau, a temporary agency within the War Department. The bureau, also known as the United States Bureau of Refugees, Freedmen, and Abandoned Lands, was administered by General Oliver Otis Howard from 1865 until it was dismantled by

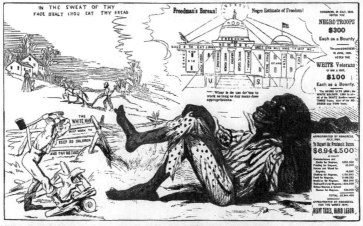

THE FREEDMAN'S BUREAU!

AN AGENCY TO KEEP THE NEGRO IN IDLENESS AT THE EXPENSE OF THE WHITE MAN.
TWICE VETOED BY THE PRESIDENT, AND MADE A LAW BY CONGRESS.
SUPPORT CONGRESS & YOU SUPPORT THE NEGRO.   SUSTAIN THE PRESIDENT & YOU PROTECT THE WHITE MAN

Northern antipathy toward the Freedmen's Bureau can be seen in this 1866 political advertisement that a Pennsylvania candidate for Congress published to attack his opponent's support of the bureau. *(Library of Congress)*

Congress in 1872. The primary objective of the Freedmen's Bureau was to help newly freed African Americans to function as free men, women, and children. In order to achieve this goal, the bureau was expected to assume responsibility for all matters related to the newly freed slaves in the southern states.

The bureau's mission was an enormous undertaking because of limited resources, political conflicts over Reconstruction policies, and a hostile environment. The work of the bureau was performed by General Howard and a network of assistant commissioners in various states, largely in the South. The Freedmen's Bureau attempted to address many of the needs of the newly freed African Americans, including labor relations, education, landownership, medical care, food distribution, family reunification, legal protection, and legal services within the African American community.

Labor and Education   In the area of labor relations, the Freedmen's Bureau dealt with labor-related issues such as transporting and relocating refugees and the newly freed persons for employment, contract and wage disputes, and harsh legislation enacted by some states. Concerning the last issue, many southern states had passed laws, called black codes, that required adult freed men and women to have lawful employment or a business.

Otherwise, they would be fined and jailed for vagrancy, and sheriffs would hire them out to anyone who would pay their fine. Given the scarcity of jobs, this policy resulted in former slave owners maintaining rigid control over newly freed African Americans. Another discriminatory law gave the former owners of orphaned African Americans the right to hire them as apprentices rather than placing them with their relatives. Again, this law resulted in the continuation of free labor for many southerners. The Freedmen's Bureau has been criticized for the failure of its agents to negotiate labor contracts in the interest of the newly freed. The bureau was frequently accused of protecting the rights of the southern planters instead.

Obtaining an education was extremely important to the newly freed African Americans. They knew that learning to read and write would enable them to enter into contracts and establish businesses, and would aid them in legal matters. The Freedmen's Bureau provided some support, by providing teachers, schools, and books and by coordinating volunteers. The bureau also made a contribution to the founding of African American colleges and universities. Southern opposition to educating African Americans was a result of the southerners' fear that education would make African Americans too independent and unwilling to work under the terms established by their former owners. Therefore, southerners instituted control over the educational administration and classrooms and the entire system. Southern planters used various methods to exert control: frequent changes in administrative personnel, the use of racial stereotypes regarding the intellectual inferiority of African Americans, and educational policy decision making based on paternalism and self-interest. Consequently, educational opportunities were significantly restricted for African American youth.

Property and Other Rights The newly freed African Americans were eager to acquire property. They demonstrated their interest in owning their own land as individuals and formed associations to purchase large tracts of land. Their sense of family and community was the basis for their strong desire to own land. The Freedmen's Bureau was initially authorized to distribute land that had been confiscated from southern plantation owners during the Civil War. The Freedmen's Bureau also attempted to provide for the social welfare of the freed persons. The agency was noted for rationing food to refugees and former slaves; it assisted families in reuniting with members who had been sold or separated in other ways during slavery.

Protecting the rights of the former slaves was a major task of the Freedmen's Bureau. Republicans believed that African Americans should have the same rights as whites. However, many southern states enacted black codes that severely restricted the civil rights of the freed men, women, and children. These laws, exacting social and economic control over African Americans, represented a new form of slavery. When state legislation prohibited African Americans' equal rights, the bureau attempted to invoke the 1866 Civil Rights Act, which offered African Americans the same legal protections and rights as whites to testify in courts, to own property, to enforce legal contracts, and to sue. The bureau found it extremely difficult to enforce the Civil Rights Act and to prosecute state officials who enforced laws that were discriminatory against African Americans. A shortage of agents and a reluctance among bureau commissioners to challenge local officials contributed to the agency's limited success in enforcing the Civil Rights Act. Finally, the Freedmen's Bureau also established tribunals to address minor legal disputes of African Americans within their own communities. In many instances, freed slaves were able to resolve their own problems. When they could not, they presented their legal concerns to bureau agents.

The task assigned to the Freedmen's Bureau was monumental. The responsibilities of the bureau significantly exceeded the resources and authority granted to it by Congress. The bureau's ability to perform its varied tasks also was impeded by personnel shortages. President Andrew Johnson's Reconstruction policies represented another major challenge to the bureau, as they were not always supportive of the bureau's mandate and objectives. Myriad problems associated with the bureau meant that the newly freed men, women, and children were not able to receive the goods and services necessary to gain economic independence. Consequently, they developed extensive self-help networks to address their needs.

K. Sue Jewell

Core Resources

Barry A. Crouch's *The Freedmen's Bureau and Black Texans* (Austin: University of Texas Press, 1982) discusses the Reconstruction era and the Freedmen's Bureau in the state of Texas. *The Freedmen's Bureau and Black Freedom* (New York: Garland, 1994), edited by Donald G. Nieman, explores the various problems that affected the bureau. Edward Magdol's *A Right to the Land: Essays on the Freedmen's Community* (Westport, Conn.: Greenwood Press, 1977) emphasizes the efforts that African Americans pursued to acquire land and their relentless quest for self-determination.

See also: Black codes; Civil Rights Acts of 1866-1875; Fourteenth Amendment; Reconstruction; Thirteenth Amendment.

Freedom Riders

Freedom Riders were civil rights activists who traveled on interstate bus lines in 1961 in order to promote enforcement of a 1960 Supreme Court ruling that prohibited racial segregation in facilities that served interstate travelers. James Farmer, the national director of the Congress of Racial Equality (CORE), modeled the protest after a similar effort that the organization had undertaken in 1947. Like their predecessors in 1947, the Freedom Riders were both African Americans and whites committed to a nonviolent approach to achieving the goal of a racially integrated United States.

The first group of Freedom Riders, seven African Americans and six whites, met in Washington, D.C., for training sessions on May 1, 1961. They left the nation's capital three days later, traveling south on two different bus lines. The Freedom Riders met with little resistance until they arrived in Rock Hill, South Carolina. When John Lewis, an African American seminary student, and Albert Bigelow, a white retired naval officer, attempted to enter the white waiting room in the bus station, a group of white youths beat them. This incident foreshadowed the violence that the Freedom Riders would meet later on their journey through the American South. Outside Anniston, Alabama, on May 14, a mob firebombed the bus on which the Freedom Riders were traveling and attacked the passengers as they hurried off the burning wreckage. That same day, another contingent of Freedom Riders suffered beatings at the bus station in Birmingham, Alabama. Because of the violence, the bus drivers refused to carry the Freedom Riders any farther, and the protest ended with a plane flight to New Orleans, Louisiana.

The premature end of the first Freedom Ride did not mark the end of the effort, which had captured the attention of the nation and placed pressure on the administration of President John F. Kennedy to enforce the Supreme Court ruling. A second group of Freedom Riders, eight African Americans and two whites, set forth from Nashville, Tennessee, just days after the first ride had ended. After a great deal of difficulty, most of this group reached Montgomery, Alabama, where they met with a second group of eleven activists who had arrived to join the protest. Angry white segregationists confronted the Freedom Riders, and the scene at Montgomery degenerated into a riot during which several Freedom Riders were badly injured. Despite this incident, supporters of civil rights throughout the nation volunteered to continue the protests. Biracial Freedom Rides continued throughout the summer of 1961, with hundreds of riders jailed in southern states for violating local ordinances. The continuing crisis prompted the Interstate Commerce Commission to issue regulations, in September, 1961, enforcing the Supreme Court ruling regarding segregation in interstate travel facilities.

The biracial nature of the Freedom Rides revealed that Americans from diverse backgrounds were willing to risk their safety, even their lives, to secure the civil rights of African Americans. The violence surrounding the Freedom Rides also proved that southerners committed to perpetuating racial segregation would attack white civil rights activists with as much abandon as they did the African American protesters.

Thomas Clarkin

See also: Children in the Civil Rights movement; Civil Rights movement; Congress of Racial Equality; Nonviolent resistance.

Freedom Summer

In 1964, the Council of Federated Organizations (COFO), comprising mostly volunteers from the Student Nonviolent Coordinating Committee (SNCC), launched a black voter registration campaign in Mississippi. Leaders sought to expose the ways that whites denied blacks the right to vote and to prod the federal government into enforcing the voting rights of black Americans. The struggle would also encourage the emergence of black community leaders.

In June, the first of nearly nine hundred white student volunteers, mainly from northeastern schools, arrived in Mississippi. White and black volunteers operated about fifty Freedom Schools and about the same number of community centers.

Local white reaction was swift and violent. Even before the project started, three civil rights workers were murdered. Throughout the summer, white segregationists burned churches, shot at volunteers, and bombed homes and civil rights headquarters. The violence had the opposite effect of what whites had intended; it galvanized national opinion that the racial situation in Mississippi and the South had to change. At the same time, continued violence contributed to growing rifts within the Civil Rights movement. The Freedom Summer convinced many black SNCC workers that nonviolence and cooperation with whites were not succeeding and that more radical measures were necessary.

Robert E. McFarland

See also: Civil Rights movement; Council of Federated Organizations; Student Nonviolent Coordinating Committee.

Friendships, interracial/interethnic

Interracial and interethnic friendships involve persons from dissimilar racial, ethnic, linguistic, or national groups. These friendships are significant for intergroup relations because they are a sign of structural assimilation or integration for the minority group. According to sociologist Milton Gordon, integration into the primary sector of society for minorities includes having acquaintances, close friends, and neighbors from the dominant group.

Since the 1950's, legislation such as the Civil Rights Act of 1964 and the Voting Rights Act of 1965 has helped to reduce discrimination against racial and ethnic groups. Similarly, the U.S. Supreme Court's 1954 decision in

Brown v. Board of Education began the movement to desegregate public schools and, as a result, did much to break down personal barriers between blacks, whites, Latinos, Asian Americans, and other groups. As a result of such factors, contact across group lines in American schools, colleges, workplaces, neighborhoods, and social gatherings has increased, but these situations do not often lead to increased acceptance and the growth of friendships across racial and ethnic boundaries. According to numerous sources, including S. Dale McLemore's *Racial and Ethnic Relations in America* (1994) and Joseph F. Healey's *Race, Ethnicity, Gender, and Class* (1998), interracial and interethnic friendships remain relatively infrequent. This is not surprising given the centuries of racism and prejudice, as well as the differences in socioeconomic status, places of residence, and levels of education, that continue to exist between groups. Moreover, the slowly changing norms concerning issues of race and ethnicity also discourage the growth of interracial and interethnic friendships. Despite significant legal and political efforts to control them, racial stereotyping and prejudice remain powerful social forces. Whereas interactions with members of the same racial or ethnic group promote social stability, interactions with members of different racial or ethnic groups mark social change and instability, which can be seen as threatening to a group's sense of security.

Intergroup Contact Though statistics regarding the incidence of interracial and interethnic friendships are substantially harder to find than are corresponding statistics regarding intermarriage, there is a body of research within the social sciences that addresses the issue of interracial/interethnic friendships. Sociologist Gordon Allport's contact hypothesis is applicable to the study of these friendships. The contact hypothesis proposes that when social, political, and economic barriers to integration and equality disappear, the social distance between racial groups should also decrease. Social distance can be defined as the degree of intimacy to which an individual is willing to admit persons of other groups, ranging from intermarriage to complete segregation.

A variety of social settings in which interracial and interethnic contact leads to friendships have been studied, but the majority of research has focused on desegregated schools. Since *Brown v. Board of Education*, the desegregation of schools has facilitated the interaction of students, teachers, and parents from different racial and ethnic groups. Yet when it comes to friendship, or social interaction outside the school context, the majority of the research has found that students prefer members of their own racial and ethnic group as friends, although the frequency of these friendships differs depending on what racial and ethnic groups are involved. For example, studies such as Nathan Glazer and Daniel P. Moynihan's *Beyond the Melting Pot* (1970) and Richard Alba's *Ethnicity and Race in the U.S.A.* (1988) have found that social distance between white ethnic groups is being reduced by interethnic friendships and intermarriage. Similarity in attitudes, values, behaviors, and socioeconomic status are often the basis of interpersonal attraction, with race an important factor in the choice of friends. Therefore, it is understandable why interethnic friendships, especially between white European Americans, would be more common than interracial friendships.

Racial stereotypes and societal norms act as barriers to the formation of interracial friendships. One study has found that students often cite the tendency of members of other groups to segregate themselves and the perception that they lack common ground upon which to build a friendship as reasons why they do not have friends from other racial or ethnic groups. Other studies have also found that some school practices, such as tracking, contribute to the low number of interracial friendships; tracking, for example, may tend to segregate African Americans and other minorities into classrooms devoted to lower academic tracks. Another barrier to the formation of interracial and interethnic friendships is the perception of negative family attitudes toward these friendships.

Among adults, research has tended to focus on the effects of residential desegregation on interracial contact and friendships. Douglas Massey and Nancy Denton's *American Apartheid* (1993) explored the issue of residential segregation and found that racial groups remain virtually segregated, even when they are of the same social class. Among adults, therefore, interracial friendships remain infrequent, both because of a lack of opportunities to interact and because of prejudices and stereotypes. One study by James E.

Among many issues addressed in the melodramatic 1934 film *Imitation of Life*, is the inability of two women of different races, played by Louise Beavers (left) and Claudette Colbert (right) to reveal their close friendship and business partnership to the world. *(Museum of Modern Art, Film Stills Archive)*

Rosenbaum et al. found that when low-income blacks moved to middle-class white suburbs as part of a housing voucher program, considerable racial integration was achieved, including a substantial number of individual friendships.

Asian Americans, Hispanic Americans, and African Americans

Rates of interracial and interethnic friendships vary depending on the groups involved. According to sources such as S. Dale McLemore's *Racial and Ethnic Relations in America* (1994) and Joseph F. Healey's *Race, Ethnicity, Gender, and Class* (1998), Asian Americans have experienced considerable assimilation in the areas of primary relations such as friendships and marriage, especially with white European Americans. Overall the extent of intimate contact between Hispanic Americans and whites is higher than for African Americans, yet lower than for Asian Americans and whites, according to Healey. For example, according to McLemore, Mexican Americans decreasingly have only Mexican friends over the passage of time. This generational trend is more pronounced among those living in desegregated neighborhoods and among those of higher income, suggesting that if Mexican Americans continue to live, work, and send their children to school in desegregated areas, the number of friendships with non-Hispanics will continue to increase. Similarly, Clara Rodriguez's *Puerto Ricans: Born in the USA* (1989) found that rates of interracial contact increase for Hispanic Americans of the more affluent social classes who live in the cities and for the presumably more Americanized younger generations.

According to the majority of research, including McLemore's *Racial and Ethnic Relations in America* and Healey's *Race, Ethnicity, Gender, and Class*, friendships between African Americans and whites are the least frequent. These two groups remain virtually separated in their personal relationships everywhere but in the schools. Even in school, the proportion of African American/white friendships remains low. According to research, it is common for black students to remain virtually segregated within primary and secondary school systems, and black college students are increasingly forming their own sororities, fraternities, and student organizations. The low level of interracial contact between African Americans and whites is further evidenced in the low rates of intermarriage between the two groups. Therefore, McLemore, for example, concludes that the level of primary assimilation of African Americans, as evidenced in the low number of interracial friendships and marriage, is low compared to that of other racial and ethnic groups.

Improving Intergroup Friendships

One of the most commonly proposed methods of improving intergroup relations is for people to establish communication, get to know one another, and participate in group activities together. This process enables individuals to judge members of a different race or ethnicity on the basis of their individual characteristics rather than their group membership. It is often maintained that such transformations are most likely to occur if the individuals involved are of equal socioeconomic status, if they are given the chance to work cooperatively together, if their interaction is supported by those in authority, and if there is a high level of intimacy. Often, intergroup contacts that occur under different circumstances do not alter prejudices and rarely result in the formation of friendships, because they simply mirror the power differentials and inequalities of the larger society. Other factors that have been shown to influence the outcome of contacts between members of different racial and ethnic groups include minimal competition, voluntary interaction, and similarities in beliefs and values.

Schools can encourage intergroup contact by offering noncompetitive, supportive environments where different racial and ethnic groups can interact and work cooperatively. Proposed methods of accomplishing this include the implementation of small-group learning teams and interracial extracurricular activities. Moreover, positive effects on the development of interracial friendships have been observed when school officials and teachers have implemented programs that reduce status differences between students of different racial and ethnic groups.

Erica Childs

Core Resources

Gordon Allport's *The Nature of Prejudice* (Garden City, N.Y.: Doubleday, 1958) explores the contact hypothesis, which is generally used in examining intergroup relations. Milton Gordon, in *Assimilation in American Life* (New York: Oxford University Press, 1964), identifies three subprocesses of assimilation, with one of the main stages, primary structural assimilation, being the formation of interracial and interethnic friendships. For a general summary of intergroup relations and the formation of intergroup friendships, S. Dale McLemore's *Racial and Ethnic Relations in America* (Boston: Allyn & Bacon, 1994) and Joseph F. Healey's *Race, Ethnicity, Gender, and Class: The Sociology of Group Conflict and Change* (Thousand Oaks, Calif.: Pine Forge Press, 1998) are good sources. A few of the most comprehensive scholarly articles that deal with student friendships include Maureen T. Hallinan and Ruy A. Teixeira's "Opportunities and Constraints: Black-White Differences in the Formation of Interracial Friendships" (*Child Development* 58, 1987); Maureen T. Hallinan and Richard A. Williams's "Interracial Friendship Choices in Secondary Schools" (*American Sociological Review* 54, 1989); and Maureen T. Hallinan and Richard A. Williams's "The Stability of Students' Interracial Friendships" (*American Sociological Review* 52, 1987). For an in-depth look at residential segregation and how it affects intergroup contact, Douglas Massey and Nancy Denton's *American Apartheid* (Cambridge, Mass.: Harvard University Press, 1993) is an excellent source.

See also: Desegregation: public schools; Interracial and interethnic marriage.

Fugitive slave laws

Although the U.S. Constitution provided for the return of fugitive slaves across state borders, it did not specify the mechanism by which this would be accomplished. Congress therefore enacted the Fugitive Slave Law of 1793, by which slaves could be seized by masters or agents crossing state lines. State officials were made responsible for the enforcement of the federal law. For the slaves, the law embodied no protection of *habeas corpus*, trial by jury, or right to testify in their own behalf. In response, many northern states passed laws granting slaves personal liberties.

So long as fugitive slave laws were in effect, African Americans fleeing southern slavery never felt safe, even after reaching northern states, unless they entered Canada. *(Library of Congress)*

The Fugitive Slave Law of 1850 made the federal government responsible for returning slaves to their owners. Interference with the law became a felony. Again, the alleged fugitive was denied personal rights. Furthermore, since commissioners received a higher fee for delivering a slave than for rejecting a claim, the law resulted in the confiscation of free people. The law's constitutionality was upheld in 1859 in *Ableman v. Booth*. Northern furor over the law and increasing abolitionist sentiment helped bring the country closer to the brink of war.

Mary E. Virginia

See also: Abolition; Compromise of 1850; Missouri Compromise; *Scott v. Sandford*; Slave codes; Slavery: history.

Fullilove v. Klutznick

In *Fullilove v. Klutznick*, the Supreme Court on July 2, 1980, ruled that setting aside a percentage of federal contracts for minority business enterprises was constitutional as long as it was intended to remedy demonstrated discrimination. In passing the Public Works Employment Act of 1977, Congress required 10 percent of local public works contracts to be "set aside" for minority businesses—businesses with at least 50 percent ownership or 51 percent stockholding by African Americans, Spanish-speaking people, Asian Americans, American Indians, Eskimos, or Aleuts. Nonminority prime contractors were required, in subcontracting to minority businesses, to provide guidance and technical assistance in making bids, to lower or waive bonding requirements, and to assist minority businesses in obtaining working capital from financial institutions and government agencies.

Shortly after Juanita Krebs, U.S. secretary of commerce, issued administrative guidelines for bidding under the new law, several potential project grantees (H. Earl Fullilove and trustees of the New York Building and Construction Industry Board of Urban Affairs Fund, two general contractor associations, and a firm engaged in heating, ventilation, and air conditioning work) filed suit against Krebs, the city and state of New York, the New York Board of Higher Education, and the Health and Hospitals Corporation for a temporary restraining order to block implementation of the law. After they lost the case in the district court (in December, 1977) and on appeal (in 1978), they took the case to the Supreme Court. When the case was decided, Philip Klutznick was U.S. secretary of commerce. Chief Justice Warren Burger wrote the majority opinion; three justices provided concurring majority opinions, and two wrote dissents.

The Court answered the argument that government should act in a color-blind manner by noting that Congress had the power to spend money for the general welfare and thus to design a remedy for minority businesses. The argument that nonminority businesses were deprived of equal access to contracts was rejected: a 10 percent set-aside rate was considered light in view of the larger percentage of minorities. The Court responded to the argument that the definition of "minority" was underinclusive and should have added other groups by noting that such a definition was entirely up to Congress. The argument that the "minority" definition was overinclusive and might favor minority businesses unqualified to do the technical work was refuted by a reference to the statutory provisions that only bona fide minorities were covered by the law and that a waiver from the set-aside could be issued if no minority business was able to do the work.

The Supreme Court thus held that a numerical goal could be designed as a remedy for a statistically demonstrated inequality for minorities, with provisions tailored to removing specific, documented barriers to the success of minorities. Plans failing these tests have been consistently rejected by the Court, as in *Richmond v. J. A. Croson Company* (1989).

Michael Haas

See also: *Adarand Constructors v. Peña*; Affirmative action; Civil Rights Act of 1964; Discrimination: racial and ethnic; Quotas; *Richmond v. J. A. Croson Company*; Set-asides.

Fusion movement

Beginning in 1890, leaders of the Populist, or People's, Party courted black votes in an effort to vote Democratic "redeemers" (southern whites who had regained control of local governments after Reconstruction had ended in the 1870's) out of office in the southern states. The appeal was based on the mutual interest of all downtrodden farmers, whatever their race. Fusionists argued that black farmers shared the same economic problems as whites and that the Republican Party only wanted to help the white business community. State organizations elected black delegates to their councils and gave them a voice in the party organization. Party rallies and speeches were attended by both races, although seating was segregated. Black Populist clubs served to indoctrinate members in party principles and to encourage speakers and leaders. Sometimes deals were made with Republican bosses to deliver black votes.

Fusion was never accepted by all white Populists. In the 1894 election, the party was divided between fusionists and antifusionists led by Tom Watson of Georgia. Watson believed that fusion would taint the party by association with the party of Lincoln (the Republicans). In any case, fusion was never a formal platform but a series of local agreements that led to success at the polls across the South. The demise of fusion and the Populist Party came in the presidential election of 1896.

Robert E. McFarland

See also: Compromise of 1877; Reconstruction.

Gandhi, Mohandas K.

The primary leader in India's nationalist movement, Mohandas K. Gandhi (1869-1948) developed and implemented a system of nonviolent resistance, or *satyagraha*, to oppose British rule in India during the first half of the twentieth century. Gandhi's legacy to the modern Civil Rights movement in the United States was the idea that persistent nonviolent agitation can bring about peaceful social change.

Trained in England, Gandhi became a successful attorney in South Africa's British-ruled Natal Colony from 1893 to 1901. Later he returned to India to join its nationalist movement. In 1920, India's British rulers made salt a government monopoly and imposed a salt tax. Gandhi led a peaceful march to Dandi and broke the Salt Law by making salt on April 5, 1920. This aroused the Indian nation to fight for freedom. He attended a roundtable conference in London in 1931 to discuss self-rule in India. He undertook many fasts to preserve Hindu-Muslim unity. In August, 1947, freedom from

British rule was granted to the Indian subcontinent; two nations were born, India and Pakistan. Martin Luther King, Jr., discovered a method for social reform in Gandhi's emphasis on nonviolence and love. Nonviolent resistance was a practical weapon that King used in the American Civil Rights movement.

Glenn Canyon

See also: Civil disobedience; Civil Rights movement; King, Martin Luther, Jr.

Grandfather clauses

After the Civil War (1861-1865), the Fifteenth Amendment to the U.S. Constitution guaranteed the voting rights of people of color in southern states. It expressly stated that the right to vote could not be "denied or abridged . . . on account of race, color, or previous condition of servitude." During the period of Reconstruction (1863-1877), the military administration in charge of the former Confederate states enforced this prescription. When Reconstruction ended, and the civil authority of these states replaced the federal military administration, white southerners devised various methods of circumventing the Fifteenth Amendment. One of these methods was the grandfather clause.

Grandfather clauses based eligibility to vote on the capacity of one's grandfather to vote. Of course, the grandfathers of the vast majority of African Americans in the South had been slaves and therefore had never been allowed to vote. Seven southern states incorporated such a clause into their state constitutions. Along with poll taxes, literacy tests, and other so-called Jim Crow measures, grandfather clauses effectively prohibited African Americans from voting for several decades. In 1915, the U.S. Supreme Court declared the grandfather clause to be an unconstitutional qualification for voting.

Aristide Sechandice

See also: Fifteenth Amendment; *Guinn v. United States*; Jim Crow laws; Literacy tests; Poll tax; Reconstruction; Voting Rights Act of 1965.

Great Migration

The Great Migration was the early twentieth century movement of more than a million African Americans from the rural South and Midwest to northern cities.

The Great Migration, a demographic shift of African Americans from southern states to midwestern and northeastern states, occurred roughly between 1910 and 1930. Because migration figures are based on the U.S. census, which is conducted every tenth year, the dating of migration events is imprecise. The data indicate only that this migration took place sometime between 1910 and 1930, but other historical evidence suggests that it began sometime during World War I (between 1914 and 1918) and ended around the onset of the Great Depression in 1929.

During the Great Migration, the industrial northern and midwestern states of New York, Illinois, Pennsylvania, Ohio, and Michigan experienced the greatest net migration of African Americans. The greatest net loss of African American population was from the southern, agricultural states of Georgia, South Carolina, Virginia, Alabama, and Mississippi. As they moved from one region to another, most of the migrants also moved from rural areas to urban areas. Between 1910 and 1920, the African American population of Detroit grew from 5,000 to 40,800; that of Cleveland from 8,400 to 34,400; that of Chicago from 44,000 to 109,400; and that of New York from 91,700 to 152,400. The transition from rural to urban locales was accompanied by a transition from employment in agriculture to employment in industrial or service occupations for increasing numbers of African Americans.

Reasons for Leaving   The reasons that African Americans did not leave the South in large numbers until fifty years after the end of the Civil War have been the subject of debate among social scientists and historians. Both social and economic factors were involved. After the Civil War, owners of plantations and farms in the South imposed new ways of controlling labor that were almost as restrictive as slavery had been. As sharecroppers, former slaves and their descendants were allowed to farm land belonging to the property owner in return for part of the harvest. These arrangements usually left the sharecroppers perpetually indebted to the landowners, so that they were financially obligated to stay on the land although legally they were free to leave. In addition, many African Americans who were born during the period of slavery were accustomed or resigned to their inferior social and economic positions and were reluctant to seek change. According to W. E. B. Du Bois, a leading African American intellectual of the period, African Americans who came of age around 1910 were the first generation for whom slavery was a distant memory. Jim Crow laws that formalized segregation and discrimination and racial violence that included lynchings motivated many in this new generation of African Americans to seek better conditions in the North.

Because the vast majority of African Americans in the South worked in agriculture, particularly in the production of cotton, several bad crop years and a boll weevil infestation in the mid-1910's contributed to the decision on the part of some to migrate when they did. The increase in out-migration was greatest in the areas that experienced the greatest crop failures.

Changing conditions in the North also played an important role in the timing of the Great Migration. Prior to World War I, immigration from Europe had supplied the labor needs of northern industry, and African Americans in northern cities usually could find work only as servants, porters, janitors, or waiters. Most industries hired African Americans only during strikes, as a way to exert pressure on Euro-American workers. Restrictions imposed during World War I reduced the number of European immigrants entering the United States by more than 90 percent, from 1.2 million in 1914 to 110,000 in 1918. This reduction in the available labor force took place just as the war increased demand for industrial production. Northern factories, mills, and workshops that previously had disdained African American workers were forced actively to recruit them, offering wages that were often twice what African Americans could earn in the South, plus inducements such as free rooms and train fare. Northward migration was encouraged by news of opportunities spread not only by personal letters home from new arrivals but also by advertisements and articles in newspapers such as the *Chicago Defender*, published by Robert Abbott, an African American editor. In some industries, managers attempted to foster racial division among their workers by encouraging segregated labor unions. The strategy was effective, and workplace competition sometimes contributed to antagonism and racial violence.

Forming of Communities   African Americans in northern cities established their own communities, including the Manhattan neighborhood of Harlem. Although it was primarily occupied by wealthy European Americans at the beginning of the twentieth century, African Americans had been in Harlem since Dutch colonial times. Philip A. Payton, Jr., was among several African American business people who saw an opportunity when a housing glut in Harlem coincided with an influx of African Americans. He leased apartment buildings and rented the apartments to African American tenants, antagonizing some of the wealthy Euro-American residents. Harlem was soon an almost exclusively African American enclave.

Harlem became not only a home for African American workers but also a center of intellectual, cultural, and political development. The Harlem Renaissance, fostered by such African American intellectuals as Du Bois and the poet Langston Hughes, was embraced by white liberals as an alternative to bourgeois American culture. Harlem also became known for African American performing arts, which attracted many white visitors seeking entertainment. Jamaican-born Marcus Garvey arrived in 1916 to establish a branch of his newly formed Universal Negro Improvement Association (UNIA), which was intended to unite all the "Negro peoples of the world." The UNIA flourished in New York and other northern cities during the 1920's. Garvey encouraged African Americans to take pride in their heritage and to establish their own businesses.

The Great Migration ended with the onset of the Great Depression. Because of poverty and the fierce competition with Euro-Americans for scarce jobs, African Americans from the South found the North to be a less desirable destination. During the 1930's, net migration of African Americans from the South was diminished by about one-half, to 347,500. The Great Migration set the stage, however, for subsequent migrations of African Americans that would be even greater in absolute numbers. By the 1940's, the trend had reversed again, with net migration growing to 1,244,700, a level that would be sustained or exceeded during subsequent decades.

James Hayes-Bohanan

Core Resources

Nicholas Lemann's *The Promised Land: The Great Black Migration and How It Changed America* (New York: Alfred A. Knopf, 1991) describes the second Great Migration, which began in the 1940's, and includes biographical sketches of individual migrant families and a comprehensive discussion of political implications. *The Black American Reference Book* (Englewood Cliffs, N.J.: Prentice-Hall, 1976), edited by Mabel M. Smythe, provides demographic details of the migration. Ronald Takaki's "To the Promised Land: Blacks in the Urban North," in *A Different Mirror: A History of Multicultural America* (Boston: Little, Brown, 1993), uses primary sources, including music, advertisements, and letters, to detail the impacts of the migration on northern urban culture and labor relations.

See also: Employment among African Americans; Racial and ethnic demographics: trends; Universal Negro Improvement Association.

Green v. County School Board of New Kent County

In *Green,* the U.S. Supreme Court on May 27, 1968, determined for the first time that school boards have an affirmative duty to desegregate their schools and disallowed freedom-of-choice desegregation plans that do not result in substantial pupil mixing.

In the wake of the Supreme Court's 1954 decision in *Brown v. Board of Education* that outlawed school segregation, few southern school boards took action to integrate their schools. Finally, in the mid-1960's, under the threat of federal fund cutoffs and adverse court decisions, most southern school boards made some effort to integrate their schools. Many such school boards did so by adopting an assignment system whereby students were permitted to choose which school they wished to attend. Most such freedom-of-choice plans resulted in little racial integration. Black students typically chose to attend traditionally black schools, whereas white students chose to attend traditionally white schools. As a result, schools remained racially segregated in many southern school districts following the introduction of free-choice plans.

One school district that adopted a free-choice plan during the 1960's was the school district in New Kent County, Virginia. New Kent County is a rural county; its student population was about half black and half white, with blacks and whites scattered throughout the county. Prior to 1965, the schools in New Kent County had been completely segregated, with all the black students attending the county's one black school and all the white students attending the county's one white school. In 1965, the school board adopted a free-choice plan whereby every student was permitted to choose between the two schools. As a result of the free choice, all the white students chose to remain in the white school and 85 percent of the black students chose to remain in the black school.

A group of black parents, with the assistance of the National Association for the Advancement of Colored People (NAACP) Legal Defense and Educational Fund, filed a lawsuit challenging this free-choice plan. These parents contended that the plan was deficient because it did not effectively dismantle the old dual school system. The Supreme Court, faced with thirteen years of southern school board recalcitrance on school desegregation, agreed that the school board's free-choice plan did not satisfy constitutional standards and announced that the school board had an affirmative duty to devise a desegregation plan that actually resulted in substantial pupil mixing. This decision, the Supreme Court's most important school desegregation decision since the 1954 *Brown* decision, helped transform school desegregation law by forcing school boards to devise assignment plans that resulted in greater integration. In the wake of the *Green* decision, lower courts throughout the South required school boards to take additional action to integrate their schools.

Davison M. Douglas

See also: *Brown v. Board of Education*; Civil Rights movement; National Association for the Advancement of Colored People; National Association for the Advancement of Colored People Legal Defense and Educational Fund; Segregation: de facto and de jure.

Greensboro sit-ins

On February 1, 1960, four black students from the North Carolina Agricultural and Technical College sat down at the whites-only lunch counter of the Woolworth's department store in Greensboro, North Carolina, and refused

Students from North Carolina A&T College on the second day of the sit-in protest at Greensboro's Woolworth lunch counter. *(Library of Congress)*

to leave until served. The next day, they returned along with twenty-six more students. By the end of the week, more than three hundred black students were involved in nonviolent demonstrations in downtown Greensboro.

The white community at first refused to make any change in the status quo, but in April, white leaders offered a plan for partial desegregation. The student leadership, the Student Executive Committee for Justice, rejected this offer as a blatant attempt at tokenism. Greensboro officials then tried arrests, sending forty-five demonstrators to jail on trespassing charges. The protesters responded with a boycott, which cut profits for retail businesspeople by one-third. Finally, six months after the protest began, the white community gave up and desegregated downtown businesses.

The sit-in at Woolworth's launched a regionwide campaign and marked the beginning of the student phase of the Civil Rights movement, led by a new organization called the Student Nonviolent Coordinating Committee (SNCC). By August of 1961, more than seventy thousand blacks and whites had taken part in similar protests and more than three thousand had been arrested.

Robert E. McFarland

See also: Civil Rights movement; Student Nonviolent Coordinating Committee.

Griffin v. Breckenridge

Griffin v. Breckenridge, decided June 7, 1971, extended federal civil rights guarantees of equal protection of the law to the protection of personal rights. On July 2, 1966, a group of African Americans who were suspected of being civil rights workers were halted on a Mississippi highway near the Alabama border by Lavon and Calvin Breckenridge, who purposely blocked the road with their car. The Breckenridges forced the African Americans from their vehicle and then subjected them to intimidation by firearms. They were clubbed about their heads, beaten with pipes and other weapons, and repeatedly threatened with death. Although terrorized and seriously injured, the African Americans (who included Griffin) survived. They subsequently filed a suit for damages, charging that they had been assaulted for the purpose of preventing them and "other Negro-Americans" from enjoying the equal rights, privileges, and immunities of citizens of the state of Mississippi and of the United States, including the rights to free speech, assembly, association, and movement and the right not to be enslaved.

A federal district court dismissed the complaint by relying on a previous U.S. Supreme Court decision, *Collins v. Hardyman* (1951), which in order to avoid difficult constitutional issues had held that federal law extended only to "conspiracies" condoned or perpetrated by states. That is, the Court tried to avoid opening questions involving congressional power or the content of state as distinct from national citizenship, or interfering in local matters such as assault and battery cases or similar illegalities that clearly fell under local jurisdiction.

The *Collins* case, however, had been decided a decade before the nationwide Civil Rights movement of the 1960's, a period marked by the enactment of a new series of federal civil rights laws as well as by attentive regard by the U.S. Supreme Court of Chief Justice Warren Burger to cases involving civil rights violations. The Burger court heard the *Griffin* case on appeal.

The Supreme Court's unanimous decision in *Griffin* was delivered by Justice Potter Stewart on June 7, 1971. The Court broadly interpreted the federal statute under which Griffin brought damages, Title 42 of the U.S. Code, section 1985. Section 1985 stipulated that if two or more persons conspired or went in disguise on public highways with the intent to deprive any person or any class of persons of equal protection of the laws or of equal privileges and immunities under the laws, a conspiracy existed and damages could be brought. The Court waived consideration of whether the *Collins* case had been correctly decided. Instead, reviewing previous civil rights legislation, starting in 1866, the justices determined that the language of the federal statute clearly indicated that state action was not required to invoke federal protection of constitutionally guaranteed personal rights from impairment by personal conspiracies. *Griffin* effectively extended federal safeguards of civil rights to reach private conspiracies under the Thirteenth Amendment as well as under congressional powers to protect the right of interstate travel.

Clifton K. Yearley

See also: Civil Rights movement; Thirteenth Amendment.

Griggs v. Duke Power Company

The Supreme Court's 1971 decision in *Griggs* established the "adverse impact" test for discrimination so that an unequal statistical pattern could be used as *prima facie* evidence.

The Civil Rights Act of 1964, Title VII, prohibited workplace segregation. Shortly after the law took effect in mid-1965, Duke Power Company in North Carolina rescinded its policy of restricting blacks to its labor department, so in principle they could transfer to other departments. Nevertheless, according to a company policy, begun in 1955, all employees but those in Duke's labor department had to have a high school diploma. Therefore, all those applying for a transfer from the labor department in 1965 needed a diploma. For those lacking a high school diploma (blacks were far less likely to have completed twelve grades than whites in that part of North Carolina), an alternative was to score at the national median on two standardized aptitude tests.

Willie Griggs and coworkers in the labor department at the company's Dan River steam-generating plant filed a class-action charge with the Equal Employment Opportunity Commission (EEOC), which ruled in favor of Griggs. When the company refused to conciliate the case, Griggs and his coworkers filed suit in district court. The court held that a claim of prior inequities was beyond the scope of Title VII and that the requirements for a high school diploma or a passing score on standardized tests were not intentionally discriminatory.

The district court's decision was overruled by the Supreme Court. Chief Justice Warren Burger delivered a unanimous Supreme Court opinion (8 to 0), setting forth the adverse impact test. According to this principle, if statistics show that a job requirement screens out one race, the employer must prove that the requirement is relevant to the performance of the job. Since the percentage of black high school graduates and percentages of blacks who passed the two tests were substantially below percentages for whites, Duke Power had to prove that the jobs sought by Griggs and his coworkers required completing high school or having a level of intelligence at the national median. Since the company advanced no such evidence, the Court ruled that Title VII discrimination had occurred and decreed that "any tests used must measure the person for the job and not the person in the abstract."

The decision had an extremely broad impact: It called into question all lists of qualifications for every job in the United States. Employers were called upon to review job qualifications and to recalibrate job duties to job qualifications or risk successful discrimination suits.

In the 1980's the Supreme Court began to chip away at the *Griggs* ruling. In *Wards Cove Packing Company v. Atonio* (1989), the Court shifted the burden of proof so that those filing suit must prove that specific job requirements alone cause statistical disparities. Congress responded by passing the Civil Rights Act of 1991, codifying the original *Griggs* ruling into law.

Michael Haas

See also: Civil Rights Act of 1964; Civil Rights Act of 1991; Discrimination: racial and ethnic; Equality of opportunity.

Grovey v. Townsend

In *Grovey v. Townsend*, the Supreme Court ruling on April 1, 1935, upheld "whites only" primaries when approved by state party conventions without any involvement or encouragement from the state legislature.

One of the most successful devices in eliminating black voters in the South was the white primary. Since the Democratic Party dominated the solid South, whoever won the Democratic primary went on to win the general election. If blacks could not participate in the primaries, they were denied any real choice in selecting public officials.

In *Newberry v. United States* (1921), the U.S. Supreme Court held that primary elections were not constitutionally protected. Although the *Newberry* case took place in Michigan and involved the issue of vote fraud rather than racial discrimination, the South immediately took advantage of the ruling. In 1924 the Texas legislature passed a law that barred blacks from participation in that state's primary elections. Three years later, a unanimous Supreme Court struck down the Texas law in *Nixon v. Herndon* (1927), finding the actions of the Texas legislature a clear violation of the equal protection clause of the Fourteenth Amendment.

The Texas legislature then passed a law authorizing the executive committees of the political parties to determine eligibility for voting in primary elections. As expected, the executive committee of the Texas Democratic Party excluded blacks from the primary. In *Nixon v. Condon* (1932), in a 5-4 decision, the U.S. Supreme Court ruled that the executive committee had acted as the agent of the state. As such, the attempt to bar black participation in the primary still violated the equal protection clause.

Texas succeeded on its third attempt to ban black voting. Immediately after the *Condon* decision, the Texas Democratic Party convention, without any authorization from the legislature, adopted a resolution restricting party membership to whites. R. R. Grovey, a black resident of Houston, brought suit against the county clerk who refused to give him a primary ballot. On April 1, 1935, a unanimous U.S. Supreme Court upheld the actions of the state party convention. According to the Court, there was no violation of the equal protection clause because there was no state action involved. The Democratic Party was a voluntary association of individuals who acted in their private capacity to exclude blacks from primary elections.

In 1941 the U.S. Supreme Court reversed *Newberry* in *United States v. Classic* (1941). The *Classic* decision brought primary elections under constitutional protection for the first time. *Classic* also paved the way for *Smith v. Allwright* (1944), the Supreme Court case banning white primaries.

Darryl Paulson

See also: National Association for the Advancement of Colored People; *Newberry v. United States; Nixon v. Herndon; Smith v. Allwright.*

Guinn v. United States

The Supreme Court's June 21, 1915, decision in *Guinn v. United States* overturned Oklahoma's grandfather clause and marked a first step in the National Association for the Advancement of Colored People's campaign to use the courts to combat racial discrimination.

Though the Fifteenth Amendment supposedly prohibited racial discrimination in voting, during the late nineteenth and early twentieth centuries southern and border states found ways to prevent African Americans from voting in significant numbers. One method was the literacy test. One potential drawback to this practice, however, was that such a test would also prevent poorly educated whites from voting. A number of states solved this problem by adopting grandfather clauses, provisions that allowed anyone registered before a certain date or anyone descended from such a person to vote regardless of literacy. Since the date selected was usually set at a point when there would have been few black voters (1866 was popular), very few blacks would qualify. Thus a measure that was nonracial on the surface was decidedly discriminatory in its effects.

Many grandfather laws had only temporary application, and most southern states moved away from them in the early twentieth century. In 1910, however, Oklahoma enacted a literacy test requirement with a permanent grandfather clause. The measure threatened not only black voting rights but also the position of the state's Republican Party. Fearing the loss of several thousand black votes, the U.S. attorney brought suit under the Reconstruction-era Enforcement Acts and won a conviction against state officials who were trying to enforce the literacy test.

The state appealed the case to the U.S. Supreme Court, attracting the attention of the National Association for the Advancement of Colored People (NAACP), which was just beginning to use litigation as a strategy for combating racial discrimination. Moorfield Story of the NAACP filed a brief in support of the government. In a unanimous decision, the Court upheld the convictions and ruled that the grandfather clause was a clear attempt to thwart the Fifteenth Amendment's ban on racial discrimination in voting.

The decision had relatively little immediate impact: Only one other state still had a grandfather clause at the time, and the Court carefully avoided declaring literacy tests themselves discriminatory. Nevertheless, the decision was not without its significance. Not only did it mark a modest revival of the Fifteenth Amendment, but it also encouraged the NAACP to continue its strategy of using litigation to put the Constitution on the side of racial equality.

William C. Lowe

See also: Civil rights; Fifteenth Amendment; Grandfather clauses; Jim Crow laws; Literacy tests; National Association for the Advancement of Colored People.

Gullah

The Gullahs came to North America in the first decades of the nineteenth century as slaves, originally from Angola (hence the name). Gullah is also a creole form of English that derives from the sea islands of Georgia and South Carolina. Gullah, once similar to the language spoken on slave plantations in the South, is very different from other African American dialects of English. The Gullah dialect combines elements of English vocabulary with grammar and punctuation elements of several West African languages such as Ewe, Mandinka, Igbo, Twi, and Yoruba.

Gullah traditions, myths, and language stayed longer with the Coastal Carolina Gullahs because of the isolation and self-sufficiency they experienced on the sea islands. As with many minority languages around the world, television, education, and increased social contact have all undermined the Gullah language and culture. Many Gullah speakers use various African American English dialects in dealing with nonislanders, though Gullah remains the language of home, family, and community. Gullah has affected culture and language beyond the Carolina sea islands with words such as goober (peanuts), gumbo, and yam. The Gullah dialect and culture were spread to mainstream America through the tales of Uncle Remus and Bre'r Rabbit.

Jason Pasch

See also: Ebonics; Slavery: history.

Haitians and Haitian refugees

Haitians have immigrated to the United States, particularly New York and Florida, in significant numbers since the 1950's. In general, U.S. policy toward Haitians has been unreceptive since the 1970's, treating them as economic migrants rather than refugees.

During the 1980's and early 1990's, many Haitians seeking asylum in the United States were intercepted at sea and forced to return to Haiti. This treatment contrasts with that of Cuban asylum seekers, who have generally received a generous welcome to U.S. shores as legitimate refugees. The U.S. government's differential treatment of Cubans fleeing the Marxist-dominated Fidel Castro government and of Haitians fleeing a very poor country governed by right-wing repressive leaders caused many to question U.S. refugee policy. In addition, Haitians speak Creole and are black, leading some to suggest latent racist motivations for the U.S. government's actions.

The Haitian Immigration Experience   Haitians, like citizens of most Caribbean countries, have for many decades participated in labor-based migration throughout the Caribbean region, including the United States. Haiti's economy is among the poorest in the Western Hemisphere, providing a significant reason for migration. However, authoritarian regimes also contributed to migration, as some people fled political repression. In the 1950's and 1960's, skilled Haitian professionals legally entered the United States and Canada as permanent or temporary immigrants. Although many left Haiti in part because of political repression, they were treated as routine immigrants rather than refugees. Legal immigration continued throughout the 1970's and 1980's, but larger numbers of much poorer people also began to leave Haiti by boat.

For many years, Haiti was governed by the authoritarian regimes of François "Papa Doc" Duvalier and his son, Jean Claude "Baby Doc" Duvalier, who finally fled the country in 1986. A series of repressive regimes continued to rule the country until Haiti's first democratically elected government, that of Jean-Bertrand Aristide, was established in 1990, but this government was overthrown by a military coup in 1991 and had to be reinstalled by the international community in 1994, after three years of devastating economic sanctions imposed by the United Nations that, coupled with domestic political repression, precipitated large flows of refugees. The refugee flows subsided once the military regime gave up power, the U.N. peacekeeping forces were deployed, the Aristide government was reestablished, and the economic sanctions were removed.

Thousands of Haitians have immigrated to the United States since the early 1970's. Many thousands more were deported because they were judged to be lacking legitimate asylum claims. Those who managed to stay in the United States concentrated around already existing Haitian communities in Florida, especially in the Miami area, and in New York City, where several hundred thousand Haitians make their home. Lacking significant public assistance, the Haitians who settled in the United States during the 1970's and 1980's were obliged to rely on aid from charitable organizations and the already established local Haitian communities.

Reactions to the Immigrants Reactions to the Haitian migration varied considerably. Generally, the earlier and more skilled migration out of Haiti was uncontroversial. As larger numbers of poorer Haitians, especially the "boat people," sought entry into the United States, however, concern about the economic implications of these undocumented migrants arose. Local politicians, especially in southern Florida, under pressure from their constituents, including elite members of the Cuban exile group, along with others concerned about the potentially disruptive Haitian flow, put pressure on Congress and successive presidents to deter the Haitian migration.

However, steps by the federal government to staunch the Haitian migratory flows eventually prompted political opposition by second-generation Cubans, voluntary agencies, human rights groups, and the Congressional Black Caucus. Many of these groups charged that the discriminatory treatment of Haitians was based at least in part on race. Efforts to detain Haitians in the United States were successfully challenged in court, and advocates for Haitians won a number of court-related victories to ensure fairer treatment for Haitian asylum seekers. The interdiction programs instituted by President Ronald Reagan, however, continued under the presidencies of George Bush and Bill Clinton. Only with the return of democracy to Haiti in 1994 did the migration pressures from Haiti to the United States ease.

Future Prospects The return of stability to the Haitian political system and the application of considerable international economic assistance holds out hope that Haiti will benefit from economic development, thus encouraging investment at home and further reducing pressures for migration abroad. The booming economy in the United States during the 1990's and the reduction in illegal and undocumented migration from Haiti helped to reduce the controversy surrounding Haitian migration.

Robert F. Gorman

Core Resources

Alex Stepick's *Haitian Refugees in the U.S.* (London: Minority Rights Group, 1982) and Jake Miller's *The Plight of Haitian Refugees* (New York: Praeger, 1984) provide critiques of the Haitian predicament in the United States. To set the Haitian situation into the wider immigration experience, see Alejandro Portes and Rubén G. Rumbaut's *Immigrant America: A Portrait* (Berkeley: University of California Press, 1990). For a contrast of the Cuban and Haitian refugee and resettlement experience, see Felix R. Masud-Piloto's *From Welcomed Exiles to Illegal Immigrants* (Lanham, Md.: Rowman & Littlefield, 1996). On the foreign policy implications of U.S. Haitian policy, see *Western Hemisphere Immigration and United States Foreign Policy* (University Park: Pennsylvania State University Press, 1992), edited by Christopher Mitchell.

See also: Congressional Black Caucus.

Harper v. Virginia Board of Elections

The Supreme Court's March 24, 1966, decision in *Harper v. Virginia Board of Elections* eliminated the use of poll taxes in state and local elections.

Poll taxes, or the payment of a fee in order to vote, were widely used in southern states as a means to restrict the electorate, and in particular black voters. Because poll taxes led to corruption—as candidates and political organizations would pay the taxes of their supporters—and because there were more effective ways of eliminating black voters, many southern states started to repeal their poll taxes. Opposition to the poll tax was led by the National Committee to Abolish the Poll Tax and the National Association for the Advancement of Colored People (NAACP). On five occasions the House of Representatives passed legislation to ban the tax, but southern senators filibustered, blocking passage in the Senate. In 1964, the Twenty-fourth Amendment to the Constitution was ratified, eliminating the use of poll taxes in federal elections. Five states—Alabama, Arkansas, Mississippi, Texas, and Virginia—continued to use poll taxes in state and local elections. Arkansas dropped its poll tax in 1964 after the passage of the Twenty-fourth Amendment.

In 1965 the U.S. House of Representatives passed a poll tax ban in state elections as part of the Voting Rights Act of 1965. The Senate failed to support the ban, however, and the final version of the Voting Rights Act merely stated that the poll tax "denied or abridged" the constitutional right to vote.

Blacks in Virginia brought suit against that state's $1.50 annual poll tax as a requirement for voting in state and local elections. The U.S. district court, citing the 1937 case *Breedlove v. Suttles,* dismissed the claim. In *Breedlove,* the U.S. Supreme Court had held that, except where constrained by the Constitution, the states may impose whatever conditions on suffrage that they deem appropriate. On appeal, a 6-3 majority in the Supreme Court overruled *Breedlove* and held that the payment of a fee in order to vote violated the Constitution.

Interestingly, although the plaintiffs were black, the ruling was based on economic discrimination rather than racial discrimination. "To introduce wealth or payment of a fee as a measure of a voter's qualifications," wrote Justice William Douglas in the majority opinion, "is to introduce a capricious or irrelevant factor." In the view of the Court's majority, voter qualifications had no relationship to wealth. The three dissenters believed that a "fairly applied" poll tax could be a reasonable basis for the right to vote. The *Harper* decision actually had little direct impact. Since only four states used poll taxes as a condition for voting at the time of the *Harper* decision, the ban on poll taxes barely generated a ripple on the surface of American politics.

Darryl Paulson

See also: Poll tax; Vote, right to; Voting Rights Act of 1965.

Head Start

Head Start is a U.S. government program established in 1965 to improve the potential for children in disadvantaged households to escape poverty and succeed later in life. The program provides early education and nutritional programs to children between the ages of three and five years old. It is targeted primarily at low-income households and children with disabilities.

In addition to the main program, the Early Head Start program targets pregnant women and infants and toddlers, and the Migrant Head Start program helps migrant workers. All the Head Start programs serve a disproportionately large number of minority children and involve federal grants to local service providers.

The programs are founded on the reasoning that early intervention is the most effective way to ensure a person's long-term success. Investment in nutrition and education during a child's early years is thought to create a solid foundation for later learning and development. Such investment would therefore reduce the need for more costly and controversial programs at later stages, such as youth counseling, welfare, drug rehabilitation, or incarceration.

Such investment is also seen as a means for increasing minority enrollment in college that is more politically acceptable than alternatives such as affirmative action. The programs are therefore highly popular with the

Pupils in a Head Start classroom practicing counting skills. *(Library of Congress)*

public and politicians of both the Democratic and Republican Parties. Nevertheless, formal long-term evaluations of Head Start programs have raised serious questions about their actual effectiveness.

Steve D. Boilard

See also: Affirmative action; Economics and race; Poverty and race; Welfare's impact on racial/ethnic relations.

Heart of Atlanta Motel v. United States

The Supreme Court's December 14, 1964, decision in *Heart of Atlanta Motel v. United States* upheld the constitutionality of the public accommodations section (Title II) of the Civil Rights Act of 1964.

After the Civil War, Congress passed the Thirteenth, Fourteenth, and Fifteenth Amendments in order to establish legal and political rights for the newly freed slaves. The Fourteenth Amendment, in part, was designed to protect black citizens from discrimination by state and local governments in the South. It did not address the issue of private discrimination against blacks in hotels, restaurants, and theaters. Was discrimination by private individuals therefore legal? The U.S. Congress addressed this question when it passed the Civil Rights Act of 1875. This law made it illegal to discriminate against individuals in public accommodations. In 1883 the U.S. Supreme Court declared the Civil Rights Act of 1875 to be unconstitutional. According to the Court, the Fourteenth Amendment only protected against state discrimination and not discrimination by private individuals in their private businesses.

Almost a century later, the U.S. Congress addressed this issue again. Congressional hearings were held concerning the difficulty African Americans faced in using public accommodations. According to the hearings, blacks traveling from Washington, D.C., to New Orleans, Louisiana, in 1963 would find that the average distance between hotel and motel accommodations available to them was 174 miles. As a result of the hearings, Congress incorporated a public accommodations section as part of the Civil Rights Act of 1964. The public accommodations section prevented discrimination in hotels, motels, restaurants, theaters, sports arenas, and other public facilities. Congress based its authority to regulate public accommodations on the "commerce clause" of the Constitution, which grants Congress the authority to "regulate Commerce with foreign Nations, and among the several States."

The Supreme Court's *Heart of Atlanta Motel* decision turned back the first major challenge to the Civil Rights Act of 1964, ensuring there would be no return to legally protected racial segregation in public accommodations such as movie theaters. *(Library of Congress)*

The *Heart of Atlanta* case involves the immediate challenge to the constitutionality of the public accommodations section of the Civil Rights Act of 1964. The Heart of Atlanta Motel, a local operation, refused to serve African Americans. As a local motel, it argued that its not serving blacks had no impact on interstate commerce. Attorneys for the U.S. government argued that interstate commerce was affected by the motel's policy because three-quarters of its clientele came from outside the state. In upholding the public accommodations section of the Civil Rights Act of 1964, a unanimous Supreme Court argued that it made no difference that the motel was a local operation. If interstate commerce is affected at all, "it does not matter how local the operation which applies the squeeze." A companion case, *Katzenbach v. McClung* (1964), involving a small, local restaurant in Birmingham, Alabama, which refused sit-down service to blacks, reached a similar conclusion. Although the Court was unanimous in upholding the public accommodations section of the Civil Rights Act of 1964, the justices did not all concur on the reasoning. A majority of the justices upheld the law on the basis of the commerce clause, but Justice William Douglas wanted to base the decision on the equal protection clause of the Fourteenth Amendment.

Darryl Paulson

See also: Civil Rights Act of 1964; Discrimination: racial and ethnic; Fair Housing Act; Freedom Riders; Greensboro sit-ins; Housing; Segregation: de facto and de jure.

Homelessness

"Homelessness" refers to a marginalized condition of detachment from society and to the lack of bonds that connect settled persons to a network of institutions and social orders. Although homelessness knows no racial bounds, those minorities living at or below the poverty level erroneously stand out in the minds of some white Americans as constituting the "homeless problem." Such a view arises from racist stereotypes rather than fact.

By the late 1980's, the homeless population in the United States, according to both governmental and advocacy reports, was estimated to be between 600,000 and 3 million. Included among these casualties were men, women, and children of all racial and ethnic backgrounds; urban and rural workers; displaced and deinstitutionalized persons; alcoholics, drug addicts, AIDS victims, and the mentally ill; physically abused mothers and their babies; sexually abused teenagers and preadolescents; neglected elderly people; and migrants, refugees, and veterans.

Like other social problems, the problem of homelessness has historically revolved around the way in which specific societal groups and class interests have defined the social issue in the first place. Generally, public policies in the United States regarding homelessness, the homeless, and the shortage of low-income or subsidized housing in America are influenced by and inseparable from local and national politics. Moreover, economic crises and considerations, grounded in the ideological perspectives of laissez-faire, free-market capitalism and liberal social reformism, are also at work. At the same time, while most people do not blame individual homeless people per se for their predicament, they still support a public policy ideology that essentially does nothing to alter the victimizing conditions of homelessness.

In part, this has to do with a legacy of viewing homeless people primarily as middle-aged men and elderly eccentric "shopping-bag ladies" rather than primarily as children, mothers, and families. When most people think about the homeless, rarely do images come to mind of teenage runaways, lacking marketable skills and financial resources, selling their bodies to the highest urban bidders. Typically, people do not think about homeless children, most of them abused or neglected, sleeping in abandoned buildings without heat, electricity, and running water. Most people do not think about homeless mothers who believe that it is better to exchange sexual services for shelter than to avail themselves of shelter opportunities that may entail the risk of losing their children to foster care or an adoption agency.

As a group of people, today's homeless may be thought of as a new subclass of people at the bottom of the U.S. stratification system. Although they are most obvious in urban areas, camping near downtown shelters or requesting aid at freeway offramps, there is also a less obvious group, the hidden homeless.

Far away from the more conspicuous sights of the urban homeless, on the rural roads of the corporate agrieconomy of the United States, thousands are doing their best to stay out of the way of local citizens and police, who may arrest and charge them for criminal trespassing, squatting, panhandling, or littering. In more than a few cases, these homeless persons have been arrested for merely trying to feed themselves. In the sparsely populated regions of the Midwest and the South, bankrupted and marginal farmers have been forced off their land, joining the ranks of other migrant workers in search of unskilled work. Crisscrossing the country, these members of a new migrant class, with and without their families, spend varying periods of time traveling the state highways and byways. If they are fortunate, they sleep in cars and trucks; if they are not, they sleep at rest stops, all-night truck stops, in plowed fields, or on the side of the road.

In many more communities, including medium-sized cities as well as urbanized metropolitan areas, a sizable majority of the homeless population remain, if not hidden, at least relatively invisible. That is to say, most of the urban homeless populations are warehoused out of sight in abandoned armories, terminals, or motels. In part, this situation is a result of governmental assistance and programs; it is also a result, in part, of the private efforts of concerned citizens and groups, especially of church-related assistance.

Programs and Policies   Temporary or emergency assistance is available through bureaucracies that operate at all levels of government. At the same time, public and private armories and shelters—some for whole families, some for couples only, some for single women, and some for battered women and their infants—protect these homeless groups from physical elements, at least during the night. There are also various secular and religious efforts to provide the homeless, hungry, and the nearly destitute with day shelters, soup kitchens, clothes closets, and food pantries. A few notable private nonprofit secular programs out of literally hundreds of programs nationwide are the Atlanta Day Shelter for Women, the Birmingham Partnership Assistance to the Homeless, and Cincinnati's Alcoholic Drop Inn Center Shelterhouse.

Without this array of programs to regulate the behavior of the new poor and homeless, these members of society would quickly become a threatening element that would call into question established political and economic arrangements. The sheer numbers of tens of thousands of homeless people roaming the urban streets in search of food and shelter would contribute to the widespread victimization of both the homeless and others. In turn, this would contribute to the further deterioration of the urban United States and to growing social disorder.

Despite these programs and other services, such as city policies that require the police to pick up homeless individuals and drive them to one of the nearby community shelters on cold nights when the temperatures drop below zero, hundreds of Americans still freeze to death every winter. As for the homeless of communities that do not or cannot provide forms of social welfare, most do not quickly perish. Even in the most caring and compassionate urban communities, where people do not necessarily look away as they step over or around homeless persons, after a while even those unfortunate souls who can be found sleeping in doorways, in metal trash receptacles, and in homemade cardboard shelters become invisible.

When one examines the significant increase in homelessness from some 10,000 to more than 1 million—within the context of an expanding base of poor persons in the United States—one finds that more and more people not only slipped down the socioeconomic ladder but also became part of a permanent group of have-nots. These people, many of whom had become members of the new homeless groups consisting of women and children, could therefore be regarded as marginal victims of a changing global political economy that has reduced the size of the unskilled and semiskilled industrial workforce in North America. These fundamental changes in the domestic economy must be reflected in the development of social housing for the nonaffluent. Until the United States adopts a public policy grounded in both a commitment to social and economic justice and a recognition of the need for the development of an alternative approach to homelessness and inexpensive housing, the delivery of adequate and permanent housing for all persons living in the United States will remain an unfulfilled dream of the thousands of homeless advocates and volunteers found nationwide.

Gregg Barak

Core Resources

Gregg Barak's *Gimme Shelter: A Social History of Homelessness in Contemporary America* (New York: Praeger, 1991) explains not only the root causes of homelessness but also why it is not going to "go away" unless a radically different social policy is introduced. Stephanie Golden's *The Women Outside: Meanings and Myths of Homelessness* (Berkeley: University of California Press, 1992) tells the story of homeless women throughout history. Valerie Polakow's *Lives on the Edge: Single Mothers and Their Children in the Other America* (Chicago: University of Chicago Press, 1993) locates crises in U.S. social and domestic policies in the history of American institutions and the history of childhood itself. Peter H. Rossi's *Down and Out in America: The Origins of Homelessness* (Chicago: University of Chicago Press, 1989) explores the incidence of homelessness in relation to such correlates as disabilities, addictions, illnesses, lack of relatives, unemployment rates, and housing costs. David A. Snow and Leon Anderson's *Down on Their Luck: A Study of Homeless Street People* (Berkeley: University of California Press, 1993) provides the best description available of the social order of homeless society and of the varieties of resourcefulness employed by the homeless to cope with their situations.

See also: Culture of poverty; Economics and race; Housing; Poverty and race.

Housing

The residential conditions and distribution of ethnic and racial minority groups in the United States are consequences of social and economic factors as well as of the characteristics of the localities in which these groups live. Principal processes are immigration, regional migration and distribution, acculturation and social mobility, racism, and discrimination.

African Americans, the largest U.S. ethnic or racial minority, are an overwhelmingly metropolitan-area population. About 90 percent of the African American population resides in urban areas, and two-thirds are central-city residents. In contrast, about three-quarters of the white population is metropolitan, and two-thirds of these are suburban. In part, this reflects the greater degree of home ownership by whites as compared to blacks, a majority of whom rent their homes. Furthermore, twice the proportion of whites compared to blacks live outside metropolitan areas.

The African American population has been predominantly southern; slightly more than half the African American population lives in the South. About one-fifth of American blacks live in the Midwest, slightly fewer in the Northeast, and fewer than 10 percent in the West. Whites, on the other hand, are rather evenly distributed, making up approximately 20 to 30 percent of the residents in each of the four regions. The state with the largest African American population is New York, with more than three million, followed by California, Texas, and Florida.

Hispanics, many of whom are recent immigrants, are concentrated primarily in four states. The border states of California and Texas are home to more than half the nation's Latinos, predominantly Mexican immigrants or people of Mexican ancestry. Florida's Latino population is largely Cuban American. Puerto Ricans make up the majority of Hispanics in New York State, although Spanish-speaking immigrants from other parts of the Caribbean, such as the Dominican Republic, represent a sizable contingent.

More than 90 percent of Hispanics are metropolitan area residents, primarily living in central-city neighborhoods; most rent their residences. The metropolitan area with the greatest Latino population is the Los Angeles-Anaheim-Riverside area of California, which contains one quarter of the U.S. Hispanic population. The majority of Hispanics in the New York metropolitan area are Puerto Rican.

Asian Americans are a diverse minority, consisting of descendants of earlier immigrants (primarily Japanese and Chinese) as well as newcomers from nations which, until recent decades, were not represented among the Asian American population (including Vietnamese, Asian Indians, and Southeast Asians). This minority includes Pacific Islanders (mostly Native Hawaiians) and recent Samoan and Guamanian immigrants. Ninety-four percent of Asian Americans are metropolitan-area residents, with slightly more than half being suburban. Unlike blacks and Hispanics, most are homeowners, and more than half are residents of the western states.

Causes of Residential Segregation   Waves of African American migrants have left the South since the early 1900's. Following World War II, a massive migration of blacks to the industrial centers of the Northeast, Midwest, and West resulted from the industrialization of southern agriculture, which displaced many tenant farmers and sharecroppers. Also, black veterans returning to the United States after World War II, having visited other areas of the country while in the military, were attracted to the job opportunities in northern factories. Consequently, in several of these cities, the numbers of African Americans doubled between 1950 and 1970.

Many strategies have been employed by whites to discourage darker-skinned newcomers from moving into white residential areas, contributing to the maintenance of residential racial segregation. History records instances of violence and other acts of intimidation in order to discourage perceived intrusions into white neighborhoods. Restrictive covenants added to property deeds have been employed in order to prevent the sale of housing to minorities. In some cohesive communities, researchers have found sales and rentals of residences conducted by means of informal communications in order to avoid the use of public advertising that might result in minority applicants. Slum clearance and public housing construction in the inner city have contributed to a concentration of minority residences. Following World War II, suburbanization, stimulated by the construction of housing developments, federally guaranteed mortgages for veterans, and new highways, contributed to flight from cities by the white middle class, further segregating minorities. Court-mandated school busing and black migration to cities contributed to white flight as well. Banks in many areas adopted the practice of "redlining," which resulted in the denial of mortgage loans to prospective buyers of homes in designated areas, usually racially transitional ones. Though illegal, the practice intensified the black concentration in central city areas.

Although some have suggested that African American preferences are the root cause of residential segregation, survey evidence has repeatedly indicated a preference for racially mixed neighborhoods on the part of blacks. Similar studies among whites indicate increased tolerance by whites of black residents living in their neighborhoods so long as they represent a numerical minority.

Social scientists have offered a variety of perspectives explaining the reasons for the persistence of residential segregation. Some theorists hold that the welfare system dulls incentives for minorities and the poor in general. The supposed predictability in subsistence provided by a monthly welfare check results in laziness and a lessened ambition to improve one's lot in life. Life becomes stagnant, as do the segregated neighborhoods in which these people reside.

The "culture of poverty" view, exemplified by the writings of anthropologist Oscar Lewis, holds that poverty conditions result in a general perspective that includes psychological depression and a view of life devoid of any hope of ever extricating oneself from one's predicament. A fatalism and the feeling that any efforts to improve one's life are doomed to failure result in a cycle of poverty that continues from generation to generation.

The institutional racism perspective attributes segregation to factors inherent in the institutions serving the poor in the inner city. Deteriorating, aging schools with inexperienced teachers lacking insight into ghetto life, a political institution concerned with servicing other populations in the society that are more likely to vote, an urban economy that no longer provides a living wage as low-paying service employment has replaced manufacturing jobs, and increasing unemployment as jobs migrate to the suburbs have left the black population behind as society has changed.

Sociologist William Julius Wilson holds the view that the upward social mobility experienced by middle-class blacks as a consequence of the civil rights revolution resulted in community leaders moving out of ghetto neighborhoods. This development, coupled with changes in the economy that reduced employment opportunities in the central cities, leaves the poor who have not benefited from civil rights advances behind in increasingly deteriorating areas abandoned by many community businesses. The result is a racially homogeneous neighborhood characterized by crime, drug use, illegitimate births, and other conditions characteristic of the underclass syndrome.

Patterns of Residential Segregation   The ethnic segregation experienced by the "new" European immigrants of the late nineteenth and early twentieth centuries was a transient phenomenon. Financial limitations and the psychological comfort of familiar cultural surroundings resulted in formation of an ethnic ghetto in the central city. With cultural assimilation attained through education and upward social mobility, later generations attained "respectable" middle-class occupations.

Research by Nancy Denton and Douglas Massey on contemporary ethnic and racial minorities indicates that this scenario is not occurring for all groups. Unlike advances made by African Americans in education and the workplace, residential segregation appears to be a relatively permanent condition of life for a large majority of blacks. This is true across social class lines. Tract data from U.S. censuses are used in calculating an index of dissimilarity, a statistical indicator of the proportion of the minority population that would have to move its census tract residence in order for proportional residential "evenness" or integration to occur. The researchers used data from sixty metropolitan areas that contained the largest populations of blacks, Hispanics, and Asians.

Denton and Massey's findings indicated that for the twenty metropolitan areas containing the largest black populations, residential segregation from whites was high regardless of black social class. Social class was measured using income, education, and occupational status, each of which was examined independently. Segregation indexes declined for blacks of higher social class but remained high. Cleveland, Detroit, and Chicago exhibited the highest degree of black/white residential segregation, Washington, D.C., and San Francisco the lowest. The authors pointed out that unlike earlier European immigrants who lived in relatively heterogeneous neighborhoods, an overwhelming majority of blacks live in racially homogeneous neighborhoods. This segregation is relatively impervious to advances in social mobility and is not transitory. Federal efforts such as the Fair Housing Act of 1968, an outgrowth of the urban disorders of the 1960's, have had little impact on this phenomenon.

Significantly smaller proportions of blacks than Hispanics and Asians live in suburbs. Data indicate that suburban blacks receive somewhat higher incomes than those residing in the inner city. The degree of residential racial segregation experienced by African Americans across class lines indicates that a high proportion of the black middle class in the suburbs lives under segregated conditions, as do their urban counterparts.

For Hispanics, in contrast to blacks, the index of dissimilarity is moderate, even for those in the lowest categories of social class. For U.S.-born Hispanics, descendants of immigrants (for research purposes, Puerto Ricans are treated as immigrants, although they are U.S. citizens), the segregation index declines with upward social mobility. For Latinos, in fact, increased education results in sharp declines in segregation, indicating a general acceptance by non-Hispanic whites of middle-class Latinos as neighbors. This decline is particularly true in Miami, where the Latino population is predominantly Cuban American and white, and in Los Angeles, where the great majority of Latinos are of Mexican ancestry. This is less the case in New York City and Newark, New Jersey, where the majority of Hispanics are of Puerto Rican descent. This Hispanic population is more segregated from whites than from blacks. Puerto Ricans are the only one of the three Hispanic populations with significant African ancestry; this may indicate that they are experiencing color prejudice, consistent with the findings for African Americans.

Federal housing studies of the residential accommodations of blacks and Latinos produce findings consistent with those groups' lower socioeconomic status. In contrast with medians for the total U.S. population, these minorities inhabit smaller living quarters, share fewer square feet per person, are less likely to have air conditioning, live in homes that are more likely to be older, and live in areas with streets or roads that are more likely to be in need of repair. Respondents from both minorities rate their neighborhoods lower as environments in which to live.

Asian Americans (including Pacific Islanders), although racially distinct from whites, experience reduced segregation with attainment of higher class status. Middle-class Asian Americans are undergoing a minority immigration experience not unlike that of the European immigrants who arrived near the beginning of the twentieth century, although they do not seem to be forming ethnic enclaves to the same extent as the European immigrants did. Most live in ethnically heterogeneous neighborhoods. In general, the dominant white population does not appear to object to sharing communities with upwardly mobile Asian Americans.

Consequences of Residential Segregation In addition to exacerbating such urban ghetto problems as poor schools, crime, and illegal drug use, residential segregation serves to limit communication between groups and, thus, precludes cooperation between populations in solving common problems. Separation promotes distrust, feelings of hostility, and occasionally open conflict. African Americans are segregated not only from whites but also from Asian Americans and from most Hispanic Americans. For African

Americans, attainment of higher education and other criteria of middle-class status do not readily translate into either acceptance as neighbors by the dominant whites or attendance at newly built, quality suburban schools by their children. Furthermore, homogeneous black neighborhoods are often perceived by political and economic powers as areas that can be sacrificed when new roads are to be built or when undesirable municipal facilities are to be erected. In addition, the ability of relatively few blacks to attain the American Dream divides the dominant whites from the largest U.S. racial or ethnic minority and breeds continual intergroup tensions.

American Indian Population   American Indians, or Native Americans, are included in a category with Eskimos and Aleuts by the U.S. Census Bureau, the two latter populations representing less than 5 percent of the total category. A little more than one third of American Indians live on reservations; however, there is substantial movement by Indians to and from reservations. Native Americans do not make up a sufficiently large population to establish enclaves equivalent to the ethnic communities of other minorities, so most urban Indians reside in heterogeneous working-class neighborhoods. Movement to the city is ordinarily for economic reasons. Returning to the reservation is often caused by loss of employment or to secure free health care from the Bureau of Indian Affairs' Indian Health Service. Poverty among Indians is two times the rate among the general population, and unemployment on some reservations may be as high as 80 percent. For many, reservation life involves overcrowded conditions, substandard housing, and lack of adequate sanitation. Government housing and mortgage programs administered by some of the individual tribes have made it easier for new home building and home improvements, and income from gaming (gambling) has promised to do more, but many Native Americans are simply too poor to consider new housing, even with the help of these agencies.

Edward V. Mednick

Core Resources
    Information on housing and segregation can be found in Nancy Denton and Douglas Massey's "Residential Segregation of Blacks, Hispanics, and Asians by Socioeconomic Status and Generation" (*Social Science Quarterly* 69, 1988) and their *American Apartheid* (Cambridge, Mass.: Harvard University Press, 1993); "Stereotypes and Segregation: Neighborhoods in the Detroit Area" (*American Journal of Sociology* 100, no. 3, 1994), by Reynolds Farley et al., and William Julius Wilson's *The Truly Disadvantaged: The Inner City, the Underclass, and Public Policy* (Chicago: University of Chicago Press, 1987).

    See also: Banking practices; Culture of poverty; Fair Housing Act; Hypersegregation; Minority and majority groups; Poverty and race; Redlining; Restrictive covenants; Segregation: de facto and de jure.

Hypersegregation

The term "hypersegregation" refers to the excessive physical and social separation of a class, ethnic, or racial group by forcing the group, usually through institutional arrangements, to reside in a limited area or neighborhood with low-quality educational facilities and few economic opportunities.

According to sociologists Norman A. Anderson and Cheryl Armstead, many minority group members, especially African Americans and Latinos who live in large metropolitan areas in the United States, experience hypersegregation. This phenomenon creates a state of extreme isolation from resources that allow people to improve their social and economic well-being. The isolation also dimishes people's ability to obtain adequate health care and thus negatively affects their health.

Hypersegregation is the result of a number of factors, one of the most prominent being pervasive housing discrimination against low-income minority group members. Noted sociologist William J. Wilson has shown that low-income nonwhites are more likely to live in impoverished residential areas than are low-income white Americans.

Gwenelle S. O'Neal

See also: Discrimination: racial and ethnic; Housing; Poverty and race; Segregation; Self-segregation.

"I Have a Dream" speech

The Reverend Dr. Martin Luther King, Jr.'s "I Have a Dream" speech called for a color-blind society, identifying a new American Dream for race relations.

The spring and summer of 1963 proved to be one of the most important times of the Civil Rights movement. On June 12, NAACP leader Medgar Evers was assassinated; white supremacist Byron de la Beckwith would not be found guilty of his murder for nearly thirty years. In April, 1963, protest against discrimination in the downtown department stores of Birmingham, Alabama, culminated in protests on April 4. King's arrest during these demonstrations and the media coverage of police violence against the demonstrators catapulted both the movement and King, the leader of the Southern Christian Leadership Conference (SCLC), into the national spotlight to an even greater degree than before. The boycotts and mass marches eventually provided sufficient pressure that white leaders promised to desegregate the stores' facilities, hire African Americans to work in the stores, and establish a biracial committee for ongoing talks concerning racial problems.

These gains were achieved at a price, however: King was jailed briefly; police brutality occurred against protesters; and arrested protesters filled Birmingham's jails. Nevertheless, the filled jails negatively affected the capacity of police to arrest and hold demonstrators, which was exactly what King and other civil rights leaders had hoped; news coverage of police brutality outraged many citizens; and, while jailed, King wrote his "Letter from Birmingham Jail," a document that delineated the need for and goals of the direct action campaigns of the Civil Rights movement. The acclaim that met this document foreshadowed the reaction to his speech at the March on Washington two months later.

March on Washington The purpose of the March on Washington (sometimes called the Poor People's March) was not merely to make an emotional plea on behalf of African Americans; its primary purpose was to expose the American public to the economic basis of racial inequality. Thus, the focus of the march was the need to increase jobs and economic opportunities for African Americans, in order for them to realize racial equality. These especially were the goals of the leaders of the March on Washington, A. Philip Randolph, labor leader and organizer of the Brotherhood of Sleeping Car Porters, and civil rights activist Bayard Rustin, one of the earliest planners of the event. In fact, the full title of the event was "The March on Washington for Jobs and Freedom." The march, therefore, had a set of important goals: more jobs, a higher minimum wage, support for President John F. Kennedy's antidiscrimination legislation, and arousing the conscience of the United States to the plight of African Americans. King's speech was especially important on this last point, for the "I Have a Dream" section of the speech was an eloquent plea for a society based on

Martin Luther King, Jr., delivering his "I Have a Dream" speech on the steps of the Lincoln Memorial. *(Library of Congress)*

racial harmony. Nevertheless, while King's speech is best remembered for his vision of racial equality, its true import lies in the fact that the renown accorded the speech helped advance the multifaceted goals of the march, thus helping to pave the way for the Civil Rights Act of 1964.

King's Vision   The passage in which King reiterates "I have a dream" should be understood in the overall context of the talk. Although King started by reading from his prepared text, he disregarded this text about halfway through the speech and incorporated a theme he had used in some previous speeches: "I have a dream." This theme introduced into the speech two of the main tenets of the SCLC: interracial cooperation and social equality. King's eloquent vision of a future without racial divisions captured the emotions of many viewers and, later, readers of the speech. In fact, the emotional power of that section of King's remarks sometimes blurs the memory of other, equally important aspects of his speech.

King's speech has become widely known as a masterpiece of rhetoric and argumentation. One rhetorical device that King used to great effect is repetition. The most obvious example is the repetition of the phrase "I have a dream" to detail different aspects of King's vision of racial harmony, but there are other, equally important examples. In the opening section of the speech, King reiterated the phrase "one hundred years later" to emphasize that one hundred years after the Emancipation Proclamation (issued in 1863), African Americans still had not achieved equality. Immediately after the "I have a dream" section, King repeated the phrase that it is "with this faith" in his dream that he and other people could hope to transform American society. These examples demonstrate King's consciousness of the use of rhetoric to produce emotional impact.

Perhaps one of the most important rhetorical strategies of King's speech is his reference to the principles voiced by the Founding Fathers in his appeal for racial equality. This strategy was especially important in light of the fact that the government (including the Federal Bureau of Investigation and the Justice Department) was concerned that the Civil Rights movement might discredit the United States abroad. Hence, it was perceptive of King to imply in the speech that he was not undermining the United States but asking the country to do justice to the principles that were asserted to be the bedrock of the U.S. political and societal character. King stated, for example, that his dream was "deeply rooted in the American dream," and that he dreamed of a day when Americans "will be able to sing with new meaning 'My country 'tis of thee, sweet land of liberty, of thee I sing.'" King then immediately used the words of that song to delineate the different areas of the country where he hoped the United States would soon "let freedom ring" for all its citizens. He referred to the Declaration of Independence and the Constitution as being a "promissory note" to all citizens, which those at the march now were claiming as their inheritance. The speech gained power from King's stressing that he was asking the United States to live up to its principles and thus to fulfill the greatness of its pronounced creed.

King's speech became not only one of the most publicized events of the Civil Rights movement but also one of the most highly regarded speeches in U.S. history. Although much of the acclaim rests on the emotionally powerful "I have a dream" section of the speech, the entire speech is a masterpiece of rhetoric and argument. One of the most essential aspects of the speech was at the end, when King stated that on the day "when we let freedom ring" the United States will only be speeding up the day—not arriving at it—when "all of God's children, black men and white men, Jews and Gentiles, Protestants and Catholics, will be able to join hands and sing in the words of the old Negro spiritual, 'Free at last! Free at last! Thank God Almighty, we are free at last!'" This stands as the lingering, haunting challenge of Martin Luther King's speech at the March on Washington.

Jane Davis

Core Resources

James Baldwin's "The Dangerous Road Before Martin Luther King," in *The Price of the Ticket* (New York: St. Martin's Press, 1985) offers a detailed consideration of the difficulties facing King. David J. Garrow's *Bearing the Cross: Martin Luther King, Jr., and the Southern Christian Leadership Conference* (New York: Vintage Books, 1986) examines the strategies of civil rights protests and conflicts between various civil rights groups. Penelope McPhee and Flip Schulke's *King Remembered* (New York: Pocket Books, 1986) ia s concise introductory biography of King that focuses on his philosophy as a leader of a nonviolent movement.

See also: Civil Rights Act of 1960; Civil Rights Act of 1964; Civil Rights movement; King, Martin Luther, Jr., assassination; Little Rock school desegregation; Montgomery bus boycott; Southern Christian Leadership Conference; Watts riot.

Ideological racism

Ideological racism is a system of beliefs in or assertions of the genetic and/or cultural inferiority of dominated racial groups. Incorporated into eugenics theories, into social scientist Daniel Patrick Moynihan's notion of "cultural deficiency" in *The Negro Family: The Case for National Action* (1965), into appeals to the Bible by some Christian fundamentalists, and into racist stereotypes held by Americans in general, ideological racism sustains white Americans' certainty that their advantages and unequal share of resources have been achieved meritoriously, thereby legitimizing both their privileges and the deprivations suffered by minorities. Ideological racism functions to blame the victims for their misery and to shunt attention away from the social circumstances of both the well-off and the impoverished that reproduce their respective superior and inferior social statuses. For example, Moynihan's report counseled "benign neglect" rather than governmental action to assist African Americans. Europeans conceptualized race as an ideology to justify colonization. They conquered, enslaved, and committed genocide remorselessly, believing non-Europeans were inferiors or members of sub-human species. Almost all scientists today discredit ideological racism and affirm the equal humanity of all racial and ethnic groups.

Gil Richard Musolf

See also: Moynihan Report; Racism as an ideology.

Individual racism

Activists Stokely Carmichael and Charles V. Hamilton, in *Black Power: The Politics of Liberation in America* (1967, p.4), defined individual racism as "individual whites acting against individual blacks." Sociologist Fred L. Pincus, in an article published in *American Behavioral Scientist* (1996, p. 186), entitled "Discrimination Comes in Many Forms," renamed and expanded Carmichael and Hamilton's concept as *individual discrimination*, which he defined as "the behavior of individual members of one race/ethnic/gender group that is intended to have a differential and/or harmful effect on the members of another race/ethnic/gender group." Individual racism is distinguished from institutional racism, which is, according to Pincus, the intentional harm of minority groups by institutional practices such as the enactment of Jim Crow laws and the internment of Japanese Americans during World War II. Individual racism is here specified as actions by members of a dominant group that are intended to harm members of other racial and ethnic groups.

A range of individual racism prevails in American society, from intolerance to hate crimes. Included are incidents such as not hiring minority members in one's place of business, scapegoating minority groups for economic problems, stereotyping that leads to anti-Semitic and nativist prejudice and de facto residential segregation, and hurling racist insults and slurs. This last problem, now called hate speech, erupted on many college campuses in the late 1980's and early 1990's. Universities enacted hate-speech codes to protect minorities, but such codes were later found unconstitutional. Violent hate crimes include intimidation, harassment, assaults, beatings, church and synagogue burnings and bombings, cross burnings, destruction of personal property, lynchings, police brutality, and even an instance of white soldiers hunting African Americans as prey in 1995 at Fort

Editorial cartoon decrying the continuing threat to American freedoms posed by the Ku Klux Klan and other white racist organizations. *(Library of Congress)*

Bragg, North Carolina. Police brutality, if isolated within a department, is an example of individual racism. However, if it is widespread with lax norms and *unenforced* formal sanctions against it, then, according to Pincus, it is an institutional harm. In the late 1990's, a flare-up of church burnings, reminiscent of those in the 1960's, terrorized the rural South. According to the Southern Poverty Law Center's Klanwatch Project, white supremacist hate groups—skinheads and those adhering to movements and groups such as Christian Identity, White Aryan Resistance, Aryan Nations, the Ku Klux Klan, and militias of various types—remain strong; some, such as the militias, are on the rise. Many sociologists argue that an increase in acts of individual racism stems from the growing racial diversity of American society and the intensifying competition for scarce resources, such as jobs, in a global economy. With frustration escalating from mounting class stratification, individual racism is a classic example of scapegoating, that is, displacing one's anger at the economy onto minority groups.

Social scientist Gunnar Myrdal, in *An American Dilemma* (1944), argued that a moral dilemma, or contradiction, flourishes in American society between the American creed (freedom, equality of opportunity, and justice) and discrimination. Inequality is maintained through a vicious cycle whereby dominated groups are despised, engendering discrimination. Discrimination, whether individual or institutional, perpetuates minority groups' inferior social circumstances and engenders ideologies and stereotypes that blame minority groups for their deprivation and justify dominant group advantages. Thus, individual and institutional racism are inextricably intertwined.

Gil Richard Musolf

See also: Discrimination: behaviors; Institutional racism; Police brutality.

Inequality

Inequality is the unequal distribution of resources, opportunities, and rewards within society. In the United States, resources such as money, power, prestige, educational degrees, access to private clubs, political offices, and housing have been unequally distributed in a manner that has excluded racial and ethnic minorities.

Two early contributors to discussions concerning inequality were Karl Marx and Friedrich Engels. Marx and Engels, in *The Communist Manifesto* (1848), argued that the most important source of inequality relates to the control or ownership of the means of production, meaning the materials, tools, resources, and organizations by which society produces and distributes goods and services. The bourgeoisie, the owners of the means of production, are in a position to exploit and coerce the proletariat, or working class, thus enabling them to claim the greatest proportion of economic resources. Max Weber, in *Economy and Society* (1921), disagreed with Marx, arguing that stratification is multidimensional and involves economics, prestige, and power. Economic inequality is based on ownership or control of property, wealth, and income. Inequality in terms of prestige is based on the amount of esteem or respect given to an individual by others. Inequality of power is based on the differing impact individuals have on the societal decision-making process. Those with more power are better able to protect their interests and achieve their goals than the less powerful.

Kingsley Davis and Wilbert Moore, in their article "Some Principles of Stratification" (*American Sociological Review*, 1945), argued that inequality is necessary, contending that some positions are of greater importance than others to the well-being of society. If all individuals received equal shares of societal resources regardless of their position, there would be no motivation for an individual to undergo the rigorous training necessary to fill the important positions. Inequality rewards the most qualified individuals, encouraging them to take important positions in society and work to the best of their ability. Therefore, Davis and Moore assert that society would not be able to motivate people to work hard and achieve without unequal reward systems.

In the United States, the constitutional basis for many court cases challenging inequality in terms of opportunities, resources, or treatment by the government, its agents, or private citizens is the Fourteenth Amendment. This amendment, in conjunction with court rulings, declares that states cannot make laws that abridge the privileges of citizens; deprive any person of life, liberty, or property without due process of law; deny any citizen the equal protection of the laws; or deny any citizen the right to vote. As a result, by defining equal treatment, the Fourteenth Amendment and court rulings since the ratification of the amendment have defined inequality as the unequal treatment of people based on race, color, ethnic background, sexual orientation, religion, sex, or previous condition of servitude.

Ione Y. DeOllos

See also: Equality; Equality of opportunity; Fourteenth Amendment.

Institutional racism

Institutional racism refers to the manner in which a society's institutions operate systematically, both directly and indirectly, to favor some groups over others regarding access to opportunities and valued resources. This concept helps explain how a society can discriminate unintentionally against particular groups.

Racial discrimination, in the most general sense, is the denial of equal opportunities and rights to groups on the basis of race or ethnicity. The study of institutional racism (sometimes called institutional discrimination), rather than looking at individual attitudes as an explanation for racial inequality, focuses on the way society itself is structured or organized. Sociologist Joe R. Feagin distinguishes among four types of discrimination, and he includes two types of institutional racism in his typology: "direct institutionalized[institutional] discrimination" and "indirect institutionalized discrimination." An example of the former, which was documented by Diana Pearce in a 1976 study in Detroit, is the practice by real estate companies of "steering" African Americans away from homes in white areas. This direct form of institutional discrimination is the easiest to identify, understand, and (given the will) eradicate. Most sociologists, however, use the term "institutional racism" to refer to the second type noted by Feagin, indirect discrimination.

The term was coined in 1967 by African American civil rights activist Stokely Carmichael (Kwame Toure) and Charles V. Hamilton. Toure and Hamilton were attempting to shift attention away from individual, overt, and direct forms of racial discrimination as the principal explanation for the persistence of racial inequality.

From the perspective of sociologists studying unintentional and indirect forms of institutional racism, consequences are the most important indicator of discrimination. If the results or consequences of a policy or practice are unequal along racial lines, then indirect institutional racism is thought to exist. As sociologist Jerome Skolnick avers, "a society in which most of the good jobs are held by one race, and the dirty jobs are held by people of another color, is a society in which racism is institutionalized no matter what the beliefs of its members are."

Statistical Evidence   In the 1980's, statistical evidence of racism could be found in every institutional area. As recently as 1980, African Americans, for example, constituted nearly 12 percent of the population of the United States but only 1.5 percent of the country's elected officials. Almost 50 percent of all prison inmates in the U.S. were black. The dropout rate for blacks in education was twice that of whites. The infant mortality rate for whites in 1985 was 9.3 per 1,000 live births, but for blacks it was 18.2 per 1,000. The maternal mortality rate in 1984 for whites was 5.4 per 100,000 live births; for black women it was 19.7. Forty-three percent of black children and 16 percent of white children under the age of eighteen lived in poverty in 1986, and the median per capita wealth for blacks in 1984 was $6,837, compared to $32,667 for whites. These inequities strongly suggested the existence of institutional racism, which persists to this day.

The fact that blacks do not own businesses proportional to their percentage of the population demonstrates another important element of institutional racism: the interrelatedness of institutions. A society's institutions are interrelated in ways such that exclusion from one frequently means exclusion from all. Harold M. Baron has called this phenomenon the "web" of urban racism. Black enterprise in the United States has been stifled by discrimination in education and the job market and by discriminatory banking practices that make it difficult for African Americans to secure loans to start businesses.

In the 1967 film *In the Heat of the Night*, Rod Steiger (right) plays a southern police chief slowly adjusting to the fact that a black policeman, played by Sidney Poitier (left), may be more competent than he is. *(Museum of Modern Art, Film Stills Archive)*

Research and Remedial Efforts   The study of institutional racism also places considerable importance on the deep historical roots and lasting effects of direct racial discrimination. The effects of earlier practices, policies, and laws that were designed purposely to exclude and harm particular groups have continued to be felt even after most of them were eliminated by legislative and other measures. The cumulative effect of this discrimination left African Americans and other racial and ethnic minorities—notably Mexican Americans/Chicanos, Native Americans, and Puerto Ricans—at a competitive disadvantage with majority group members in virtually every institutional area.

Knowledge gained from the study of institutional racism is applied in a number of ways in attempts to counter institutional racism. Among the many approaches are civil rights legislation; executive orders, such as those for affirmative action; and changes in the criteria used by admissions offices in higher education.

College Admissions   Historically, college admissions officers have relied on so-called objective criteria in their decisions. The most important of these criteria have been class rank, grade point average, scores on the Scholastic Aptitude Test (SAT), participation in extracurricular activities, and the quality of the high school attended by applicants. While it was not necessarily the intent of colleges to discriminate against members of minority groups, reliance on these criteria, in effect, did so. Minority-group applicants, for example, are disproportionately poorer than majority-group applicants. As a consequence, they are more likely to have attended poorly funded schools that offer fewer extracurricular activities and that generally provide a lower-quality education. Minority students also are more likely to have to work and to care for siblings, which in turn affects their academic performance and limits their participation in extracurricular activities.

Because of studies of institutional racism, universities and colleges were able to see how their admissions policies were discriminating against members of certain groups. In the 1960's, most of these institutions adjusted their admissions processes, including the criteria used to determine admissibility and predict academic potential, to take into account the disadvantaged positions in which members of minority groups find themselves. Instead of automatically penalizing students for not participating in extracurricular activities, for example, admissions officers obtained information from applicants and high school guidance counselors on the activities available in the school and on applicants' responsibilities, including work, which may have made it difficult for them to participate in school-sponsored programs. Admissions officers also began to consider possible biases in standardized tests and accorded test scores less weight in their decision to admit or not to admit a student.

Hiring Practices   Affirmative action programs are principally intended to be remedies for institutional discrimination. Affirmative action requires race consciousness rather than "color blindness," because (as studies of institutional racism have shown) society is structured in such a way that race-neutral or color-blind policies exclude members of minority groups. In the area of employment, for example, affirmative action programs were created to increase the pool of qualified minority candidates and to eliminate discriminatory practices from the selection process. Approaches include advertising positions in places where potential candidates from minority groups can be reached more effectively.

A long-standing and common recruitment practice has been to hire new workers through personal connections. Because of prior racial discrimination, however, the people doing the hiring were disproportionately white, and their connections tended to be white as well. Hence, African Americans and members of other minority groups often were excluded. Affirmative action programs have sought to eliminate this practice, which, even if its practitioners did not intend it to be, is discriminatory. Advertising positions widely, even nationally when possible, has been one remedy prescribed.

A seemingly innocuous practice used by some police agencies provides another example of institutional racism. Many police forces maintained a minimum height requirement, which placed Latinos, Asians, and women at a disadvantage. Because members of these groups generally tend to be shorter than white or black males, this requirement reduced significantly the pool of qualified applicants from these groups. Although the height require- ment seemed to be neutral, or nondiscriminatory, it in fact discriminated against particular groups; intent is not necessary for a requirement to be discriminatory. In many instances, such discriminatory job requirements have been eliminated or modified.

In yet another example, seniority systems, established to provide job security for longtime employees, discriminate against minority group mem- bers. Blacks are adversely affected in disproportionate numbers by this practice because, as a group, they were denied job opportunities on the basis of race until court decisions and legislative initiatives made it illegal to discriminate on this basis. Being the most recently hired employees, they would be the first fired when layoffs became necessary. While seniority systems may not have been established to discriminate intentionally against members of certain groups, they did so nevertheless. As a consequence, the courts in a number of instances have ordered employers to cease the practice.

The Civil Rights Act of 1991, signed into law by President George Bush, was drafted partly in response to a number of Supreme Court decisions that, in effect, required plaintiffs in discrimination suits to prove intent on the part of the defendant, usually an employer. The bill stipulates that once the plaintiff is able to show that an employer's practice adversely affects a particular group, then the burden falls on the employer to "demonstrate that the challenged practice is job related for the position in question and consistent with business necessity." The bill is consistent with an approach designed to counter institutional discrimination. A practice is deemed discriminatory if it has a disparate impact on any group, irrespective of intent.

Between the election of President Ronald Reagan in 1980 and the passage of this bill, the tendency had been to place the burden of proof increasingly on plaintiffs in discrimination cases. In other words, a plaintiff had to prove that an employer intended to discriminate against him or her—a very difficult, often impossible, task. This approach of the 1980's was a departure from the approach that began in the 1960's, based on countering institutional discrimination. The Civil Rights Bill of 1991 returned, although in a somewhat weakened fashion, to the earlier approach intended to counter institutional racism.

Context   Prior to the 1920's, few sociologists studied race relations. When they did, beginning with the work of such sociologists as Edward Ross, Lester Ward, and William Sumner, the tendency was to view discrimination as conscious acts performed by prejudiced individuals; this view continued to dominate until the 1960's. The assumption inherent in this "prejudice causes discrimination" model, as noted by Joe Feagin and Clairece Feagin, is that the way to eradicate racial discrimination is to eliminate racial prejudice. It was believed that, with time, this would happen. Racial discrimination was seen as an aberration, inconsistent with American ideals of equality and justice. Swedish sociologist Gunnar Myrdal captured this belief well in the title of his classic and influential work on discrimination in the United States, *An American Dilemma: The Negro Problem and Modern Democracy* (1944).

Beginning with the pioneering work on immigration by American sociologist Robert Ezra Park in the first half of the twentieth century, immigration scholars as a rule predicted the eventual assimilation of various ethnic groups. While most conceded that the situation of African Americans was unique in some respects, their assimilation into American society was also predicted. Along with this, it was thought, would come the diminution and eventual elimination of racial prejudice. Milton Gordon, in the 1960's, developed a more sophisticated theory of assimilation, in which he distinguished between cultural and structural assimilation. Structural assimilation refers to the ability of members of a minority group to participate in such societal groups and institutions as businesses, government, and private clubs; Gordon pointed out that cultural assimilation does not assure equal opportunities in these areas.

In the 1950's and 1960's, the Civil Rights movement made great strides in attaining legal equality for African Americans and other minorities. Robert Blauner observed that initially the Civil Rights movement adopted the view that blacks, if guaranteed legal equality, would be able to assimilate into American society. In time, however, it became increasingly apparent to civil rights activists as well as to many scholars that racist ideologies and prejudiced attitudes were not the "essence" of racism. Rather, racism was inherent in society's institutions. This realization quickly led to a fundamental change in the study of race relations, a change spurred by the cultural climate of social unrest and protest during the 1960's. The Black Power movement of the 1960's called attention to how little the status of blacks had changed or promised to change despite progressive civil rights legislation and a reduction in racial prejudice. This relatively new way of analyzing racial stratification shifted the focus from individual expressions of racism to the manner in which society itself was structured and operated to favor some groups over others.

Héctor L. Delgado

Core Resources

James Baldwin's *The Fire Next Time* (New York: Dell, 1963) presents a beautifully written analysis of racism and an unrivaled statement on being black in the United States. Robert Blauner's *Racial Oppression in America* (New York: Harper & Row, 1972) presents the thesis is that racial minorities in the United States are internal colonies created by the capitalist system. Stokely Carmichael and Charles V. Hamilton's *Black Power: The Politics of Liberation in America* (New York: Vintage Books, 1967) exhorts African Americans to seize the initiative in effecting social change. Joe R. Feagin's *Racial and Ethnic Relations* (Englewood Cliffs, N.J.: Prentice-Hall, 1989) discusses racial and ethnic minorities in their broader social contexts. Joe R. Feagin and Clairece Booher Feagin's *Discrimination American Style: Institutional Racism and Sexism* (Englewood Cliffs, N.J.: Prentice-Hall, 1978) remains one of the best and most accessible discussions of institutional racism and sexism. *Institutional Racism in America* (Englewood Cliffs, N.J.: Prentice-Hall, 1969), edited by Louis L. Knowles and Kenneth Prewitt, is a collection of essays that analyze institutional racism in various institutional areas, such as the economy and education.

See also: College admissions; Racism: history of the concept.

Integration

Crucial changes in U.S. public policy beginning in the 1940's helped promote the goal of racial integration. Legally, whites and nonwhites were given equal access to workplaces, schools, and neighborhoods; however, many social and economic factors acted to slow or prevent the complete intermingling of races.

A racially integrated society would be one in which African Americans and other racial or ethnic groups could participate in all aspects of national life

Residents of Englewood, New Jersey, demonstrating in favor of integrating one of the city's high schools in 1962. *(National Archives)*

without being handicapped by their color. In such a society, there should be no neighborhood where an African American could not reside simply because of being black; no hotel, restaurant, or other public facility that an African American could not use on equal terms with whites; no school that an African American child could not attend because of being black; no kind of vocational training, university education, or line of work from which an African American would be barred because of being black; and no public office for which an African American could not contend. In an integrated society, whites would see African Americans not as pariahs but as fellow Americans, fellow veterans, coworkers, and neighbors. This goal of a racially integrated society, despite much progress, is only half achieved; the role that public policy should play in creating a more racially integrated society remains a matter of lively debate.

Those who discuss the ethics of integration are dealing with the ethics of public policy rather than (as is the case, to some extent, with prejudice and racism) the morality of private behavior. The promotion of racial integration has been seen by its proponents as essential to the realization of an important value in public policy ethics: that of equality under the law regardless of race or color. This principle was publicly recognized in the United States by the Fourteenth Amendment to the Constitution (ratified in 1868), which mandated that every state guarantee its citizens the equal protection of the laws. Nevertheless, de facto segregation reigned for nearly three-quarters of a century before significant steps were taken to break down racial barriers.

Milestones in Integration: 1945 to 1968   Signposts of progress during these years (which witnessed the flowering of the Civil Rights movement) included the gradual desegregation of the American military, which began with President Harry S Truman's Executive Order 9981 in 1948; the Supreme Court decision of 1954, that struck down the constitutionality of segregated schools; the admission of African Americans into southern state universities; the Civil Rights Act of 1964, which established the right of equal access to public accommodations and banned discrimination in employment; the Voting Rights Act of 1965; the Supreme Court decision of 1967 that overturned state laws against black-white intermarriage; and the federal Fair Housing Act of 1968. By 1990, many of these changes had achieved general acceptance; efforts to integrate employment, schools, and housing, however, continued to arouse controversy.

The Affirmative Action Controversy   By the late 1970's, affirmative action, in which the presence or absence of a fixed percentage of African Americans in a business, government department, or university is used to determine whether that institution discriminates, had become the chief tool by which the federal government tried to open up opportunities for African Americans. In 1975, in the book *Affirmative Discrimination*, the white sociologist Nathan Glazer condemned the application of this policy in both private businesses and government employment. Glazer argued that affirmative action undermines respect for merit and encourages ethnic and racial divisiveness; unlike many liberals, he denied that the underrepresentation of African Americans in a particular job or profession is necessarily evidence of discrimination. In the 1990's African American conservatives asserted that affirmative action stigmatizes as inferior those African Americans who do gain entrance to prestigious universities or get good jobs. Yet other thinkers—white as well as African American—argue that many employers would hire no African Americans at all if they were not prodded to do so by the existence of a numerical goal.

Racial Integration of Elementary and Secondary Schools   In *Brown v. Board of Education*, in 1954, the Supreme Court declared that officially enforced school segregation by race (then found mostly in the southern states) violated the Fourteenth Amendment to the Constitution. In a 1968 decision, the Supreme Court exerted pressure on southern school boards to end segregation more quickly; in a 1971 decision, *Swann v. Charlotte-Mecklenburg Board of Education*, the Court held that school busing—the transportation of children out of their neighborhoods for schooling—might be an appropriate tool for achieving desegregation.

In the 1960's, the question arose of what to do about the de facto racial segregation of the schools, based on neighborhood racial patterns rather than on the law, found in many northern cities. In 1973, the Supreme Court ordered, for the first time, a northern school district (Denver, Colorado) to institute a desegregation plan. In 1974, however, the Court, in a sudden shift (in the decision *Milliken v. Bradley*) banned busing for integration purposes across city-suburban boundaries. In general, the Court has ordered steps toward ending de facto segregation only when evidence exists that local authorities have deliberately rigged school district boundaries to keep the races apart.

Ever since 1954, people have argued about how necessary integration of the races in the classroom is to providing equal educational opportunities for African American children. In the 1980's, some African American thinkers, such as Thomas Sowell and Robert Woodson, had their doubts. Woodson argued that a neighborhood school, even if it is exclusively African American, can become a valuable focus of neighborhood pride for low-income city dwellers; Sowell pointed nostalgically to a high-quality African American secondary school of the pre-1954 era of segregation, Dunbar High School in Washington, D.C. (Critics stress how atypical Dunbar was.)

Integrationist scholars, however, argue that forcible exclusion from the company of white schoolchildren stigmatizes and psychically wounds African American children. The African American journalist Carl Rowan thinks that such exclusion is psychically wounding even if it results from white flight to the suburbs rather than government edict. White liberal political scientist Gary Orfield suggests that racial integration of the schools is necessary if African American children are to have greater access to information about jobs and other opportunities; white liberal education writer Jonathan Kozol contends, like many African American thinkers, that all African American public schools are more likely than integrated ones to be starved of money by legislatures that are beholden to white-majority electorates.

Although the compulsory busing of children into schools predominantly of the other race may be necessary to achieve racial integration in some cases, it does severely limit the rights of parents, thereby causing some resentment. However, the rights of parents over their children are, as the African American philosopher Bernard R. Boxill points out, by no means absolute. There is a societal interest in promoting interracial harmony, Boxill suggests, that perhaps should be allowed to prevail over the wish of bigoted white parents to preserve their children from all contact with African American children, and perhaps even over the wishes of parents who simply wish to spare their children the additional time spent traveling to and from home. Rejecting the notion (found in the writings of African American conservative Glenn Loury) of an unresolvable tension between integrationist goals and individual rights, Boxill also argues that government can use inducements as well as penalties to promote integration, in education and in other areas.

To promote integration of the schools while keeping busing to a minimum, some local school authorities have instituted so-called magnet schools. By placing elementary and secondary schools with above-average endowment in facilities and curricula in the middle of African American neighborhoods, authorities have sometimes persuaded, rather than forced, white parents to accept racial integration of the schools. Yet because funds are limited, the number of magnet schools that can be established is also limited; inevitably, some African American schoolchildren have often remained in primarily minority schools.

Housing Integration By 1990, neither the federal Fair Housing Act of 1968 nor the many state and local laws banning discrimination in the sale or rental of housing had solved the problem of racially segregated neighborhoods. One troublesome issue that arises with respect to housing integration is the tension between individual rights and the goal of keeping a neighborhood integrated over time. Many whites are reluctant to live in a neighborhood or an apartment complex when the percentage of African American residents exceeds a certain number. To prevent wholesale evacuation by whites, so-called benign quotas have been introduced limiting the African American influx in the interest of stable integration. Benign quotas have been used by real estate agents in the Chicago suburb of Oak Park and by the management of the Starrett City apartment complex in New York City; in the latter case, the constitutionality of benign quotas was challenged in the 1980's.

Another difficult question is whether poor as well as middle- or upper-income African Americans should be given the chance to live in the prosperous and mostly white suburbs. White suburbanites who might tolerate the occasional prosperous African American homeowner as a neighbor might also oppose the building of public housing projects in suburbia; yet it is the poorer African American who might benefit most from the greater employment opportunities found in the suburbs. In Chicago, the Gautreaux program attempted to circumvent the problem by settling small numbers of carefully selected poor African American families in prosperous white suburbs.

Nathan Glazer, in a 1993 magazine essay, argued that only an extremely intrusive government could make racially integrated neighborhoods remain racially integrated over time. Bernard Boxill contends, however, that not every action that is beyond the penalties of law is necessarily moral, and that government, if it cannot force whites to stay in integrated neighborhoods, can at least offer inducements for them to do so.

Paul D. Mageli

Core Resources

Useful studies of integration can be found in Bernard R. Boxill's *Blacks and Social Justice* (Totowa, N.J.: Rowman & Allanheld, 1984); Gertrude Ezorsky's *Racism and Justice: The Case for Affirmative Action* (Ithaca, N.Y.: Cornell University Press, 1991); Nathan Glazer's *Affirmative Discrimination: Ethnic Inequality and Public Policy* (New York: Basic Books, 1975); Andrew Hacker's *Two Nations: Black and White, Separate, Hostile, Unequal* (New York: Charles Scribner's Sons, 1992); Jonathan Kozol's *Savage Inequalities: Children in America's Schools* (New York: Crown, 1991); Glenn C. Loury's "Matters of Color—Blacks and the Constitutional Order," in *Slavery and Its Consequences: The Constitution, Equality, and Race,* edited by Robert A. Goldwin and Art Kaufman (Washington, D.C.: American Enterprise Institute Press, 1988); Douglas S. Massey and Nancy A. Denton's *American Apartheid: Segregation and the Making of the Underclass* (Cambridge, Mass.: Harvard University Press, 1993); and Harvey Molotch's *Managed Integration: Dilemmas of Doing Good in the City* (Berkeley: University of California Press, 1972).

See also: Affirmative action; *Brown v. Board of Education*; Civil Rights Act of 1964; Civil Rights movement; Desegregation: defense; Desegregation: public schools; Housing; Military desegregation; Racism: history of the concept; Segregation; Segregation: de facto and de jure; Segregation vs. integration.

Intelligence and race

Observed differences in mean IQ levels for racial/ethnic groups have generated prolonged and intense controversy on whether intelligence is determined by environment or genetics. The fact that human DNA is nearly identical across racial and ethnic groups argues against race-based genetic differences. Consequences of the position taken on this issue are enormous for social policy, education, and overall race relations.

Contemporary debate on the relationship between intelligence and race can be traced to the nineteenth century eugenics movement initiated by Francis Galton, Charles Darwin's half-cousin. Eugenics is a science that aims to improve the hereditary characteristics of a race or breed, usually through selective mating. Galton proposed eugenics as a means of promoting the chances of "superior" races to prevail over the rapid growth of "inferior" races. In *Hereditary Genius* (1869), Galton concluded that mental traits were as inheritable as physical features. Galton's colleague, Karl Pearson, the founder of statistical correlation, shared his anxiety about a dysgenic trend, one that favored the "weaker races," which were reproducing at a higher rate than the "mentally better stock."

Galton's efforts to measure intelligence using the speed and accuracy of mental processes as criteria led to attempts to create mental tests. The term "mental test" itself was coined in 1890 by British scientist James McKeen Cattell.

Test Development   During this time, French psychologist Alfred Binet was conducting experiments on his two daughters to develop an accurate method of measuring intelligence. Binet's major concern was not eugenics but helping schoolteachers distinguish the "malicious" (students who lacked motivation) from the "stupid" (students who lacked the intellectual capacity to succeed). In 1904, Binet created a scale known as the Binet-Simon Scale and advocated that all students be tested with it to separate the "malicious" from the "stupid."

At the start of the twentieth century, several U.S. psychologists including Edward L. Thorndike, Naomi Norsworthy, Henry Goddard, and Lewis Terman, all believers in eugenics, were also developing methods to test intelligence. The first version of the Stanford-Binet Intelligence Test, which improved on the Binet-Simon Scale, was produced by Terman at Stanford University in 1916. The notion of intelligence quotient, or IQ—mental age divided by chronological age of the person tested and multiplied by 100—was introduced by Wilhelm Stern, making it possible to compare people's performances. Finding that the average IQ of children from upper-class families was 107 and that of working-class children was only 93, Terman concluded that the difference was genetic, not an outcome of home environment. He questioned the utility of education to help lower-class children become "intelligent voters or capable citizens."

During World War I, Terman convinced the United States army to use psychological testing to assess the mental fitness of soldiers. Because many of the 1.7 million men who were tested were not proficient in English or hailed from impoverished backgrounds, their test scores were depressed, leading the researchers to conclude that immigrants from the non-English-speaking world and lower-class Americans were genetically inferior. This led to a policy of testing all immigrants who arrived at Ellis Island, spreading the view that immigrants who were not white Anglo-Saxon Protestants were of "moron grade."

In 1939, David Wechsler developed a new IQ test, the Wechsler-Bellevue test. It was very similar to the Stanford-Binet; however, it measured not only verbal skills but also performance skills. In 1955, it was renamed the Wechsler Adult Intelligence Scale (WAIS). Modifications were added later to create the Wechsler Intelligence Scale for Children (WISC-R) and the Wechsler Preschool and Primary Scale Intelligence (WPPSI). By the end of the twentieth century, hundreds of other tests, including tests designed to measure scholastic aptitude and achievement, had been created and used, revealing the United States' fascination with intelligence.

Challenges to IQ Testing   Objections to intelligence testing were first raised as early as 1913 by J. E. Wallace Wallin, a clinical psychologist from Iowa who noticed that children judged to be morons were sometimes unfairly institutionalized. Robert M. Yerks, a psychologist from Harvard University, also warned about the dangers of untrained examiners clinically diagnosing people. In response, the American Psychological Association, at its 1915 meeting, passed a resolution discouraging unqualified individuals from administering psychological testing.

Herrnstein and Murray's controversial 1994 book, *The Bell Curve.*

Widespread criticism of psychological testing arose in the 1960's in response to two conclusions that had been reached by most psychologists: Blacks as a group consistently scored fifteen points lower than whites on standardized IQ tests, and blacks did better or at least as well as whites on test items involving simple tasks and rote memorization. These conclusions reinforced prevalent negative stereotypes of African Americans, providing justification for continued discrimination against them in education and jobs. As criticism of intelligence testing became louder, the validity of the tests was challenged in court. Civil rights activists protested against placing children in special education programs based on IQ tests. Charges of racism and examiner bias were made in professional circles as well as in the media. An avalanche of books, articles, and dissertations were produced, mostly challenging the black inferiority thesis.

Racial and Ethnic Differences and IQ Few contest the fact that a definite difference exists in mean IQ between blacks and whites in the United States. Most people also acknowledged that regardless of race, class differences exist in mean IQ scores: Upper-class whites perform better than lower-class whites. What is contentious is the interpretation of these observed differences, that is, whether they stem from the genetic makeups of different groups or are determined by environmental factors.

The controversy was sharpened by an article published by A. R. Jensen, an educational psychologist, in the *Harvard Educational Review* in 1969. This article held that inherited factors largely accounted for individual differences in human intelligence. Jensen asserted that because of their genetic limitations, educational programs designed to raise the IQs of African American children were largely ineffective. Although he did not deny the influence of environmental factors, he claimed that they were merely "threshold variables."

Two other prominent psychologists who have for decades defended the hereditarian thesis are H. J. Eysenck, a British psychologist, and Richard Herrnstein, a psychologist from Harvard University. Eysenck supported Jensen's position and distinguished between two main types of intellectual abilities: abstract reasoning ability, which IQ is based on, and associative learning ability, which involves memory and rote learning. In his estimation, large racial and social class differences exist in abstract reasoning, although virtually no such differences are found in associative learning.

Herrnstein has also long maintained that genetics is a significant factor in IQ differences between racial and ethnic groups. His definitive statement, coauthored by Charles Murray, is *The Bell Curve: Intelligence and Class Structure in American Life* (1994). Herrnstein and Murray insist that race and IQ are genetically linked. Problems of the poor—unemployment, crime, poverty, and the like—are to be blamed, at least in part, on low IQ. Herrnstein and Murray are pessimistic in their assessment of programs designed to raise people's intellectual abilities. Evoking Galton's fears of a dysgenic trend, the authors believe that the United States is irrevocably turning into a caste society, stratified by IQ differences.

Critics of *The Bell Curve* question the findings of this book on several grounds: Data collected in this book are unreliable; available data do not support the thesis that intelligence is unequally distributed among various races; its authors reach conclusions that are far beyond what the data warrant; and, finally, even if genetics is a factor in intelligence, by the authors' own admission, it accounts for no more than 5 percent to 10 percent of the variance, far from what is needed to justify their fatalistic view on social stratification.

What Is Intelligence?   The difficulties in resolving the IQ controversy are many: There is no reliable method of isolating the influence of environmental variables from genetics in measuring intelligence, and the concepts used—intelligence, race, and ethnicity in particular—are not precisely definable.

Perhaps the most difficult problem is determining what constitutes intelligence. Intelligence is generally understood as a concept, rather than an objective entity, that is constructed to account for certain cognitive abilities. Intelligence tests are designed to identify and measure cognitive abilities, using quantitative methods based on some theoretical conception of intelligence. Existing intelligence tests measure such abilities as the ability to master common information (such as how many days there are in a year), verbal comprehension (such as what "serendipity" means), knowledge of culturally/legally acceptable ways to deal with problems (such as what one would do if one were the first person in a movie theater to notice smoke and fire), basic mathematical ability (such as the abilities to add, subtract, and multiply), the ability to reason abstractly, the ability to compare and contrast different objects or ideas, the ability to recall information, the ability to manipulate situations mentally, the ability to analyze and solve practical problems, the ability to distinguish what is essential from what is merely accidental, and the ability to learn a new task.

Considerable discussion exists on whether human intelligence is a unitary idea or whether there are several kinds of intelligence. In 1904, British psychologist Charles Spearman proposed that intelligence is made up of two parts: general intelligence (g) and the specific ability measured by particular test items(s). In 1941, R. B. Cattell distinguished between fluid (Gf) and crystallized (Gc) intelligences. Going beyond Cattell, some have recognized the need to consider intelligence as comprising several types, some of which are not measured by available IQ tests. Psychologist Howard Gardner has identified many types and forms of intelligence other than cognitive. Studies also show that intelligence is not fixed but remains changeable over time, depending on new opportunities and experiences. For example, one study found that the IQs of African American college students rise significantly higher as a result of their receiving a college education.

Cultural and Other Biases It has been pointed out that IQ tests measure, more than anything else, knowledge of white middle-class culture. Researchers have noted that subcultural differences play a decisive role in the ways in which people grasp and process information, their learning styles, and their attitudes toward test taking. Not all groups are equally familiar with the content of the test items presented to them; words are not univocal across subcultures. Researcher Janet E. Helms has suggested that socioeconomic status, culture, and race may influence a person's performance on the Wechsler Adult Intelligence Scale-Revised (WAIS-R). For example, persons from lower socioeconomic classes may not establish a trusting relationship with the examiner, and individual characteristics of the examiner and their biases in interpretation of ambiguous answers affect test scores. African Americans score lower when tested by whites than when tested by blacks, a fact that was known as early as 1936 but ignored until the 1960's. Also, people with limited vocabulary may not understand the instructions given and the explanations offered in response to their questions.

Impact on Social Policy Intelligence testing has become an incendiary issue because of its linkages with a variety of other historically sensitive issues, including a belief in the superiority of the Anglo-Saxon race, eugenics movements, black slavery, discriminatory immigration policies, and efforts to remedy past injustices. Some observers have pointed out that the intense interest in IQ today parallels its ideological beginnings toward the end of the nineteenth century.

In the nineteenth century, when industrialization was in full swing, the pressures of the marketplace demanded greater social equality and inclusion of all social strata in the social processes. Eugenics and Social

Darwinism arose as reactionary movements to oppose programs and policies designed to open up greater opportunity to the poor and the working
classes.

The second half of the twentieth century saw a social revolution that in
many ways paralleled the Industrial Revolution. In the United States, disadvantaged people demanded fundamental changes in social institutions and
abolition of racist policies. Following the civil rights victories of the 1960's,
social and educational programs were put in place to remedy the effects of
past discrimination. The 1980's and 1990's witnessed the rise of a white
reactionary movement that resulted in the progressive dismantling of many
of these programs. Some fear that recent interest in resurrecting old arguments in support of the genetic basis of intelligence through such publications as *The Bell Curve* may well be part of a renewed attempt to reinstitute
the castelike structure of racism through other means.

Mathew J. Kanjirathinkal

Core Resources

Those who believe that intelligence is linked to race set forth their
positions in a number of books and articles, including H. J. Eysenck's *The IQ
Argument* (New York: Library Press, 1971) and *The Measurement of Intelligence*
(Baltimore: Williams and Wilkins Company, 1973); A. R. Jensen's "How
Much Can We Boost IQ and Scholastic Achievement?" reprinted in *Environ-
ment, Heredity, and Intelligence*, a compilation of studies and commentaries
(Cambridge, Mass.: Harvard Education Review, 1969); and Richard
Herrnstein and Charles Murray's *The Bell Curve: Intelligence and Class Structure
in American Life* (New York: Free Press, 1994).

Books and articles stating the case against a race-intelligence link include
James Flyn's *Race, IQ, and Jensen* (London: Routledge, 1980); Douglas Lee
Eckberg's *Intelligence and Race* (New York: Praeger, 1979); and Linda Darling-
Hammond's "Cracks in the Bell Curve: How Education Matters" in *Journal
of Negro Education* (64, 3, Summer, 1995).

More neutral treatments of the issue include chapters 10 and 11 in *The
Legacy of Malthus: The Social Costs of the New Scientific Racism* (Urbana: Univer-
sity of Illinois Press, 1980), by Allan Chase; Janet E. Helms's "The Triple
Quandary of Race, Culture, and Social Class in Standardized Cognitive
Ability Testing" in *Contemporary Intellectual Assessment: Theories, Tests, and
Issues*, edited by Dawn P. Flanagan et al. (New York: Guilford Press, 1997);
Sandra Scarr's *Race, Social Class, and Individual Differences* (Hillsdale, N.J.:
Lawrence Erlbaum, 1981); *The IQ Controversy: Critical Readings*, edited by N. J.
Block and Gerald Dworkin (New York: Pantheon Books, 1976); and *The Bell
Curve Debate: History, Documents, Opinions* (New York: Random House, 1997),
edited by Russel Jacoby and Naomi Galuberman.

See also: Education and African Americans; Education and racial/ethnic
relations; Equal educational opportunity.

Internal colonialism

An ethnic or racial group that is a victim of internal colonialism lacks the ability to guide its own destiny economically, politically, and socially because it has been singled out for exclusion from the mainstream by the dominant ethnic group.

Some observers believe that certain subordinate ethnic and racial groups are colonies within their own countries, controlled by the dominant ethnic group. The applicability of this concept is disputed by other observers, who point out difficulties in the analogy between external and internal colonialism.

External Colonialism   A nation can establish an external colony by imposing control over a territory located beyond its existing borders. To maintain control, the colonial power must send civilian and military personnel to live in the country. Military personnel are sent to keep order, that is, to suppress any opposition to the colonial power, which displaces the former indigenous power structure. Civilian personnel are sent to maintain control through economic, political, and social means.

Economic control is maintained by such methods as restricting licenses to operate local businesses, imposing heavy taxes, buying out local businesses and property, importing workers from other countries, paying lower wages to the subordinate group for the same work performed by members of the dominant ethnic group, setting up absentee landlords, turning areas into ghettos, and banning local businesses. The colonial power's objective is to dominate the market so that the colonized people will lack economic autonomy, become economically marginalized, and can be exploited in order to enrich the colonizers. Money can then flow from the dominated peoples to the rulers.

Political control is maintained by arresting independent leaders, banning opposition groups, locating pliable local leaders who will carry out the colonial agenda, and restricting civil liberties. The aim of the colonial power is to dominate the political system so that the colonized people lack any ability to influence public policy. Compliance can then result from a belief that resistance is useless.

Social control is maintained by banning the local language, controlling the educational system and the media, geographically displacing the subordinate ethnic group, moving in settlers from the home country of the colonial power, and ridiculing the supposed backwardness of the subordinate ethnic group. The aim of the colonial power is to dominate society to the extent that the colonized people believe in their own inferiority. The ruling group can then break the spirit of the subordinate population.

One example of external colonialism occurred a century ago, when the United States attempted to seize control of the Philippine islands by suppressing an armed independence struggle in 1901. U.S. military personnel arrived first, followed by bureaucrats, educators, media, traders, and others, who established themselves as colonists. This classical form of external colonialism ended in 1946, when the Philippines became an independent country and U.S. bureaucrats withdrew. U.S. armed forces, however, remained in the Philippines for more than four decades after 1946 on bases that were transferred to Philippine sovereignty.

Native Americans as Colonized People In external colonialism, a dominant and powerful country goes overseas to take over a country that is weak and can be dominated. However, the same methods can be used inside a country: A dominant ethnic group can act as a colonial power in subordinating a weaker ethnic group inside the same country.

For many centuries, the natives of North and South America lived in isolation from the rest of the world. When Europeans set foot in the Western Hemisphere with the intent of occupying the land, conflict between the two groups was inevitable. The history of the European conquest of the Americas began as a form of external colonialism. When the countries of North and South America became independent, internal colonialism existed because the population that was of European origin continued to hold a dominant position over the indigenous population and imposed economic, political, and social control.

Today, Native Americans in the United States can live on reservations, that is, plots of land in which they alone are permitted to reside. Although tribal authorities are allowed to make some decisions on behalf of the reservation population, ultimate political authority is held by the U.S. Department of the Interior's Bureau of Indian Affairs (BIA). Native Americans can develop their own sources of income, but the BIA runs the schools in a manner quite similar to the educational systems that operate in colonies.

Many examples of internal colonialism abound outside the United States. In the seventeenth century, after suppressing an Irish rebellion, Henry VIII of England encouraged British settlers to move to Ulster, in the northern part of Ireland; the result was a colonization of Ireland. Later in the same century, Dutch settlers arrived to establish colonial enclaves amid the indigenous peoples of South Africa; however, when apartheid was adopted in 1948, it was the Africans who were forcibly relocated into enclaves. After the United States gained control of the Philippine islands from Spain in 1901, the indigenous peoples of Mindanao Island and the Sulu archipelago refused to recognize the authority of the new colonial power, so the U.S. authorities encouraged Filipinos to move to Mindanao in the role of internal colonists.

African Americans as Colonized People Some observers claim that a form of internal colonialism involving African Americans exists in the United States. They believe that African Americans who live primarily in segregated housing and territorial enclaves have been treated as colonial subjects. For example, businesses in these enclaves tend not to be run by

African Americans. As further evidence, they cite how African Americans, for more than three centuries, were denied positions of political authority, rendering them politically dependent. The dominant white population made sure that the Africans lost their own culture and, during the era of slavery, would not have an opportunity to acquire American culture.

Robert Blauner's *Racial Oppression in America* (1972) is one of the most famous statements of the thesis that African Americans have been internally colonized. Economically, African Americans have worked for white Americans in low-paying jobs. Until the 1960's, blacks rarely held executive positions in government. Indeed, the practice among whites was to deal with captive leaders in the African American community, that is, blacks who represented the interests of whites more than the needs of blacks. Moreover, blacks lost African culture and have been excluded from the mainstream of American culture. Advocates of the concept of internal colonialism argue that these facts establish the existence of a separate caste status for African Americans, who are forced to confront a split labor market in which they are the lowest-paid workers, are harassed by police, ignored by politicians, and subjected to inferior schooling so that they will not acquire the skills needed for upward mobility.

Critics of the concept of internal colonialism point out several reasons why they believe that the concept of internal colonialism does not fit the situation of African Americans. Whites and blacks can be found in all classes: Some African Americans are economically much better off than the average white American. Also, African Americans are not confined to a specific bounded territory but live in many neighborhoods. Similarly, African Americans have been elected mayors of most larger American cities, so they are hardly politically impotent. Finally, African Americans have developed their own distinctive culture within the United States, and most Americans are well acquainted with the African American entertainers and other cultural leaders. Marxists argue that the real divisions in society are not between racial groups but rather between social classes.

Impact on Public Policy   When members of an ethnic or racial group believe that they are being colonized, at least four courses of action are open to them. One is to assimilate to the dominant culture, thereby ending discriminatory treatment. European ethnic groups in the United States, many of which initially formed enclaves such as Little Italies, have generally been successful in becoming part of the mainstream.

A second course is to leave the country to escape persecution. In the early part of the twentieth century, Turkey instituted massacres of Armenians, many of whom chose to emigrate to the United States. Chinese left Indonesia and Malaysia in the 1960's for similar reasons.

A third course is to protest unequal treatment with the aim of reversing an ethnic group's colonial status. The American Civil Rights movement of the 1960's agitated successfully for the passage of legislation to outlaw discrimination on the basis of race and sex, though enforcement of the legislation has not eliminated discrimination.

The fourth alternative is nationalism and the establishment of a separate country. However, the weaker ethnic group can expect to lose if it engages in a war of independence unless it can find an ally abroad. In 1971, for example, the peoples of East Pakistan believed that they were being exploited and badly governed by authorities in West Pakistan. After a war successfully waged with the help of India, East Pakistan was recognized as the new nation of Bangladesh. Similarly, some of the Moros of Mindanao and the Sulu archipelago have continued to agitate for an independent state consisting of the territories of the former Sultanate of Sulu. Within the United States, some members of the African American liberation movement of the 1960's, inspired by the agenda in Stokely Carmichael and Charles V. Hamilton's *Black Power* (1967), have urged the United Nations to hold plebiscites in the "black colonies of America."

Michael Haas

Core Resources

The concept of internal colonialism is developed in several publications. An excellent discussion is found in Harold Wolpe's "The Theory of Internal Colonialism," in *Beyond the Sociology of Development: Economy and Society in Latin America and Africa*, edited by Ivar Oxaal, Tony Barnett, and David Booth (London: Routledge & Kegan Paul, 1975) and Pablo Gonzales-Casanova's "Internal Colonialism and National Development," in *Latin American Radicalism*, edited by Irving Louis Horowitz (New York: Random House, 1969). The concept is applied to Britain by Michael Hechter in *Internal Colonialism: The Celtic Fringe in British National Development* (Berkeley: University of California Press, 1975), to France by Suzanne Berger in *Peasants Against Politics: Rural Organization in Brittany, 1911-1967* (Cambridge, Mass.: Harvard University Press, 1972), and to Peru by Julio Cotler in "The Mechanism of Internal Domination and Social Change in Peru," in *Masses in Latin America*, edited by Irving Louis Horowitz (New York: Oxford University Press, 1970).

Applications to the United States were developed by Stokely Carmichael (later Kwame Toure) and Charles V. Hamilton in *Black Power: The Politics of Liberation in America* (New York: Random House, 1967) and Robert Blauner's *Racial Oppression in America* (New York: Harper & Row, 1972), Ronald Bailey and Guillermo Flores's "Internal Colonialism and Racial Minorities in the U.S.: An Overview," in *Structures of Dependency*, edited by Frank Bonilla and Robert Girling (East Palo Alto, Calif.: Nairobi Bookstore, 1973), and "The Barrio as Internal Colony," by Mario Barrera et al. in *People and Politics in Urban Society*, edited by Harlan Hahn (Beverly Hills, Calif.: Sage Publications, 1972). For critiques of the concept of internal colonialism as applied to the United States, see Michael Burawoy's "Race, Class, and Colonialism," in *Social and Economic Studies* (24, December, 1974), and Michael Omi and Howard

Winant's *Racial Formation in the United States: From the 1960's to the 1980's* (New York: Routledge & Kegan Paul, 1986).

See also: Discrimination: racial and ethnic; Slavery: history.

Internalized racism

A foundational principle in sociology is that the self is socially constructed through the role-taking aspect of socialization, whereby we see ourselves from the perspectives of significant others and the general perspective of our culture. Other people and the media provide a looking glass, supplying us with reflected appraisals of the self and racial or ethnic groups. Because racist stereotypes prevail in American culture, it is possible for some minority members to internalize them and to denigrate themselves by thinking about, feeling toward, and treating themselves in the same way members of the dominant culture may. However, a caveat is warranted here, as minority members are not passive victims of oppression; if a minority individual has a favorable self-feeling through, for example, internalizing a positive racial or ethnic group identity from significant others and his or her primary groups, then the ability to resist racist evaluations is greatly enhanced. Individuals are also able to interpret situations reflectively, enabling some minority members to realize that many dominant-group representations of their groups and cultural heritages are stereotypical and ideological. Nevertheless, an individual can succumb to the enormous influence that a media-saturated culture exerts on the construction of his or her identity.

Internalized racism has been poignantly illustrated in such portraits as African American writer Jean Toomer's book *Cane* (1923) and African American novelist Toni Morrison's *The Bluest Eye* (1970). The latter novel tells the story of Pecola Breedlove, an adolescent African American girl tormented by her internalization of the white standards of beauty as symbolized by blue eyes. Social psychologist Kurt Lewin researched the phenomenon of group self-hatred. Another social psychologist, Kenneth Clark, documented the prevalence of internalized racism, providing persuasive testimony to the U.S. Supreme Court in *Brown v. Board of Education* (1954) that segregated schools taught black children that they were inferior, engendering emotional devastation and psychological harm. Along similar lines, social theorist bell hooks, in *Black Looks: Race and Representation* (1992), describes internalized racism as a "colonization of the mind."

In the United States, the Declaration of Independence declares that those who rule must have the "consent of the governed." If minority members believe that their status in society is a result of *natural* inequality in a system of fair play, meritocracy, or equality of opportunity, then their internalized racism manufactures the consent needed to be governed although oppressed. Internalizing a view of innate inferiority dissuades minorities from seeking redress for their grievances, encouraging instead accommodation, acquiescence, and resignation. Nevertheless, many minority individuals have resisted white supremacy, developing a consciousness of social injustice, igniting a movement for civil rights, and, occasionally, sparking violent protest (expressed in the slogan "No justice, no peace!"). Over the years, African Americans have forged positive self and group identities as "New Negroes" of the 1920's Harlem Renaissance and have transformed their identity from Negro to black, epitomized by the 1960's phrase, "Black is beautiful." Native Americans have acted similarly through such activities as a revival of tribal consciousness and of powwows, the rise of the American Indian Movement (AIM), and the concept of Red Power. Many Mexican Americans have responded similarly by adopting "Chicano" as a term of group pride and Chicanismo as a counterideology and by forming the political movement of La Raza Unida.

Gil Richard Musolf

See also: Accommodationism; Black Is Beautiful movement; *Brown v. Board of Education.*

Interracial and interethnic marriage

Interracial and interethnic marriages involve people from dissimilar racial, ethnic, linguistic, or national groups. These marriages are significant for intergroup relations because they are a sign of assimilation or integration for the minority group. Intermarriage can be understood as an indication of the state of race and ethnic relations, as well as an agent of assimilation. Intermarriage blurs racial and ethnic boundaries by bringing together diverse groups and producing children who can assume new multiracial and multiethnic identities.

In the United States, racial and ethnic groups have tended to marry within their own group. Throughout U.S. history, there have been laws against various types of interracial and interethnic marriage; such laws were usually directed at African Americans, Native Americans, and Asian Americans. For example, in the early twentieth century, Chinese and Japanese immigrants were denied "white" status, which meant, among other things, that they were subject to restrictions on their right to marry outside their own groups. Since the institution of slavery, interracial relations between African Americans and whites have been closely monitored and restricted. Up until 1966, seventeen states still had formal prohibitions against one or more forms of interracial marriage, and forty states at one time had laws prohibiting blacks from marrying whites. On June 12, 1967, the U.S. Supreme Court rendered a decision in *Loving v. Virginia* that overturned the sixteen existing state antimiscegenation statutes.

Intermarriage Rates   Rates of intermarriage thus differ depending on the racial or ethnic groups involved. According to numerous studies, such as Richard Alba's *Ethnicity and Race in the U.S.A.* (1988), interethnic marriages, especially between European Americans, are common. Alba has concluded that among white ethnic groups there has been a steady increase in interethnic marriage. For example, only 20 percent of Italian American men born after 1949 were married to Italian American women. Similarly, Nathan Glazer and Daniel P. Moynihan's *Beyond the Melting Pot* (1970) analyzed ethnic groups in New York City and found that distinctions between white ethnic groups were being reduced by intermarriage. Despite this increase in interethnic marriages, these two studies both found that individuals are still somewhat more likely to choose mates from their own ethnic group than from another.

Interethnic marriage, though, is different from interracial marriage. People are often willing to cross ethnic boundaries to marry, but there is a much greater resistance to crossing racial boundaries. In addition, there are disparities between rates of intermarriage for the various racial groups. Hispanic Americans are an interesting example, since this group can be classed as both an ethnic minority group and a racial minority group. Marriages between Hispanic Americans and whites account for only 2.6 percent of all U.S. marriages, according to 1996 U.S. Census Bureau data; however, this represents a substantial increase from 1970, when the rate was closer to 1 percent. Some studies, such as Clara Rodriguez's *Puerto Ricans: Born in the USA* (1989), have found that rates of intermarriage increase for Hispanic Americans of the more affluent social classes who live in the cities and for the presumably more Americanized younger generations.

Asian Americans have higher rates of intermarriage than African Americans and Hispanic Americans, according to scholars Sharon Lee and Keiko Yamanaka, who found the outmarriage rate for Chinese Americans to be 15 percent and for Japanese Americans 34 percent. However, not all Asian American groups have high rates of intermarriage. Robert Jiobu's *Ethnicity and Assimilation* (1988) found that Vietnamese Americans have very low rates of intermarriage.

African Americans have the lowest rates of intermarriage among all racial groups. According to the U.S. Census Bureau, in 1995, black-white marriages accounted for less than 1 percent of all U.S. marriages. Black males have traditionally outmarried at higher rates than black women. This is consistent with a 1990 study by Tucker and Mitchell-Kernan, which found that 3.6

percent of all married black men are married to white women, while only 1.2 percent of married black women are married to white men.

Intermarriage and Prejudice Despite the increasing occurrence of intermarriage, there is still prejudice against these unions, especially marriages between blacks and whites. This disapproval is communicated through formal channels such as social institutions as well as via informal channels such as families and friends. According to scholars Paul Rosenblatt, Terri A. Karis, and Richard D. Powell, there are various ways in which white families express their opposition to intermarriage. Not allowing black individuals in their homes is one manifestation of the rejection by whites of the possibility that blacks could become part of the family; by not allowing them in, they maintain their image as "pure" whites, thus protecting the family from losing any status or privilege with other whites. Another way that the white family demonstrates its opposition to interracial relationships is to boycott a holiday gathering that a black individual will attend, or even more directly, the interracial wedding of a family member. Refusing to attend such a wedding can be seen as a symbolic refusal to witness and endorse the public entrance of an unacceptable individual into the family. Many white families also disown a member who marries interracially, thus declaring that the offender is no longer a member of the family (and of the white community in general). Ultimately many whites choose to marginalize the white member of their family rather than accept a black individual into their primary group. According to Rosenblatt et al., the reasons given by white families for their opposition are the disapproval of others; issues of safety and well-being; the alleged clannishness of the nonwhite racial group; the problems that children of the union would have; and the likelihood of a poor economic future. By citing such reasons for their behavior, whites are able to reflect stereotypes of racial minorities and acknowledge societal disapproval without implicating themselves personally.

Other forms of opposition that the interracial couple may face come from outside the family. According to Rosenblatt et al., the refusal to accept or acknowledge interracial marriages occurs in a variety of ways, such as not selling a house or not renting a hotel room to an interracial couple. Other typical examples are restaurant hostesses asking one member of an interracial couple if it is "one for dinner" or supermarket cashiers trying to separate their food items in line at the grocery store, which are both refusals to acknowledge that the two are a couple. Religious reasons are also widely used, with Christian groups distributing information over the Internet that "interracial marriages are not biblical" or preachers interpreting the scriptures as explicitly opposing interracial marriages. Interracial couples also cite police harassment, getting "pulled over" a disproportionate number of times when together, and being told that the white woman fits the description of a kidnap victim. Popular culture and the mass media also work against the acceptance of interracial couples by presenting negative images of interracial couples on television talk shows or by rarely casting interracial couples in television shows or films. Often, whites who intermarry are marginalized and stereotyped in much the same way as minorities, with the assumption that they have pathological problems or are "white trash." Thus, although intermarriages are often seen as representative of the improving state of race and ethnic relations, opposition to and prejudice against these marriages still exist.

Erica Childs

Core Resources

Milton Gordon, in *Assimilation in American Life* (New York: Oxford University Press, 1964), identifies seven subprocesses of assimilation, including marital assimilation, or the formation of interracial and interethnic marriages. S. Dale McLemore's *Racial and Ethnic Relations in America* (Boston: Allyn & Bacon, 1994) and Joseph F. Healey's *Race, Ethnicity, Gender, and Class: The Sociology of Group Conflict and Change* (Thousand Oaks, Calif.: Pine Forge Press, 1998) both offer a summary of interracial and interethnic marriage trends. Richard Alba's *Ethnicity and Race in the U.S.A* (New York: Routledge, 1988) and Nathan Glazer and Daniel Moynihan's *Beyond the Melting Pot* (Cambridge, Mass.: MIT Press, 1970) explore interethnic marriage. Clara Rodriguez's *Puerto Ricans: Born in the USA* (Boston: Unwin Hyman, 1989) deals with the issue of intermarriage among Hispanics, focusing primarily on Puerto Ricans. Matthew Snipp's *American Indians: The First of This Land* (New York: Russell Sage Foundation, 1989) explores interracial marriage among Native Americans. Both Sharon Lee and Keiko Yamanaka's "Patterns of Asian American Intermarriage and Marital Assimilation" (*Journal of Comparative Family Studies* 21, 1990) and Robert Jiobu's *Ethnicity and Assimilation* (Albany: State University of New York Press, 1988) explore the issue of intermarriage among Asian Americans. There are many works that look at the issue of black-white marriage, including Belinda Tucker and Claudia Mitchell-Kernan's "New Trends in Black American Interracial Marriage: The Social Structural Context" (*The Journal of Marriage and Family* 52). Paul Spickard's *Mixed Blood: Intermarriage and Ethnic Identity in Twentieth-Century America* (Madison: University of Wisconsin Press, 1989) and Paul Rosenblatt, Terri A. Karis, and Richard D. Powell's *Multiracial Couples: Black and White Voices* (Thousand Oaks, Calif.: Sage Publications, 1995) offer a more qualitative approach that explores the actual experiences of interracial and interethnic couples. For an understanding of interethnic marriage in Canada, Clifford Jansen's "Inter-Ethnic Marriages" (*International Journal of Comparative Sociology* 23, 1982) offers a good analysis.

See also: Discrimination: behaviors; Friendships, interracial/interethnic; Miscegenation laws.

Jewish-African American relations

When relations between Jews and African Americans were good, both groups dramatically advanced the cause of civil rights. Their joint efforts helped bring about the end of legal segregation.

Although the leaders of the African American and Jewish communities enjoyed undeniably good relations in the thirty years after World War II, their friendship was not the historical norm. The periods before and after these years of closeness and cooperation were marked by ambivalence. The relationship between the two communities has varied across time, depending upon economic developments, geographical proximity, and the presence of other ethnic groups.

Early U.S. History Although both Africans and Jews came to North America early, their interaction was very limited. Most of the Africans were slaves on plantations; however, almost no Jews owned slaves or had reason to interact with them. Minimal contact began in the mid-nineteenth century in southern and border-state towns that had a population of freed slaves and a scattering of Jews from Central Europe. The Jews, many of whom opposed slavery, were among the few merchants willing to trade with the former slaves. Both groups shared a sense of being outsiders, a strong attachment to the Hebrew Bible and its message of freedom for the slaves, and support for Abraham Lincoln and the liberal Republican Party during the Civil War (1861-1865).

Turn of the Century Large-scale immigration of Eastern European Jews did not start until the mid-1880's. They came to the United States to escape legal discrimination, religious persecution, pogroms, and dire poverty. Very few of them had experienced any contact with blacks; however, they firmly believed in equality and the rights of the workers, the oppressed, and the poor. Therefore, they were sympathetic to the plight of the African Americans, many of whom had moved from the rural South to northern cities in which Jews lived to escape problems very similar to those from which the Jews had fled.

Depression and World War II During the Great Depression of the 1930's, the Jewish and African American communities came into contact in large industrial cities, but relations were mixed. Both groups shared poverty and persecution and liberal Democratic affiliation. However, as some of the Jews began to prosper, conflict ensued. Many Jews went into business for themselves, partly because of prejudice against them in the workforce.

Because they had limited resources, they opened small stores and later bought small apartment buildings in their urban neighborhoods. Normal shopkeeper-customer and landlord-tenant conflicts developed, intensified by the racial and ethnic differences.

During World War II, the events in Germany provided a common enemy for Jews and African Americans, but that did not eliminate problems. Nazism was not a salient issue for most African Americans. One of the serious rifts between the two groups involved a charismatic member of the Nation of Islam, Sufi Abdul Hamid, who built a reputation for himself partly by insulting Jews and their religion.

Post-World War II   World War II and its aftermath provided opportunities for both groups. African Americans, still fleeing the South, moved into the neighborhoods evacuated by Jews. A decline in public anti-Semitism, combined with higher education, allowed Jews to move from blue-collar to white-collar jobs and to escape the inner-city ghettos. Many Jews who went to college were exposed to and apparently moved by the plight of African Americans.

Early in the twentieth century, Jews had formed a number of organizations, such as the Anti-Defamation League, to protect their rights. Several Jews worked with African American leaders to help them bolster parallel institutions to protect black people's rights, including the National Association for the Advancement of Colored People (NAACP), which had a significant Jewish presence both in funding and in legal staffing.

These civil rights organizations grew in number and in strength, especially after the sit-ins in the South during the early 1960's. The NAACP Legal Defense and Educational Fund, later headed by Jack Greenberg, took the lead in prosecuting the civil rights cases that broke down the legal support for segregation. In the most famous case, *Brown v. Board of Education* (1954), a number of Jewish defense organizations acted as supporting counsel and argued, along with Thurgood Marshall, before the U.S. Supreme Court against the segregation laws. It was this cooperation at the top that led to the golden age of Jewish-African American relations.

Cooperation and support by Jews pervaded the Civil Rights movement. Jews offered much stronger support for racial equality than did other white Americans. Jews constituted more than one-third of all the northern Freedom Riders who went to the South to help organize and register African American citizens to vote. The 1964 murder of two Jewish civil rights activists, Michael Schwerner and Andrew Goodman, and of African American activist James Chaney, was one of the defining moments of the Civil Rights movement.

The Mid-1960's and Black Power   The bond between the Jews and African Americans began to unglue with the increasingly antiwhite and anti-Semitic rhetoric of young black radicals such as Stokely Carmichael (later Kwame Toure) of the Student Nonviolent Coordinating Committee. Leaders of the nascent Black Power movement wanted complete control over their destiny; they wanted to run their own organizations and to live by their own cultural standards, not those of white Europeans. The role of Jews in these movements, therefore, began to diminish.

As the Black Power movement grew, several radical African Americans started attacking Israel, hastening the departure of most Jews. Many young secular Jews grew up with a strong affinity for civil rights but were ambivalent or had weak feelings toward Israel. However, because of the shrill anti-Israel rhetoric and the threat to Israel's existence in 1967 by numerically larger Arab forces, American Jews started to become more supportive of the Israelis. As the younger generation of Jews left the Civil Rights movement in response to the rise of black power, they turned their attention to issues involving Israeli and Russian Jews, and their sense of themselves as an ethnic group increased.

Although Carmichael was critical of the Jewish people, civil rights activist Martin Luther King, Jr., had many friends among Jewish leaders. King was a hero not just to African Americans but also to Jews, in part because of his intolerance for anti-Semitism and his support for Israel. King's death accelerated the split between African Americans and Jews. In the terrible riots following his assassination, a disproportionate amount of loss was sustained by Jewish shopkeepers and landlords who had stayed in the ghetto because they could not afford to relocate. The remaining Jews left quickly.

At the end of the 1960's, a series of hostile confrontations occurred, many in New York, where unionized Jewish teachers battled local African American leaders. Disputes also arose over a proposed housing project in a middle-class Jewish neighborhood and among white-collar municipal employees over jobs and promotions. After the 1970's, many of these inner-city conflicts subsided as Jews moved to the suburbs. For example, in the Los Angeles riots of 1992, friction arose between African Americans and Koreans, not Jews. In other cities, conflicts involved African Americans and Latinos rather than Jews.

1980's and 1990's   Although friction between the two groups was more limited, it did not disappear. Black leader Jesse Jackson angered Jews during his 1984 bid for the presidency by referring to New York, which has a large Jewish population, as "Hymietown" ("hymie" is a derogatory term used to describe Jews) and courting Arab leader Yasser Arafat. On college campuses, a conflict of opinion arose over affirmative action. Jews, who had suffered from quotas that limited their enrollment in higher education, tended to oppose affirmative action, although perhaps less strongly than many white Americans. In 1991, in the racially mixed community of Crown Heights, Brooklyn, a car driven by a Hasidic Jew hit and killed an African American boy and injured his companion. In the rioting that followed, a Hasidic Jew was killed.

Cornel West, coauthor, with Michael Lerner, of *Jews and Blacks* (1995), a book calling for reconciliation between African Americans and Jews. *(Jon Chase/ Harvard News Office)*

An ongoing source of tension in the 1980's and 1990's was Louis Farrakhan, a dynamic and media-sensitive member of the Nation of Islam with a passionate hatred of Jews and Judaism, which he called a "gutter religion." For many Jews, he was the devil incarnate; for many African Americans, he was an articulate spokesperson for black self-determinism and for self-respect and dignity.

The ties between the two groups were never completely severed, however. Both groups tended to be liberal and Democratic, so they had a common political predisposition. They typically lived in the same metropolitan areas and had a partial common history. Nonetheless, at the end of the twentieth century, their political interests diverged. African Americans were focused on the large numbers of blacks in what seemed like a permanent American underclass; Jews were worried about overseas Jews and their declining numbers due to widespread intermarriage and low birthrates. To many African Americans, Jews were just "white folks"; to many Jews, African Americans were ungrateful for the help that Jews had given in the past.

Alan M. Fisher

Core Resources

Murray Friedman's *What Went Wrong: The Creation and Collapse of the Black-Jewish Alliance* (New York: Free Press, 1995) provides the best single overview of relations between the two groups form a Jewish perspective. Hasia R. Diner's *In the Almost Promised Land: American Jews and Blacks, 1919-1935* (Westport, Conn.: Westview, 1977) examines the reasons behind Jewish leaders' support of African Americans. *Blacks and Jews: Alliance and Arguments*, edited by Paul Berman (New York: Delacorte Press, 1994), is a collection of stimulating essays from African Americans and Jews, many close to the New York world of race and politics. Jonathan Kaufman's *Broken Alliance: The Turbulent Times Between Blacks and Jews in America* (New York:

Scribner's, 1988) brings a sensitive, human perspective on change from the 1950's to the 1980's. Mary Berry and John W. Blassingame, two revisionist African American historians, address the role of whites, especially Jews, in *Long Memory: The Black Experience* (New York: Oxford University Press, 1982).

See also: Black Power movement; Civil Rights movement; Nation of Islam; National Association for the Advancement of Colored People.

Jim Crow laws

Jim Crow laws were part of an organized attempt throughout the American South to keep African Americans permanently in a socially subordinate status in all walks of life and to limit possibilities for any form of contact between people of different racial backgrounds.

The precise origins of the term "Jim Crow" are unknown. It may have first appeared in 1832, in a minstrel play by Thomas D. "Big Daddy" Rice. The play contained a song about a slave titled "Jim Crow." The expression was used commonly beginning in the 1890's. In 1904, the *Dictionary of American English* listed the term "Jim Crow law" for the first time.

Jim Crow laws had predecessors in the so-called black codes, passed in many southern states after the Civil War (1861-1865) to limit the freedom of African Americans and assure a continuous labor supply for the southern plantation economy. Radical Reconstruction, which placed most parts of the South under military government, put an end to this. Even after the official end of Reconstruction in 1877, race relations in the South remained in a state of flux.

The Jim Crow Era   Jim Crow laws emerged during the 1880's and 1890's as conflict over political control in the South between different parties and between factions within parties intensified. Disfranchisement of African Americans and the segregation of whites and blacks were intended to assure the permanent subjugation of the latter and the prevention of future biracial political movements which could challenge white rule in the South. Domestic politics do not bear the sole responsibility, however: Jim Crow laws emerged at a time when the United States acquired colonies in the Pacific and the Caribbean and in the process subjugated the indigenous populations of those areas. Race theories used to justify American imperialism did not substantially differ from the white supremacy rhetoric of southern politicians.

The first Jim Crow law was passed by the state of Florida in 1887, followed by Mississippi in 1888, Texas in 1889, Louisiana in 1890, Alabama, Arkansas,

Georgia, and Tennessee in 1891, and Kentucky in 1892. North Carolina passed a Jim Crow law in 1898, South Carolina in 1899, and Virginia in 1900. Statutes requiring racial segregation had been quite common in northern states before the Civil War, but only in the post-Reconstruction South did racial segregation develop into a pervasive system regulating the separation of white and black in all walks of life. Jim Crow laws segregated public carriers, restaurants, telephone booths, residential areas, workplaces, public parks, and other recreational spaces. Mobile, Alabama, passed a special curfew law for African Americans in 1909. In Florida, the law required separate textbooks, which had to be separately stored. The city of New Orleans segregated white and black prostitutes in separate districts. Many states outlawed interracial marriages. Jim Crow laws were not even limited to life: Cemeteries, undertakers, and medical school cadavers were all subjects of segregation under the laws.

These laws, however, represented only symptoms of larger and even more pervasive patterns of discrimination and racial oppression. White vigilante groups, such as the Ku Klux Klan, often enforced their own brand of racial justice through violent means, frequently with the quiet consent and even cooperation of law enforcement officers. In addition, contract labor laws and corrupt law enforcement and prison officials created a system of peonage, which kept large numbers of African Americans in the turpentine and cotton belts in debt slavery.

U.S. Supreme Court   In the process of legally entrenching racial segregation through so-called Jim Crow laws, the U.S. Supreme Court served as a willing handmaiden. In the 1883 *Civil Rights* cases, the Supreme Court ruled that segregation in privately owned railroads, theaters, hotels, restaurants, and similar places comprised private acts of discrimination and as such did not fall under the Fourteenth Amendment. In the 1896 case of *Plessy v. Ferguson*, concerning the constitutionality of a Louisiana Jim Crow law, the Supreme Court redefined segregation from a matter of private prejudice into a mandate of state law. In *Plessy v. Ferguson*, the Supreme Court approved of segregation as long as facilities were "separate but equal." In the 1930's and 1940's, the Supreme Court began to strike down segregation. Eventually, on May 17, 1954, the Supreme Court, in the landmark decision in *Brown v. Board of Education*, declared that separate facilities by their very nature were unequal, thereby reversing previous decisions.

Thomas Winter

Core Resources

An excellent starting point in understanding the Jim Crow era is C. Vann Woodward's *The Strange Career of Jim Crow* (3d rev. ed., New York: Oxford University Press, 1974). For a valuable survey of the relations between African Americans and the law, see Loren Miller's *The Petitioners: The Story of the Supreme Court of the United States and the Negro* (New York: Pantheon Books,

1966). See also Paul Finkelman, ed., *Race, Law, and American History, 1700-1900* (11 vols., New York: Garland, 1992). Of particular interest in this series is volume 4, *The Age of Jim Crow: Segregation from the End of Reconstruction to the Great Depression.* On peonage, see Pete Daniel, *The Shadow of Slavery: Peonage in the South, 1901-1969* (Urbana: University of Illinois Press, 1972).

See also: Black codes; *Brown v. Board of Education*; Civil rights; *Civil Rights* cases; Discrimination (all entries); Ku Klux Klan; Literacy tests; Lynchings; Miscegenation laws; National Association for the Advancement of Colored People; *Plessy v. Ferguson*; Poll tax; Restrictive covenants; Segregation: de facto and de jure; Slavery and race relations.

John Brown's raid

This attempt by a militant abolitionist to liberate and arm Virginia slaves hastened the Civil War.

John Brown's abortive raid on the federal arsenal at Harpers Ferry, Virginia (now West Virginia), on October 16-18, 1859, stands out as a critical episode in the spiraling sequence of events that led Northerners and Southerners into the Civil War in 1861. Brown, long a militant abolitionist, emigrated to Kansas Territory in 1855 with five of his sons to participate in the struggle between proslavery and Free State forces for control of the territory. Their insurrection was in the same spirit as earlier violence perpetrated by abolitionist, Free State militias such as the Border Ruffians following election of a proslavery, territorial legislature in 1854. With a small band of Free State men, Brown helped initiate civil war in Kansas by murdering five allegedly proslavery settlers along Pottawatomie Creek, in May, 1856. Historians would later dub this era "Bleeding Kansas."

Brown's Plan Brown's experience in the Kansas civil war convinced him that a conspiracy existed to seize the national territories for slavery. Having long since lost faith in combating slavery by peaceful means, Brown vowed to strike a violent blow at the heart of slavery. An intense Calvinist, Brown had come to believe that he was God's personal instrument to eradicate the inhuman institution. As early as 1857, he had decided to seize a mountain fortress in Virginia with a small guerrilla force and incite a bloody slave rebellion that would overthrow the slave powers throughout the South.

To that end, Brown sought funds and arms from abolitionists in the North. Under the guise of seeking money to continue the Free State fight in Kansas, Brown secured the friendship and financial aid of the Massachusetts State

Kansas Committee—a group dedicated to helping the Free-Soil forces in Kansas and elsewhere. The resolute and persuasive Brown won the support of six prominent antislavery figures, who agreed to form a secret Committee of Six to advise him and raise money for his still-secret mission. The Secret Six consisted of a well-educated group of dedicated abolitionists and reformers: Franklin B. Sanborn, a young Concord schoolteacher and secretary of the Massachusetts State Kansas Committee; Thomas Wentworth Higginson, a "disunion abolitionist" and outspoken Unitarian minister; Theodore Parker, a controversial theologian-preacher; Samuel Gridley Howe, a prominent physician and educator; George Luther Stearns, a prosperous merchant and chairman of the Massachusetts State Kansas Committee; and Gerrit Smith, a wealthy New York landowner and reformer.

Throughout the remainder of 1857, the indefatigable Brown trained a small group of adventurers and militant abolitionists in preparation for his mission. In May, 1858, Brown moved on to Chatham, Canada, holding a secret "Constitutional Convention" attended by thirty-four African Americans and twelve whites. There, he outlined his plans to invade Virginia, liberate and arm the slaves, defeat any military force brought against them, organize the African Americans into a government, and force the southern states to concede emancipation. Under Brown's leadership, the convention approved a constitution for a new state once the slaves were freed and elected Brown commander in chief with John Kagi, his chief lieutenant, as secretary of war.

Brown's proposed invasion was delayed in 1858, when a disgruntled follower partially betrayed the plans to several prominent politicians. The exposé so frightened the Secret Six that they urged Brown to return to Kansas and create a diversionary operation until rumors of the Virginia plan dissipated. Brown also agreed not to inform the Secret Six of the details of his plans, so that they could not be held responsible in case the invasion failed. In December, 1858, Brown conducted the diversion as planned, by leading a raid into Missouri, liberating eleven slaves, and escorting them to Canada. He then began final preparations for the invasion of Virginia.

The Raid Harpers Ferry, situated at the confluence of the Potomac and Shenandoah Rivers in northern Virginia, was the initial target in Brown's plan, because he needed weapons from the federal arsenal there to arm the liberated slaves. Brown and three of his men arrived at Harpers Ferry on July 3, 1859, and set up headquarters at the Kennedy farm, seven miles east of Harpers Ferry in Maryland. The rest of Brown's twenty-one young recruits (sixteen whites and five African Americans) slowly trickled in. On the night of October 16, 1859, after several months of refining his plans, Brown led eighteen of his followers in an assault on the arsenal and rifle works at Harpers Ferry. They quickly captured the arsenal, the armory, and a nearby rifle works, and then seized hostages from the townspeople and surrounding countryside.

Fearing a slave insurrection, the armed townspeople gathered in the streets, and church bells tolled the alarm over the countryside. Brown stood his ground, anxiously waiting for the slaves from the countryside to rally to his cause. By 11:00 A.M. the next day, Brown's men—holed up in the small fire-enginehouse of the armory—engaged in a pitched battle with the assembled townspeople, farmers, and militia. By dawn the following morning, a company of horse Marines under the command of Colonel Robert E. Lee took up positions in front of the armory. When Brown refused Lee's summons to surrender unconditionally, the Marines stormed the armory, wounded Brown, and routed his followers. Seventeen people died in the raid; ten of the dead, including two of Brown's sons, were raiders. Five raiders were captured, two were taken prisoner several days later, but five escaped without a trace.

The Consequences   Governor Henry A. Wise of Virginia decided that Brown and his coconspirators should be tried in Virginia rather than by federal authorities, even though their attack had been against federal property. Brown and the captured raiders stood trial at Charles Town, Virginia; on October 31, the jury found them guilty of inciting a slave rebellion,

Imaginative depiction of John Brown's raid, in a mural painted in the Topeka, Kansas, state capitol by John Stuart Curry during the late 1930's. *(National Archives)*

murder, and treason against the state of Virginia. After the trial, in a final attempt to save his life, Brown's lawyers collected affidavits from many of his friends and relatives alleging that Brown suffered from hereditary insanity and monomania. Brown rejected his defense, claiming that he was sane. He knew that he could better serve the abolitionist cause as a martyr, a sentiment shared by Northern abolitionists. Governor Wise agreed that Brown was sane, and on December 2, 1859, John Brown was hanged at Charles Town. Six of his fellow conspirators met a similar fate.

Brown's raid intensified the sectional bitterness that led to the Civil War. Although the vast majority of Northerners condemned the incident as the work of a fanatic, the outraged South, racked by rumors of a slave insurrection, suspected all Northerners of abetting Brown's crime. Republican denials of any link with Brown were of little avail. Northern abolitionists, including the Secret Six, who had been cleared of complicity, gathered by the hundreds throughout the North to honor and acclaim Brown's martyrdom. The South was in no mood to distinguish between the Northern Republicans who wanted to contain slavery and the small group of abolitionists who sought to destroy the institution. The South withdrew even further into a defense of its peculiar institution, stifled internal criticism, and intensified its hatred and suspicion of the "Black Republican" Party. In 1861, Northerners marched to war to the tune of "John Brown's Body"—fulfilling Brown's prophecy that "the crimes of this guilty land will never be purged away; but with Blood."

Terry L. Seip, updated by Richard Whitworth

Core Resources

Richard O. Boyer's *The Legend of John Brown: A Biography and a History* (New York: Alfred A. Knopf, 1972) covers not only the events but also the temper of the era that culminated in the Civil War. Stephen B. Oates's *Our Fiery Trial: Abraham Lincoln, John Brown, and the Civil War Era* (Amherst: University of Massachusetts Press, 1979) shows how Lincoln, Brown, and Nat Turner were interconnected in the events that hurled the United States toward civil war. Oates's *To Purge This Land with Blood: A Biography of John Brown* (2d ed., Amherst: University of Massachusetts Press, 1984) is an evenhanded account of Brown and the events he precipitated. *Blacks on John Brown* (Urbana: University of Illinois Press, 1972), compiled by Benjamin Quarles, includes selections by Frederick Douglass, W. E. B. Du Bois, Countee Cullen, and Langston Hughes. Edward J. Renehan's *The Secret Six: The True Tale of the Men Who Conspired with John Brown* (New York: Crown, 1995) details the lives of the six unlikely revolutionaries—five aristocratic Bostonians and one mon-eyed New Yorker—who financed John Brown's bloody raid.

See also: Abolition; Bleeding Kansas; Compromise of 1850; Kansas-Nebraska Act.

Jones v. Alfred H. Mayer Company

Reversing many precedents, the Supreme Court held in this 1968 decision that the 1866 Civil Rights Act prohibited both private and state-backed discrimination and that the Thirteenth Amendment authorized Congress to prohibit private acts of discrimination as "the badges of slavery."

Joseph Lee Jones, alleging that a real estate company had refused to sell him a house because he was African American, sought relief in a federal district court. Since the case appeared before the passage of the Civil Rights Act of 1968, Jones and his lawyer relied primarily on a provision of the 1866 Civil Rights Act that gave all citizens the same rights as white citizens in property transactions. Both the district court and the court of appeals dismissed the complaint based on the established view that the 1866 law applied only to state action and did not address private acts of discrimination. The U.S. Supreme Court, however, accepted the case for review.

All the precedents of the Supreme Court supported the conclusions of the lower courts. In the *Civil Rights* cases (1883) the Court had ruled that the Thirteenth Amendment allowed Congress to abolish "all badges and incidents of slavery," but the Court had narrowly interpreted these badges or incidents as not applying to private acts of discrimination. In *Hodges v. United States* (1906) the Court held that Congress might prohibit only private actions that marked "a state of entire subjection of one person to the will of another," and even in *Shelley v. Kraemer* (1948) the Court recognized the right of individuals to make racially restrictive covenants.

In *Jones*, however, the Court surprised observers by voting 7 to 2 to overturn its precedents. Writing for the majority, Justice Potter Stewart asserted that Congress under the Thirteenth Amendment possessed the power "to determine what are the badges and incidents of slavery, and the authority to translate that determination into effective legislation." In addition, the majority reinterpreted the 1866 law so that it proscribed both governmental and private discrimination in property transactions—an interpretation that is questioned by many authorities.

Justice John M. Harlan wrote a dissenting opinion which argued that the majority probably was wrong in its interpretation of the 1866 law. Harlan also wrote that the passage of the Fair Housing Act of 1968 eliminated the need to render this decision that relied on such questionable history.

Since the *Jones* decision was based on the Thirteenth rather than the Fourteenth Amendment, it was important in diluting the Court's traditional distinction between state and private action, and it appeared to grant Congress almost unlimited power to outlaw private racial discrimination. *Jones* became a precedent for new applications of the almost forgotten post-Civil War statutes in cases such as *Griffin v. Breckenridge* (1971) and

Runyon v. McCrary (1976). In the quarter-century after *Jones,* however, the Congress did not pass any major legislation based upon the authority of the Thirteenth Amendment.

Thomas T. Lewis

See also: Civil rights; Civil Rights Act of 1968; Civil Rights Acts of 1866-1875; *Civil Rights* cases; *Griffin v. Breckenridge; Moose Lodge No. 107 v. Irvis; Runyon v. McCrary;* Segregation: de facto and de jure; *Shelley v. Kraemer.*

Judicial review

Judicial review is the power of a court to determine whether actions of government officials are in accord with the U.S. Constitution, when the matter is before the court in a proper case. Changing interpretations of the Constitution have enabled the eighteenth century document to respond to modern problems.

Under the Articles of Confederation, the first governing document of the United States, there was no national court system. When that document was replaced by the U.S. Constitution in 1789, the latter's Article III provided that the new government would have a court system. It stated that the judicial power of the United States would be lodged in one Supreme Court and whatever lower courts Congress would create. Much of Article III is devoted to defining the jurisdiction of the Supreme Court. There is no statement in the judicial article that the Supreme Court was being given the power to review the constitutionality of the actions of Congress or the president.

Had U.S. political and legal development faithfully followed British tradition, U.S. courts would not have had the power of judicial review. Many other legal practices in the United States have their roots in the nation's British heritage, but not judicial review. In the largely unwritten British constitution, the legislative branch of government is supreme.

The United States, however, has a written Constitution that explicitly states that the "Constitution" is the "supreme Law of the Land." This is known as the supremacy clause. It further states that laws passed by Congress are the supreme law of the land, but only if they are pursuant to the Constitution. It does not say that all laws passed by Congress are supreme. If all laws are not supreme, then there must be a decision maker to decide which laws of the Congress are the supreme law of the land and which laws are unconstitutional. That decision maker might also be called upon by persons who claimed that the president had exceeded the authority conferred on that office by the Constitution. Although the language of the Constitution appeared to have abandoned the British tradition of legislative supremacy, it did not identify any particular decision maker in the government as having the power to decide which laws were constitutional and which were not. The Supreme Court was not expressly given that power.

Origins of Judicial Review The Supreme Court assumed the power of judicial review in 1803, in the case of *Marbury v. Madison*. In that case, steeped in the partisan politics of the period, the Supreme Court for the first time held congressional legislation unconstitutional. Since the Constitution did not explicitly confer on the Court the authority to do this, the task fell to Chief Justice John Marshall to write a judicial opinion justifying the Court's decision. Marshall observed that the Constitution is law and that it is the function of the justices to interpret and apply the law. When a law enacted by Congress conflicts with the law of the Constitution, the Supreme Court is obliged to apply the law of the Constitution rather than the law of Congress, because the Constitution is the supreme law of the land, and the justices of the Supreme Court swore to uphold the Constitution when they took their oaths of office. Thus, Chief Justice Marshall justified the Supreme Court's exercise of judicial review.

Although Marshall's opinion was well reasoned, it did not win universal acceptance. Critics of his opinion accurately observed that all public officials, not just Supreme Court justices, take an oath to support the Constitution. The doctrine of judicial review was opposed because it was believed that it would make the Supreme Court, whose members were appointed to office, superior to the president and Congress, both of which were elected to office. Marshall denied that judicial review meant judicial supremacy, contending that it merely implied the supremacy of the Constitution over all three branches of government. He contended that without judicial review, a written constitution would be meaningless.

During the remainder of Marshall's years as chief justice, the Supreme Court did not again hold congressional legislation unconstitutional. That does not mean, however, that the court did not exercise judicial review. In 1819, in the case of *McCulloch v. Maryland*, it used judicial review to uphold a congressional statute that created the Bank of the United States, when the constitutionality of that legislation was challenged by the state of Maryland. Although the creation of a bank was not among the enumerated powers of Congress, the Supreme Court found ample constitutional authority for the legislation in the necessary and proper clause of Article I, section 8. Over the years, the Court used its power of judicial review far more often to legitimize the actions of the elected branches of government than to hold them unconstitutional.

Even the legitimizing use of judicial review could result in controversy and rejection of the judiciary's special role as constitutional interpreter. Although Congress had seen fit to create a national bank, and the Supreme Court had exercised judicial review to uphold the power of Congress to do so, President Andrew Jackson vetoed similar legislation in 1832, when Congress rechartered the bank. Jackson contended that the legislation was unconstitutional and that he was not bound by the Court's contrary interpretation of congressional power. He too had taken an oath to support the Constitution and so had the right and the responsibility to interpret the document himself in the exercise of the powers of his office. Judicial review had not yet won universal acceptance. That would not come until the post-Civil War period, when the Court aligned itself with the dominant political and economic forces of industrialization.

Whatever doubts remained concerning the Supreme Court's power in relation to Congress and the president, the two elected branches that were considered co-equal with the Court, there were few real doubts about the authority of the Supreme Court to review the constitutionality of state actions, when they were brought before the Court in a proper case. After the Constitution went into effect, the first Congress passed the Judiciary Act of 1789, the statute that set forth the structure of the national judicial system. Section 25 of that act gave the Supreme Court the power to review state legislation challenged as being inconsistent with the Constitution. Even though the Court was clearly given the power of judicial review over state legislation at various times throughout American history, individual states have defied, or attempted to defy, the Court's authority when it held their legislation unconstitutional. Defiant states were rarely able to win the support of a significant number of states not directly involved in the controversy. Those not directly involved have tended to recognize the Supreme Court's power of judicial review over state legislation. They have recognized that such power is necessary, if the federal union is to be maintained.

Whether called upon to exercise judicial review of congressional actions, executive actions, or state actions, the constitutional decisions of the Supreme Court are relatively permanent. They may be reversed by constitutional amendment, but the amending process is difficult; it requires extraordinary majorities in Congress and the states. If a constitutional decision is to be changed, it is far more likely to be done by the Court itself. After the passage of time, the Court may overrule an earlier decision. An overruling decision is generally the result of new justices having been appointed to the Court who interpret the Constitution differently than earlier justices did.

Judicial Review and Civil Rights   Among the Supreme Court's more controversial exercises of judicial review have been those in the area of civil rights. At various times, the Court has reviewed actions of Congress and actions of state governments, sometimes legitimizing those actions and sometimes holding them unconstitutional.

In the aftermath of the Civil War, the Fourteenth Amendment was adopted to overturn the pre-Civil War Supreme Court decision *Dred Scott v. Sandford* (1857). In the *Dred Scott* decision, the Supreme Court said that slaves were not citizens of the United States, could not be citizens, and had no rights under the Constitution. The Fourteenth Amendment overturned the *Dred Scott* decision by extending citizenship to all persons born or naturalized in the United States and under its authority.

The Fourteenth Amendment, however, did more than extend citizenship to the recently freed slaves; it prohibited the states from denying them "the equal protection of the laws." The amendment concluded with an authorization to Congress to enforce the amendment by appropriate legislation.

Relying upon that authorization, Congress passed the Civil Rights Act of 1875. The law prohibited persons who operated various kinds of businesses, such as hotels, restaurants, theaters, and coaches, from discriminating against potential customers on the basis of their race. Challenges to the constitutionality of the law came from business operators in various parts of the nation who denied service to blacks. They argued that in enacting this law, Congress had exceeded its constitutional authority.

The Supreme Court agreed. In the *Civil Rights* cases of 1883, the Supreme Court exercised its power of judicial review to hold the Civil Rights Act of 1875 unconstitutional. The Court concluded that the Civil Rights Act was not appropriate legislation for enforcing the terms of the amendment because it was directed at the operators of private businesses, but the Fourteenth Amendment did not restrict the activity of private businesses, only that of states. In a dissenting opinion, Justice John Marshall Harlan criticized the Court's majority for its interpretation of the language of the Fourteenth Amendment, which he believed violated the spirit of the amendment.

Title II of the Civil Rights Act of 1964 represented a twentieth century attempt to accomplish what the Supreme Court had held unconstitutional in the *Civil Rights* cases of 1883. It prohibited racial discrimination in public accommodations. In passing the 1964 statute, however, Congress did not rely upon the Fourteenth Amendment alone as the source of its authority to enact the legislation. Congress also asserted its authority under the commerce clause, which has been a major source of congressional power in the twentieth century.

Like the Civil Rights Act of 1875, the Civil Rights Act of 1964 was challenged as unconstitutional. In *Heart of Atlanta Motel v. United States* (1964), however, the Supreme Court handed down a decision that legitimized the use of the commerce power to prohibit racial discrimination in public accommodations. The Court examined the legislative history of the 1964 Civil Rights Act and found that there was considerable testimony at congressional hearings that discrimination continued to exist in all parts of the country and that this discrimination in public accommodations had a detrimental effect on interstate travel by African Americans. The Court held that Congress had acted within its legitimate commerce power when it passed the Civil Rights Act. Since the commerce clause provided ample support for this legislation, the Court did not find it necessary to reexamine the extent of congressional authority under the Fourteenth Amendment; thus, it did not overrule the *Civil Rights* cases of 1883.

Judicial review of state legislation requiring segregation of the races followed a path somewhat similar to that of congressional legislation banning discrimination in public accommodations, in that the Court initially legitimized state segregation statutes but years later adopted a different interpretation of the Constitution. In *Plessy v. Ferguson* (1896), the Supreme Court upheld a Louisiana law requiring that black passengers and white passengers ride in separate railroad cars. Homer Plessy, legally considered black although racially mixed, had challenged the constitutionality of the state law, arguing that it denied him the equal protection of the laws which the Fourteenth Amendment guaranteed. He argued that this state-imposed segregation placed a badge of inferiority on black people.

The Supreme Court rejected Plessy's argument and legitimized state-imposed segregation of the races. The Court considered the Louisiana law to be a reasonable regulation that took into consideration the customs and traditions of the people. Out of this came the "separate but equal" doctrine, which came to be applied not just to railroad transportation but to virtually all areas of life in the southern states.

By 1954, the Supreme Court was using its power of judicial review to begin dismantling the segregated society that it had previously legitimized. In that year, it rendered a decision that state-imposed racial segregation violated the equal protection clause of the Fourteenth Amendment. In the landmark case of *Brown v. Board of Education*, the Supreme Court overruled *Plessy v. Ferguson*, insofar as it applied to public education. Writing for a unanimous Supreme Court, Chief Justice Earl Warren stated that it was impossible to determine how those who proposed and ratified the Fourteenth Amendment intended for its equal protection clause to apply to public education, for the simple reason that public education was virtually nonexistent then. By the mid-twentieth century, however, public education was among the most important functions of state and local governments, as their own compulsory school attendance laws recognized. The Court concluded that in this modern context, legally imposed racial segregation could never provide equal education, even if all tangible elements were equal, because of the psychological damage done to black children. In the view of the Court, such segregation generated feelings of inferiority in black children, which had a detrimental effect on their motivation to learn. Thus, the Court rejected "separate but equal" in public education.

Broader Applications of Judicial Review

Judicial review is not a power that belongs solely to the Supreme Court of the United States. It may also be exercised by federal district courts and federal courts of appeals. The decisions of those courts, however, may be appealed to the Supreme Court. State courts may also exercise judicial review and determine whether challenged actions of their own state officials are in accord with the United States Constitution. The decisions of the highest court of a state on such matters may be appealed to the Supreme Court of the United States. Thus, the Supreme Court provides uniformity in constitutional interpretation.

The decisions of the Court have involved a multitude of constitutional issues, not just civil rights. The Supreme Court has defined the constitutional authority of the states and of the three branches of the national government. In the late twentieth century, for example, the Court held that the legislative veto—that is, the power of one house of Congress to pass a resolution negating a decision of administrative officials—was unconstitutional. Another decision legitimized congressional legislation creating the position of independent counsel.

Because the justices of the Supreme Court are politically appointed, the Court's exercise of judicial review has generally reflected the dominant values of U.S. society. As those values change over time, the Court's interpretation of the Constitution changes. The flexible language of the Constitution and the infusion of new ideas and values as new justices join the Court have enabled the United States Constitution, adopted by a young nation in the eighteenth century, to remain the basic governing document of the United States for more than two hundred years. Judicial review has become as much a part of the constitutional system in the United States as those powers specifically written in the Constitution.

Patricia A. Behlar

Core Resources

A good introduction to the subject is John A. Garraty, ed., *Quarrels That Have Shaped the Constitution* (Rev. ed. New York: Perennial Library, 1987), a collection of case studies of important constitutional decisions by the Supreme Court, written for nonspecialists. Robert Lowry Clinton's *Marbury v. Madison and Judicial Review* (Lawrence: University Press of Kansas, 1989) argues that current interpretations of *Marbury v. Madison* have given the Supreme Court more power than John Marshall ever did. Charles Warren, *The Making of the Constitution* (New York: Barnes & Noble, 1967) offers a day-by-day summary of the Constitutional Convention for the general reader.

See also: Civil rights; Civil Rights Act of 1875; Civil Rights Act of 1964; *Civil Rights* cases; Fourteenth Amendment; *Plessy v. Ferguson*; *Scott v. Sandford*.

Jury selection

Equal protection of the law is at the heart of ensuring that no category of people is systematically favored over any other. If any category of people is limited in its access to participation in the U.S. legal system—especially in passing judgment on a member of that category who may have been accused of a crime—justice may be imperiled. If members of different racial or ethnic groups have the perception that justice is not blind, their full participation in society is jeopardized.

Before the Civil War (1861-1865), Massachusetts was the only state that permitted nonwhites to serve on juries. After the war, most southern states enacted legislation that effectively barred African Americans and other minorities from jury service, irrespective of the protections of the Fourteenth Amendment. Northern states tended to produce largely the same outcome mostly through the use of an exclusive *venire* (jury pool) process, whereby "prominent" citizens (which effectively left out minorities) filled out the rolls.

The exclusionary laws typical in the southern states were struck down when the U.S. Congress criminalized racism in jury selection in 1875. However, Congress left the exclusionary *venire* procedures common in the North unaddressed. These procedures soon became quite prevalent in the South as well.

Twentieth Century Reforms   Although nonexclusionary *voir dire* (selection to sit on a jury) became the standard guideline by the middle of the twentieth century, major changes were not initiated until the 1960's, when the United States Fifth Circuit Court began overturning convictions and indictments within its jurisdiction (mostly southern states) on the basis of exclusionary selection. Although the U.S. Supreme Court ruled in *Swain v. Alabama* (1965) that constitutional requirements were satisfied as long as minorities were on the *venire* and part of the grand jury that brought down an indictment, it was not until the Jury Selection and Service Act (1968) that Congress outlawed "blue ribbon" juries in federal courts. Consequently, the *venire* process had to be more open. In *Taylor v. Louisiana* (1975) the Supreme Court extended this requirement to the state and local courts.

Nevertheless, exclusion persisted through use of the peremptory challenge in petit (trial) jury *voir dire*—whereby attorneys have the right to strike potential jurors without stating any reason. Such screening of potential grand jurors is less prevalent. In *Batson v. Kentucky* (1986), the Supreme Court curtailed unrestricted use of peremptory challenge in petit juries by allowing judges to inquire as to the rationale for and to limit strikes (dismissals) of potential jurors when there appeared to be a pattern of exclusion. However, it is difficult to determine motivation definitively unless the prosecutor is unusually inept or unusually honest. The fact that more minorities have had adverse contacts with the criminal justice system can be used as a rationale for exclusion.

Consequently, some experts argued that "affirmative action" is necessary to guarantee representative juries. Others criticized this idea, saying that affirmative action in jury selection would translate into imposing quotas of minorities on juries, and some local jurisdictions did impose quotas on jury selection. However, in *Holland v. Illinois* (1990), the Supreme Court held that as long as the *venire* provided an appropriate cross section of the community, *voir dire* did not have to produce representative results because the Constitution merely guarantees equality of opportunity, not necessarily representativeness.

Jury Nullification The most potentially problematic issue in the late twentieth century involved the Fully Informed Jury Association (FIJA) and related initiatives. FIJA proponents tend to be opposed to governmental authority in that they try to encourage potential jurors—especially those who may be judging antigovernment activists—to ignore the facts and/or the law in order to acquit. This "jury nullification," about which the government has no legal appeal (unless there is evidence of something like jury tampering), may contribute to even greater use of "scientific" jury selection. This innovation uses social research and psychological studies to profile and include or exclude (through peremptory challenge) jurors who may be more or less favorable to the case presented.

The jury nullification notions of the FIJA appear to be shared by some minority activists, who argue that members of their communities on juries judging their peers have a duty to vote for acquittal in almost all instances in order to redress the social injustices visited upon their community by the majority. Although this might accomplish nothing more than "hung" (unable to decide) juries—which permit the government to retry the cases—if minority members on subsequent juries act the same way, government efforts to convict members of the minority will be stymied. If such postures become widespread, racially based peremptory challenges might become acceptable with the rationale that these minorities have an antigovernment bias such that they cannot meet the requirement of impartiality.

Scott Magnuson-Martinson

Core Resources

Randall Kennedy's *Race, Crime, and the Law* (New York: Pantheon, 1997) offers a comprehensive history of race and criminal justice in the United States—with several chapters on how it affects the composition of juries. Hirosaki Fukarai, Edgar W. Butler, and Richard Krooth elaborate the history of discrimination in U.S. jury selection in *Race and the Jury: Racial Disenfranchisement and the Search for Justice* (New York: Plenum, 1993). In *Guilty: The Collapse of Criminal Justice* (New York: Random House, 1996), Judge Harold J. Rothwax criticizes past legal methods of excluding minority participation on juries as well as some of the more extreme modern remedies. Albert W. Alschuler makes an argument for affirmative action in jury selection in "Racial Quotas and the Jury," in *Duke Law Journal* (44, 1995), and Paul Butler proposes that certain minorities use their jury participation to protect their communities in "Racially Based Jury Nullification: Black Power in the Criminal Justice System," in *Yale Law Journal* (105, 1995).

See also: *Batson v. Kentucky*; Crime and race/ethnicity; Criminal justice system.

Kansas-Nebraska Act

Senator Stephen A. Douglas, chairman of the Committee on Territories, introduced legislation to organize the land west of Missouri and Iowa as the Nebraska Territory. New settlements in the region and the potential for a transcontinental rail route prompted Douglas's action. It soon became apparent to Douglas that obtaining support from the South required two major revisions. First, the region was split into the Kansas and Nebraska territories. Second, the bill called for repeal of that part of the Missouri Compromise of 1820 which prohibited slavery north of 36° 30' latitude. Rather, settlers in each territory would vote to accept or prohibit slavery.

Douglas viewed slavery from economic rather than moral grounds, reasoning that its unprofitability in northern climates would be its demise. Douglas's concessions to slave states reflected both the desire to get on with nation building and the necessity of obtaining Southern support for his presidential ambitions. The act, which became law May 30, 1854, widened the growing rift between North and South and encouraged the formation of the Republican Party.

John A. Sondey

See also: Abolition; Bleeding Kansas; John Brown's raid; Lincoln-Douglas debates; Missouri Compromise; Slavery: history.

Kerner Report

The Kerner Report was a formal attempt to explain one of the greatest explosions of urban racial violence in the history of the United States. The report, the product of a commission appointed by President Lyndon B. Johnson, blamed pervasive racist attitudes and practices for the riots in the nation's cities.

Beginning in 1963, the United States experienced an unprecedented number of urban racial disorders. In 1967 alone, more than one hundred U.S. cities exploded in episodes of violence and looting. In November, 1967, President Johnson appointed the Kerner Commission (formally known as the National Advisory Commission on Civil Disorders), headed by Governor Otto Kerner of Illinois, to conduct an investigation to determine exactly what had happened and why and to make recommendations to solve the problem.

The commission reported that the basic cause of the urban disorders was white racism and that white, moderate, responsible America was where the responsibility for the riots ultimately lay. It had conducted detailed case studies of cities where violence had erupted and found that the riots had not been caused by any single factor or precipitating incident and were not the

President Lyndon B. Johnson (below bust of Abraham Lincoln) convenes the first meeting of the Kerner Commission in 1967. *(National Archives)*

result of an organized plan or conspiracy. Its report stated that "the single overriding cause of rioting in the cities was not any one thing commonly adduced—unemployment, lack of education, poverty, exploitation—but that it was all of those things and more, expressed in the insidious and pervasive white sense of the inferiority of black men." The commission emphasized that the source of the problems was the very structure of American society; it did not seek explanations in the psychology of individuals. The report pointed out, "What white Americans have never fully understood—but what the Negro can never forget—is that white society is deeply implicated in the ghetto. White institutions created it, white institutions maintain it, and white society condones it." The report concluded, "Our nation is moving toward two societies, one black, one white—separate and unequal."

According to the commission, although racism was behind the riots, the more proximate causes of the unrest were pervasive discrimination and segregation in employment, education, and housing and the concentration of impoverished blacks in the inner city, produced by black migration into and white exodus from urban areas. Other contributing factors included the frustration of African Americans with civil rights legislation that failed to deliver the greater opportunity it promised; dissatisfaction with police practices that, for many African Americans, symbolized the oppression associated with racism; and society's apparent tendency to approve of violence against civil rights activists. The commission also noted enhanced racial pride, especially among young African Americans, and a feeling of powerlessness that led some to conclude that violence was the only effective means of change.

The Kerner Commission concluded that discrimination and segregation were serious problems that presented a threat to the future of the nation and must be eliminated. It indicated that three options were open to the nation: to maintain existing, admittedly inadequate policies regarding integration and the elimination of poverty; to focus on improving life in African American ghettos and ignore the goal of integration; or to pursue integration by improving conditions in the ghetto and implementing policies that would encourage movement out of the inner city.

The commission stated that the first option, to maintain existing policies, would permanently divide the United States into two separate and unequal societies and create an irreversible, polarized, police state rather than a democracy. The second option, described as "gilding the ghetto," would enrich the inner city but would further promote a separate, segregated society. Option three, a national commitment to change that involved moving a substantial number of African Americans out of the ghettos, was viewed as the most viable. This option was designed to create a single society in which all citizens would be free to live and work according to their capabilities and desires, not their color.

The Kerner Commission made a series of recommendations related to jobs, housing, education, law enforcement agencies, and nearly every other aspect of American life. It asked Americans to tax themselves to the extent necessary to meet the vital needs of the nation. Specific goals included the elimination of barriers to job choice, education, and housing and increasing the responsiveness of public institutions to relieve feelings of powerlessness. Other goals were to increase communication across racial lines to destroy stereotypes; to halt polarization, distrust, and hostility; and to create common ground for efforts toward public order and social justice.

Frank E. Hagan

See also: Civil Rights movement; Detroit riot; Newark race riots; Race riots of the twentieth century; Watts riot.

Keyes v. Denver School District No. 1

Decided June 21, 1973, this ruling outlawed de facto desegregation and expanded prohibitions on segregation. *Brown v. Board of Education* (1954) invalidated laws that required or permitted segregated black and white schools. Nevertheless, many school districts remained segregated, in part because of de facto segregation (segregation "in fact" rather than de jure, or "by law"). Wilfred Keyes did not want his daughter, Christi Keyes, to attend any kind of segregated school in Denver. In 1970, when a newly elected school board rescinded a desegregation plan adopted by the previous board in 1969, he brought a class-action suit.

In 1970, the district court ordered Park Hill schools desegregated after hearing evidence that the school board deliberately segregated its schools through school site selection, excessive use of mobile classroom units, gerrymandered attendance zones, student transportation routes, a restrictive transfer policy, and segregated faculty assignment to schools. Keyes was also successful before the court in arguing that inner-city schools, with substantial black and Hispanic student populations, should also be desegregated, but Denver prevailed on appeal in 1971, arguing that the large percentages of black and Hispanic students in these schools resulted from a "neighborhood school" policy.

Justice William J. Brennan delivered the opinion of the U.S. Supreme Court. Six justices joined Brennan, one justice affirmed the decision in part and dissented in part, and the remaining justice dissented. The Supreme Court ruled that since intentional segregation was proved in one part of the city, there was a presumption of intentional discrimination in the other case. The burden of proof thus shifted to the school board to prove that the intentional segregation of one section of the district was isolated, separate, and unrelated to the pattern of pupil assignment to the "core city schools."

When the case was sent back to the district court in 1973, Denver was determined to have practiced unlawful segregation in both areas of the city, and the school board was required to desegregate. When the school board failed to design an adequate plan to desegregate by 1974, the court drew up a plan of its own.

The effect of *Keyes* was to open all northern school districts to the possibility of desegregation lawsuits. Eventually almost every city of at least moderate size then grappled with desegregation plans, voluntary or court ordered. The lone exception is the statewide school district of Hawaii, which has never been desegregated despite the existence of schools situated to serve certain geographic areas where only persons of Hawaiian ancestry by law can reside.

Michael Haas

See also: *Brown v. Board of Education*; Segregation: de facto and de jure; *Sweatt v. Painter.*

King, Martin Luther, Jr.

As founding president of the Southern Christian Leadership Conference, King (1929-1968) spearheaded the nonviolent movement that led to the 1964 Civil Rights Act and the 1965 Voting Rights Act.

Martin Luther King, Jr., was born in Atlanta, Georgia, on January 15, 1929, the second child of the Reverend Michael Luther and Alberta Williams King.

Martin Luther King, Jr. *(Library of Congress)*

He was originally named Michael Luther King, Jr., but after the death of his paternal grandfather in 1933, King's father changed their first name to Martin to honor the grandfather's insistence that he had originally given that name to his son in the days when birth certificates were rare for blacks. Nevertheless, King was known as M. L. or Mike throughout his childhood. In 1931, King's father became pastor of the Ebenezer Baptist Church on Auburn Avenue, only a block away from the house where King was born.

King's father was both a minister and a bold advocate of racial equality. His mother was the daughter of the Reverend Adam Daniel Williams, who had preceded King's father as pastor of Ebenezer and had established it as one of Atlanta's most influential black churches. Both of King's parents believed in nonviolent resistance to racial discrimination. He grew up under the strong influence of the church and this family tradition of independence.

Though small as a boy, King was vigorously athletic and intellectually curious. He enjoyed competitive games as well as words and ideas. Intrigued by the influence of his father and other ministers over their congregations, young King dreamed of being a great speaker. Lerone Bennett noted:

> To form words into sentences, to fling them out on the waves of air in a crescendo of sound, to watch people weep, shout, *respond*: this fascinated young Martin. . . . The idea of using words as weapons of defense and offense was thus early implanted and seems to have grown in King as naturally as a flower.

Early Education King excelled as a student and was able to skip two grades at Booker T. Washington High School and to enter Morehouse College in 1944 at age fifteen. At first he intended to study medicine, but religion and philosophy increasingly appealed to him as the influence of Morehouse president Dr. Benjamin E. Mays and Dr. George D. Kelsey of the religion department grew. Mays, a strong advocate of Christian nonviolence, sensed in King a profound talent in this area. In 1947, King was ordained a

Baptist minister, and after graduation the following year he entered theological studies at Crozer Theological Seminary in Pennsylvania.

During his studies at Crozer and later in a doctoral program at Boston University (1951-1954), King deepened his knowledge of the great ideas of the past. Especially influential upon his formative mind were the Social Gospel concept of Walter Rauschenbusch, the realist theology of Reinhold Niebuhr, and above all, the nonviolent reformism of Mohandas K. Gandhi. In Gandhi, King found the key to synthesizing his Christian faith, his passion for helping oppressed people, and his sense of realism sharpened by Niebuhrian theology. Later King wrote:

> Gandhi was probably the first person in history to lift the love ethic of Jesus above mere interaction between individuals to a powerful and effective social force on a large scale. . . . It was in this Gandhian emphasis on love and nonviolence that I discovered the method for social reform.

King realized that nonviolence could not be applied in the United States exactly the way Gandhi had used it in India, but throughout his career King was devoted to the nonviolent method. In his mind, Gandhi's concept of *satyagraha* (force of truth) and *ahimsa* (active love) were similar to the Christian idea of *agape*, or unselfish love.

In Boston, King experienced love of another kind. In 1952, he met Coretta Scott, an attractive student at the New England Conservatory of Music. They were married at her home in Marion, Alabama, by King's father the following year. Neither wanted to return to the segregated South, but in 1954, while King was finishing his doctoral dissertation on the concepts of God in the thinking of Paul Tillich and Henry Nelson Wieman, he received a call to pastor the Dexter Avenue Baptist Church in Montgomery, Alabama. Their acceptance marked a major turning point in their own lives, as well as in American history.

By then King was twenty-five years old and still rather small at five feet, seven inches. With a strong build, large pensive eyes, and a slow, articulate speaking style, he was an unusually well-educated young minister anxious to begin his first pastorate. As the Kings moved to the city which had once been the capital of the Confederacy, they believed that God was leading them into an important future.

Pastoral Work   King quickly established himself as a hardworking pastor who guided his middle-class congregation into public service. He encouraged his parishioners to help the needy and to be active in organizations such as the NAACP. Montgomery was a rigidly segregated city with thousands of blacks living on mere subsistence wages and barred from mainstream social life. The U.S. Supreme Court's *Brown v. Board of Education* decision of 1954, requiring integration of public schools, had hardly touched the city, and most blacks apparently had little hope that their lives would ever improve.

An unexpected event in late 1955, however, changed the situation and drew King into his first significant civil rights activism. On December 1, Rosa Parks, a local black seamstress, was ordered by a bus driver to yield her seat to a white man. She refused, and her arrest triggered a 381-day bus boycott that led to a U.S. Supreme Court decision declaring the segregated transit system unconstitutional. King became the principal leader of the Montgomery Improvement Association, which administered the boycott, as thousands of local blacks cooperated in an effective nonviolent response to legally sanctioned segregation.

Quickly, the "Montgomery way" became a model for other southern cities: Tallahassee, Mobile, Nashville, Birmingham, and others. In January, 1957, King, his close friend Ralph David Abernathy, and about two dozen other black ministers and laymen met at the Ebenezer Baptist Church to form a Southwide movement. Subsequent meetings in New Orleans and Montgomery led to the formal creation of the Southern Christian Leadership Conference (SCLC), which King used as the organizational arm of his movement.

From this point onward, King's life was bound with the SCLC's nonviolent movement. Its driving force was the heightened confidence of thousands of blacks and their white supporters, but King was its symbol and spokesman. He suffered greatly in the process. In 1958, while promoting his first book, Stride Toward Freedom (1958), an account of the Montgomery boycott, he was stabbed by a black woman. He was frequently arrested and berated by detractors as an "outside agitator" as he led various campaigns across the South. By early 1960, he had left his pastorate in Montgomery to become copastor (with his father) of the Ebenezer Baptist Church and to give his time more fully to the SCLC.

Not all of King's efforts were successful. A campaign in Albany, Georgia, in 1961 and 1962 failed to desegregate that city. At times there were overt tensions between King's SCLC and the more militant young people of the Student Nonviolent Coordinating Committee (SNCC), which was created in the wake of the first significant sit-in, in Greensboro, North Carolina, in February, 1960. King supported the sit-in and freedom ride movements of the early 1960's and was the overarching hero and spiritual mentor of the young activists, but his style was more patient and gradualist than theirs.

King's greatest successes occurred from 1963 to 1965. To offset the image of failure in Albany, the SCLC carefully planned a nonviolent confrontation in Birmingham, Alabama, in the spring of 1963. As the industrial hub of the South, Birmingham was viewed as the key to desegregating the entire region. The campaign there was launched during the Easter shopping season to maximize its economic effects. As the "battle of Birmingham" unfolded, King was arrested and wrote his famous "letter from a Birmingham Jail" in which he articulated the principles of nonviolent resistance and countered the argument that he was an "outside agitator" with the affirmation that all people are bound "in an inextricable network of mutuality" and that "injustice anywhere is a threat to justice everywhere."

The Birmingham campaign was an important victory. Nationally televised scenes of police chief Eugene "Bull" Connor's forces using fire hoses and trained dogs to attack nonviolent demonstrators stirred the public conscience. The Kennedy administration was moved to take an overt stand on behalf of civil rights. President John F. Kennedy strongly urged the Congress to pass his comprehensive civil rights bill. That bill was still pending in August, 1963, when King and many others led a march by more than 200,000 people to Washington, D.C. At the Lincoln Memorial on August 28, King delivered his most important speech, "I Have a Dream," calling upon the nation to "rise up and live out the true meaning of its creed 'that all men are created equal.'"

After the March on Washington, King reached the height of his influence. Violence returned to Birmingham in September when four black girls were killed at the Sixteenth Street Baptist Church. In November, President Kennedy was assassinated. Yet in July, 1964, President Lyndon B. Johnson signed into law the Civil Rights Act that ended most legally sanctioned segregation in the United States. Later in 1964, King was awarded the Nobel Prize for Peace. Increasingly, he turned his attention to world peace and economic advancement.

In 1965, King led a major campaign in Selma, Alabama, to underscore the need for stronger voting rights provisions than those of the 1964 Civil Rights Act. The result was the 1965 Voting Rights Act, which gave the federal government more power to enforce blacks' right to vote. Ironically, as these important laws went into effect, the ghettos of northern and western cities were erupting in violent riots. At the same time, the United States was becoming more deeply involved in the Vietnam War, and King was distressed by both of these trends. In 1966 and beyond, he attempted nonviolent campaigns in Chicago and other northern cities, but with less dramatic successes than those of Birmingham and Selma.

King's opposition to the Vietnam War alienated him from some of his black associates and many white supporters. Furthermore, it damaged his relationship with the FBI and the Johnson administration. Many observers have seen his last two years as a period of waning influence. Yet King continued to believe in nonviolent reform. In 1968, he was planning another march on Washington, this time to accentuate the plight of the poor of all races. In April he traveled to Memphis, Tennessee, to support a local sanitation workers' strike. On the balcony of the Lorraine Motel on April 4, he was shot to death by James Earl Ray. King's successor, Ralph David Abernathy, carried through with the Poor People's March on Washington in June. King was survived by Coretta and their four children: Yolanda Denise (Yoki), Martin Luther III (Marty), Dexter, and Bernice Albertine (Bunny). Soon Coretta established the Martin Luther King, Jr., Center for Nonviolent Social Change to carry on, like the SCLC, his work.

Summary Martin Luther King, Jr., embodied a number of historical trends to which he added his own unique contributions. He was the author of five major books and hundreds of articles and speeches. His principal accomplishment was to raise the hopes of black Americans and to bind them in effective direct-action campaigns. Although he was the major spokesman of the black movement, he was modest about his contributions. Just before his death he declared in a sermon that he wanted to be remembered as a "drum major for justice." Essentially, he is. The campaigns he led paved the way for legal changes that ended more than a century of racial segregation.

Above all, King espoused nonviolence. That theme runs through his career and historical legacy. He left a decisive mark on American and world history. His dream of a peaceful world has inspired many individuals and movements. In 1983, the United States Congress passed a law designating the third Monday in January a national holiday in his honor. Only one other American, George Washington, had been so honored.

Thomas R. Peake

Core Resources

King's life has been the subject of many biographies. For example, John J. Ansbro's *Martin Luther King, Jr.: The Making of a Mind* (Maryknoll, N.Y.: Orbis Books, 1982) is an excellent study of King's intellectual and spiritual development, based on extensive primary material. First published in 1964 while King was still living, Lerone Bennett, Jr.'s *What Manner of Man: A Biography of Martin Luther King, Jr.* (Rev. ed. New York: Johnson Publishing, 1976) captures the meaning of King's personality and faith. Shortly after King was killed, his widow, Coretta Scott King, wrote *My Life with Martin Luther King, Jr.* (New York: Holt, Rinehart and Winston, 1969), a valuable personal account of the King family, the Montgomery bus boycott, and other SCLC campaigns. This book should be balanced by more scholarly accounts. David Levering Lewis, *King: A Critical Biography* (2d ed. Urbana: University of Illinois Press, 1978), is a critical account of King's public career and is particularly incisive on the Birmingham campaign of 1963. More recent biographies include Brian Ward and Tony Badger, *The Making of Martin Luther King and the Civil Rights Movement* (New York: New York University Press, 1995), and James R. Ralph, Jr., *Northern Protest: Martin Luther King, Jr., Chicago, and the Civil Rights Movement* (Cambridge, Mass.: Harvard University Press, 1993). The most thorough recounting of the life of King, with extensive material on SCLC as well, is David J. Garrow, *Bearing the Cross: Martin Luther King, Jr., and the Southern Christian Leadership Conference, a Personal Portrait* (New York: William Morrow, 1986). Garrow carefully documents King's personal life and the origins and progress of his movement, with special attention to King's internal struggles. Garrow also wrote *The FBI and Martin Luther King, Jr.: From "Solo" to Memphis* (New York: W. W. Norton, 1981), which examines the roots and nature of the FBI's opposition to King and the SCLC. Any deeper research into King's life should not overlook *The*

Papers of Martin Luther King, Jr., edited by Clayborn Carson and others, which the University of California Press began publishing during the early 1990's.

See also: Civil disobedience; Civil Rights movement; "I Have a Dream" speech; Montgomery bus boycott; Southern Christian Leadership Conference.

King, Martin Luther, Jr., assassination

The murder in 1968 of the nation's most prominent civil rights leader touched off widespread urban unrest and dealt a severe blow to the Civil Rights movement.

For more than a decade, Martin Luther King, Jr., led the Southern Christian Leadership Conference (SCLC) and was, for many people, the quintessential symbol and spokesman for nonviolence. By the spring of 1968, however, King had lost some of his mystique, as the relatively simpler issues of voting rights and access to public facilities were superseded by more costly and divisive social and economic problems, accompanied by the deepening U.S. involvement in the Vietnam War.

King had lost his close alliance with President Lyndon B. Johnson because of his opposition to the president's Vietnam policy. King also faced challenges from younger, more militant African American leaders, for whom King's philosophy of passive resistance seemed too slow.

On the evening of April 4, King walked onto the balcony of his Memphis motel and was struck down by a bullet, fired from a building across the street. He died almost instantly. Initial attempts to identify and apprehend the killer failed, and while fires and riots raged in several cities in protest of King's death, an intensive search began, spreading eventually to Canada and Great Britain. On June 8, British immigration officials arrested an escaped U.S. convict traveling under the name of Roman George Sneyd and returned him to the United States to stand trial for the murder of King. The prisoner, whose real name was James Earl Ray, pleaded guilty to the charge in March, 1969, and was sentenced to ninety-nine years in prison. Later, Ray changed his position, claimed innocence, and wrote a book entitled *Who Killed Martin Luther King?* (1992), with a foreword by the Reverend Jesse Jackson that cautiously endorsed Ray's conspiracy argument.

The immediate aftermath of King's death was marked by serious urban rioting in several cities, and somewhat later, by the granting of a substantial number of the strikers' demands in Memphis. More difficult to appraise is the place that his martyrdom earned for him and for his ideas in the Civil

Rights movement. At a time when his influence was threatened by men such as H. Rap Brown and Huey P. Newton, King was killed in a way that served to restore his prestige among many African Americans. Under the leadership of King's longtime assistant Ralph David Abernathy, the SCLC continued to play a leading role in the Civil Rights movement after King's death. On the other hand, some African Americans, finding in King's death a confirmation of the futility of passive resistance, turned instead to more militant tactics.

In death, King remained an inspiring symbol, even a martyr, to many people who supported his causes. The SCLC, which King helped to found and which he led for eleven years as its president, continued under presidents Ralph Abernathy and Joseph E. Lowery to keep the vision of a nonviolent society central to their organizational and personal goals.

Courtney B. Ross, updated by Thomas R. Peake

Core Resources

Gerold Frank's *An American Death: The True Story of the Assassination of Dr. Martin Luther King, Jr.* (Garden City, N.Y.: Doubleday, 1972) is a well-documented analysis of King's assassination that argues that Ray acted alone. William Bradford Huie's *He Slew the Dreamer: My Search for the Truth About James Earl Ray and the Murder of Martin Luther King* (New York: Delacorte Press, 1970) rejects Ray's contention that King was the victim of a conspiracy and that Ray had been framed for the murder. James Earl Ray's *Who Killed Martin Luther King? The True Story by the Alleged Assassin* (Washington, D.C.: National Press Books, 1992), an apparently self-serving account by King's convicted assassin, argues that Ray did not commit the murder but was a scapegoat set up by the Federal Bureau of Investigation and other agencies.

See also: Black Power movement; Civil Rights movement; Southern Christian Leadership Conference.

King, Rodney, case

The arrest and beating by police of Rodney King, a black man, sparked a major investigation of police brutality in Los Angeles and violent race riots after a California court acquitted the officers involved.

Following a high-speed chase along a Los Angeles highway that ended just after midnight on March 3, 1991, California Highway Patrol officers Timothy and Melanie Singer stopped driver Rodney Glen King and his two passengers, Bryant Allen and Freddie Helms, for questioning. More than twenty Los Angeles Police Department (LAPD) officers soon arrived on the scene in Los Angeles' Lake View Terrace neighborhood. Police sergeant Stacey Koon, assisted by officers Theodore Briseno, Laurence Powell, and Timothy Wind, took over the investigation. The police quickly subdued and handcuffed Allen and Helms without incident. Their encounter with King, however, caused a controversy with far-reaching legal and social consequences.

King's Arrest   According to the four white police officers who arrested King, a black man, King refused at first to leave the car and then resisted arrest with such vigor that the officers considered it necessary to apply two jolts from a Taser electric stun gun, fifty-six blows from aluminum batons, and six kicks (primarily from Briseno) to subdue King before they success-fully handcuffed and cordcuffed King to restrain his arms and legs. The event probably would have gone unnoticed had not George Holliday, an amateur cameraman who witnessed the incident, videotaped the arrest and sold the tape to a local television station news program. The videotape became the crucial piece of evidence that the state of California used to charge the four LAPD arresting officers with criminal assault and that a federal grand jury subsequently used to charge the officers with civil rights violations.

Broadcast of Holliday's tape on national news programs elicited several responses from the LAPD. On March 6, 1991, the LAPD released King from custody and admitted that officers failed to prove that King had resisted arrest. On March 7, Los Angeles Police Chief Daryl Gates announced that he would investigate King's arrest and, if the investigation warranted it, would pursue criminal assault charges against the arresting officers. On March 14, a Los Angeles County grand jury indicted Sergeant Koon and officers Briseno, Powell, and Wind for criminal assault, and they sub-sequently pleaded not guilty.

Investigation of Police Brutality   Overwhelming public sympathy for King following the national broadcast of Holliday's videotape prompted Los Angeles Mayor Thomas Bradley to investigate charges that instances of police brutality motivated by racism were commonplace during LAPD arrest opera-tions. On April 1, 1991, Mayor Bradley appointed a nonpartisan commission, headed by Warren Christopher (who had formerly served as President Jimmy Carter's deputy secretary of state), to study the LAPD's past record of complaints regarding police misconduct. On April 2, Mayor Bradley called on Police Chief Gates, who had served on the LAPD since 1949 and had been police chief since 1978, to resign. In May, the LAPD suspended Sergeant Koon and officers Briseno and Powell without pay and dismissed officer Wind, a rookie without tenure, pending the outcome of their criminal trial. King then filed a civil rights lawsuit against the city of Los Angeles.

Several significant developments occurred as the officers awaited trial. On July 9, 1991, the Christopher Commission released the results of its investi-gation and its recommendations to the five-member Los Angeles Police Commission. The Police Commission employed the police chief and was responsible for the management of the LAPD. The Christopher Commission found that the LAPD, composed of 67.8 percent white officers in 1991, suffered from a "siege mentality" in a city where 63 percent of the population were people of color. The commission also found that a small but significant proportion of officers repeatedly used excessive force when making arrests and that the LAPD did not punish those officers when citizens filed complaints. Finally, the commission recommended measures to exert more control over the LAPD's operations, including limiting the police chief's tenure to a five-year term, renewable by the Police Commission for one additional term only. After the release of the Christopher Commission report, Police Chief Gates announced his retirement, effective April, 1992 (which he later amended to July, 1992). On July 23, 1991, a California court of appeal granted the police defendants' request for a change of venue for the upcoming criminal trial.

The State of California Court Trial The trial of the four officers began on March 4, 1992, in the new venue—the primarily white community of Simi Valley in Ventura County. The jury who heard the state of California's case against the four officers consisted of ten whites, one Latino, and one Asian. The officers' defense lawyers presented Holliday's videotape broken down into a series of individual still pictures. They asked the jury to judge whether excessive force—that is, force that was not warranted by King's "aggressive" actions—was employed at any single moment during the arrest. Referring often to the "thin blue line" that protected society from the "likes of Rodney King," the defense built a case that justified the police officers' actions. King's lawyer, Steven Lerman, a personal injury specialist, advised

In May, 1992, in the aftermath of the violence that devastated Los Angeles when the police officers charged with beating Rodney King were acquitted, King publicly appealed for an end to the violence, asking why people cannot "just get along." (*Reuters/Lou Dematteis/Archive Photos*)

King not to testify at the trial out of concern that King's "confused and frightened" state of mind since the beating might impair his memory of events and discredit his testimony. The Simi Valley jury acquitted the four officers of all charges of criminal assault, with the exception of one count against officer Powell on which the jury was deadlocked.

The acquittal of the four police officers on April 29, 1992, ignited widespread and destructive riots led by poor and angry black Angelenos. The riots affected areas throughout Los Angeles but particularly devastated parts of impoverished South Central Los Angeles. Fifty-three people died during the riots, which raged until May 2, and more than one billion dollars' worth of property was damaged. There had long been friction between Los Angeles' neighboring Korean and black communities, and the Korean American community bore the brunt of the rioters' destructive attacks.

The Federal Court Civil Rights Trial   On August 5, 1992, a federal grand jury indicted the four officers for violating King's civil rights. The grand jury charged Sergeant Koon with violating the Fourteenth Amendment, which obligated Koon, as the officer in charge of the arrest, to protect King while he was in police custody. Officers Briseno, Powell, and Wind were charged with violating the Fourth Amendment in using more force than necessary, and using that excessive force willfully, when they arrested King. King testified during the federal trial. On April 17, 1993, a jury of nine whites, two blacks, and one Latino found Koon and Powell guilty and Briseno and Wind not guilty. On August 4, 1993, Koon and Powell were sentenced to two-and-one-half-year prison terms. In May, 1994, a Los Angeles jury awarded King $3.8 million in compensatory damages in his civil rights lawsuit against the city, but on June 1, 1994, the jury denied King's request for additional punitive damages.

Karen Garner

Core Resources

For accounts of the Rodney King incident that are sympathetic to King, see H. Khalif Khalifah, ed., *Rodney King and the L.A. Rebellion: Analysis and Commentary by Thirteen Best-Selling Black Writers* (Hampton, Va.: U.B. & U.S. Communications Systems, 1992), and Tom Owens with Rod Browning, *Lying Eyes: The Truth Behind the Corruption and Brutality of the LAPD and the Beating of Rodney King* (New York: Thunder's Mouth Press, 1994). For an account of the police officers' point of view, see Stacey Koon with Robert Deitz, *Presumed Guilty: The Tragedy of the Rodney King Affair* (Washington, D.C.: Regnery Gateway, 1992). For a collection of essays that places the Rodney King incident in the context of race relations in the United States, see Robert Gooding-Williams, ed., *Reading Rodney King/Reading Urban Uprising* (New York: Routledge, 1993).

See also: Los Angeles riots of 1992; Police brutality; Race riots of the twentieth century.

Know-Nothing Party

The Know-Nothing Party was a political organization that prospered in the United States between 1852 and 1856. During that period, the antiforeign and anti-Catholic feelings of Americans concerned about the large numbers of immigrants arriving in the United States, especially from Ireland, led to the creation of political organizations grounded in prejudice. The secret Order of the Star-Spangled Banner, informally known as the Know-Nothings because "I know nothing" was the response of members queried regarding the organization, emerged as the most prominent of the nativist organizations.

The Know-Nothings eventually dropped their secrecy to become a force in U.S. politics. Under a new name, the American Party, the Know-Nothings surprised the nation with electoral victories in 1854 and 1855. The new party successfully shifted attention away from the issue of slavery in many parts of the country by playing on unrealistic fears of foreign and papal plots to control the United States. The American Party platform called for reforming immigration laws by limiting the number of immigrants and extending the time requirement for naturalization. Former president Millard Fillmore, the American Party candidate for president in 1856, received 21 percent of the popular vote but carried only the state of Maryland. Unable to emerge as a dominant force in national politics, the American Party split into factions over the issue of slavery.

Donald C. Simmons, Jr.

See also: Slavery: history.

Ku Klux Klan

A group of white supremacists, disaffected by the outcome of the Civil War, grew into an organization of institutionalized race hatred.

With the end of the Civil War and the emancipation of African American slaves in the South, tension arose between old-order Southern whites and Radical Republicans devoted to a strict plan of Reconstruction that required Southern states to repeal their black codes and guarantee voting and other civil rights to African Americans. Federal instruments for ensuring African American rights included the Freedmen's Bureau and the Union Leagues. In reaction to the activities of these organizations, white supremacist organizations sprouted in the years immediately following the Civil War: the Knights of the White Camelia, the White League, the Invisible Circle, the Pale Faces, and the Ku Klux Klan (KKK).

Beginnings The last of these would eventually lend its name to a confederation of such organizations, but in 1866 it was born in Pulaski, Tennessee, as a fraternal order for white, male, Anglo-Saxon Protestants joined by their opposition to Radical Reconstructionism and an agenda to promote white, Southern dominance. This incarnation of the Klan established many of the weird rituals and violent activities for which the KKK became known throughout its history. They named the South the "invisible empire," with "realms" consisting of the Southern states. A "grand dragon" headed each realm, and the entire "empire" was led by Grand Wizard General Nathan B. Forrest. Positions of leadership were dubbed "giant," "cyclops," "geni," "hydra," "goblin." The white robes and pointed cowls stem from this era; these were donned in the belief that blacks were superstitious and would be intimidated by the menacing, ghostlike appearance of their oppressors, who thus also maintained anonymity while conducting their activities.

Soon the Klan was perpetrating acts of violence, including whippings, house-burnings, kidnappings, and lynchings. As the violence escalated, Forrest disbanded the Klan in 1869, and on May 31, 1870, and April 20, 1871, Congress passed the Ku Klux Klan Acts, or Force Acts, designed to break up the white supremacist groups.

Second Rise of the Klan The next rise of the Klan presaged the period of the Red Scare (1919-1920) and the Immigration Act of 1921, the first such legislation in the United States to establish immigration quotas on the basis of national origin. In November, 1915, on Stone Mountain, Georgia, a second Ku Klux Klan was founded by preacher William J. Simmons, proclaiming it a "high-class, mystic, social, patriotic" society devoted to defending womanhood, white Protestant values, and "native-born, white, gentile Americans." Such an image of the Klan was perpetrated by the popular 1915 film *Birth of a Nation*, in which a lustful African American is shown attempting to attack a white woman, and the Klan, in robes and cowls, rides to the rescue.

The new Klan cloaked itself as a patriotic organization devoted to preserving traditional American values against enemies in the nation's midst. An upsurge of nationalist fervor swelled the ranks of the Klan, this time far beyond the borders of the South. This second Klan adopted the rituals and regalia of its predecessor as well as the same anti-black ideology, to which it added anti-Catholic, anti-Semitic, anti-immigrant, anti-birth-control, anti-Darwinist, and anti-Prohibition stances. Promoted by ad-man Edward Y. Clarke, its membership reached approximately 100,000 by 1921 and over the next five years, by some estimates, grew to 5 million, including even members of Congress.

The second Klan perpetrated more than five hundred hangings and burnings of African Americans. In 1924, forty thousand Klansmen marched down Pennsylvania Avenue in Washington, D.C., sending a message to the federal government that there should be a white, Protestant United States. Finally, the Klan's growing wave of violence alienated many

Hooded klansmen meeting in Chicago in 1924. *(Library of Congress)*

of its members, whose numbers dropped to about 30,000 by 1930.

Klan activities increased again prior to World War II, and membership rose toward the 100,000 mark, but in 1944 Congress assessed the organization more than a half million dollars in back taxes, and the Klan dissolved itself to escape. Two years later, however, Atlanta physician Samuel Green united smaller Klan groups into the Association of Georgia Klans and was soon joined by other reincarnations, such as the Federated Ku Klux Klans, the Original Southern Klans, and the Knights of the Ku Klux Klan. These groups revived the agenda of previous Klans and were responsible for hundreds of criminal acts. Of equal concern was the Klan's political influence: A governor of Texas was elected with the support of the Klan, as was a senator from Maine. Even a Supreme Court justice, Hugo L. Black, revealed in 1937 that he had been a member of the Ku Klux Klan.

Challenges In the 1940's, many states passed laws that revoked Klan charters, and many southern communities issued regulations against masks. The U.S. Justice Department placed the Klan on its list of subversive elements, and in 1952 the Federal Bureau of Investigation used the Lindbergh law (one of the 1934 Crime Control Acts) against the Klan. Another direct challenge to the principles of the KKK came in the 1960's with the advent of the Civil Rights movement and civil rights legislation. Martin Luther King, Jr., prophesied early in the decade that it would be a "season of suffering." On September 15, 1963, a Klan bomb tore apart the Sixteenth Street Baptist Church in Birmingham, Alabama, killing four young children. Despite the outrage of much of the nation, the violence continued, led by members of the Klan who made a mockery of the courts and the laws that they had broken. Less than a year after the bombing, three civil rights workers were killed in Mississippi, including one African American and two whites from the North involved in voter registration. This infamous event was later documented in the motion picture *Mississippi Burning*. Viola Lee Liuzzo was killed for driving freedom marchers from site to site. Such acts prompted President Lyndon B. Johnson, in a televised speech in March, 1965, to denounce the Klan as he announced the arrest of four Klansmen for murder.

After the conviction of many of its members in the 1960's, the organization became somewhat dormant, and its roster of members reflected low numbers. Still, as it had in previous periods of dormancy, the Klan refused to die. Busing for integration of public schools in the 1970's engendered Klan opposition in the South and the North. In 1979, in Greensboro, North Carolina, Klan members killed several members of the Communist Party in a daylight battle on an open street. Klan members have patrolled the Mexican border, armed with weapons and citizen-band radios, trying to send illegal aliens back to Mexico. The Klan has been active in suburban California, at times driving out African Americans who attempted to move there. On the Gulf Coast, many boats fly the infamous AKIA flag, an acronym for "A Klansman I Am," a motto that dates back to the 1920's. Klan members have tried to discourage or run out Vietnamese fishers. Klan leaders active since 1970 include James Venable, for whom the Klan became little more than a hobby, and Bill Wilkinson, a former disciple of David Duke. Robert Shelton, long a grand dragon, helped elect two Alabama governors. Duke, a Klan leader until the late 1980's, decided to run for political office and was elected a congressman from Louisiana despite his well-publicized past associations; in 1991, he ran for governor, almost winning. In the 1980's the Klan stepped up its anti-Semitic activities, planning multiple bombings in Nashville. Klan leaders in the 1990's have trained their members and their children for what they believe is an imminent race war, learning survival skills and weaponry at remote camps throughout the country.

A major blow was struck against the Klan by the Klanwatch Project of the Southern Poverty Law Center, in Montgomery, Alabama, when, in 1984, attorney Morris Dees began pressing civil suits against several Klan members, effectively removing their personal assets, funds received from members, and even buildings owned by the Klan.

Core Resources

Tyler Bridges's *The Rise of David Duke* (Jackson: University Press of Mississippi, 1994) is a thorough discussion of a notorious Klan member. David Mark Chalmers's *Hooded Americanism: The History of the Ku Klux Klan* (New York: F. Watts, 1981) is considered the bible of books about the Klan. Raphael Ezekiel's *The Racist Mind: Portraits of American Neo-Nazis and Klansmen* (New York: Viking Press, 1995) explores conditions of childhood, education, and other factors in an attempt to explain racist behavior. Bill Stanton's *Klanwatch: Bringing the Ku Klux Klan to Justice* (New York: Weidenfeld, 1991), by a former Klanwatch director, explains initiatives to disable the Klan, most of which have been effective. Wyn Draig Wade's *The Fiery Cross: The Ku Klux Klan in America* (New York: Simon & Schuster, 1987) recounts the Klan's history and episodes of violence.

See also: Freedmen's Bureau; Ku Klux Klan Acts; Reconstruction.

Ku Klux Klan Acts

Also known as the Enforcement Acts, or Force Acts, these three laws were enacted by the U.S. Congress in response to the terrorist activities of the Ku Klux Klan and other groups committed to white supremacy in the South during the era of Reconstruction, immediately following the Confederate defeat at the end of the Civil War. The first act, passed in May, 1870, made night riding (the practice of riding on horseback at night and committing various acts of intimidation and harassment) a federal felony and reaffirmed the rights of African Americans provided for in the Fourteenth and Fifteenth Amendments. Congress passed a second act in February, 1871, which provided for election supervisors to ensure against fraud and racial discrimination. Two months later, Congress approved a third statute aimed specifically at the activities of the Ku Klux Klan. This law made it a federal offense to violate anyone's voting rights. In addition, it allowed the president to proclaim areas in which state governments failed to curb domestic violence to be in "rebellion" and authorized the use of military force and the suspension of the writ of *habeas corpus* to end rebellions. In October, 1871, President Ulysses S. Grant used the law to declare nine counties in South Carolina to be in rebellion. These laws proved effective in suppressing white supremacy organizations.

Thomas Clarkin

See also: Fifteenth Amendment; Fourteenth Amendment; Ku Klux Klan; Reconstruction.

Labor movement

The history of the American labor movement has both reflected and influenced racial and ethnic relations.

An unusually diverse mix of racial and ethnic groups have formed and replenished the labor force of the United States since the Reconstruction era following the Civil War. Emancipated slaves and their descendants rapidly expanded the American labor ranks, with many entering agricultural and industrial production in both the North and the South. In a similar manner, immigration began to alter the appearance and form of American labor. In the late nineteenth century, the United States opened its doors to foreign migrants, in large part because the nation's rapidly expanding economy needed labor. Between 1880 and 1924, more than 25 million immigrants (primarily from Asia and Europe) poured into the country to join people of other nationalities working in factories and industries. Through their collective labor as workers, their actions as union members, and their varied responses to exploitation and insecurity, this varied ethnic mix was a crucial element in shaping the American economy and labor force through the twentieth century.

Such heterogeneity has had both negative and positive consequences for the American labor movement as a whole. It has produced interethnic and interracial conflict among working people; such conflict has often been purposefully exacerbated by employers to lessen the threat of worker solidarity. Yet this heterogeneity has also fostered strong ethnic identification and has been utilized toward worker mobilization for protection and advancement. Both tendencies can be seen within some of the key labor organizations that emerged during the United States' two "labor eras" (the 1880's and the 1930's) and in minority and immigrant labor activity in later decades.

Knights of Labor   The Noble Order of the Knights of Labor (KOL) was initially organized in Philadelphia in 1869; however, the period of its most successful accomplishment did not come until the 1880's. Led by Terence Powderly, a machinist from Scranton, Pennsylvania, the KOL aimed to unite all those who worked (except for liquor dealers, lawyers, gamblers, and bankers) into one huge union that would produce and distribute goods on a cooperative basis.

Recognizing the need for a broad-based labor solidarity to achieve this goal, the Knights of Labor opened its membership to men and women of all ethnic and racial groups. Powderly traveled the country gathering all those who advocated equal pay for equal work and the abolition of child labor. This recruitment campaign was quite successful, and more than thirty cooperative enterprises were established with membership that spanned national and racial boundaries. At its peak, the Knights of Labor included about seventy thousand black members and thousands of Asian and European laborers.

The results of such multiethnic labor solidarity can be seen in the strike against the Missouri Pacific Railroad in 1885. Through work stoppages and interruptions, certain unions affiliated with the Knights of Labor forced railroad mogul Jay Gould to restore wages he had cut the previous year and to rehire hundreds of fired union members. This victory so raised the KOL's standing that membership grew from about 100,000 to more than 700,000 within a year.

American Federation of Labor The American Federation of Labor (AFL), formed in Philadelphia in 1886, was a very different organization. Its members were not individual workers but rather craft unions encompassing laborers from specific trades. Regular dues from these members provided the federation with money to fund strikes and to hire full-time organizers and labor-dispute negotiators.

Although the AFL provided these supportive labor services, it did so for a narrow spectrum of workers. The way in which AFL leader Samuel Gompers structured the organization made it racially and ethnically divisive and restrictive. In his recruitment campaigns, Gompers made membership appeals only to the elite males of the working class, the skilled workers. Few minority group members fit this description; even those who did were excluded from membership. Gompers's position was that allowing members of various ethnic and immigrant groups (especially blacks) to join the federation would embroil the organization in the controversial issue of race in the labor movement; he wished to avoid ethnic entanglements at all costs. Believing that the AFL had more "imperative" and "concrete" matters on which to focus, he closed the ranks of the AFL to minority workers. By the early 1920's, the AFL was the dominant workers' organization in the United States, but fewer than 10 percent of the nation's wage earners were organized into unions eligible for AFL membership.

The Twentieth Century Evidence of the ways in which racial diversity can be utilized both to help and to hinder the labor movement is not restricted to the nineteenth century. Similar examples can be found in the second wave of labor organization that hit the United States in the 1930's.

The American Federation of Labor had survived into this decade despite the continuance of its strategies of labor elitism and racial division. The descendants of the craft union leaders who had come together in the federation of the 1880's sought to retain the legacy of their power and standing as the "aristocracy of labor." They continued to deny membership to unskilled or semiskilled immigrant labor from the mass-production industries; they also prohibited other leaders from organizing these workers in new unions.

AFL leaders doubted the ability of immigrant groups to provide valuable support for the labor movement. Racist and nativist ideologies led many to see these groups not as a possibly valuable coalition in the advancement of labor policies but as individual nationalities whose differences were potentially subversive to the labor movement. As a source of cheap labor, immigrant groups emerged as second only to capitalists themselves as organizers' and native workers' enemies.

Debate over this issue culminated between 1935 and 1938, when John L. Lewis and seven other AFL leaders broke from the Federation to form the Congress of Industrial Organizations (CIO). They asserted that the same defensive mindset that manifested itself within the AFL in exclusionary impulses could also impart great cohesion toward resistance to employers. To this extent, the CIO was organized to solidify those workers whom the AFL ignored or overlooked: the semiskilled and unskilled immigrant and minority ranks. Altogether, more than 1.8 million workers were organized by the CIO, and they proved to be a valuable tool toward labor advancement.

The CIO utilized its large membership (and the ethnic and ideological solidarity it often represented) to challenge repressive labor practices in the steel and automobile industries. In these challenges, the tool of the CIO was the sit-down strike: Instead of walking off the job and picketing, workers went to their posts in the plants and stayed there, making it difficult for others to replace them. In 1937, successful sit-down strikes against General Motors, Chrysler, and U.S. Steel won the CIO recognition as the bargaining agent for workers previously thought unorganizable.

The eventual merger of the AFL and the CIO in 1955 was of great interest to minority labor. CIO leader Walter Reuther and AFL leader George Meany worked declarations of opposition to racial discrimination into the new organization's merger agreement and subsequent constitution. Members of both organizations hailed these statements, but they still waited anxiously to see if the words would be backed by actions. These members would be both pleased and disappointed. The AFL-CIO won respect in the black community early in its career when its executive council called on President Dwight D. Eisenhower to comply with the U.S. Supreme Court's 1954 decision on school desegregation and deny school-construction funds to any state that defied the ruling. Yet it also antagonized the black community by remaining aloof during the great Montgomery bus boycott of 1955 and 1956.

The 1950's were charged with racial strife, and racial tensions often exacerbated difficulties in labor organization and negotiation. Specifically, most AFL-CIO union leaders feared regional political and economic repercussions and avoided adopting a stand clearly in favor of egalitarian racial principles. The ultimate result was the alienation of black workers from the AFL-CIO. Indeed, the National Association for the Advancement of Colored People (NAACP) issued a report in 1959 announcing that the AFL-CIO had not achieved its merger goals, having failed to unify racial and labor issues.

African Americans   Even before the CIO's split from the AFL, A. Philip Randolph had welded a powerful union from the many African Americans who worked on the nation's passenger railroads. Randolph's organization, the Brotherhood of Sleeping Car Porters, won significant concessions from the Pullman Company in the 1930's and later provided a solid base from which black labor could challenge discrimination on a variety of fronts. In 1941, Randolph organized a march on Washington to protest discrimination in the defense industry; he canceled the march when President Franklin D. Roosevelt agreed to issue an executive order forbidding employment discrimination by defense contractors. Further pressure by Randolph and the union helped prompt President Harry S Truman to end segregation in the armed forces in 1948. After the AFL-CIO merger in 1955, Randolph became the only black member of the union's executive council.

The 1960's and 1970's saw more African American and Mexican American laborers attempt to assert their political, economic, and social identities. During these decades, a movement was begun to unify labor and civil rights issues and to extend that cause through the nation. Such a movement began locally, however, with significant labor strikes among black sanitation workers in Memphis, Tennessee, and black hospital workers in Charleston, South Carolina.

The strikes at Memphis and Charleston were among previously unorganized, heavily exploited, poverty-level workers who desired safer working conditions, better pay, and job security. Both strikes were bitterly opposed by the power structure in the communities involved, yet both were supported by top civil rights leaders, including Ralph Abernathy and Coretta Scott King. The strikes also won the support of powerful unions, including the United AutoWorkers' Union, the United Steelworkers of America, the United Rubber Workers, and the Tobacco Workers' International Union. Further, the black community at large bolstered the strikers through marches, mass meetings, boycotts, and financial aid. Despite their overall success, both strikes received only limited support from white workers.

Latinos   This struggle for black equality was paralleled by the rising aspirations of Hispanic Americans, including Cubans, Puerto Ricans, and Mexicans. Although these groups were linked by similar ethnic roots and by a common language and religious heritage, their labor experiences differed. Mexican American laborers, in particular, advanced under the leadership of César Chávez, the son of migrant farm workers. In the early 1960's, pressure from Chávez and other activists helped force the end of the Bracero program, a government-sponsored importation of Mexican laborers that had undercut the agricultural labor market since the early part of World War II. In 1965, Chávez's leadership launched the Delano Grape Strike, which brought national attention to the plight of migrant farm workers; he subsequently became head of the newly formed United Farm Workers. Chávez continued to use strikes and national boycotts against fruit- and vegetable-raising agribusinesses to win concessions from California grape growers. Yet as important as the victories of the United Farm Workers were, in both an economic and a cultural sense, the union, in an increasingly urbanized nation, could not become a major organizational base among the primarily rural Mexican American population as a whole.

Asian Americans   In recent decades, Hispanic and black workers have continued their struggle for labor and ethnic recognition and have been joined in this effort by other minority labor groups. One of the most active since the early 1990's has been the Asian Pacific American Labor Alliance (APALA), founded in 1992 to address the needs of the Asian and Pacific

Island American labor community. APALA's commitment to labor includes the empowerment of all Asian Pacific workers through unionization on a national level and the provision of national support for individual, local unionization efforts. The organization actively promotes the formation of AFL-CIO legislation to create jobs, ensure national health insurance, and reform labor law. It also supports national governmental action to prevent workplace discrimination against immigrant laborers and to prosecute perpetrators of racially motivated crimes.

These efforts of the Asian Pacific American Labor Alliance are certainly not the final word on the relevance of racial and ethnic diversity to the labor movement. Their successes have not resolved the debate about the role of immigrant and minority workers in American labor, but they have ensured the continuance of discussion. Indeed, many of the same issues that have captured the attention of American labor organizers since the late nineteenth century continue to spark debate: the means to secure humane treatment, higher wages, and other improvements in working conditions, and the role of racial and ethnic workers in those efforts.

Thomas J. Edward Walker and Cynthia Gwynne Yaudes

Core Resources

Labor Divided: Race and Ethnicity in United States Labor Struggles, 1835-1960 (Albany: State University of New York Press, 1990), edited by Robert Asher and Charles Stephenson, is a collection of case studies that explores both the potential divisiveness of racial and ethnic heterogeneity in the American labor force and the ability of these diverse groups to coalesce toward united action. *Culture, Gender, Race and U.S. Labor History* (Westport, Conn.: Greenwood Press, 1993), edited by Ronald C. Kent et al., is a collection of essays unified through their "recollection of dissident historical movements—when individuals and collectives attempted to change perceived reality, to confront injustices in the general polity, and seek alternative paths to a shared future." Robert D. Parmet's *Labor and Immigration in Industrial America* (Boston: Twayne, 1981) describes the restrictionist attitudes and actions used in the attempt to prevent solidarity between "native" and "foreign" workers and discusses Samuel Gompers's role in promoting immigration restriction and exclusion. *Unions and Immigrants: Organization and Struggle* (New York: Garland Press, 1991), edited by George E. Pozzetta, is a collection of essays that discuss patterns of immigrant assimilation into the United States, their effect on American industrialization, and their role in creating an American working class. Thomas J. Edward Walker's *Pluralistic Fraternity: The History of the International Worker's Order* (New York: Garland Press, 1991) examines the seemingly unique ability of Communist-backed labor organizations to create worker solidarity across racial and national lines.

See also: Brotherhood of Sleeping Car Porters; Employment among African Americans.

Liberator, The

The weekly newspaper The Liberator *served as a major vehicle for advocacy of the immediate abolition of slavery.*

The initial publication of white abolitionist William Lloyd Garrison's weekly newspaper, *The Liberator*, in Boston, on January 1, 1831, helped to transform the antislavery movement in the United States. It symbolized the beginning of a radical effort to abolish slavery and secure equal rights for African Americans throughout the country.

Garrison and his newspaper were products of the religious revival called the Second Great Awakening, which transformed Protestant theology in the United States. The Awakening engendered moral reform movements in New England and other parts of the North during the early decades of the nineteenth century. Unlike their Calvinist predecessors, those who engaged in moral reform assumed that human beings, by their actions, could create a perfect society and bring about the millennial return of Jesus Christ. In his perception of the sinfulness and criminality of slave-holding, which he believed deprived both slaves and masters of a chance for salvation, Garrison went beyond most of the other reformers of his time.

Garrison's Beliefs   Garrison was born in Newburyport, Massachusetts, in 1805. Deserted by his seafaring father in 1808, Garrison was raised in poverty by his devout Baptist mother, who instilled in him her strict moral code. At thirteen years of age, he apprenticed with a printer at the *Newburyport Herald*, where he learned the newspaper business. By 1828, he was in Boston as the editor of *The National Philanthropist*, advocating the temperance movement. Garrison also supported what he and others perceived to be the antislavery efforts of the American Colonization Society (ACS), founded in 1817. As the dominant antislavery organization of the 1820's, the ACS advocated the gradual abolition of slavery, combined with the colonization of free black Americans in Africa.

It was Garrison's decision, later in 1828, to join Quaker abolitionist Benjamin Lundy in Baltimore as coeditor of Lundy's weekly newspaper, *The Genius of Universal Emancipation*, that led to *The Liberator* and a more radical antislavery movement. In Baltimore, Garrison observed slavery in practice. Influenced by members of Baltimore's African American community, Garrison came to believe that gradualism would never end the "peculiar institution." African American influences also led Garrison to conclude that the ACS perpetuated a racist assumption that blacks and whites could not live together as equals in the United States.

Garrison's increasing militancy made cooperation with the more conservative Lundy difficult. Garrison's radicalism also led to his imprisonment for libel in the Baltimore jail and to his decision to return to New England to begin his own antislavery newspaper.

Garrison Makes a Statement   In the first issue of *The Liberator*, Garrison proclaimed his conversion to immediate abolitionism. Harshly condemning slaveholders as sinners and thieves, he pointed out that one did not ask sinners to stop sinning gradually or require that thieves gradually stop committing crimes. Christian morality and justice, he insisted, required that slaveholders immediately and unconditionally free their bondspeople.

Garrison was not the first to advocate immediate emancipation. What was significant was his rejection of moderation and his linkage of immediatism with a demand that the rights of the formerly enslaved be recognized in the United States. In his most famous statement, Garrison proclaimed, "I am in earnest—I will not equivocate—I will not excuse—I will not retreat a single inch—AND I WILL BE HEARD."

The initiation of *The Liberator* also is significant for its reflection of biracial cooperation in the antislavery movement. Although Garrison, like other white abolitionists, never entirely escaped the racial prejudices of his time, he and his newspaper enjoyed the strong support of African Americans. Wealthy black abolitionist James Forten of Philadelphia provided crucial financial support to *The Liberator* in its early years. During the same period, Garrison employed black subscription agents, and three-quarters of the newspaper's subscribers were black. In Boston, where white antiabolition sentiment could produce violent confrontations, Garrison enjoyed the physical protection of African Americans.

The Paper's Effects   Meanwhile, Garrison and *The Liberator* played an essential role in the formation of the American Anti-Slavery Society (AASS). Founded in December, 1833, under the leadership of Garrison and New York City businessmen Arthur and Lewis Tappan, the AASS united immediate abolitionists in the United States during most of the 1830's. Reflecting the pacifistic views of Garrison, the Tappans, and others, the society pledged in its Declaration of Sentiments (modeled on the Declaration of Independence) to use peaceful means to bring about the immediate, uncompensated emancipation of all U.S. slaves, without colonization. Promoted by *The Liberator*, dozens of other antislavery newspapers, and thousands of antislavery pamphlets, the AASS grew exponentially. By 1838, it had a membership in the North of approximately one-quarter million and as many as 1,350 local affiliates.

By the late 1830's, however, internal tensions were tearing the AASS apart. The essential problem was that Garrison and his closest New England associates, including Maria Weston Chapman, Wendell Phillips, and Henry C. Wright, had concluded that the spirit of slavery had so permeated the nation that the North—not just the South—had to be fundamentally changed.

Although other abolitionists were reaching similar conclusions in the late 1830's, many of them objected to the specific policies advocated in the columns of *The Liberator* to effect those changes. In particular, an increasingly unorthodox Garrison antagonized church-oriented abolitionists by his wholesale condemnation of organized religion. He also seemed to threaten traditional concepts of patriarchy by his championing of women's rights and, specifically, female equality within the AASS. He appeared to threaten government through his advocacy of nonresistance, the pacifist doctrine that physical force is never justified, even in self-defense or on behalf of law and order. He frustrated those who desired a separate abolitionist political party by condemning political parties as inherently corrupt.

As a result, the abolitionist movement splintered in 1840. Garrison, his New England associates, and a few others across the North retained control of the AASS, but the great majority of abolitionists left the organization. Lewis Tappan began the American and Foreign Anti-Slavery Society, which, until 1855, maintained a church-oriented antislavery campaign. Politically inclined abolitionists organized the Liberty Party. By the 1850's, a majority of non-Garrisonian abolitionists had come to support the Republican Party, which advocated neither immediate abolition nor equal rights for African Americans.

In the 1840's and 1850's, Garrison, in *The Liberator* and elsewhere, continued to promote anticlericalism, women's rights, and nonresistance, as well as immediate emancipation and equal rights for African Americans. Although he and his former AASS colleagues remained in agreement on many points, there was also considerable mutual antagonism. Chances for reconciliation among them diminished in 1842, when Garrison began to call on the people of the North to dissolve the Union. He argued that it was Northern support that kept slavery in existence in the South, implying that, when the North withdrew its support through disunion, the slaves could free themselves. His abolitionist critics responded that disunion was tantamount to the North's exculpating itself from the slavery issue.

When the South, rather than the North, initiated disunion in 1860 and 1861, however, changing circumstances caused Garrison to draw back from some of his more radical positions. He compromised his pacifism and his opposition to party politics by supporting Republican president Abraham Lincoln's war to preserve the Union and free the slaves. When the war ended successfully for the North and slavery was formally abolished, Garrison, old, tired, and seeking vindication, announced that his work was done—although it was clear that black equality had not been achieved with the end of slavery. The last issue of *The Liberator* rolled off its press on December 29, 1865.

Stanley Harrold

Core Resources

Robert H. Abzug's *Cosmos Crumbling: American Reform and the Religious Imagination* (New York: Oxford University Press, 1994) demonstrates Garrison's radicalism in the context of early nineteenth century U.S. Protestantism. Lawrence J. Friedman's *Gregarious Saints: Self and Community in American Abolitionism, 1830-1870* (New York: Cambridge University Press, 1982) includes a description of Garrison's circle of abolitionists and his leadership style. Aileen S. Kraditor's *Means and Ends in American Abolitionism: Garrison and His Critics on Strategy and Tactics, 1834-1850* (New York: Vintage Books, 1970) is a probing analysis of Garrison's tactics in comparison with those of other abolitionists. Walter M. Merrill's *Against Wind and Tide: A Biography of William Lloyd Garrison* (Cambridge, Mass.: Harvard University Press, 1963) is the most detailed biography of Garrison to date. James Brewer Stewart's *William Lloyd Garrison and the Challenge of Emancipation* (Arlington Heights, Ill.: Harlan Davidson, 1992) explores the personal choices that initiated and maintained Garrison's career as an abolitionist. John L. Thomas's *The Liberator: William Lloyd Garrison, A Biography* (Boston: Little, Brown, 1963) portrays Garrison as a romantic individualist who defied authority for psychological reasons.

See also: Abolition; American Anti-Slavery Society; Lincoln-Douglas debates; Proslavery argument; Turner's slave insurrection.

Lincoln-Douglas debates

The most famous and consequential campaign debates in American history, the dialogue between Abraham Lincoln and Stephen A. Douglas, clarified how Democratic and Republican conceptions of justice differed and laid a foundation for a renewed national commitment to principles of freedom.

In 1858, Lincoln, a leader of Illinois' recently formed Republican Party and a former one-term member of the House of Representatives, ran for the Senate against incumbent Douglas. A national leader of the Democratic Party, Douglas based his campaign, and his future presidential ambitions, on "the great fundamental principle" of "self-government," or "popular sovereignty." People of the federal territories, he argued, had the right to vote for or against allowing slavery, as they saw fit, and no outsiders had a right to interfere with their decisions. To Douglas, no principle was more fundamental to American democracy than this right of self-government, even if it meant countenancing slavery.

Lincoln viewed Douglas's position as a repudiation of the principles of freedom enshrined in the Declaration of Independence, which, if they meant anything, meant that slavery was wrong. Slavery had existed in the nation since before it began, but Lincoln echoed Thomas Jefferson in recognizing that the founders had been keenly aware of its incompatibility

Illinois senator Stephen A. Douglas, Abraham Lincoln's opponent in the famous debates of 1858. *(Library of Congress)*

with principles of freedom and that they hoped for its eventual end. For Lincoln and other Republican Party leaders, the issue of extending slavery into the territories—the dominant political controversy of the 1850's—demanded that the nation make a choice. It must either recommit itself to the principles of freedom by refusing to extend this odious institution to new areas or adopt a position of moral neutrality toward slavery, thereby allowing it to spread into the territories and eventually into the free states. At stake was not only the fate of African Americans but also the freedom of all Americans. If the American credo were to abandon the idea that "all men are created equal," tyranny of one form or other would surely follow.

These issues focused the seven debates that Lincoln and Douglas conducted throughout Illinois between August and October of 1858. In a format quite unlike modern political "debates," one man spoke for an hour, the other responded for an hour and a half, then the first finished with a half-hour rejoinder. They alternated speaking first.

Although Douglas was reelected to the Senate (the actual vote was by state legislators, who had pledged themselves to either Lincoln or Douglas in their own election campaigns), Lincoln's forceful defense of the antislavery position won him fame outside Illinois and greatly contributed to his election to the presidency in 1860. His elevation to the presidency, in turn, marked the political defeat of Douglas's position of moral indifference to slavery and led to a national reaffirmation that American justice would remain rooted in freedom and equality.

Joseph M. Bessette

See also: Abolition; Free-Soil Party; Kansas-Nebraska Act; *Liberator, The;* Missouri Compromise; Proslavery argument; *Scott v. Sandford;* Slavery: history.